Are the Androids Dreaming Yet?

Amazing Brain.
Human
Communication,
Creativity &
Free Will.

How Alan Turing invented the computer, helped win World War II and left us with one of the greatest puzzles of our time: are humans simply computers or are we more than that? Many scientists think we have a tenuous hold on the title, "most intelligent being on the planet". They think it's just a matter of time before computers become smarter than us, and then what? This book charts a journey through the science of information, from the origins of language and logic, to the frontiers of modern physics. From Lewis Carroll's logic puzzles, through Alan Turing and his work on Enigma and the imitation game, to John Bell's inequality, and finally the Conway-Kochen 'Free Will' Theorem. How do the laws of physics give us our creativity, our rich experience of communication and, especially, our free will?

Can a computer win the imitation game and pass the Turing Test?
Why do creative people make better mates than rich people?
Why are humans bad at mathematics, yet so creative?
Could an infinite number of monkeys write Hamlet?
Is our brain a quantum computer?
Is free will an illusion?

James Tagg is an inventor and entrepreneur. A pioneer of touchscreen technology, he has founded several companies, including Truphone, the world's first global mobile network. He holds numerous patents, filed in over a hundred countries. He studied Physics and Computer Science at Manchester University, Design at Lancaster University and Engineering at Cambridge University. He lives with his family on a farm in Kent, England.

www.jamestagg.com

“I can’t tell you when the last time was that I had this much fun reading and using my brain. From the very beginning, James Tagg had me hooked with the premise; the question of whether or not humans are the most intelligent beings on the planet....”

Janet, Netgalley

“This is a fantastic book. It seams together cutting edge neuroscience, psychology, thought experiments, artificial intelligence/ machine learning, mathematics and even some history!...”

PFJ H., Amazon

“Hard work to read, but makes you think about the nature of human intelligence and AI...”

Brian Clegg, Popular Science

“This is a fat book that covers a huge amount of ground. James’ topic is primarily the brain and how we think, but there is a running theme contrasting the human brain with computers. His thesis is that computers can never think like humans (for example, that they can never be truly creative) and he explores many fields from philosophy and logic to mathematics in pursuit of this proof....”

R. Hanbury, Amazon

If you have enjoyed reading this book please leave a review and if you would like to hear more, or come to one of my talks, please join the mailing list at: www.jamestagg.com/updates.

Are the Androids Dreaming Yet?

Amazing Brain.
Human
Communication,
Creativity &
Free Will.

JAMES TAGG

Hurst Farm Books
An Imprint of
Hurst Farm Enterprises

Published by Hurst Farm Books

Hurst Farm, Dairy Lane, Crockham Hill, TN8 6RA.
+44 1732 807246
12 Williams Road, Chatham, NJ 07928
+1 646 355 1250
www.jamestagg.com
bookinfo@jamestagg.com

A catalogue record for this book is available from the British Library.

Publisher's Cataloging-in-Publication Data

Tagg, James, 1964-
Are the Androids Dreaming Yet?: Amazing Brain.
Human Communication, Creativity & Free Will. /
James Tagg.
pages cm

Includes bibliographical reference and index
ISBN: 978-1-910464-03-8 (softcover)
ISBN: 978-1-910464-01-4 (ebook)

1. Creative ability. 2. Communication—Social aspects.
3. Technology—Social aspects. 4. Mind and body. 5.
Computers and civilization. I. Title.
T174 .T24 2015
303.48`34—dc23

Library of Congress Control Number: 2014945686
(hardback)

p2 220415 postc

To my family,
who have patiently listened to my interminable
ramblings about 'Elephantine' Equations.

PREFACE

ACPMM, Wolfson College, Cambridge

"A man may have twenty years of experience, or one year of experience twenty times."

Mike Sharman

"Rules are for the obedience of fools and the guidance of wise men."

Douglas Bader

I am an inventor. I've always been an inventor. Ever since childhood I've tinkered with electronics and computers, taking things apart and putting them back together. There is no academic course for inventing, so I had to choose my own path through school and University. I studied design, physics and mathematics at secondary school, and engineering and management at University. Part of that time was spent in the Engineering Department of Cambridge University on a particularly special course.

Mathematical Bridge, Cambridge

Every autumn about thirty graduate students arrive at the Engineering Department in Cambridge to join the Advanced Course in Design, Manufacturing and Management. They expect to spend the year walking among the city's hallowed spires, attending lectures, bumping into Stephen Hawking and punting on the River Cam.

Instead, they get quite a shock!

In 1989, I joined the course. There were twenty-six engineers, a psychologist and a physicist – me. There was no prescribed syllabus; instead the course used learning-by-experience and lectures from the experts in a given field. To study advertising, you might visit a top London agency, for shipbuilding a shipyard on the Clyde. If you were unlucky enough to find these two lectures scheduled for the same week, you had to travel the length of Britain. The course runs a half dozen minibuses to solve this transport problem. Every four weeks we would undertake a project in a different company. I remember designing pit props for coal mines and imaging software for a weaving company. At the end of each project we presented our findings to each other and, with eight projects and thirty students, this made for a great many presentations. To keep the process manageable, the course put great store in teaching us the art of communication.

These days I design large complex systems, and clear communication is extremely important. My ideas are often turned into working products and, if those products have flaws, a post-mortem usually shows the cause was a breakdown in communication. Of course, this may be a purely personal failing, but when I talk to people in other companies they report the same problem. It seems we all find communication difficult.

have wondered for many years why it is called the 'art of communication'. Surely it's a science, governed by bits, bytes and bandwidth. That might be true of the symbols in an email – they are clearly encoded symbolically – but is the understanding in our brains simply encoded by symbols? What is the physics that underlies human understanding?

Each summer I go on holiday to escape engineering for a couple of weeks. While away I indulge my passion for reading books by the likes of Douglas Hofstadter, David Deutsch and Stephen Hawking. One book that struck me years ago was Roger Penrose's *The Emperor's New Mind*. In it, he tackles the question of what happens in the human brain when we understand something. He extends an idea put forward by J.R. Lucas of Oxford University that minds must be more powerful than computers because they do something computers cannot: namely to step beyond mere rules and see truth. Colloquially we call this 'common sense' or 'stepping outside the box'.

The Lucas argument uses the theories of Gödel and Turing to show computer algorithms have limitations. Some things are simply not computable. Computers can do many useful things, but they cannot discover new mathematical theorems, such as a proof of Fermat's Last Theorem. In 1996, Andrew Wiles succeeded in finding a solution to this problem. This presents a paradox, solved only if we conclude Andrew Wiles is not a computer. Indeed, since most mathematicians discover at least one theorem during their lives, we must conclude no mathematician is a computer! This is controversial. Most philosophers tend to the view put forward by Daniel Dennett that the Universe is an entirely determined place and any personal sense of free will and creativity is an illusion. In Dennett's worldview, Andrew Wiles is a special purpose machine that was always destined to solve Fermat's Last Theorem. I believe this model is flawed. It is my aim in this book to show you why. Indeed I am going to go further and argue all human creativity is non-computational; art, communication, understanding – all are based on non-algorithmic principles.

If you consider creative thinking deeply enough you're inevitably drawn into the question of whether we have free will. When I get to work each morning, the first thing I do – after a cup of coffee, obviously – is choose which creative task to tackle first. I feel this choice is freely made, but the determined determinists assure me I am wrong and my decision was already made. As Daniel Dennett says, "You have no free will. Get over it!" They say I am effectively an avatar in some giant cosmic computer game, going about my business in an entirely predefined way. I do not agree! If they are right all the coincidences and chance actions of my life were fixed at the time of the Big Bang. I feel this must be wrong, but finding a chink in the determinist armor is hard work; the laws of physics as we know them today are almost exclusively deterministic. This book lays out the options – the chinks – that would allow free will to enter our Universe.

To understand human thinking we would really like to look inside a working human brain. We can't do this yet. All we can do is observe minds at work when they communicate with one another. If our minds think non-computationally – as I believe – we should be able to see them struggle when they have to translate thoughts into symbolic form. The more symbolic, the harder it will be. This is indeed what we observe: face-to-face communication is easy, while formal written modes are much harder. We will explore the difference between human and computer communication as our first step in locating the weakness in the armor of determinism.

What do I Believe?

As a scientist, I ought not to have beliefs. I should have theories and working assumptions. But, as a human being, I must admit believing certain things are true. Science does not forbid beliefs. It just requires you to be prepared to have one overturned if a better one comes along. Richard Feynman summed this up in a lecture he delivered at Cal Tech: "If you want to discover a theorem," he said, "first, you guess, then you work out some effect predicted by the theorem. Finally, you see if the effect happens in the real world. If it does, you have a good theory. If the effect happens a little differently, you will need to look for a better theory." Here are some of my overturn-able beliefs.

Beliefs

- We have true free will. We consciously decide our actions and these decisions are in no way predetermined. We shape the future. Allowing for free will is, therefore, a boundary condition for any theory of our Universe.

- The world is an amazing place, but understandable. We can understand the Universe through the application of thought and reason.

- There is only one Universe and it appears to make sense.

- Humans think creatively, computers do not.

- The process of understanding and communication is complex, much more complex than the digital theorems of Claude Shannon and Harry Nyquist.

- Understanding is hard.

- The communication of understanding is even harder.

CONTENTS

Preface **ix**

Introduction – Experiments, Multimedia and Puzzles **1**

Chapter 1 – Mind Over Computer **3**
- Deep Blue 5
- Man v Machine 11
- Intelligence 25
- The Learning Brain 35
- Determinism 41
- Creative Theories 49

Chapter 2 – Understanding **53**
- Bad Understanding Can Kill 59
- The Imitation Game 65

Chapter 3 – Body Language & Banter **77**

Chapter 4 – The Brain **95**
- Thinking 117

Chapter 5 – Knowledge **127**

Chapter 6 – Kittens & Gorillas **147**

Chapter 7 – Complexity & Chaos **161**
- Chaos 171

Chapter 8 – ∞ **177**

Chapter 9 – Known Unknowns **191**
- The Game of Math 199

Chapter 10 – Turing's Machine 209
The Machine 221

Chapter 11 – Software 229
Silver Bullets Can't be Fired 233
Consequences 257

Chapter 12 – Hyper-Computing 273

Chapter 13 – Hyper-Communication 285

Chapter 14 – Creativity 295

Chapter 15 – Free Will 313
Schrödinger's Cat 325
Twins 331
Does God have Free Will? 339
The Free Will Theorem 343
Free Will Universe 351

Chapter 16 – The Quest for Knowledge 355
Awards for Discovery 365

Chapter 17 – The Future 371

Appendix 1 – Acknowledgments 374
Appendix 2 – Bibliography 382
Appendix 3 – Puzzles and Experiments 395
Appendix 4 – Conventions in the Book 397
Appendix 5 – Index of Theorems 401
Index 405

*"It is no good getting furious if
you get stuck. What I do is keep
thinking about the problem
but work on something else.
Sometimes it is years before I see
the way forward. In the case of
information loss and black holes,
it was 29 years."*

Stephen Hawking

Introduction

EXPERIMENTS, MULTIMEDIA AND PUZZLES

Throughout this book you will come across experiments to try, multimedia references to track down, and puzzles to solve. You can get additional information at www.jamestagg.com/understanding.

If you undertake an experiment I would appreciate your leaving a note of your results on the website and making useful comments on the blog.

Most of the experiments and puzzles are quick and simple. The puzzles I have set often benefit from creative thinking. I have made finding the answers to these problems a little hard, so you are not tempted to cheat. I want you to try to solve the problems and 'feel' your brain working.

This book argues that intuitive thought solves problems in a different way to analytical thought. The process takes time and often benefits from putting a problem to one side while you use your mind to process foreground tasks. I hope you read this book at a time when the website is not available – or at least don't peek. Give your intuitive thought processes time to work.

Graham Wallas described the process of creative thinking in 1926 and I think it is still one of the best models we have:

> First you must prepare and become fully acquainted with the problem. It might seem impossible but don't despair, just commit to it. Next, you should leave the problem to stew – incubation, he called it. After a while, you will feel a solution is at hand. You don't quite have it yet but you are

> sure you will. This is intimation. Finally, some inspiration or insight will pop into your head – this is the Eureka moment. Now you have a solution but intuitive thinking is far from infallible. You will need to check the solution and may find your answer wrong the first few times. Persevere; you will get there in the end.

As a warm-up exercise, let me give you a simple childhood riddle to solve.

> *A man lives on the twentieth floor of a skyscraper with an old elevator. Each morning he gets into the elevator and goes down to the ground floor, but each evening he gets into the elevator, travels up to the tenth floor, gets out, and walks the rest of the way. Why?*

ANSWER IN YOUR OWN TIME

Chapter 1

MIND OVER COMPUTER

Computer versus Human

"I visualize a time when we will be to robots what dogs are to humans, and I'm rooting for the machines."

Claude Shannon

"The question of whether computers can think is just like the question of whether submarines can swim."

Edgar Dijkstra

Kasparov versus Deep Blue

"The Three Laws of Robotics:

1. *A robot may not injure a human being or, through inaction, allow a human being to come to harm;*
2. *A robot must obey the orders given it by humanbeings except where such orders would conflict with the First Law;*
3. *A robot must protect its own existence as long as such protection does not conflict with the First or Second Law. The Zeroth Law: A robot may not harm humanity, or, by inaction, allow humanity to come to harm."*

Isaac Asimov, *I, Robot*

Deep Blue

It is 1997 and we are on the 39th story of the Equitable Center in New York, watching a chess match. It's no ordinary match. Two men sit opposite each other. One, a neatly suited figure, stares intently at the board. You can almost see the heat rising from his head as he processes the possibilities before him. The other, sits implacably calm and, before each turn, looks to a screen at the side of the board, reads the instruction, and makes his move.

This is the famous match between Garry Kasparov and IBM's Deep Blue. Kasparov, a child prodigy, became world chess champion at the age of fifteen and, to this day, holds the record for the highest chess ranking ever achieved. Some consider him one of the most intelligent people on the planet. His opponent, Deep Blue, is a massively parallel chess-playing computer built by IBM's Watson Research Laboratory. The machine itself sits a few blocks north of the tournament in an air-conditioned room, and relays the moves over a phone line to Joe Hoane, the IBM researcher who moves the pieces.

Six months earlier, in Philadelphia, Kasparov won against Deep Blue. This is the rematch and has generated a worldwide media frenzy. Tickets to the event are sold out and most news organizations give a blow-by-blow report each day. On the eighth day of the tournament Kasparov and Deep Blue are level pegging. Kasparov is playing an opening he knows well. It's one designed to be hard for computers to play and has been tested extensively against Fritz, a chess computer Grand Masters use for practice. But Deep Blue doesn't seem fazed. Kasparov is visibly tired. On the 16th move he makes a dreadful blunder and sinks into despair. An hour later, after some moments of quiet contemplation, he tips over his king, gets up, and leaves the room. Kasparov has resigned, Deep Blue has beaten him 3½ to 2½ points and is now the most powerful chess player on the planet.

Later, when interviewed about his experience, Kasparov thought Deep Blue must have been assisted by humans during the games because the program appeared to play intuitively. The rules of the tournament allowed humans to work on the program between matches, but not during actual play. The argument has never been settled, and Deep Blue was long ago dismantled. These days chess players avoid big public matches against computers, arguing it is really a different sort of game. A computer's ability to crunch mathematically through all the many possibilities means a chess player must play without error against a machine, but can play a more interesting and fluid match against a fellow human.

Chess is computer-friendly because it is a finite problem. You always win, lose or draw. The game can't go on forever because any position that repeats itself more than three times is declared a draw, and if a player makes 50 moves without moving a pawn or taking a piece, the game is also declared a draw. In a typical game, each player makes 40 moves, and on each turn you can choose from 30 possible moves. Although this equates to a huge number of options, it is still a finite number.

It is possible, therefore, to create a perfect chess-playing machine. Such a machine would project any position it encountered through every permutation to the endgame. But, although chess is solvable using brute force this might not be practical in our Universe. The storage required to hold all the possible positions being analyzed would be vast – needing most of the atoms in the Universe. You would need to pack this information into a small enough space to allow fast retrieval in order to play the first 40 moves in two hours. This would require storing all the information within a sphere no larger than three light minutes. Putting that much data in such a small space would exceed the Hawking Bekenstein bound – a limit on the information carrying capacity of space-time put forward by Stephen Hawking and Jacob Bekenstein – causing the region of space-time to collapse to a black hole! Despite these minor technical problems, an ingenious algorithm could be made that was unbeatable: chess is essentially computable.

The term algorithm will often arise in the book, so it is worth giving a little history. The word comes from the name of an 8th Century Persian mathematician, Al-Khwarizmi, and means a step-by-step procedure. We use one whenever we do long division or look up a phone number on

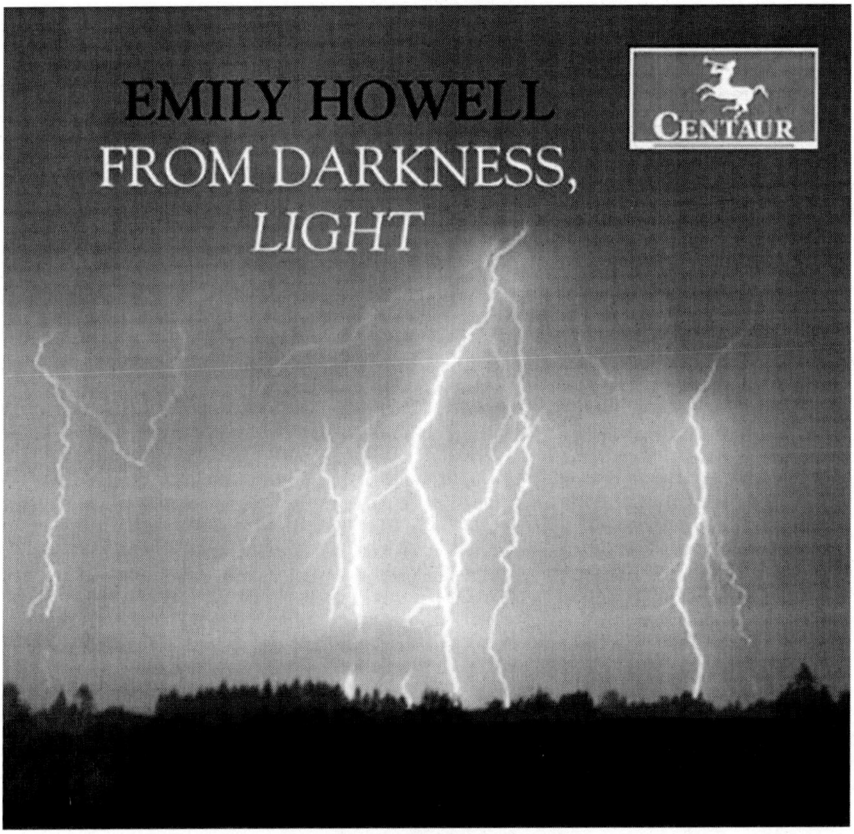

The Music of Emily Howell

our mobile phone. It is any mechanical procedure you perform without thinking about it. Computers are always executing an algorithm; that's what they do.

Fast forward to 2010 and Centaur Records releases a new classical music CD featuring the piano music of Emily Howell. Critics are enthusiastic about the new talent. She has composed music in a broad range of classical and contemporary styles. You can find some examples on my website.

But, it transpires, Emily is a computer, the brainchild of David Cope from the University of Santa Cruz. On hearing this news critics revise their opinion of the compositions – "repetitive and formulaic," "not real music," "pastiche". Listen again to the music and see whether you have changed your opinion. Whatever you think, Emily has made a good attempt at composing in the style of several great composers: J.S. Bach and Franz Liszt, as well as modern ones such as Stockhausen and

Philip Glass. The compositions would get a reasonable technical score in an exam, better than many of my attempts, but are these compositions truly art?

There's no question computers are gaining ground on us in certain mathematically oriented tasks – playing chess, musical composition, and various modeling tasks. But attempts to have them work with words and ideas have generally produced dismal results. Until now.

In 2008, IBM unveiled Watson: a computer capable of answering general knowledge questions. Watson has an enormous database of human knowledge: the Encyclopedia Britannica, a billion web pages, the entire text of Wikipedia and millions of books. It uses artificial intelligence to trawl through this vast reservoir of knowledge and answer questions using a statistical approach. In 2011, Watson featured as a contestant on Jeopardy, the American quiz show, where it beat the two record-holding contestants – the one with the highest number of wins and the one with most consecutive wins. Let me give you a few sample questions and see how you fare.

Question 1.	It can mean to develop gradually in the mind or to carry during pregnancy.
Question 2.	William Wilkinson's "An Account of the Principalities of Wallachia and Moldavia" inspired this author's most famous Novel.
Question 3.	Its largest airport is named for a World War II hero; its second largest, for a World War II battle.

Watson answered questions one and two correctly but failed on question three. You can probably see the final question is posed in poorly structured English and this threw off Watson's comprehension algorithm.

IBM's Watson Plays Jeopardy

Ignoring the odd hiccup, Watson is much better at Jeopardy than a human. Should humans be worried? First chess, then music, now general knowledge, will all human endeavors succumb to a computer? What will be our purpose on the planet if this happens?

Steve Wozniak

"Machines will run the world,
humans will become idle pets."

Steve Wozniak

Man v Machine

Are humans advanced computers with a temporary hold on the title, 'most intelligent being on the planet,' or are we fundamentally different?

We are extraordinarily creative, but we can't add up as well as a cheap pocket calculator. We have poor memories, but we can use common sense to solve problems we have never seen before. Our communication skills are woefully imprecise, but we can tell jokes that send our fellow humans into paroxysms of laughter. We might conclude humans are not computers, but the scientific consensus is that brains are 'wet computers'. I don't agree with this and I'm going to set out the argument to show why man is not a computing machine.

There is an urban legend we think with only 10% of our brains. This is not true. Science has mapped the vast majority of the human brain using two methods. The first, an amazing set of noninvasive imaging techniques, allows us to 'see' the brain as it thinks. The second is more macabre: with seven billion humans on the planet, enough accidents occur through sports injuries, car crashes and surgical mistakes to provide a large enough sample to conduct research. Questioning patients with brain-damage allows us to work out what the injured part did before the accident.

One famous patient had an accident where the blade of a toy sword went up his nose and damaged a small part of his amygdala and hippocampus, the area of the brain responsible for storing memory. This rendered the man unable to lay down permanent memories after the accident. Events before the accident remained clear but he could not memorize new information. You could tell a joke and he would find it

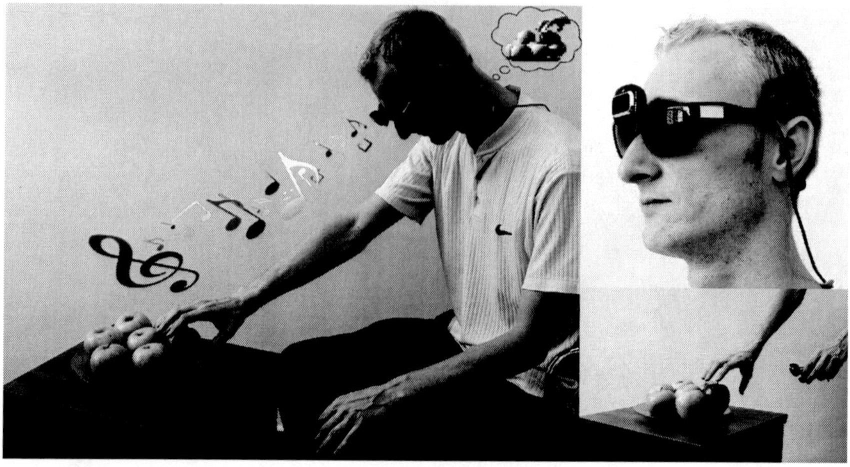

Turning Images to Music

funny and laugh uproariously. A few minutes later, you could tell the same joke and he would find it just as funny as the first time. For him, every time was the first time, because he had lost the ability to record long-term memories. The syndrome is wonderfully depicted in the film *50 First Dates* starring Adam Sandler and Drew Barrymore. Another patient with specific stroke damage was unable to recall the names of fruits but, oddly, could still name vegetables. Interestingly tomatoes presented a particular problem. He had probably never known how to catalogue them so they were partially remembered in both areas.

There are many such medical cases. In Oliver Sachs' *The Man who Mistook his Wife for a Hat*, the author relates the tale of a man with visual agnosia who could not reliably name familiar objects, including his own wife! He had a perfectly loving relationship with her but simply could not name her from a picture. Sachs, Professor of Neurology at New York University School of Medicine, provides many such fascinating stories, along with their medical backgrounds.

The fruit and vegetable case suggests our brains are organized like a filing cabinet. When we damage a part of the brain, it's like losing a drawer: All the information stored in that drawer is lost. Quite a few experiments contradict this model and indicate many tasks are distributed around the brain. The curious case of blindsight is one such example. People with a damaged visual cortex can often recognize objects despite reporting they have no sensation of vision. Show them a shape and they will report they can see nothing. Ask them to name the shape and they might even get a little irritated by the question; they are blind after all. But, ask them to guess the shape and they will get it right every time. Seeing is more

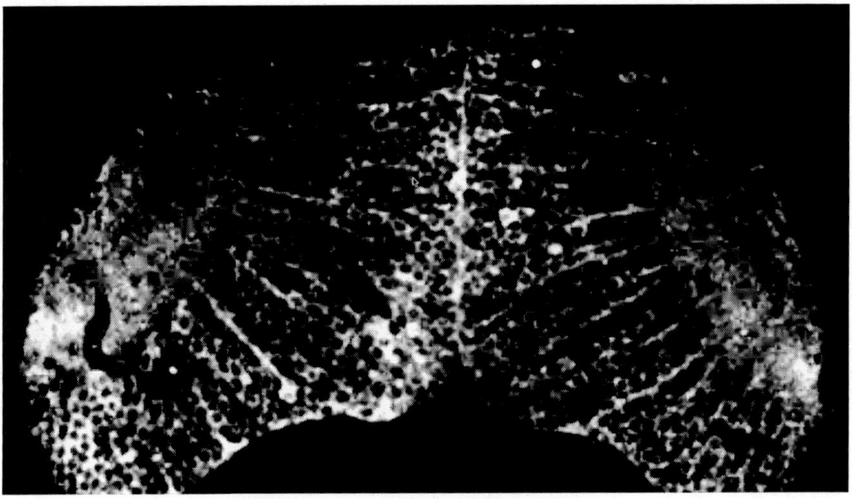

Brain Image of Fish Hunting Prey

widely distributed in the brain than was first thought. Conscious seeing is based in the visual cortex, but there are older pathways still active in the brain that facilitate this unconscious seeing.

The brain is very plastic. Lose your sight through damage to the eye or optic nerve, and the brain can repurpose the visual cortex to other uses such as processing sound or touch. Daniel Kish has developed this to such a high level that he can ride a bicycle despite being blind. He clicks his tongue against the roof of his mouth and uses echolocation to form an auditory model of the world around him. Using a similar approach, Amir Amedi from the Hebrew University of Jerusalem has built an audio imager that turns pictures of the world into musical sound patterns. CAT scans of people using this system show they use the visual cortex to convert these sound images into models of the world in similar parts of the brain to a sighted person.

We now know roughly *what* each part of the brain does, but we have no idea *how* it does it. The scale of an individual thought is too small to see in a brain scan. All we can do is observe large-scale electrical activity associated with those thoughts. A video, from a group at Tokyo University, shows an example of electrical activity filmed in real time as a fish hunts for its prey. Fish have transparent bodies and thin skulls facilitating this sort of imaging. Humans are much harder subjects to work with!

The most popular theory to explain how brains work is as some form of computer. Computers are easy to study because we manufacture them. They tend to crash quite frequently – usually at the most inconvenient moments – so we have packed them with diagnostic monitoring systems. These systems allow us to watch a computer think and, since they think symbolically, we can easily read their minds.

Unfortunately computers don't display many human-like thoughts. They don't laugh and cry, they don't report consciousness and they don't appear to exercise free will or display creative impulses. This is frustrating because these are the thoughts we would most like to study. It might be that computers are not yet powerful enough, and in another few years they will be giving Mozart a run for his money. But there may also be a fundamental difference which renders them incapable of this sort of thinking. This is the crux of the modern scientific debate: do humans think differently?

Computer Brains

On the face of it, humans and computers *behave* very differently. Our memories are poor, but we understand things. We are creative, but bad at mathematics. We learn by example, computers are programmed. We are emotional, impulsive and appear to have free will. Computers are ordered, predictable, but lack common sense. Both humans and computers appear to be physical, discrete systems. We both take inputs, generate outputs and are capable of solving similar problems. Indeed, each time we examine a problem solved by humans we usually find we can automate it. This is known as 'knowledge engineering' and there are many examples; from aerospace to finance, and architecture to medicine.

An example of where computers excel is in medical diagnosis. ISABEL is a clinical diagnosis program designed to help ER doctors quickly diagnose critical patients. It was created by the parents of Isabel Maude, a little girl who presented with multiple symptoms to an ER unit. Doctors were initially confused by the symptoms and misdiagnosed her condition. She was later diagnosed with meningitis. Isabel suffered multiple organ failure but survived. Her parents realized there was something wrong with the ER triage process. They got together with some computer scientists and built the expert system 'ISABEL'. When ER doctors are presented with symptoms, they must mentally scan a vast array of literature to rule in and out possible diagnoses. The problem-solving process is not linear; if you've ever watched the TV series *House* it gives a great dramatization of the process. Certain symptoms might suggest a diagnosis but are not conclusive, and there are many paths to explore. Programmers have taken the heuristic rules from many doctors and codified them into software. ISABEL allows a doctor to input a set of symptoms and it will spit out a range of possible alternative diagnoses with probability weightings and suggested further tests. Similar systems are widely deployed in other fields, to build racing cars, design dams and fight crime. Even the game consoles in our living rooms implement artificial intelligence to make the aliens more believable and our hearts pump faster.

Origin of Computers

Alan Turing effectively invented the modern day computer in a paper he submitted to the London Mathematical Society in the summer of 1936. He was not the first person to come up with the idea – that honor probably goes to Charles Babbage – but he was the first to fully understand its power. When we talk about computers today we mean machines, but it is worth noting computers in Turing's time were more often humans using pencil and paper. The mechanical computers before Turing were elementary at best.

Rudimentary calculating machines were developed in Greece, Persia and China as far back as the Ming Dynasty. An astrolabe recovered from a ship wreck off the Greek Island of Antikythera had cogs and gears and could accurately predict the motions of the sun and planets. Many

Babbage's Difference Engine No. 2, Computer History Museum, CA

of these skills were lost in the Dark Ages but, once the Renaissance was underway in the 16th and 17th centuries, complex mechanical clocks were devised that were capable of predicting the motions of the planets to a high degree of precision. Mechanical, hand-cranked calculators appeared in the mid-18th century, and in 1886 Charles Babbage conceived the first programmable computing machine, The Analytical Engine. It was designed to read programs from cards, and used cogs and wheels to perform the calculations. His first machine – The Difference Engine – was designed to help the Admiralty calculate tide tables, but Babbage realized he could generalize it to compute almost any function. He ran out of money to complete any of his machines, but in the 20th century a dedicated band of enthusiasts built a working model of Difference Engine No.2. One copy sits in the London Science Museum and another in the Computer History Museum in California. These difference machines are not Turing complete and his Analytical Engine has never been built.

19th Century Calculators

Model of the Antikythera Mechanism

In 1935, Turing was made a Fellow of King's College, Cambridge, and became interested in whether mathematical proofs could be found automatically. He wanted to know whether solving a mathematical puzzle was simply a matter of working through all the possibilities in a methodical manner, or whether something more subtle was required. Although chess is a fantastically complex game, it is finite, a big enough, fast enough computer can play the perfect game. Is this the case with discovering knowledge? Could a big enough, fast enough computer calculate all the knowledge in the Universe? Is Douglas Adams' fabled computer Deep Thought a possibility, able to calculate the answer to the ultimate question of 'life, the Universe and everything', albeit with a more enlightening answer than 42?

Turing boiled down the process of pencil and paper computation to a systematic program – a computer program. He proposed a thought experiment where he would run every possible program and see if such a procedure would yield the solution to every imaginable mathematical problem. He was able to show this would lead to a paradox and concluded the universal problem solver could not exist. His discovery is one of the most important of the 20th century – in the same league as relativity and quantum mechanics – and I will use it as my main tool in trying to explain the difference between brains and computers.

Although Turing's original paper was not intended as a blueprint for a practical device, he was one of those rare mathematicians who also liked to tinker with real world machines. The outbreak of the Second World War made the practical application of his work very important, and in Chapter 8 I will relate some of the code breaking stories that were to make him famous and caused Churchill to credit him with shortening the war by two years.

Calling Turing's work an 'invention' is probably the wrong term; 'discovery' might be more appropriate. Whatever you call it, people immediately equated human brains with computers. This is not new.

Each time a new advance in technology is made, people use it to explain the working of the brain. The ancient Greeks thought the brain was a fire consuming oxygen. When Alexander Graham Bell invented the telephone, the nervous system resembled a maze of wires and the brain an exchange. Brains were obviously a sophisticated telephone system. This idea has some potentially frightening consequences, particularly in light of the speed at which computers are improving.

The most striking feature of computer technology is the rate of development. Cars travel faster than a person's legs will carry them, machines manufacture things faster than our hands are capable of working. If brains are computers, surely it is just a matter of time before they will think faster than humans. Turing predicted this would happen when computers reached the level of storing around 10 billion units of information. This happened some time in mid-2000. But today, in the year 2014, I can report that although my computer can beat me at chess, it still cannot fill out my expense report for me. So I am still ahead!

Maybe Turing just got the mathematics wrong. The human brain has about 10,000 times more neurons than our most powerful computers have logic gates. By this calculation, it's not a billion units of storage we need but, a trillion trillion units to put the computer on a par with a human brain. It's just a matter of time!

The worrying thing – especially for fans of the 'computers taking over the world' science fiction genre – is that computers are improving exponentially fast in line with Moore's Law, and the parity point is coming soon. Gordon Moore founded Intel with Andy Grove, and ran the engineering department there for more than 20 years. According to Moore's Law, the power of a computer doubles approximately every 18 months. The next significant event in the computer versus human competition is the gate count parity point – the moment when the number of logic gates and the number of neurons become equal. By my reckoning this will happen some time in 2053.

Don't despair. There may be a few dodges yet. The gate parity point assumes a logic gate and a neuron are equally powerful. However, some single cell organisms with only one neuron are capable of complex behaviors, such as hunting prey and avoiding obstacles. To perform these simple behaviors, a computer would need as many as 10,000 logic gates, about the complexity of my TV remote control. This gives us a bit more breathing space. The extra four orders of magnitude push the gate parity point out to around 2080, too late for me to see, but certainly within the bounds of some readers of this book.

To give you some idea of how Moore's Law works, the graph shows growth in computing power over time; the y-axis is a logarithmic plot using engineering notation. Because the growth is exponential we rapidly end up with very large numbers. Scientists use a special notation to cope with these large and small numbers. In scientific notation a number is written out in a compact form. For example, three hundred can be written as 3.0×10^2. To expand it back to a regular number you move the decimal point in 3.0 two spots to the right, making the number 300.0. A similar technique is used for small numbers. To expand 3.0×10^{-2} move the decimal point 2 points to the left, giving 0.03. Why use scientific notation? Well, once the numbers get large they would no longer fit on a page! We can shorten the representation of numbers even further by dropping the '3.0 ×' part and just looking at the order of magnitude. The number 10^{80}, one with eighty zeroes after it, is the number of atoms in the Earth, and 10^{120} the number of particles in the known Universe. 10^{-43} meters is the 'plank number', believed to be the smallest dimension you can have, and 10^{100} is called a googol, named by Milton Sirotta, the

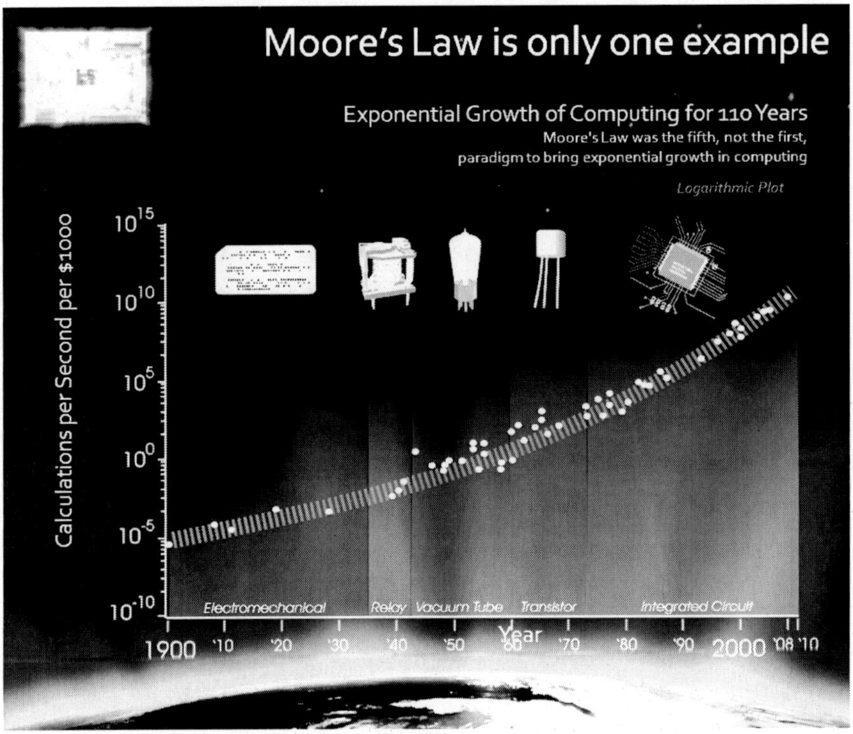

Moore's Law Extended by Ray Kurzweil

nephew of the famous American mathematician Edward Kasner, and subsequently the inspiration for the name 'Google', the Internet search engine.

Ray Kurzweil, the prolific inventor and futurologist, is fascinated by this exponential growth. Exponential curves grow slowly to start with but they pick up speed rapidly and, in the end, growth tends towards infinity. We are all painfully acquainted with one example of exponential growth: The common cold. Each infected cell in our body releases virus particles into the blood which infect further cells, leading to an exponential increase. This makes us feel rotten. Luckily our immune system can also respond exponentially, albeit somewhat delayed, so we survive. In the case of computer power there is no opposing immune system fighting back, so Kurzweil thinks computers will achieve almost limitless processing power; perhaps even within our lifetime. He thinks this will lead to some interesting consequences, for example, allowing people to live forever! Far-fetched? Follow his argument.

The two most important elements in keeping us alive are medical imaging, to see what is wrong; and genetic engineering, to fix those things. Both are improving in line with digital technology, doubling in power every 18 months. As computers get better at seeing into our bodies, and our ability to sequence and synthesize spare parts improves, we will reach a point where we can fix almost any problem. Kurzweil figures technology is improving and his body is decaying at just the right rate to mean by the time he needs heavy duty medical intervention it will be available. Barring a traffic accident or mad-axe-murderer, he should live forever. Even if his calculation is slightly off, the next generation will definitely have this option.

You might dismiss this as science fiction, but some amazing things are already happening. Recently a female patient in the USA suffering from bone cancer had her jaw replaced with a 3D printed component. Doctors were able to scan her head and take an image of the good side of her jaw, flip it right to left within the computer and repair any problems they saw. Then they sent the image to a 3D printer. The printer made a new jaw from tungsten powder, which was fused in a kiln. The final stage was to cover the metal part with an inert bone-like substance to give the human body a scaffolding on which to build real bone. They then performed the operation to remove her old jaw and replace it with the new one: result, brand new healthy jaw.

There are some practical limits to the power of computers on the horizon. Currently, the wires in a silicon chip are about twenty-two nanometers wide. That's around a thousandth of the width of a human hair, or approximately two hundred atoms wide. To match the complexity of a brain we will need to pack an order of ten million more gates into a silicon chip. One way to achieve this is to simply shrink the wires, but when we get down to around ten atoms wide, quantum effects begin to dominate. Signals in today's chips involve tens of thousands of electrons. We normally think of these electrons as a group, but in these tiny circuits we need to consider the behavior of each individual electron. Problems arise as this behavior is subject to quantum uncertainty. With only ten electrons there is a finite probability that none of them will be where you were expecting them to be. This causes problems for digital logic. You can't put a '1' in a memory location and be sure when you come to read it you will get a '1' back. You have to factor in the possibility of error.

Quantum effects can be annoying – requiring us to devise all manner of error checking hardware – but they can also be helpful. Richard Feynman proposed using quantum bits, 'qubits', to perform computation. Quantum computers can calculate many times faster than a classical computer because a single bit can represent more than one piece of information. Enterprising entrepreneurs are making use of this effect to build the next generation of devices, and you can already buy a 512 qubit computer from a Canadian company called D-Wave.

The biggest problem with building more powerful conventional chips is their area is reaching the manufacturing limit for economic viability. Silicon wafers contain random spots of damage and, as a chip gets larger, the chance it will have one of these spots approaches certainty. One solution is to use the third dimension and print the logic

3D Chip, Intel

gates so that they communicate in the vertical direction as well. Intel demonstrated the first three-dimensional chip in 2004, and these chips should begin to appear in our laptops by around 2020.

Taking a chip into the third dimension solves the economic problem but adding logic gates to a 3D chip presents a new problem – heat. Heat is generated in proportion to the volume of the chip but it can only be lost through the surface area. Result: the chip overheats. Large animals have the same problem which is why elephants have huge ears, filled with blood vessels, they can flap to cool themselves and really big mammals, such as whales, live in the ocean. The thermal problem is now the biggest problem in most computer designs. One data point suggests we could solve this problem, the human brain. We pack huge processing power into our skulls without overheating by using a variety of techniques, including folding the surface of the brain, running each neuron very slowly and maybe even using quantum mechanics. A very recent discovery is that brains could be using quantum effects to transmit signals. If true – and the research has only been recently published – it means we may use a form of high-temperature superconductivity to avoid overheating. More on this in Chapter 4.

Excluding exotic quantum effects, the main difference between computer and human brains is their processing architecture. Brains use slow, asynchronous logic to process information rather than the fast, synchronous type used in modern day computers. Logic gates in today's computers work all the time, even when there is nothing to do. For example, if I multiply 2 by 3 on my laptop the entire multiply circuit, designed to work on 20 digit numbers will still operate, and, even worse, it will operate on every tick of the master clock even if there is nothing to multiply. The brain, by contrast, works only as it needs; unused gates don't operate. This gives a massive reduction in unnecessary power consumption. We'd like to use this technique in modern computers but it is very difficult to implement. Tiny changes in timing cause completely different operation and this makes them hard to test. We accept this sort of problem in humans, calling it 'human error', but we count on computers to behave absolutely reliably, so full-blown asynchronous logic is not likely to appear anytime soon. Some of these ideas, however, have made their way into today's consumer devices. For example, the chips in the latest iPhone contain two CPUs: a small slow one operating when the phone is dormant in your pocket, and a large fast one that switches on when you need the power for a game or other high performance task.

All things considered there doesn't appear to be a fundamental engineering problem that would prevent computer hardware reaching the complexity of the human brain. But, even with all this hardware, it's not clear we would have something intelligent.

Richard Branson

"I was dyslexic, I had no understanding of schoolwork whatsoever. I certainly would have failed IQ tests. And it was one of the reasons I left school when I was 15 years old. And if I – if I'm not interested in something, I don't grasp it."

Richard Branson

Intelligence

Although my computer appears to have a mischievous sense of humor – deleting files and crashing just before important presentations – it does not appear to enjoy listening to Bach, nor does it ever ask me to put it near the window to admire the view. I think this means it's not intelligent, but what is 'intelligence'?

Intelligence is hard to define; I usually conclude someone is intelligent if I have an interesting conversation with them. In the workplace we typically hire people based on interview, rather than practical tests. Could a computer hold a conversation with me and persuade me it is intelligent? Meet Eliza.

Invented by Joseph Weizenbaum of the Massachusetts Institute of Technology, and named after George Bernard Shaw's character in *Pygmalion*, Eliza runs an algorithm pretending to be a psychiatrist offering a sympathetic ear to anyone who cares to talk. Try her out at my website or read the sample dialogue below!

User: Men are all alike.

Eliza: In what way?

USER: Men are all alike.

ELIZA: In what way ?

USER: They're always bugging us about something or other.

ELIZA: Can you think of a specific example ?

USER: Well, my boyfriend made me come here.

ELIZA: Your boyfriend made you come here ?

USER: He says I'm depressed much of the time.

ELIZA: I am sorry to hear that you are depressed.

USER: It's true. I am unhappy.

ELIZA: Do you think coming here will help you not to be unhappy ?
USER: I need some help, that much seems certain.
ELIZA: What would it mean to you if you got some help ?
USER: Perhaps I could learn to get along with my mother.
ELIZA: Tell me more about your family.
USER: My mother takes care of me.
ELIZA: Who else in your family takes care of you ?
USER: My father.
ELIZA: Your father ?
USER: You are like my father in some ways.
ELIZA: What resemblence do you see ?
USER: You are not very aggressive but I think you don't want me to notice that.
ELIZA: What makes you think I am not very aggressive ?
USER: You don't argue with me.
ELIZA: Why do you think I don't argue with you ?
USER: You are afraid of me.
ELIZA: Does it please you to believe I am afraid of you ?
USER: My father is afraid of everybody.
ELIZA: What else comes to your mind when you think of your father ?
USER: Bullies.
ELIZA: Does that have anything to do with the fact that your boyfriend made you come here ?

If you think Eliza a bit odd, you are right. Perhaps you won't hire her just yet. The program looks for keywords in speech, and parrots them back at you interspersed with a few stock phrases. If you type a sentence containing the word "job", the computer will say, "Tell me more about your job." It's a simple program and runs to only three pages of text. It shows how good a job you can do with very few resources and how far we are away from a real human being. More complex programs with a larger repertoire have been built and can hold a plausible conversation. People are occasionally taken in by them and are quite shocked when told they have been conversing with a machine. If you're on your guard, they are easy to spot. So far, no one has built a computer capable of holding an extended human conversation and fooling a human into thinking it's a person. Incidentally, having a sympathetic listener is so important to human beings these programs are used in psychotherapy and can be as effective as drugs.

Turing proposed a test to tell whether a computer had truly achieved human intelligence called the imitation game. His argument is as follows:

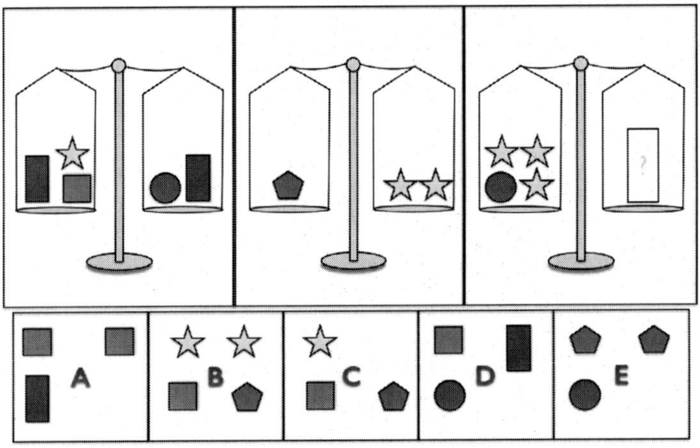

IQ Test

Humans are intelligent. (If you disagree with this premise then you're going to have a problem with this argument!) If you talk to a computer and cannot tell it from a human, it must also be intelligent: QED. The logic is sound but somehow feels wrong. It neatly, but irritatingly, sidesteps the whole problem of defining intelligence.

In 1912, William Stern devised a method for measuring intelligence in children. He named it 'IQ' from the German Intelligenz-Quotient. You may have taken one of these tests at school. The tests consist of a series of abstract reasoning problems that minimize cultural references. For example, you might be asked to look at a set of blocks with dots on them and identify which is the odd one out. Numerous versions of the test have been developed over the years, but nowadays we mostly use one of three standard tests, Wechsler being the most common.

Measuring intelligence is complicated. Culture and language play a big part. If we take a tribe of Amazonian Indians and ask them to list the presidents of the United States, they will fail. That does not mean they're stupid. Drop me into the Amazon Rainforest and I will probably starve to death; they, on the other hand, can live off the land as hunter-gatherers with only a few hours work per day. Who is more intelligent?

One problem with IQ is that individual candidate scores can differ wildly from test to test, sometimes by as much as 20 points. That's huge. At the high end of the scale it can be the difference between being classified as smart or as a genius; and, at the low end, between being average or mentally subnormal. These variations don't usually matter and most universities and colleges take IQ with a pinch of salt, preferring more specific tests such as SATs in America, the Baccalaureate in Europe or A levels in the UK. IQ can be very important; and is sometimes a matter of life or death. In Atkins v. Virginia, the US Supreme Court found a person with mental disability, defined as having an IQ of less than 80, cannot be executed.

IQ is not really a measurement, in the normal sense. Most measurements in life are absolute, for example, distance, weight, and time. I can prove my house is bigger than yours using a tape measure. We each ensure our measures are the same by calibrating them against a common reference. In the 1900s we could have walked down to the local town hall and checked our measurements against a 'yardstick'. As measurements became standardized, these sticks were compared with a common central reference. For example, the *metre* was a platinum-iridium bar kept at the Pavillon de Breteuil near Paris. In the 1960s, a laser superseded the metal reference, and today a *metre* is defined as 1,650,763.73 wavelengths of the orange-red emission line in the electromagnetic spectrum of krypton-86 in a vacuum. Measurement has become very precise!

Intelligence is different. It has no yardstick. If I were to ask, "How much intelligence does it take to design a building?" there's no simple answer. IQ is not an absolute measurement – it's a relative score. Test 100 people and list their scores in order. The ones in the middle get a score of 100; the top 5 a score of at least 130 and the top person a score of 140. Similarly at the lower end. A person with a high IQ is probably smarter than one with a low IQ, but it doesn't tell you if the building they designed will stand up. It's rather like quoting the odds of a horse winning the Derby. Quoting the odds does not give the speed of the horse, nor often the winner of the race!

Despite attempts by test creators to remove cultural bias, it can never be completely eliminated. Certain Amazonian tribes have no concept of counting above five. For them, numbers are an alien idea and serve no useful purpose in their habitat. In the jungle there are always enough trees to make spears, and as a hunter-gatherer you simply need to know where to find your prey. There is no need to count animals into an enclosure at night. Another interesting environment is the Australian Outback. Aboriginal Australians appear to have a remarkable aptitude for visio-spatial memory and can remember maps or collections of objects much better than you or I. Tests for this skill involve playing a variant of Pelmanism. A collection of objects is placed on a tray and covered with a cloth. The cloth is lifted for 60 seconds to reveal the location and type of objects and then replaced. Subjects are then given a bucket full of objects and asked to recreate the tray. You and I do a modest job. Native Australians do this almost perfectly. Why?

In the vast, inhospitable Outback it is vitally important you remember that water can be found at the two rocks near the old gnarled tree. Forget this and you will die of thirst. It was once thought the skill evolved through natural selection, but this might not be the correct explanation. Recent studies show many of us can use mnemonic tricks to significantly improve our memory. Aboriginal skills might actually be learned and passed on from generation to generation.

IQ gives us a way to sum up intelligence using a single number but is this too simplistic? We all have friends who would be our first call if we met that special someone or lost our jobs. They are often not the smartest people we know, but they are highly empathetic. These people have 'social intelligence'. Other friends may fail academic tests yet demonstrate wonderful musical or artistic ability. They have creative intelligence. As we dig deeper, more talents emerge: sporting prowess, organizational brilliance, the ability to inspire loyalty. All these traits appear independently of academic brilliance.

During the last century, scientists worked hard to understand these different intelligence traits. The most influential theory came out of studies done at the United States Army Educational testing service, by Raymond Cattell and John Horn, and later added to by John Carroll. Their initials give the theory its name. CHC theory breaks down the general idea of intelligence into many different subgroups: 'G' factors.

If you are good at recalling all the kings and queens of England in chronological order, or can name every member of the 1966 English World Cup team or, perhaps, all the members of the baseball Hall of Fame, you would have high 'crystalized intelligence' – 'Gc'. It measures the sum total of all the *things* you have learned and retained in your long-term memory, your store of useful, and useless, facts. On the other hand there is innate intelligence, the sort that allows you to solve problems where tapping memory banks is not useful. My family often buy me puzzles for Christmas, the sort where you manipulate bits of bent metal that appear linked, but can be separated with a little ingenuity. These puzzles test our ability to work with problems we have never seen before and is called 'fluid intelligence' – 'Gf'.

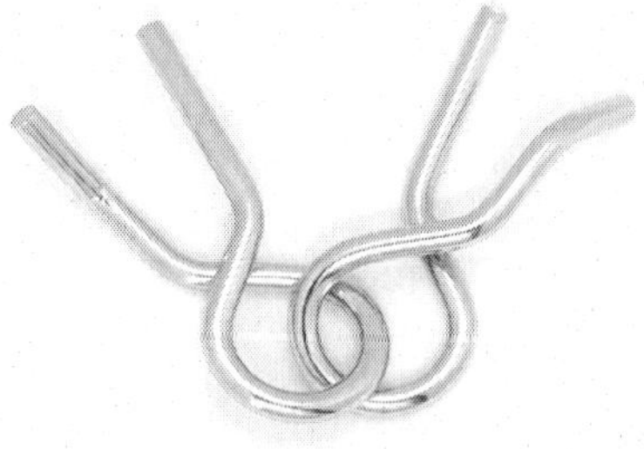

Metal Puzzle

We can go further. A good tennis player will have high 'Gt' and 'Gv' scores: 't' for time and 'v' for vision, a good pub quiz contestant a high 'Glr' score – 'lr' denoting for long-term retrieval. Carol Vorderman, a UK game show presenter famous for mental arithmetic, would have a good 'Gq' score, 'q' for quantitative numerical skills. With all these types of intelligence to choose from it begs the question, "Is there a single master intelligence from which the rest follow?"

Political correctness plays a part here. It feels rather elitist to say smart people are good at everything. It is far nicer to think we each have our individual talents and some just have a few more than others. But that's not what the science tells us. 'Group Intelligence' – the overall G score – does appear to be the underlying cause of the other types of intelligence, and smart people do tend to be good all-rounders. However, there is one major flaw in the analysis; the studies only measure the subjects' ability to pass academic tests, they don't look at our success in real-life, nor our creativity.

Lewis Terman began the longest running study of intelligence and its relationship to life success back in the 1920s. It continues to this day. A group of 1500 children with high IQs were selected and tracked throughout their lives. Terman assumed their high IQs would result in them being very successful. They certainly did well, but studies show they did no better than if they had been chosen randomly from the same area (all the children came from around Stanford University). Famously two children, William Shockley and Luis Alvarez, tested too low to be chosen for the study but went on to win Nobel Prizes for Physics in 1956 and 1968, respectively.

There are many similar anecdotes: Apparently stupid people go on to great things. Einstein's teacher famously stated he would never amount to anything and Sir John Gurdon's school report said he was 'too stupid' for science. He went on to discover monoclonal antibodies for which he was awarded a Nobel Prize! Scientists have now devised the alternative theory of an intelligence tidemark. Once above this level – an IQ of about 130 – you can pretty much do anything you want to. This might be because one very important type of intelligence – creative intelligence – is not highly correlated with the rest. Creative people tend to be sufficiently intelligent for their field but once above that threshold the relationship breaks down. Success in creative endeavors seems to reflect strength of character and creative aptitude rather than raw brainpower.

Physical Basis of Intelligence

The high correlation between different sorts of academic intelligence suggests we might find a physical process within the brain leading to high IQ. Functional MRI scans show intelligent people use more neurons when tackling a given mental task, perhaps bringing to bear greater raw horsepower, but this is not really an explanation. It is akin to saying Usain Bolt runs faster because he gets more power to his legs. This is obvious. What we want to know is *how*.

The problem with looking at brains for a common cause is the variation from brain to brain. We all have different genes and life experiences. On top of this, we really only see brains post mortem and this tends to confound comparisons of brain structure. One way to minimize the variation is to use separated identical twins. Twins have identical genes so their fundamental hardware is the same. We should be able to see features of the brain that are common to smart sets of twins but absent in less smart pairs. If a feature is not shared it can be discounted as something accidental, caused by disease, environment, or the like.

When we examine smart twins, they appear to have greater myelination of their neurons. Myelin is a flat protein that acts as an insulating sheath, wrapping the nerves and the neurons in our brain. Myelination appears to be part of the mechanism involved in laying down long-term memory – more myelin, more memories. It may also help sustain signals and allow them to move faster over a longer distance: the increased insulation allowing the brain to include information from more distant parts of the brain within a given thought. But increased myelination may be an effect of higher intelligence rather than a cause. The brain is responsible for a significant part of our overall energy consumption so insulating the neurons might simply help with energy conservation. This is an active area of research.

Evolution also gives a clue to the causes of intelligence. Humans, nonhuman primates, and dolphins all share spindle neurons. These spread across the brain and appear to help us coordinate complex actions between the different parts. The high function intelligence that characterizes these disparate species requires a great deal of cooperation between different areas of the brain. Take playing a musical instrument. This uses physical coordination (motor cortex), sound processing (auditory cortex), rhythm (another part of the motor cortex), along with emotional interpretation (amygdala). Humans have more spindle cells than other animals so this might explain our superior ability in performing these complex tasks.

However plausible these ideas, they are all hardware arguments. It is like me saying my word processor is better than yours because it has gold plated connectors. That might be true – it might allow the machine to run a little faster without electrical errors creeping in, but we all know it's software that matters. A great computer game is great because it is cleverly written and has beautiful graphics. The speed of the hardware might help, but it does not define 'great'.

Can we see these software effects in the brain?

No, unfortunately, this is where our imaging technologies fail. They lack sufficient resolution. We would need 100,000 times more resolution to see our thoughts, even assuming we would recognize thought if we saw it. There is no reason to believe the brain lays out thinking in anything resembling the computer software we are accustomed to reading.

There is one exceptional group of people that *does* show a software difference on a large-scale – chess players. It seems Chess Masters use a different part of their brain to process information about chess than you and I. This can be clearly seen on scans of the brain and is such a gross effect it even shows up in old-fashioned EEGs – where electrodes are taped to your head. Interestingly the effect can be used to predict greatness. Players likely to become Grand Masters show they use a different part of their brain from the rest of us at an early age. Chess players possess the only large scale *wiring* difference we know of, but there is another group with a visible physical difference, London taxi drivers. Their hippocampi are noticeably larger than the rest of ours. The hippocampus does many things, but one of its most significant jobs is to memorize maps. The three years it takes to acquire 'the knowledge' and the subsequent years of navigating London's complex streets give cabbies a 30% larger hippocampus than the average London resident.

Is Intelligence Static?

We've all seen the headline. Every summer public examination results come out and every year is pronounced a record breaker! Year after year, students get better and better grades. This creates a problem. There's is no better grade than an A – and eventually all students get As. Welcome to grade inflation – a problem affecting systems the world over, from British 'A' levels to Harvard grade point averages. Newspapers are awash with stories bemoaning the dumbing down of today's tests. "Examinations aren't what they used to be."

Grade inflation undoubtedly exists and studies of undergraduate grades show progressive compression into the top grades, most competent students get 'A's, making it difficult to distinguish a good student from a great one.

At first glance, the problem appears to be one of social engineering. Teachers don't want to disappoint, and academic institutions want to improve on last year's results. The people awarding the grades often have a vested interest in those grades improving. Even a tiny positive bias in the most scrupulously honest teacher is enough for grades to creep up. However, grade inflation might not be purely a matter of over enthusiastic teachers. IQ scores are also rising. Welcome to the Flynn Effect.

James Flynn, Emeritus Professor of Political Studies at the University of Otago in Dunedin, New Zealand, reported in 1987 that IQ scores rise over time throughout the world. All told the population gains about one IQ point every three years, and approximately every ten years IQ tests have to be re-calibrated, so the average student once again receives the average grade. This is a mystery. It is a large effect and cannot be explained by the rote learning of lots of sample questions. The human race is either rapidly getting smarter or the least smart members of society are coming up to the general average fast; either way it means there are fewer dumb people around. The Flynn Effect has recently slowed in western countries, suggesting it might be that intelligence is converging rather than increasing overall. Another interesting fact is people become more intelligent as they age, gaining about one IQ point every ten years. Against the stereotype, it's not all downhill after forty. There is hope for me yet!

Until recently we thought IQ was fixed, but new research contradicts this. Muscles get stronger with exercise, physical skills, such as playing golf and tennis, improve with practice; why not intelligence? Scientists used to believe brains couldn't get smarter; you had the IQ you were born with. You might learn more 'stuff' during your life, but the G factor stayed the same. It looks like this is wrong and we were simply not using the right exercises.

In 2008, Susanne Jaeggi and Martin Buschkuehl, of the University of Maryland, modified an intelligence test into a game and showed playing the game improved 'fluid' intelligence and increases IQ. They believe playing their game helps improve working memory – the short-term memory we use for storing sums as we do mental arithmetic – or remembering telephone numbers. Previous attempts to improve IQ through practice had not shown much success as the skills did not transfer between tests, but working memory is such a useful thing it appears to help across the board.

These factors argue against intelligence being a hardware feature of our brain. It does not remain static but instead improves with age, time, and education.

At the beginning of the chapter, I said Garry Kasparov was once thought to be one of the most intelligent people on the planet. When his IQ was eventually tested – the German magazine *Der Spiegel* put up the money – he scored 135. That means, in academic terms, he is smart but no genius. Yet, he is undoubtedly a genius by any common sense definition: the best chess player to ever live. These days he involves himself in politics rather than chess and is still uniquely able to concentrate for long periods of time. Concentration seems a very important factor. Einstein was once asked where his genius came from. He replied that he did not consider himself a genius but instead put his success down to his persistence and ability to concentrate on a problem for many years. IQ tests say nothing of our ability to concentrate over extended periods and nothing about our drive to change the world. The tests are, at best, a useful but dangerous diagnostic tool for educators. One of the worst things IQ can do is pigeonhole people. Would Kasparov have become world champion if he had been given his IQ score of 135 as a teenager rather than late in his thirties after he had conquered the world?

Hole-in-the-Wall Experiment

"Education is what is left after what has been learnt has been forgotten."

B.F. Skinner

The Learning Brain

Human beings are born with an extraordinary ability to learn through experiencing the world around them. Studies show babies as young as three weeks understand musical ideas, smiling as you play music to them in a major key and frowning at music in a minor key. By six months, babies have learned to distinguish the relationship between objects, and by two, they have a command of language and are beginning to develop a theory of self. They understand how to lie and become adept at playing parents off against each other!

Sugata Mitra, of Newcastle University, has run an experiment in India to test minimally invasive education called the 'Hole in the Wall Project'. As the name suggests, he cut a hole in the wall of a building in Delhi and put a computer in it. The hole opens out onto a slum district and local children rapidly discovered the computer. Without any formal training they picked up the necessary skills and very soon became adept at searching the Web. Remember, in order to 'pick up' this skill they often had to learn the English language as well.

Another example showing children's innate ability to learn is Nicolas Negroponte's 'One Laptop per Child' program, which gives computers to children in remote villages around the world. The laptops are a triumph of cost engineering but are fully functional and can connect to the Internet. The inspiration for the project came from an analysis of the economics of the computer industry. Huge capital investment in the western world is driving most costs down, but one cost that seems to have stuck fast is the access device. Laptops tend to remain at a floor price of around \$500, far too high for much of the developing world. At \$500, a computer store makes \$80 when they sell you a laptop. This is as low as is cost-effective

Laptops Galore

for them to stock the machine, employ someone to tell you about it, and fix it if it goes wrong in the first year. Value for money improvements have all focused on faster processors, more memory, sharper displays and larger hard drives, not lower prices. These improvements are useful if you want to shoot aliens, but overkill if you only want to surf the Internet and learn the '3 Rs'. So the 'One Laptop per Child' project has developed a device for $100.

Negroponte is often asked how he deals with the maintenance and repair issues. His answer, "There aren't any." The computers are treasured possessions and rarely broken or lost. Children become empowered by the machines and can access knowledge and information far beyond the wildest dreams of their parents' generation. Stories abound of children checking the spot prices for wheat or coffee on the Chicago Stock Exchange, and advising their parents on the price to accept for their crop. Negroponte estimates there are currently 500,000 children in South America teaching their parents to read!

It's interesting to speculate whether children learn spontaneously or are somehow 'programmed' by the adult members of society. In both the 'Hole in the Wall' experiment and the 'One Laptop per Child' program the children could simply be learning from adults and older children, but there is a novel way to eliminate this influence. Negroponte and Mitra have teamed up to run an experiment to see how children learn for themselves. They are planning to air-drop laptops into remote villages in the Andes. In this scenario, the children can't possibly learn from the

One Laptop per Child

adults – the adults have never even seen a computer before. Instead, they must rely entirely on their innate learning ability. At this point, the experiment has only just started; I will put details on my website as the experiment progresses.

The 10,000 Hour Club

Learning by experience takes humans quite a bit of time. Anders Ericsson, Professor of Psychology at Florida State University, studied musicians in the early 1990s and found they had accumulated a huge number of practice hours by the time they became experts. His research was popularized by Malcolm Gladwell, in the book *Outliers*, and by Daniel Coyle in *The Talent Code*. The idea is that humans need around ten thousand hours of practice to become proficient at a skill. The more skilled players seem to have simply accumulated even more

Dan McLaughlin

practice. A number of people have wondered whether you can take this literally, and if you devote 10,000 hours to practicing something you can become world class. Dan McLaughlin from the USA used to be a professional photographer and decided he might like to become a professional golfer. He quit his job and is now 3,500 hours in. So far, he has achieved a 4 handicap. I also personally got bitten by this bug and am learning the piano. I am about 3,000 hours in and am making good progress.

Piano Practice

Gladwell's interpretation of Ericsson's results is not without controversy. Ericsson stresses 'purposeful practice' is the important element. Practicing the wrong thing for ten thousand hours will just make you good at doing something wrong. Practicing without concentration and attention will equally have little effect. One illustrative example is the story of Edward Sanford, a supreme court judge, who read the morning prayer aloud every day over a 25 year period. After he retired he was asked if he could recite it from memory. Despite reading it as many as 5000 times during his working life, he was unable to remember it. It seems you must purposefully practice the exact thing you want to do if you wish to learn it, in this case recall.

Computers don't require practice to learn a skill. If their program is right they work correctly, and if it is wrong, they are always wrong. Computers can be programmed to learn but so far this learning has been limited to specific problem domains, such as face recognition. They do not have the general-purpose capability humans enjoy.

Astrological Clock at Hampton Court Palace

"The die is cast"

Shakespeare

"How does the water of the brain turn into the wine of consciousness?"

David Chalmers

Determinism

I have free will.

Look…

I can choose to type any word I like.

Giotto...

Many philosophers tell me I am deluded. I was always going to type that word and I have no free will. Everything in my life is predetermined. I'm rather like a character in an enormous video game. The character might think it was free to act, and its actions would appear random. Yet from the moment the player clicked the button to start the game, every action the character takes is determined by a preprogrammed set of rules. This is the free will debate. How can we tell we are free? Would there be any observable effect?

One of the big problems is that philosophers codified much of our modern theory of free will in the 19th century, at a time when all the known physical laws were deterministic and reversible. They could not see a way for free will to emerge from such physical laws. There was even a group called the Compatibilists lead by David Hume that thought free will could coexist with determinism. Provided you felt free it did not matter that your actions were inevitable.

We all want free will to mean actual freedom to make conscious choices. We would like to affect the world in which we live; not the other way around. I dislike making definitions – I find they take away from the core argument and only result in linguistic jousting, but it seems that two centuries of philosophers have avoided a proper discussion of free will by loosely defining the term. Here is my definition:

'We consciously, and through the exercise of will, make decisions between different choices without anyone or anything causing the decision in advance. Others can influence decisions – by offering advice or even holding a gun to our head, but we choose.'

If you can devise a better, stronger definition please email me and I will revise my definition to your better one. I'm searching for the most powerful definition of free will – totally free and born out of the exercise of will.

The human mind appears to have free will. At least this is my personal conscious experience. Computers, on the other hand, do not. They run programs that dictate exactly how they will operate in every situation. Could a computer be programmed to have free will? That's hard to do. Let's see why.

Thinking with Clockwork

Astronomers have been predicting the motions of the heavens for centuries and to do this they need accurate clocks. The very first clocks were sundials. These suffered the obvious disadvantage of not working at night, but it was also unsatisfactory to use the motion of the sun to predict the motion of the sun. The earliest 'heaven independent' clocks used water flowing through small holes in pottery vessels. They were effective over short intervals but plagued by dust, dirt and evaporation. It was the invention of the anchor escapement that enabled the first accurate mechanical clocks.

By the sixteenth century clockmakers had gone to town developing astrological clocks with more and more gears, to show all manner of information; the phases of the moon, the motions of planets, even the motion of moons orbiting those planets. These clocks became hugely ornate. The astrological clock at Hampton Court Palace was built for Henry VIII circa 1542 and, as well as showing phases of the moon and the signs of the zodiac, it accurately calculated the time of high tide at London Bridge, allowing Henry to travel quickly to the Tower of London. You might also notice it shows the sun orbiting the earth! Copernicus published his book, *De revolutionibus orbium coelestium (On the Revolutions of the Celestial Spheres)* showing the earth orbited the sun a year later in 1543, and it took centuries before it became accepted fact.

Clocks need gears. The humble gear is a simple machine. They work because wheels of different size have different circumferences – the distance around the edge – but one full turn is the same for all wheels. Imagine you have a circular sweet such as a Life Saver – or Polo for

British readers – and you roll it once around the wheel of your car. The small sweet will turn many times. Now put a pencil through the hole in the sweet, jack up your car so the wheel is off the ground, hold the sweet next to the wheel of your car and press the accelerator. The sweet will spin round very fast and probably disintegrate in a shower of minty sugar. This is the principle of gearing. A small circle has to do a lot of work to keep up with a big circle. It's very predictable. The sweet will turn a set number of times for each rotation of the car wheel, equal to the ratio of the circumferences of the two circles.

Gears usually have teeth to lock the wheels together, but this is really just to make sure they can't slip against one another when they transfer huge forces, such as in racing cars. Some passenger cars have been built with smooth gears; a friend of mine had one at university. If he put his foot down too hard, the gears would slip, heat up and you would get a terrific smell of burning rubber. If you were lucky you could leave the car for a few hours and all would be well. But, if not, you had to replace the rubber belt, which was very expensive. Toothed gears generally win out.

Toothed gears also have the enormous benefit of being digital. This is quite important if you want to keep things accurate. Gears can't move a fraction of a tooth so if a toothed gear has 'slipped' forward a small amount, it will be kicked back into position when it meshes with another gear.

In a modern mechanical clock, a balance wheel swings back and forth on a spring and moves the main gear one notch forward each time it passes its central position. Gears divide this down to move the hour and minute hands. If I put the hands of a clock at midday and let the clock tick 86,400 times, the clock hands will come back to the same place. Once you understand how a clock works you can play a trick. If you tell me the number of ticks the clock has tocked, I can tell you the exact position the hands will be in. To a small child this might be dressed up as a magicians trick – but, of course, it is simply a matter of dividing the number of ticks by 60 and then 60 again to calculate the amount of time elapsed. This type of precisely predictable behavior is called deterministic behavior. Something is deterministic if you can set it up in a particular way and know the exact state later or, conversely, examine something and trace it back into the past.

Modern computers scale up clockwork and make it much more efficient; gears are translated into electronic logic gates and a quartz crystal vibrates at 1000 million ticks per second to give us the clock tick. On each tick, the computer can do a mathematical operation, store and retrieve information, or branch down an avenue in its program. Using these simple building blocks the computer allows us to play computer games or process the words of this book as I write. Importantly, all these operations are deterministic; given a set of inputs the computer will always generate the same outputs and that means a computer has no free will.

"Ah," I hear you say, "but my computer plays games with me and is not predictable, otherwise I would always beat it." You are right, but the computer has a clever trick to fake non-deterministic behavior: it uses you!

Computers on their own cannot generate random numbers. All a computer can do is generate a pseudo-random number and it does this by working its way through a very long calculation. It could, for example, calculate the first thousand digits of π (pi), and then start using the subsequent digits as random numbers. The digits look jumbled up but we know they follow an entirely predictable pattern. The computer appears to behave randomly because when I press the button to kill an alien the computer picks the number it had counted up to at that moment, say the $55{,}678^{th}$ digit of π, and uses that. It is I, the human, who unconsciously picks the precise moment in time and therefore provides the random element. My choice is governed by all sorts of extraneous quantum influences: Did I have coffee this morning? Was it a big mug or a small cup? How hot was it? All these things will be important as they determine the amount of caffeine absorbed across the brain blood barrier and the exact timing of my actions.

Humans are not good at consciously generating random numbers. We tend to choose the same numbers too often. If I ask you to pick a number between one and ten, you are likely to choose three or seven. This effect is called social stereotyping; magicians often use it when they pretend to read your mind. The problem arises because we tend to over think the problem. I asked you to pick a random number between one and ten. You won't pick one or ten. Five is too obviously the mid-point. Even numbers don't feel random. Nine is too large. That just leaves three and seven. So the mind reading magician has you! Humans can unlearn this social programming and become quite good random number generators but normally we tend to conform.

There is a way two humans can generate a truly random number without training. Find a friend for this experiment. One of you should pick any number between one and ten and start counting under your breath, when you get to ten just go back to one and keep repeating. The other should wait a while and then shout stop. The number reached should be genuinely random. Please post the results on my website and I'll tell

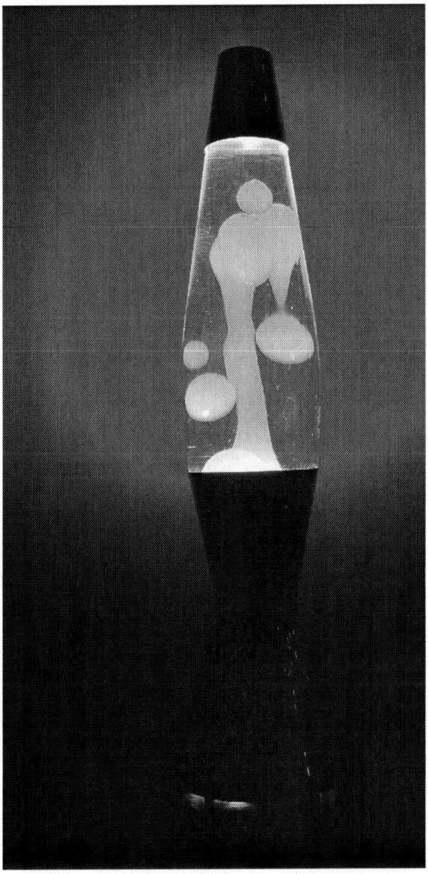

Lava Lamp

you if this crowd-sourced random number generator really works. There should be no way to predict the resulting number as both of you are affected by quantum randomness and, provided you wait a little before shouting stop, any social stereotyping should be overcome. If you want to be scientific, remember the random number you started with and the length of time before your friend shouted stop. There should be an improvement in randomness with the amount of time they wait.

In the absence of human interaction another way to give a computer access to a random number is from a quantum device. A lava lamp works well! The Lavarand, developed by Silicon Graphics, is a hardware random number generator which uses images of a lava lamp to seed a random number generator. It is covered by U.S. Patent 5,732,138, titled "Method for seeding a pseudo-random number generator with a cryptographic hash of a digitization of a chaotic system." Got that!

A computer does not acquire free will just through the injection of randomness. You could simply put an intercept on the link from the lava lamp to the computer and completely predict the computer's behavior. The system as a whole will certainly do unpredictable things, but the computer did not make a choice; behaving randomly is not exercising free will. Where is the will?

Consciousness

I remember my first trip to Death Valley in the United States. We were driving along the main east-west highway at the bottom of the valley and a sign said, "Turn off your air conditioning now." I did as I was told and to cool down I opened the window. When I put my hand out I felt nothing; no wind chill, nothing. The air was so hot the wind carried no heat from my hand. When I imagine hot weather it always brings back this memory. It's my conscious experience of the world.

Humans experience the world through a vivid lens we call consciousness. It allows us to think about the world as we watch it and plan actions. But, it also summons associated memories, something scientists call 'qualia'. Most writers describe consciousness as an internal dialogue with themselves and see it as a consequence of human language. That's probably because most writers are linguists. Non-linguists, perhaps even dyslexic engineers like me, experience consciousness as more of a visual dialogue.

It's hard to pin down consciousness as the difference between humans and computers. Computers do have something that resembles consciousness; they have watchdog functions, they plan and anticipate actions and are aware of their own existence. But they don't understand or make free choices based on this consciousness. It is an entirely mechanistic affair. A computer might know its CPU is overheating and send a notification message to the administrator, but it does not really appreciate what this means. It does not have our sensation of a near death experience. This self-awareness is the 'hard question' of consciousness. Why, despite the computer knowing it is overheating, does this not translate into the intense experience we have? Philosophers, such as Daniel Dennett, think this lack of consciousness is only a matter of time; once computers live long enough and have sufficient internal complexity they will begin to experience the world the way we do. We are nothing special.

The problem with consciousness is it does not seem to have any externally discernible effect. Anesthetics can take it away and brain scanners can see that it has been switched off, but what is it for? I think it comes hand in hand with our faculty of creativity. Consciousness allows us to shape the world – not the other way round.

Steve Jobs

"We can't solve problems by using the same kind of thinking we used when we created them."

Albert Einstein

Creative Theories

Once I have exercised my free will by getting out of bed in the morning, I often decide to do something creative. Humans seem driven to create. We compose music, draw, paint, and solve mathematical puzzles. Computers are not naturally creative; they spend most of their time doing exactly the opposite – following preset rules. Is this a fundamental limitation distinguishing the computational world from the real world?

The Conventional View

Most scientists believe pattern-matching algorithms in the brain allow us to be creative. To see how this might work, imagine our brains are chaotic – not hard to do – and process many competing ideas at the same time. The neurons in our brains build millions of useful, and useless, connections based on the patterns in the data we see and hear. Then a selection process goes to work – something akin to natural selection – to sift and prune the connections until something bubbles to the surface and we get that, 'aha' feeling.

Douglas Hofstadter, Professor of Cognitive Science at Indiana University, famous for the book *Gödel Escher Bach*, has written a computer program using pattern matching to discover number theorems; things like any number ending in a zero is divisible by 5. The program produces interesting results, even perhaps generating some new theorems. He argues the human brain is essentially a scaled up version of his program. By the way, if you like trivia, his book *Fluid Concepts & Creative Analogies* was the first book ever sold on Amazon.com.

The Unconventional View

Roger Penrose, Professor of Mathematics at Oxford University, holds a completely different view. He thinks brains operate in a non-algorithmic manner and provides a sketch of the possible mechanism in two books – *The Emperor's New Mind* and *Shadows of the Mind.* He suggests tubulin molecules, which form the skeleton of our neurons, exploit quantum-gravitational effects to calculate non-computable functions. The scientific community was initially highly skeptical that quantum effects could survive the warm, wet environment of biological systems, but in January of 2014, Edward O'Reilly and others at UCL discovered plants use quantum effects to improve the efficiency of photosynthesis. No prize has yet been awarded for this discovery but it must be a contender for a Nobel Prize at some point. Recently Travis Craddock, now of the Nova Institute in Florida, has submitted a paper showing a very similar geometry of proteins exists within tubulin microtubules in the brain. He believes this is evidence quantum effects may exist there as well.

A simple quantum effect in the brain could merely reduce the resistance of the wiring in the brain to help conserve power and avoid overheating. We recognize this is a major problem in building small, powerful conventional computers. Roger Penrose suggests an altogether more radical idea. He proposes our brains are quantum gravity computers capable of calculating non-computable functions. We don't yet have a theory for quantum gravity so his idea is at the cutting edge of physics – read highly controversial. He raises a deep mathematical question. If the Universe is deterministic and effectively equivalent to a computation, how does 'creative' knowledge emerge within it? Lots of knowledge can be manufactured by simply mechanically rearranging data. That's what happens when I watch a DVD or play a computer game, but, at some point in the past, a director or a programmer had to put in the creative effort to make the movie or write the computer program. How did that happen? Was it baked into the fabric of the Universe at the moment of the Big Bang? Is what we take for a Universe really nothing more complex than putting a DVD in the slot and hitting play?

One last piece of trivia links Hofstadter with Penrose: Roger Penrose and his father invented the Penrose Steps, inspiring the never-ending staircase in the Escher prints featured in Hofstadter's book. For movie buffs, the Penrose steps appear in the film *Inception,* starring Leonardo DiCaprio. The fact we get pleasure from these trivial links tells me something is going on in our brains that is not so mechanical.

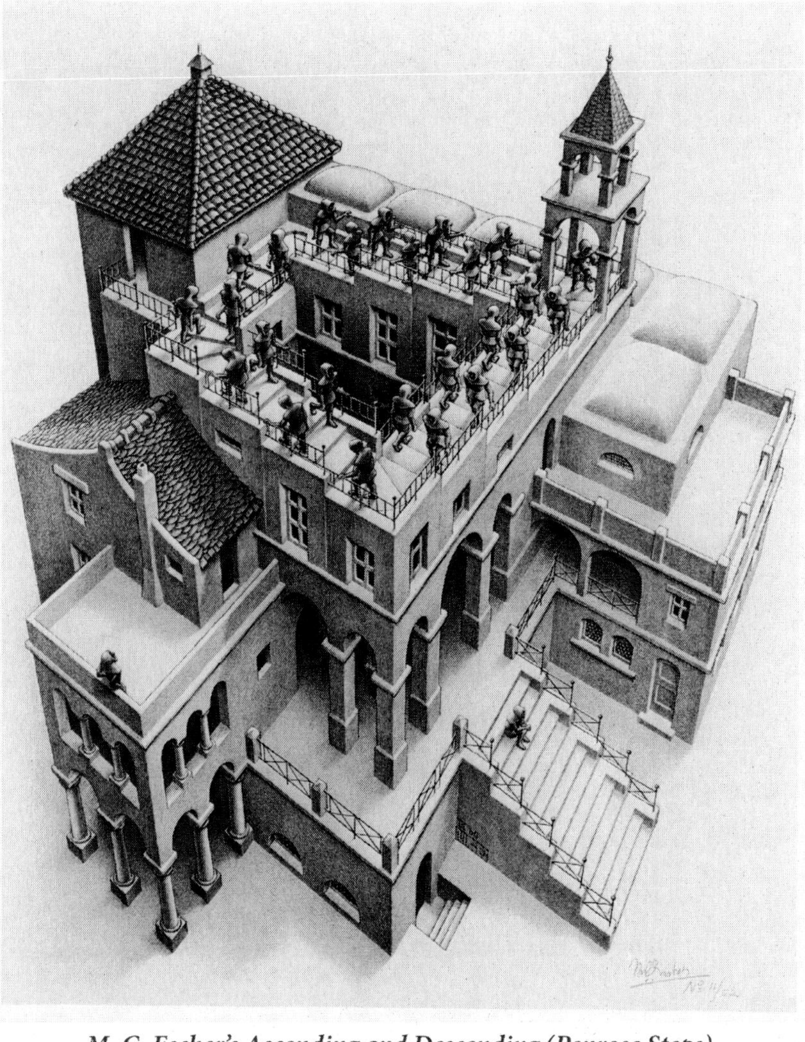

M. C. Escher's Ascending and Descending (Penrose Steps)

Chapter 2

UNDERSTANDING

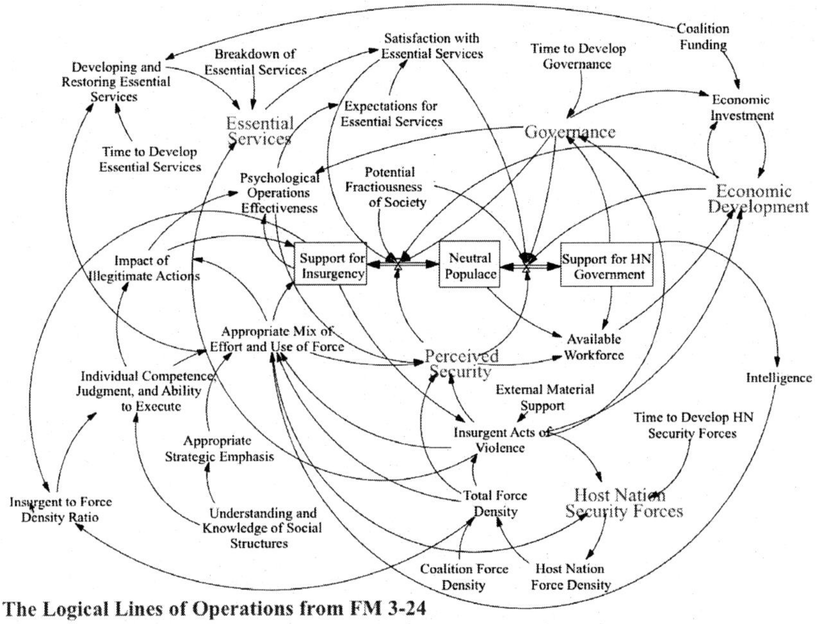

The Logical Lines of Operations from FM 3-24

Afghanistan COIN Dynamics

"Power corrupts, PowerPoint corrupts absolutely."

Ed Tufte

"No battle plan survives contact with the enemy."

Colin Powell
Originally, Helmuth von Moltke

John Masters stood up to address General Stanley A. McChrystal and his military staff in Kabul. The topic, of course, the war in Afghanistan. The main war lasted only eight weeks, but this did not end the conflict. A level of tribal violence and insurgent warfare rumbled on for years, killing around 30 people a week. Masters' job was to explain the dynamics of Afghanistan and provide politicians and military commanders a framework to understand what was going on.

Think about your country for a moment. What maintains the fabric of society – police, family, the local charity club, church, newspapers, the broadcast media? All these institutions work to keep us civilized, but what happens if a country loses them? There are institutions in Afghanistan, good and bad: tribes, gangs, corrupt officials, families. Masters had spent a year investigating these interactions, and questioning the returning commanders. He and his team believed that understanding the dynamics of the conflict was the key to bringing peace to Afghanistan.

If you live in an industrialized country, you rarely see society without its civilizing web in place. One interesting 'experiment' that shows what happens when it fails was the 1976 traffic police strike in Finland. Finland is a fantastically law abiding country where most people obey both the written and unwritten laws. During the strike, this behavior changed. Many people began parking illegally but refrained from blocking the roads. A few took advantage of the absence of police to drive incredibly fast – twice the national limit. These would be labeled as 'defectors' in game theory. Without traffic police, a different automotive

General Stanley A. McChrystal

morality emerged, a different structure to society. Of course all the other parts of society remained the same. People paid their taxes and went about their lives normally; only the traffic behavior was affected.

Afghanistan has had most of its social structures removed over the last forty or so years. First the Soviets, and then the Taliban, took apart much of the fabric until finally the Allied Forces swept the Taliban out, leaving very little behind. There were no police or courts, and few laws – or at least none enforced by the rule of law. The Allied Forces have spent a decade rebuilding these structures. Before we examine Masters' presentation, let's look at the daily life of an Afghan farmer.

If you are an Afghan farmer you have a dilemma. Your most reliable crop is opium. It grows well in the arid soil, does not require irrigation, and is resistant to most pests. For this crop there is a financial infrastructure to rival the Chicago Commodities Exchange. You get interest free loans secured against the crop, and you can forward sell your product on a futures market. Your investors can 'add value' by dealing with the major pest – the US military. They do this through the simple expedience of taking pot shots at them if they get too close to the crop. Since a field of opium is worth $30,000 and a militia wage for the year is $350, you can easily employ a few men to protect your investment. Of course, you are indebted to thugs and criminals, but they are at least reliable thugs and criminals.

On the other hand, the traditional products of the Himalayas – walnuts, pomegranates and vines – need years to cultivate. There is no forward market and the timescales over which you must take risks are far greater. If you believe your American protectors will leave before the crops mature, you will be loath to plant and care for them. But, if you make the decision to take this risk, you have a strong incentive to foster stability and reap the rewards of your effort. There is a feedback effect: the balance of power between all the different parties is important to the decisions you make, and the decisions you make affect your desire to invest in future stability.

Masters' team built a slide pack to demonstrate the complex interactions between the groups: farmers, security, stability, markets, military power, and emerging institutions. The COIN – COunter INsurgency – dynamics slide shows just how hard it is to communicate complex topics between human beings. The presentation is beautifully crafted but it was a public relations disaster. At the end of the presentation General McChrystal said jokingly, "When we understand that slide, we will have won the war." The slide was paraded in the press as, "the most complicated PowerPoint slide in history."

If you invest a little time on the slide you will understand it and may even see it as a thing of beauty. But Masters' audience was obviously expecting something different and, presented with this level of complexity, went into shutdown. Perhaps they wanted a simpler presentation, a high-level summary, a few bullet points. Of course, there is no simple presentation on Afghanistan. The lesson is that context, timing and expectation are often as important to good communication as the elegance of the content, and that information is a complex thing.

If you want a lighthearted poke at PowerPoint here is Peter Norvig's PowerPoint version of the Gettysburg Address.

Understanding

Next time you are in a business meeting, count the number of times the word 'understand' is used. If you ask the people around you what it means you'll stump many of them. That's because understanding has two very different meanings. Most people don't separate these meanings but the distinction is important. Understanding means to decode information, to comprehend – but, more importantly, it also means to absorb and internalize information. That feeling you have when you 'get it'.

If I say, "I understand" I mean I have taken in the question you asked and decoded it into ideas so I can provide an answer. This can be quite a mechanical process and computers routinely understand natural language and answer questions – Apple's digital assistant Siri being a case in point.

When I say, "I understand a problem" or "understand a culture" I mean something far less tangible. Somehow the information I have gathered over my life is formed into a matrix within my brain that allows me to ponder and run scenarios. I can predict the effects of my actions before I do them, and often anticipate your responses. That's clearly a very useful evolutionary adaption, but is there more to it than that? Roger Penrose and David Deutsch think understanding allows us to transfer non-symbolic information from one brain to another. We don't run programs in our brains, nor do we store precise information such as lists and tables. We have, therefore, had to evolve a creative approach to communicating skills and understanding each other. One of the most closely studied areas in the field of communication is when it breaks down in the lead up to a disaster.

"The human mind tends to look for clear linear relationships, we like solutions that are close to the problem in time and space and make sense when we think about it quickly, unfortunately, those simple solutions are usually wrong and come from acting on a complex system as if it was a simple one."

Brett Piersen

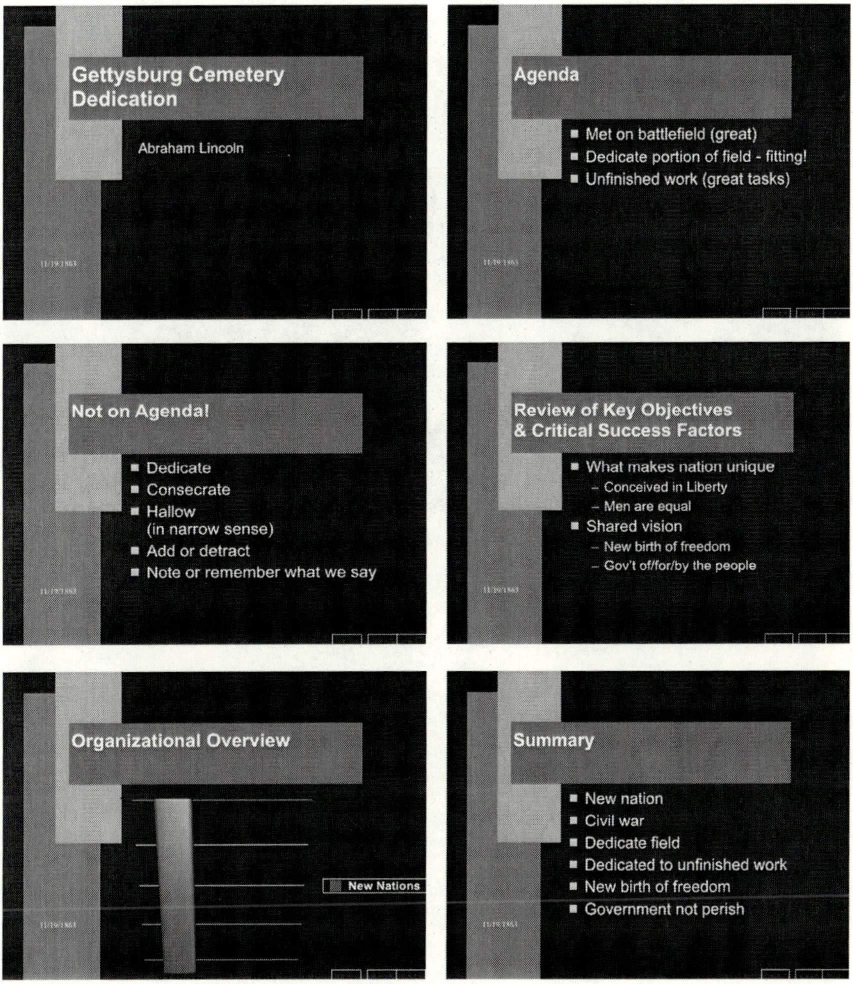

Gettysburg Address, Peter Norvig

Space Shuttle Columbia Crew Photo

*"For a successful technology,
reality must take precedence
over public relations, for Nature
cannot be fooled."*

Richard Feynman

Bad Understanding Can Kill

On January 16, 2003, at 3:39pm, the Columbia space shuttle took off from Cape Canaveral. During the launch a small piece of foam insulation broke off the fuel tank and hit the shuttlecraft. The event was recorded on a few low-resolution video frames. They show a tiny white object hitting the shuttle and a plume of dusty material splattering outward. The shuttle made it safely into orbit and for two weeks engineers on the ground debated what to do. In the end, it was decided the risk was minimal and the shuttle could safely return to Earth. On reentry, the shuttle disintegrated, killing seven astronauts.

NASA managers had decided the shuttle was undamaged based on a series of presentations by the engineers. One image in particular analyzed the potential damage to the shuttle's tiles from an impact. Read the slide, look at the key frames, and decide for yourself what action you would have taken.

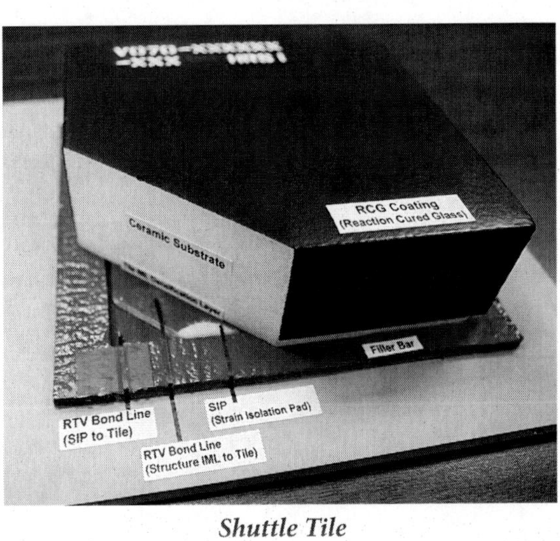

Shuttle Tile

Review of Test Data Indicates Conservatism for Tile Penetration

- **The existing SOFI on tile test data used to create Crater was reviewed along with STS-87 Southwest Research data**
  - **Crater overpredicted penetration of tile coating significantly**
    - **Initial penetration to described by normal velocity**
      - Varies with volume/mass of projectile (e.g., 200ft/sec for 3cu. In)
    - **Significant energy is required for the softer SOFI particle to penetrate the relatively hard tile coating**
      - Test results do show that it is possible at sufficient mass and velocity
    - **Conversely, once tile is penetrated SOFI can cause significant damage**
      - Minor variations in total energy (above penetration level) can cause significant tile damage
  - **Flight condition is significantly outside of test database**
    - **Volume of ramp is 1920cu in vs 3 cu in for test**

BOEING 2/21/03 6

NASA Internal Slide

WHAT DO YOU UNDERSTAND FROM THE SLIDE?

Some images of the launch are shown on the right

Here is what you should have understood from the slide: tiles are really tough but if the foam dislodged from the fuel tank broke through the outer coating it would cause significant damage. The estimated speed of the foam hitting the tile was 640 times greater than anything previously tested. Worried?

Is this a proper understanding of the problem? You have the slide and the images. Take another look and think hard. If you want, you can check a video of a similar launch on YouTube to get a feel for the scale of things, but the still frames shown all the information you need to make your conclusion.

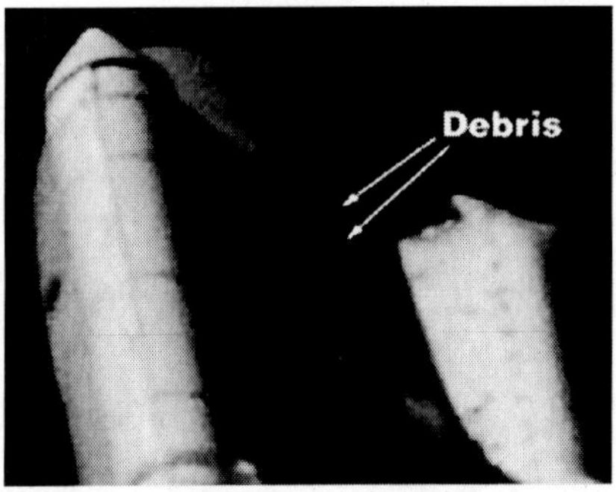

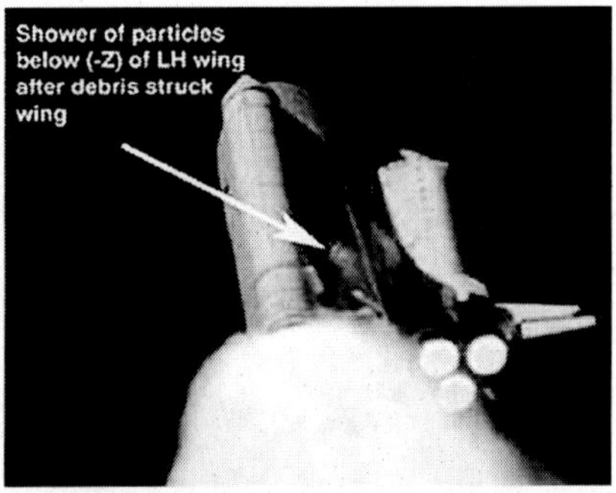

Photographs of the Foam Impact from Video Footage

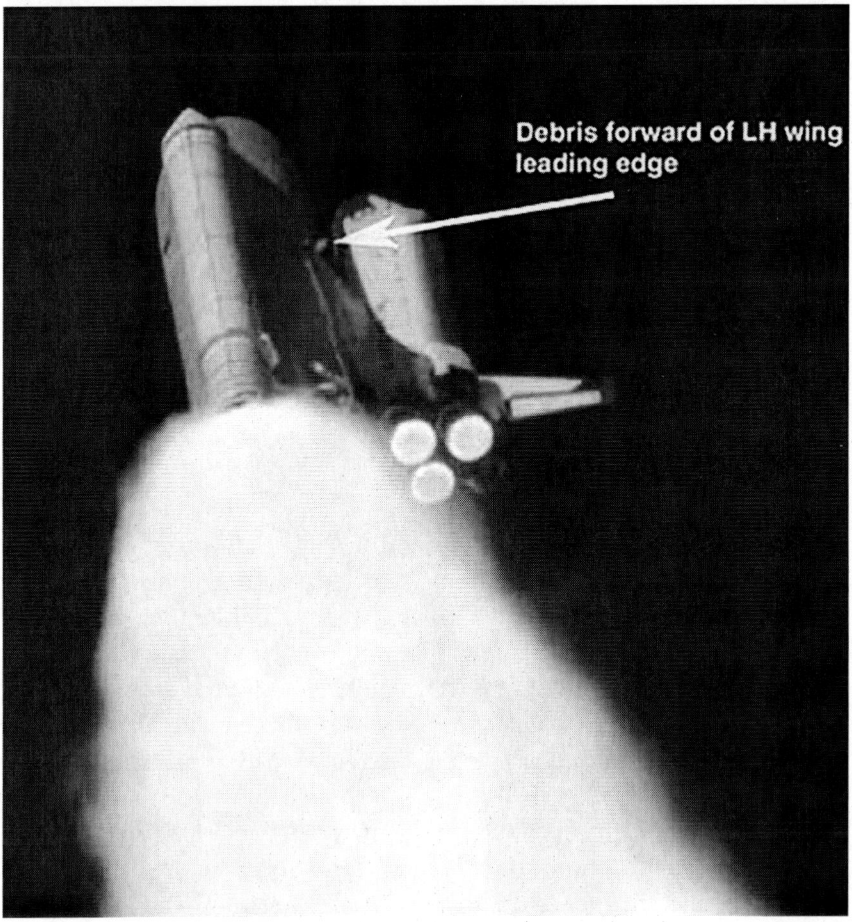

Frame Showing Foam Dislodging

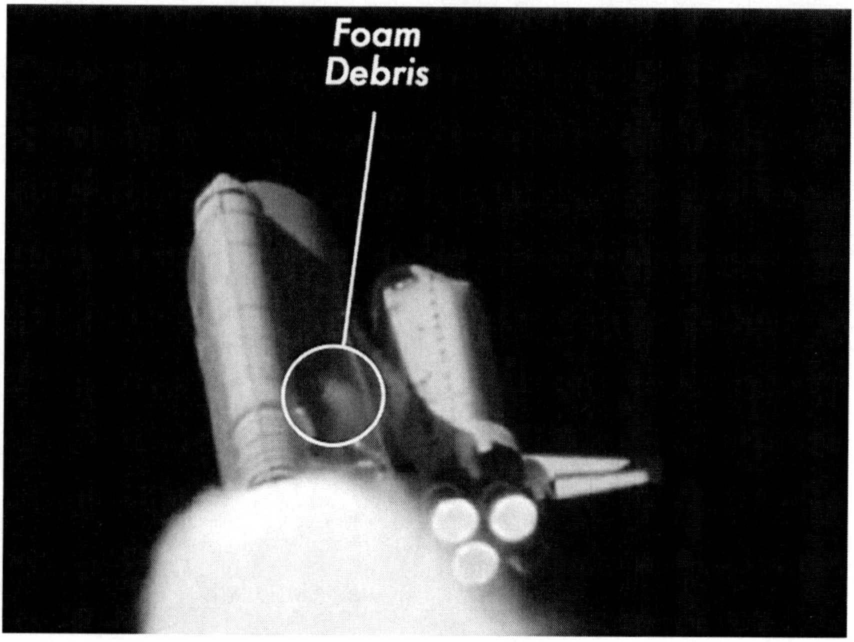

Still from Ground Camera

LOOK AT THE IMAGES, WHAT HAPPENED?

The truth is you simply don't know. If you are puzzling over the strength of tiles, you have been misdirected. There is video footage of some sort of impact on a wing mostly covered in white tiles, and a slide describing the effect of a benign sounding 'foam' hitting those tiles. But what is the evidence for an impact on a tile? The shuttle is certainly not made entirely from tiles; I can see a window in the picture. You should instead be asking more questions, "What happened?" "What hit what?" and "How bad is that?"

It was bad. The foam, a very tough material, had hit the leading edge of the wing, a weak point, punching a hole through it. The wing failed on reentry and tore the shuttle apart. Clearly, a full discussion of the possibilities did not occur amongst the shuttle team, or perhaps it only happened amongst the engineers in private. Once the analysis was tidied up and presented to 'management' it was a one-way communication of the conclusions, not a discussion of the underlying ambiguous thought process. The result: people passively listened to the information rather than interactively understanding it and agreed on the recommendation that it was safe to return. Clearly they did not understand the ambiguity otherwise they would have realized they did not have enough information to form a conclusion. This is the tragedy of lack of understanding. If they had known how little they knew, they could have deployed a spy satellite to take pictures of the damage – one was available nearby and would have taken a few hours to re-task – but they did not.

Ed Tufte served on the second shuttle disaster commission and provided an analysis of the disaster. He views slides as a poor medium for communicating complex problems and thinks documents are far better. The danger with slides is they force you to simplify information in a way that destroys the essence of the information. His analysis of the failure of communication at NASA formed a major part of the final report on the disaster. Later he coined the paraphrase "All Power corrupts; PowerPoint corrupts absolutely." Good communication benefits from stories and narrative, not bullet points and graphic fluff. Instead of using bullet points, speak! After all, we have evolved for 250,000 years to understand language, but only 25 to read PowerPoints. '

If you write presentations, Ed Tufte's book *The Cognitive Style of PowerPoint* is compulsory reading. He argues that much of the information you want to communicate is complex and interconnected. PowerPoint or any similar presentation software encourages you to simplify it into hierarchical bullets. The format implies simple causal relationships where none exists. This is dangerous. Communication should convey understanding – which is very important – and not just information. What, you ask, is the difference?

Searle's Chinese Room

"The hardest thing to understand is why we can understand anything at all."

Albert Einstein

The Imitation Game

As an experiment, I am going to ask a student to spend a week in a locked room. The room is perfectly nice; it has a bed, a light, a desk, some reading matter, oh, and we'll give him some washing facilities too! Every now and then I post some food under the door to keep him going, Pop-tarts and pizza (thin-crust) work well.

On the first evening a note is pushed under his door with a symbol on it. The student puzzles for a while, then opens the book sitting on the desk. The book says, "If you get a piece of paper with symbols on it look them up and follow the instructions." He looks up the symbols and the entry in the book says, "Go to page 44, write down the third symbol on a piece of paper then post it back under the door." He follows the instruction and is rewarded with another piece of paper, this time with a larger set of symbols on it. Again he follows the instructions in the book and posts his answer back under the door. This goes on for several days. He is somewhat bemused, but it passes the time, and he diligently looks up the symbols and performs all the complicated actions as instructed.

Meanwhile, I meet our new Chinese graduate student and explain to her she needs to interview a potential translator for the department. He has just come in from Hong Kong and there is a health scare, so we have quarantined him in the lab room. He is bored and I have some paper for writing messages. She writes "hello" in Chinese on a piece of paper and posts it under the door.

The exchange of notes goes on for a few days and the two seem to be getting on well. There is even a little romance in the air. When the week is over I open the door and the two meet. The graduate student says, "Hello. It's nice to finally meet you in person." The man is puzzled because, of course, she has spoken to him in Chinese. He knows no Chinese.

"I'm terribly sorry, but I don't speak Chinese," he says.

She is puzzled, "But I spoke with you this last week!"

"No, I really don't speak it," he says.

And, of course, he is telling the truth. The book he has been using contains the rules for answering questions in Chinese, but he has absolutely no knowledge of the language. I'll leave to your imagination whether the two strike up a real relationship and live happily ever after.

This is the Story of the Chinese Room. The setup is able to fool someone into believing there is a Chinese speaking person in the room, yet there is not. Where does the understanding of Chinese lie? The man definitely does not understand Chinese. And the book clearly does not understand Chinese because it is an inanimate object. Yet the person outside the room is convinced she is communicating with a Chinese speaker. The analogy to a computer is clear. The book is software and the man blindly following instructions is the hardware. John Searle, who devised the thought experiment uses it to show computers can never understand because there is no place in a mechanistic system for understanding to exist.

The Chinese Room has sparked huge argument in philosophical circles; let me boil it down to its simplest form. First, let's refute Searle's position with the 'System Argument'.

The man plus the book form a system. Systems understand; their individual components do not. My blood does not understand. My brain without blood would not understand – it would be dead! Plug my brain into a good supply of blood; add a dash of glucose, and it will understand the most complex of things.

The systems argument is elegant and most scientists think this is the definitive argument against Searle, but Searle has a neat way to counter it. "Imagine", he says, "that the man memorizes the book and leaves the room. Now there is no system, there is just the man, but the man still does not understand Chinese; he is just parroting rote-memorized words and rules." Computers, Searle argues, process syntax – the rules of language; humans understand semantics – the contextual meaning of language.

Artificial Intelligence (AI) proponents hate the Searle argument. They believe the memorization of a set of words and rules is exactly what gives us knowledge of Chinese. That is why we go to school!

A key problem posed by Searle's Chinese Room is whether you can know everything about a situation from just looking at the inputs and outputs. This is very similar to the restriction posed by the Turing Test. In that case if we were to trace the wire from our computer terminal to the other room we would either find a human typing messages or a large box covered in flashing lights. This would definitively answer the question whether we were talking to a man or a machine. Similarly, if we opened the door to the Chinese Room we would immediately know whether there was a real Chinese speaker in there or not. But opening the door on both tests misses the point. The question asks, "if the inputs and outputs are the same does it matter what is *really* going on inside a closed system?"

Black Boxes

Experiments involving closed systems are known as Black Box experiments. They presume you can learn *everything* about the inner workings of a box simply by probing it from the outside. Young electronic engineers are often given black boxes as a test. Electronic components hidden in the box are connected to three external terminals on the outside. The student is asked to deduce what is in the box using only an electric meter to probe those terminals. Here are a few examples of the possible contents of a black box. They would all show up identically on the student's meter. Although internally different they are externally identical. Even my 'silly' fourth choice with a cat in the box does not give

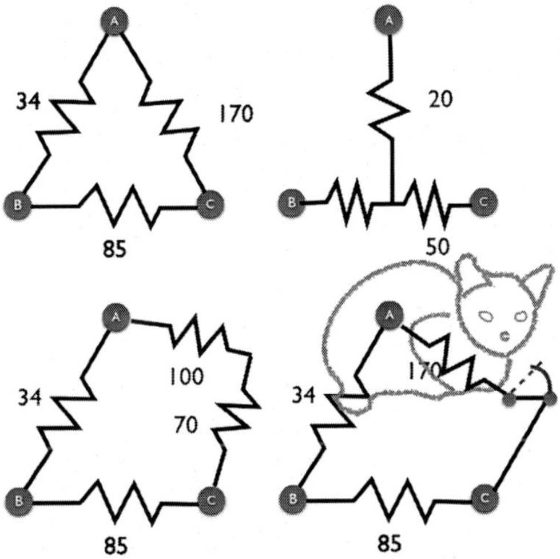

Black Box Equivalence

itself away if all you have to go on are electrical readings. (I dare say the cat would make its displeasure know if left in there for any time.) The contents are, therefore, said to be black box equivalent.

The reason for teaching engineers about black boxes is to help them understand how to simplify things. We could construct option four, with a cat and some food, but it would cost a great deal of money. Option 1 is functionally identical from an electrical point of view, but for a fraction of the cost. Steve Wozniak and Steve Jobs were so successful when they started Apple because Wozniak was brilliant at simplifying logic circuits. He could take a design with thirty chips and come back with a black box equivalent solution using only five. It was a fraction of the cost and far more reliable.

Scientists put great store in black box equivalence because of a principle called Occam's Razor. William of Occam was an English Franciscan friar living in the fourteenth century. He proposed the idea of minimal explanation. It states that, 'among competing hypotheses, the hypothesis with the fewest assumptions should be selected'. When trying to explain the workings of a black box, the more complicated inner workings should be discarded, as they have no externally verifiable effect over the simpler mechanism. Our extraneous animal must be eliminated! Sorry.

Ironically, given his calling, Occam's Razor is sometimes wheeled out as a disproof of the existence of God. Surely God is a complication unnecessary to the explanation of our Universe. The argument is illustrated beautifully in Carl Sagan's book *Contact* and the film of the same name. God gets the last laugh in Sagan's book when the difficulty with Occam's Razor is brought into sharp focus. Occam's Razor contains an inherent paradox. At any moment in time we only have evidence to support the simplest of explanations, yet we know many of these simple explanations are incomplete. We regularly discover new phenomenon – dark matter and dark energy being some recent examples. If we stopped discovering new things, Occam's Razor would be a good way to simplify our thoughts. Occam's Razor is a useful intellectual tool to prevent us over complicating explanations, but there will often be explanations that are correct, but for which there is not yet any observed effect.

If we go back to our black box example, we see the flaw in concluding the boxes are identical from examining only their inputs and outputs. Opening them would clearly show they are not identical! But, how would this fact reveal itself if they remain closed? The answer is: over time. If something in the box has memory or understanding, it could present one set of results for a while and a completely different set of results later.

In my trivial example, the cat could eat a wire and change the operation of the black box. Now there is an open circuit where none existed before. If this happened, the output would change and we would need a new theory to explain it. If the circuit was attached to a missile control system or a life support system, you would really want a full understanding without waiting. It's humans nature to try to open black boxes. This is what MRI scans, X-rays, particle accelerators and all our other tools of scientific investigation are for. We want to open all the black boxes of nature and see what is going on inside: simply waiting to see what happens is not acceptable.

In a sense, we live in a black box. We experience the world through our senses, seeing with our eyes and feeling with our hands. The brain never directly experiences anything; it only infers the likelihood of

Scene from The Miracle Worker. Helen Keller pictured at the moment she understood language.

something from the signals it receives. This is similar to our engineer probing the terminals of the circuit of a black box. How can we know our experience of the world is real?

Understanding the World

The French philosopher Descartes gave us an explanation for this paradox. He spent a long time looking skeptically at everything we perceive. For example, when we poke a stick into a pond, the surface of the water bends light and the stick appears to have a kink in it. Our eyes tell us the stick is bent, but our brain 'knows' the stick is straight: it's an illusion. Descartes wondered if something so simple could be an illusion, perhaps the whole of our experience is too.

His eventual solution underpins much of modern philosophy – 'I think therefore I am', *cogito ergo sum*. Even if we doubt everything else, we cannot doubt we are thinking about this doubt. At least we can rely upon the existence of this 'thought' as some reality. Descartes built up from this bedrock the real world we live in. We can be sure we experience things and can apply logic and use thought. We can use this intellectual faculty to tell a great deal about our Universe.

True Understanding

In the QED lecture series, *The Strange Thing about Light and Matter*, Richard Feynman relates the story of the ancient Mayan astronomers. 3000 years ago they were able to predict the motion of Venus in the sky using only pebbles. They had a simple system that could predict when the planet would rise over the horizon. Put a stone in the jar every day, take out a stone once a week, add a stone at every new moon. If the number of stones in the jar is divisible by 23, Venus will rise. I'm making up the details but you see the idea... It's a very simple algorithm. What should we conclude if the Mayans had perfected their calculations to predict the motion of Venus and it proved reliable over a whole century? Would this constitute understanding?

Feynman would say no: the Mayan understanding was not complete. It was only black box equivalent to our modern understanding over a limited period. We known that once the Sun begins to run out of fuel it will swell to a red giant and explode, destroying Venus and the Earth. Their model could not predict this catastrophic failure. Our modern deeper understanding of the workings of the solar system allows us to predict this future even though there is no clue from the motion of Venus today. Understanding allows us to predict discontinuous events: a system changing its state or a star running out of fuel.

We see the same predicament in stock markets. Stock markets normally behave in a linear fashion but, when they go wrong; they go *very* wrong. Recent recessions have been made much worse by the failure of hedging systems to handle market disruption. Some even think the crises were caused by the automatic trading strategies of these hedging systems.

The quants – as mathematicians in banks are called – spend considerable effort modeling financial instruments to show that if one stock goes down, another will go up at the same time. If the stocks are held together your investment is safe because, on average they will remain constant. The problem with these correlations, which often hold reliably for many years, is that when trouble hits they fall apart. Historical correlations don't give us understanding of the future: something that was only meant to happen once in a million years has happened within six months. As they say on your investment papers, past performance is no predictor of future results.

Do Computers Understand?

Today's computers don't have our general-purpose ability to understand. Watson was thrown off by badly formatted English. The human contestants, by contrast, had no problem with this. Just how good would Watson have to be, to call it – or should I say 'him' – intelligent? How could I judge this had happened? Alan Turing proposed an ingenious test in his 1950 paper Computing Machinery and Intelligence using 'The Imitation Game.' We now call the Turing Test.

If we ask a series of questions to a computer and we cannot tell its responses from those a human would give, then the computer is, for all practical purposes, the same as a human. Since we are intelligent – or at least we hope we are – the computer must also be intelligent. QED.

That's all there is to the Turing Test. Puzzled? Let's pick his argument apart.

Imagine you are chatting away on Facebook with someone you don't know. They may have posted a photograph so you can see what they look like. The photo might be a fake; you have no real way to tell. What question would you ask the other 'person' to prove they were human and not a computer? There are obviously some giveaway questions. Please multiply the numbers 342,321 and 23,294 and give me the answer. This would be very hard for a human but easy for a computer. If you got a very quick answer; the computer would have given itself away. But, the computer has been programmed not to give itself away, and it is free to give the answer slowly or even reply that the calculation is too hard. Our computer can say anything it likes, including lying to pass the test! If the computer can fool a questioner into believing it is a human then Turing argued the computer has shown it is at least as intelligent as we are.

It used to be assumed that the field of broad general knowledge would be hard for a computer, but Watson has shown this is not so. With enough storage and a reasonable algorithm, winning a pub quiz is well within the capability of a modern computer.

The really difficult questions for a computer are philosophical ones, novel questions and things that don't fall into a pattern. For example,

"Are you happy?"

"What do you think of Shakespeare's Hamlet?"

"Is there life after death?"

"How went it?"

"Think Differ..."

If a computer could plausibly answer this sort of questioning for an extended period, say fifteen minutes, should we conclude it is intelligent, or do we need more time to be certain?

Turing's approach to certainty was simple. Just ask lots of questions. As you ask more and more questions, you will become increasingly certain you are talking to an intelligent being. He characterized it as a linear process; after 15 minutes of questioning you might be 99% certain and after a few hours 99.9% certain and after a few days completely certain. The problem with this approach is it does not flush out discontinuities. What if the questioning suddenly stopped without warning or explanation? A human responder is likely to worry that the questioner has had a heart attack and do something to find out what is going on including leaving the room. Humans can make creative leaps, solve non-computable puzzles or come up with a clever new joke. A humans could even announce the test is a waste of time and walk off. They just exercised free will! A computer cannot do these things.

Each year a group of scientists enters a competition run by Cambridge University to win the Loebner prize, a competition to see how close a machine can come to passing the Turing Test. If you can beat the test you win $100,000. So far no one has come close and scientists are beginning to realize just how hard it is.

"On the Internet, nobody knows you're a dog."

New Yorker Cartoon

With the anonymity the Internet provides we can imagine all sorts of strange scenarios if the Turing test could be passed. You would have no way of knowing what you were talking to. The New Yorker ran a cartoon back in 2000. "On the Internet no one knows you are a dog." We come across a similar problem the other way around when we encounter bad customer support. A few years ago, while trying to get an answer to a computer problem, I became convinced the thing responding to my emails was a machine. The company did use machine responder technology so it could well have been. I asked it to prove it was human by putting the word marmalade into an English sentence and fixing my problem. The human pretending to be a machine saw the joke, fixed my problem and replied "Marmalade is served with butter and toast." The test worked!

Uncannily not Human

The sister test in robotics is equally hard. The goal is to simulate the physical human form, its movements and mannerisms. It's easy to get close, but close is not good enough. The term 'Uncanny Valley' has been coined to describe the discomfort humans have with something that tries to simulate a human being but does not quite get there. I think it is part of the reason Madam Tussaud's waxworks are so fascinating. Humans have a love-hate relationship with facsimiles of themselves. They love the flattery but feel a sense of revulsion at anything that comes too close.

Searle and Turing

In the Turing Test, we limited our senses to the purely symbolic: using only typed words on a screen. I could break the lock on the door and go into the room to see what was there.

"Aha!" I would say.

"I can see you're a computer, I, therefore, know you'll be good at sums and bad at creativity."

But Turing wants us to see if the difference is given away purely through intellect. He argues there is no way to tell. But if you follow my argument from chapter 1, there is one way: ask the computer to find a non-computable solution to a mathematical puzzle. This is, in practice, a difficult test to pose because it might take a *very* long time. Twenty-five billion people have lived on planet Earth during the last 350 years, and about 5 million of them were mathematicians. None of them was able to solve the problem posed by Pierre de Fermat until Andrew Wiles turned up but this is a clear difference between humans and computers. However long you give a computer it would never be able to solve the problem.

This creativity test would take centuries to run if non-computable thought was rare, but I think we see it often – on display even when we tell jokes. In which case computers and humans should be easy to tell apart: humans are the funny ones. I am not saying you can't build a brain; our brains are physical devices, after all. I just believe a computer or a mechanistic machine, cannot think like a human being.

I like the Searle argument but qualitative arguments are insufficient. We need a quantitative argument. In the forthcoming chapters, I am going to look at the mathematical argument underlying the difference between human intelligence and computer processing. Before we do this let's take one last look at a qualitative difference; the way computers and humans communicate.

Chapter 3

BODY LANGUAGE & BANTER

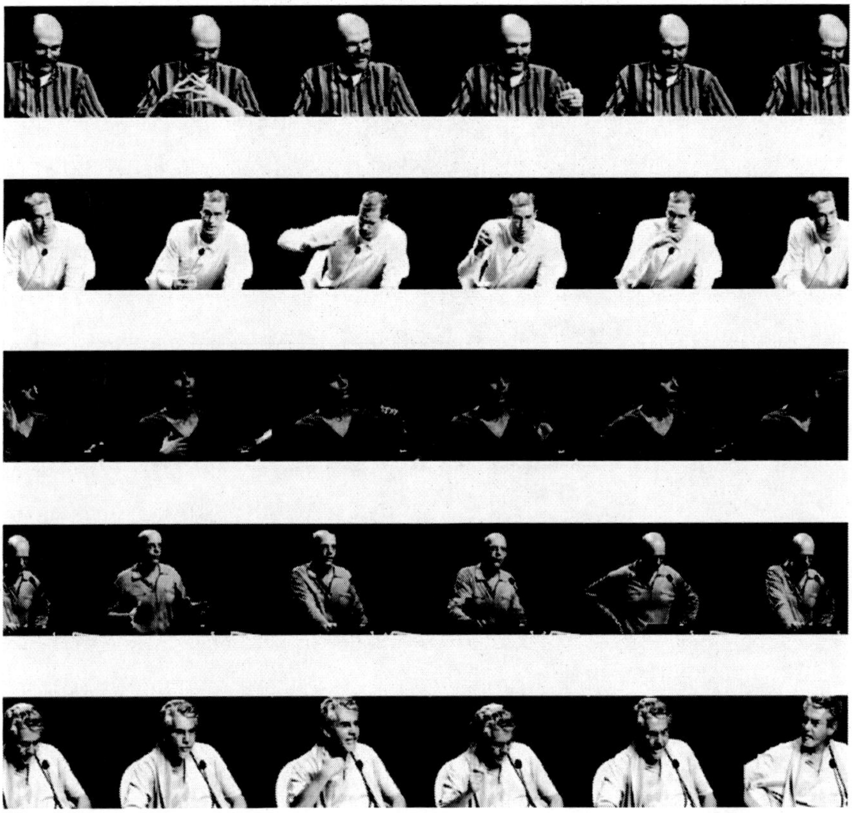

Body Language

“England and America are two countries separated by a common language.”

George Bernard Shaw

“I speak two languages, Body and English.”

Mae West

“The body never lies.”

Martha Graham

In the summer of 1986 Ronald Reagan and Mikael Gorbachev met in person for their second negotiation session, this time at the Höfði House in Reykjavik. For five days, the leaders talked alone except for interpreters. Reagan badly wanted to develop the Strategic Defense Initiative; known by its nickname, 'Star Wars'. The idea was to put smart weaponry in space that could destroy ballistic missiles before they reentered the atmosphere. Reagan believed this would remove the threat of imminent destruction that had hung over the world since 1945. Gorbachev, on the other hand, felt this was just another escalation in the Cold War, and the Soviet Union would be forced to build yet more weapons to overcome the American defenses. He wanted Reagan's plans shelved, arguing that it broke the Anti-Ballistic Missile Treaty. He was probably right. The leaders talked back and forth, unable to overcome the impasse. At the end of the summit there was a mad scramble to announce some sort of deal, but this proved difficult. In the last moments before they had to conclude a communiqué, Reagan suggested they abolish *all* nuclear weapons. Reagan's negotiating team was horrified and shut the door.

For decades, the American strategy had been to use nuclear weapons as a deterrent against the apparent numerical advantage of the Soviets. In all the potential scenarios analyzed by the Pentagon, Russian forces ended up overrunning American forward positions – otherwise known as Western Europe! The only way to stop them was through a release of nuclear weapons, which, inevitably escalated to all-out nuclear

Ronald Reagan and Mikael Gorbachev

war. It was assumed this inevitable progression deterred the aggression in the first place, and the threat of mutually assured destruction kept the world peaceful. Giving up this tenet of defense strategy was something the American military just could not contemplate. Many people did not think it a rational defense strategy; it seemed appropriate the acronym for mutually assured destruction is MAD, but this was the status quo.

We now know our worry over Russian superiority was groundless. The West's technological advantage, founded on the invention of computing and sophisticated materials technology, gave us a huge advantage. In the only battle to be fought in the 20th century between Russian and Western tanks, during the first Iraq war, most of the Russian tanks were destroyed with no losses to American tanks. We know this now, but we are talking of a time when paranoia over the Soviet advantage was the common view.

There is speculation that Reagan had muddled intercontinental ballistic missiles with all nuclear weapons. I do not think this is true. Reagan was a man of vision, quite comfortable with using his folksy way to convey sincere belief, and I think abolishing all nuclear weapons was in his mind. It would have been a breathtaking moment.

In the end a rather feeble communiqué was put together and the talks declared a technical failure. But, both leaders had seen eye-to-eye; both were prepared to make major concessions and both wanted an end to the old strategy of mutually assured destruction. Wiping each other out was no longer considered a successful outcome! The meeting, and

Höfði House in Reykjavik

the fundamental thawing of relations between East and West, was to lead to the Intermediate-Range Nuclear Forces Treaty and the end of the Cold War.

Face-to-Face Communication

What really happened between these two leaders when they met and talked? Was it a mechanical process of offer and counter-offer, as easily executed by fax, or is human interaction more complex than this?

Reagan, as a young man, had been a liberal, sympathetic to socialist ideals until a painful strike in California caused him to lose faith in the politics of the left. Gorbachev, a lifelong Communist, was desperate to reform the Soviet economy and make it more competitive. He, also, had come to see the hypocrisies that could emerge in far left-wing ideology. I don't believe this common experience could have been communicated by fax or email. Indeed, I am sure these specific points were never made, but the nonverbal communication must have conveyed something of their common background and purpose.

When we phone someone or exchange emails, the interaction is factual, there is no body language, and we rarely laugh. When we travel to meet someone, we spend a great deal of time with them. The average length of a phone call is two and a half minutes, but meetings, especially when one party has travelled to see the other, can be hours long. When humans meet they greet each other, shake hands, sit in the same room, talk at length, and laugh. Body language is important; people mirror each other's postures, adopt open and receptive stances, and make eye contact. You can see this in the picture of Reagan and Gorbachev above. Body language allows us to convey qualitatively different things, such as trust and happiness. It is very expressive; you can see the more guarded postures of Yasser Arafat and Shimon Pérez below, just after they negotiated a landmark peace deal. Can you tell if the leaders smiles are false?

Communication

Communication is one of mankind's greatest expenditures. The US telephone system is arguably the largest machine on the planet, while the world's mobile phone networks have a capital value of $2.5 trillion, greater by an order of magnitude than all the steel plants in the world put

Yasser Arafat and Shimon Pérez

together. This lifeblood of our existence – long-distance communication between human beings – turns out to be amazingly difficult, even with all our clever technology.

In recent years the Internet has, in theory, allowed each and every person to communicate freely with any other person on the planet. In some of the most distant parts of the world mobile phones, and projects such as; 'One Laptop per Child' are rapidly bringing unlimited communication to all. This communication can be personal, one-to-one, or broadcast: I can talk to people interested in a particular topic directly. As we watch the Arab world democratize, catalyzed by the Internet, there is no question that digital communication has now become a major force in the world. Yet, people don't communicate over the Internet as much as you would expect; they often use the Internet to set up phone calls during which they arrange meetings! This is odd. We have a fantastic phone system and sophisticated communication technologies; email, video and instant messaging. Yet, we still choose to travel when we want to communicate.

On the face of it, there should be no difference between a phone call and a meeting. In principle the same information can be conveyed. Yet when we want to really understand someone, we always go to meet

Smiles Fake or Real

in person. No great treaty or big industrial contract has been negotiated without a face-to-face meeting. We see this daily: people talking on the phone get to a certain point, give up, and arrange to meet in person.

The consequence is that we spend $550 billion annually, flying around the globe to meet each other. Each day the world's population takes three million plane flights. Around 80% of these are business flights. Some are people emigrating or going to do specific manual tasks, but most are to have meetings. We have always assumed that this is because the parties are unable to reach a sufficient level of trust over the phone and need face-to-face interaction to build that trust, but it may be that the parties are not able to convey sufficient information to fully understand each other. Face-to-face meeting may convey much more information than we think.

Smiles

When we smile naturally we use a full set of facial muscles, including the muscles around our eyes. When the smile is forced those eye muscles remain passive and the smile, although superficially the same, is missing something. You can't put your finger on it, but the look is insincere. A study of marriages in the USA analyzed smiles in wedding photographs. The couples with false smiles divorced much earlier than the genuinely happy couples. Similarly for high school photos; people with genuine smiles at 18 years of age were happier later in life and in more stable relationships. Smiling is really important. It is good to be around people who smile, they are more successful – and nicer.

There is also a curious reverse effect. The link between our minds and bodies is much more fundamental than we thought. If you grasp a pencil between your teeth, it forces you to smile. Try it. The mere act of smiling is found to make you happier, it causes the release of the chemicals called endorphins which improve your feeling of well-being.

Micro-expression Analysis

Since the involuntary movements of the muscles around our eyes give away genuine happiness, a whole science has evolved looking for other biological cues to mood. The two most interested groups are the FBI, trying to detect lies, and poker players, trying to make money! Much has been written on the topic, including a few best sellers, but the evidence for micro expressions is mixed. Regardless of whether involuntary actions give away our emotions, humans voluntarily use a great deal of body language when talking.

Body Language

A study by Albert Mehrabian is often cited to say 93% of the information in a conversation comes through nonverbal cues. This is misquoted. The study really stated 93% of the *emotional* content is nonverbal. That's more believable. And further studies have shown when there is doubt, nonverbal cues win over verbal information every time. The rule is sometimes laid out as the 7%-38%-55% rule – 7% words, 38% tone of voice and 55% body language. Remember this is emotional content, your conviction and sincerity. You will still have to get over the factual information you want to convey.

Learning Swedish with The Two Ronnies

Try this experiment on a friend. Tell them you like their shirt using different tones of voice: sarcastic, sincere, amazed. Then see what they understood. You will find it difficult to appear sincere because I have told you to say you like their shirt – unless of course you really do. When you use sarcasm they will find it hard to process your statement. It is revealing how we use the information.

Interestingly, a piece of research described in *Scientific American* shows even insincere flattery is effective. If you want a pay rise from your boss, any form of flattery will do. Vanity appears to override skepticism!

Interaction

The normal cadence of communication between people includes a great deal of mutual interruption. When a meeting breaks down we often see people begin to say things like, "Please don't interrupt me," "Do you mind, I was talking," "Pleeeease, let me finish." If the meeting is really getting out of hand, third parties will often step in and tell one to wait for the other. This is where the mechanics of face-to-face interaction fail, as we need to interact in order to communicate effectively.

Because we have a lot more time in a face-to-face meeting people can wander 'off topic'. This is an important part of the process of communicating. After all since most phone calls are 2-3 minutes and most meetings an hour, there are another 57 minutes to fill! These off topic items bring in social experience and help us form the background context we need to properly communicate.

What is Background Context?

Alex and Bella are both fans of the British comedy duo, the Two Ronnies, and enjoy their learning Swedish sketch. Bella asks Alex what kind of sandwich he wants for lunch. Alex replies 'M'. Bella laughs. If you have seen the sketch you will understand the background context to the joke. If not this paragraph might as well have been in Swedish. Take a look at the sketch on YouTube and reread this paragraph... Now you understand.

Do I think in English?

Most scientists believe we think thoughts using language, but most scientists writing about thought are linguists or psychologists. If you are a dyslexic engineer like me, language is a long way down the processing chain. I think abstractly and then translate those thoughts into words. Some ideas don't map between languages and often, one language adopts the words of another to fill in the gaps. Some interesting examples are:

Zeitgeist	German, spirit of the times
Schadenfreude	German, enjoying others misfortune
Chutzpah	Hebrew, audacity

All of these are fully signed up, card carrying entries in the Oxford English Dictionary.

Some languages have fewer distinctions between ideas: truth and law are the same word, 'torah', in Hebrew. Languages have different tenses and structure. In Chinese all words are one syllable and the script is pictographic rather than phonetic. This is unusual, even Egyptian and linear-B, which look pictographic are mostly phonetic. With single syllable words, Chinese uses voice inflection to change meaning; a rising or falling tone can change the meaning of a word from 'grey' to 'girl'. In many Western languages rising voice inflection is used to indicate a question, as in Australian English or irritation, as in English English. So how do the Chinese show if they are annoyed or want to ask a question? They elongate their words and accentuate the changes in intonation. An argument in Chinese can sound quite alarming to the Western ear, with its percussive monosyllables and extreme inflection changes. This degree of inflection is used in English, but only in extreme emotional contexts: A Chinese argument over cold tea can sound like an accusation of murder to a Western ear.

Symbolic Communication

The earliest recorded permanent human communication is cave painting, dating to 33,000BCE. Written communication emerged in Sumer, the southern part of Mesopotamia (now Iraq), using a script called Cuneiform, written on clay tablets. It was used primarily for accounting. The Sumerians are responsible for our common use of base twelve. Twelve hours in a day, inches in a foot, and notes in the scale; all stem from their civilization.

Although not the first to write stories, the Greeks perfected the dramatic forms we use today: poetry, prose and plays. Watch an episode of 'Law and Order' and you are seeing a direct descendant of a Greek tragedy, complete with suffering and justice denied. All this permanent *thought art* is made possible by the translation of ideas into symbols.

Scripts and Symbols

The world supports a huge variety of scripts split roughly into phonetic, representing the component sound of words, and pictographic, stylized pictures of the ideas.

Traditional	開	圖	學
Simplified	开	表	学
	Open	Picture	Learn

Chinese Traditional and Simplified

Some scripts have interesting quirks. Ancient Hebrew, although phonetic, is a script where vowels are omitted. Modern Hebrew often leaves them out as well. This means words can be ambiguous and need context to decipher them. A common set of Chinese characters has long been used by Mandarin, Cantonese, and Japanese speakers even though their spoken languages are entirely different. The script languages of these people are gradually diverging and might in time become entirely separate languages too.

The Chinese government in Beijing has moved to using simplified Chinese for Mandarin speakers, while Hong Kong continues with the traditional form. Japanese has developed many new characters for

Latin	Hello Reader
Japanese	読者こんにちは
Russian	Здравствуй читатель
Greek	Γεια σας αναγνώστη
Hebrew	שלום קורא
Arabic	مرحبا قارئ
Chinese	讀者： 您好！
Chinese	读者： 您好！ *simplified*
Korean	리더 인사
Japanese	読者こんにちは
Linear-a	can't be translated!
Linear-b	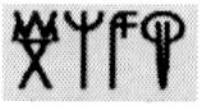 (best I could do is 'new wine')
Lao	ສະບາຍດີຜູ້ອ່ານ
Hindi	पाठक (hello)
Persian	سلام خواننده
Hieroglyphics	

modern ideas, such as computers, that differ from the Chinese, and mixes in a great deal of Katakana, a script allowing the phonetic representation of foreign words. If you walk around these countries their signage looks quite different, although I am told Cantonese speakers can still read simplified Chinese. Take a look and normally you will find them to be quite different. Each example in the figure is my best attempt to translate the phrase "Hello Reader" into a script and the corresponding language.

Symbols of the World

English is one of the most irritating script languages of all. It commonly uses etymological elements, showing the history or origin of the word that has nothing to do with the sound of the word. A word like school has the 'k' sound spelt 'ch', showing its historical derivation from the Greek, but confusing for pronunciation. English has 53 sounds derived from only 26 letters, so there are plenty of letter combinations, many of which are irregular. Because the language favors historical convention over simplicity, sugar is pronounced "shu-gar" whereas sand is strictly phonetic. As for Leicestershire I'll leave that as a test for the American readers amongst you. If you're British, try Mattapoisett, a town in Massachusetts named in Native American.

Yet English is also a 'lovely' language. Because of its richness there are often twenty different ways to say something, and a dozen words to choose on any topic. One of my own favorite words is 'jump'. It is phonetic, but also onomatopoeic and even pictographic. Jump both sounds like a jump and looks like a *jump*.

Two scripts that puzzled scholars for many years are Linear-b and Hieroglyphics. Linear-b – found on clay tablets on the Island of Crete – turned out to be a coded form of ancient Greek with some slight quirks, such as dropping the letter 's' from the ends of words. The 's' is superfluous in most Greek words, and dropping it saved precious clay space!

Hieroglyphics was a real puzzle. It looks so like a pictographic language that it fooled many people for centuries. The Rosetta Stone was discovered in 1799 and became the key to their deciphering. This stone had the same edict written out in 3 languages – Greek, Egyptian and Demotic. The French adventurer Jean-François Champollion decoded hieroglyphics in 1822 and although it *looks* pictographic, it was found to be predominantly phonetic. Linear-a, another script found on the Island of Crete has yet to be decoded and remains one of the world's great-unsolved mysteries.

All these different ways to code ideas into symbols present the children of the world a great learning challenge. Because written language is so young, in evolutionary terms, our brains have not had enough time to evolve to master it. Instead words co-opt parts of our brains originally evolved for different purposes. As languages differ in their construction they co-opt different bits of the brain. It is possible to see this using brain imaging.

Dyslexics – and I am one – have difficulty in translating between the realm of conceptual thought and written script. This translation is subtly different for each language. Chinese speakers use their motor cortex to process characters. Young children write out the characters over and over, to memorize them, so the 'muscle' memory is highly involved. French and Spanish children use the audio pathways, as most of their language is phonetic, the motor part of writing is then an add-on and does not process meaning. English children must use portions of their visual cortex to process the meaning of words, as many words have spelling quirks that have nothing to do with the sound of the words. Some studies even suggest a child dyslexic in one language, because, for example, their audio pathway is impaired, might not suffer the condition in another language that relied on a visual or motor skill.

Can Objects Communicate?

The process of communication has many components, starting with something capable of communicating. Communication usually – perhaps always – is something that occurs between sentient beings. I don't think of my computer as communicating with me, but rather think of it as a medium for communication or a dumb machine. But colloquial language around the subject is a little muddled. We all agree a lighthouse does not communicate, even though it can signal danger, but what do we mean when we say, "That song really spoke to me." No one believes the song is actually communicating, but some kind of communication was made nonetheless. When we talk of communication do we mean the agent or the message?

Stories

Humans enjoy communicating; we create works of art, music and literature that transcend simple analysis. The COIN dynamic slide, which we saw earlier detailing the strategic situation in Afghanistan, would probably have been better communicated with a story. Humans, unlike computers, do not cope well with large quantities of unrelated information, and studies of memory and comprehension show we benefit from a narrative structure. Let me give you a basic example. One simple trick the human brain uses is chunking. Give yourself a moment to try to learn this string of characters.

HALTNTIBMGTATLAMATLOLPOMSGTG

TRY TO MEMORIZE THE STRING WITHOUT READING ON

Now, if I divide it into chunks, you will see it includes meaningful information.

HAL TNT IBM GTA TLA MAT LOL POMS GTG

You probably won't recognize all the acronyms unless you are under 10. Even then, you will find memorizing it hard, but if you put the sequence into the context of a story then it is much easier to learn.

HAL uses TNT to blow up the IBM building in Grand Theft Auto. "Three Letter Acronyms are annoying," says MAT. I'm Laughing Out Loud; Parents Over My Shoulder. Got To Go.

We find it easier to fit new information into existing structures within our brains rather than memorizing by rote. I've used quite a bit of modern Internet slang here. You'll find young people recall this information better than older people for whom GTG and POMS are nonsense.

If you want to memorize something, experts recommend you imagine bizarre images and relate them to a story pictured in the mind's eye. Try it and you may very well find you can still remember my sentence in ten years time!

Let's try something else. The following sentences are a little different, yet the recall scores for information in the two are dramatically different:

1. I met an old tramp on 42nd Street wearing a dirty grey rain coat.

2. New York on a cold damp November day; as I cross the street I bump into an old man wearing a dirty grey Macintosh. His shuffling gait suggests some sordid intent. I think nothing of it, but this brief meeting was to change my life.

The addition of contextual cues allows you to form a mental picture. By withholding some information at the end I have used a dramatic trick to cause your brain to free wheel and imagine what happens next. You are involved in the story. Notice the *longer* story, with more data in it, is paradoxically more comprehensible and memorable.

Ed Tufte makes the point about our ability to process information very forcefully. He believes presentation experts are wrong when they recommend you keep your slides to a few words! He points out the common advice to use only six bullets per slide and six words per bullet comes from a misconception that has blighted a generation of presenters. Studies performed on memory in the 1960s measured unrelated word recall. Six words are all you can remember if the words are meaningless. But if the words have meaning we can comprehend and absorb many pages of data. Hundreds of millions of people throughout the world read a newspaper every morning and can recall the stories throughout the day; the poems, songs and plays we memorize when young are usually long, comprising thousands of words, yet we are able to remember them verbatim for the rest of our lives.

When we tell a story, we are trying to draw the reader in so they can to experience our imaginary world and be 'in' the story. When I read a story – perhaps *Harry Potter* – I don't think about the grammar and punctuation, or even the accuracy of character portrayal. I'm transported to a different place. I experience a piece of the reality or 'imaginality' the storyteller has created. I can describe the characters, the scene, the sounds and the smells. A good author forms a complete world in our heads corresponding with the world they have in their heads. With more abstract information, comprehension and retention is harder. Often if the information does not hang together in a linear narrative it can be impossible to take in at a single sitting. However, if it forms a story and is well told so you 'get it', you do not need it repeated. We experience something of this effect when we watch a good movie. "I've already seen that one," means you have absorbed the whole story in a single sitting. You don't need to watch it over again to comprehend it.

Comedy

Finally, when you mix all the elements up, emotional understanding, body language, in-person communication and empathy; you get comedy. Humans 'do' comedy from a very young age and it's vitally important to the fabric of our lives. What purpose comedy serves in communication

My XBox is Broken
The One Ronnie

Dead Parrot Sketch
Monty Python

Gerald the Gorilla
Not the 9 O'Clock News

Fork Handles
The Two Ronnies

Andre Previn
Morecambe and Wise

Self Defense Against Fruit
Monty Python

is not clear. In life, telling a joke will make another person smile. This causes people to be happy and happy people release chemicals into their bloodstream which make them healthier. Happy people then tell jokes to others. This circular process improves the well-being of communities and helps bond people together. But why on Earth did comedy evolve to be the mechanism that does this?

Comedy may be an important way to avoid an argument when context is unclear. Much of what we say can be taken the wrong way. Simple communication of fact can sound like criticism or challenge, and humans are naturally hierarchical – not unlike packs of dogs or beached walruses. Humor allows us to test the response of others to statements, which might otherwise be taken the wrong way. Something said in a 'jokey' tone of voice may not generate a negative response, even though the raw content might be quite provocative. "Ah, late again I see…"

It is worth taking a look at some great comedy sketches because they bring home the richness of human interaction. Here are some of my favorite links as an antidote to the heavy-duty mathematics I am about to inflict on you.

The World's Funniest Joke

> *Two hunters are out in the woods when one of them collapses. He doesn't seem to be breathing and his eyes are glazed. The other guy whips out his phone and calls the emergency services. He gasps, "My friend is dead! What can I do?" The operator says, "Calm down. I can help. First, let's make sure he's dead." There is a silence, then a gunshot is heard. Back on the phone, the guy says, "OK, now what?"*
>
> Spike Milligan, from *The Goon Show*

I think comedy is a fitness display. It demonstrates to those around us – particularly of the opposite sex – that we can be creative and use non- computable thought processes, just as dancing is a fitness display of our agility and coordination. When we tell a joke we are showing others we can 'think outside the box', a valuable survival skill.

At a simple level it has been proven that animals with the ability to behave randomly escape being eaten more often than animals that follow a pattern. Non-computability is the ultimate behavioral randomizer since it is not an algorithm and cannot be copied. The ability to take non-computable thinking to its logical conclusion to create and invent has clearly taken off for humans.

Of course, another explanation might be that making people happy is fun. People like to be around other fun people so humor encourages crowds to form. If a saber-toothed tiger attacks you, and you are in a crowd, you're more likely to survive. You only have to outrun one member of the crowd!

Chapter 4

THE BRAIN

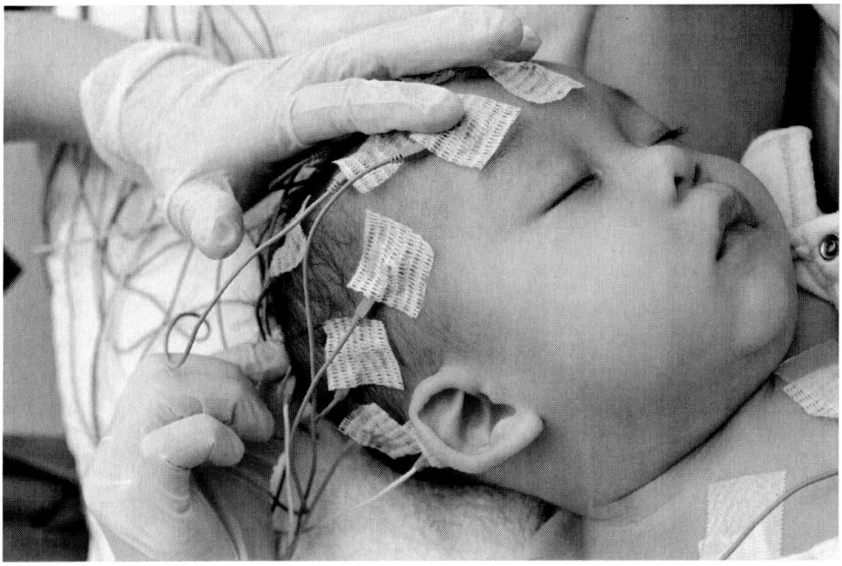

Baby EEG

*"The brain is a wonderful organ;
it starts working the moment
you get up in the morning and
does not stop until you get into
the office."*

Robert Frost

*"The brain looks like nothing
more than a bowl of cold
porridge."*

Alan Turing

Physically the human brain is very boring. Alan Turing described it as looking like a bowl of cold porridge. To get to the porridge you must first cut through the skull, a two-millimeter thick protective layer of bone. The adult human skull has almost no gaps in it, and the only ways into the brain without a bone saw are through the eye sockets or the soft area of bone at the back of the nose. Egyptian mummies had their brains removed through the nose and preserved in a jar for the afterlife!

Thinking with Porridge

Protecting the brain is very important and the skull does a good job by being a tough, impenetrable barrier. But sometimes this toughness backfires. In 2009, Richard Hammond, one of the presenters of the TV motoring series Top Gear, suffered a crash while testing a land speed record-breaking car. Although he was in a multipoint harness, the crash, at over 200 miles per hour, bounced his helmeted head around the inside of the cockpit and his brain was badly bruised. As you know from experience, when you bruise you get swelling, and the brain is no exception. However, the brain is encased in bone, so this swelling has nowhere to escape. The resulting buildup of pressure is dangerous, causing an interruption of blood supply to the un-bruised parts. Brain damage in such accidents is often fatal; Richard Hammond was very lucky to live through the experience.

Surgeons often need to cut into the skull to relieve pressure on the brain, or to gain access to remove tumors. Going through the scalp involves a great deal of blood, but once you have a clean hole in the skull you can peel back the thin membranes, called the meninges, to reveal a wrinkly folded whitish thing that looks a bit like a cauliflower. This is the outer surface of the brain where much of our thinking is done. Unfolded, this surface layer would cover the area of a football field and this intense folding distinguishes the human brain from the brains of simpler animals. Some animals, such as elephants and dolphins, have larger brains than ours, but the area of their folded surface is considerably smaller. It is thought that this efficient folding is key to giving us the ability to think complex thoughts.

Analysis of Einstein's brain held at Princeton University shows it is not particularly massive, but it is strikingly more folded than average, and has a shorter lateral sulcus – the fissure between the front and back

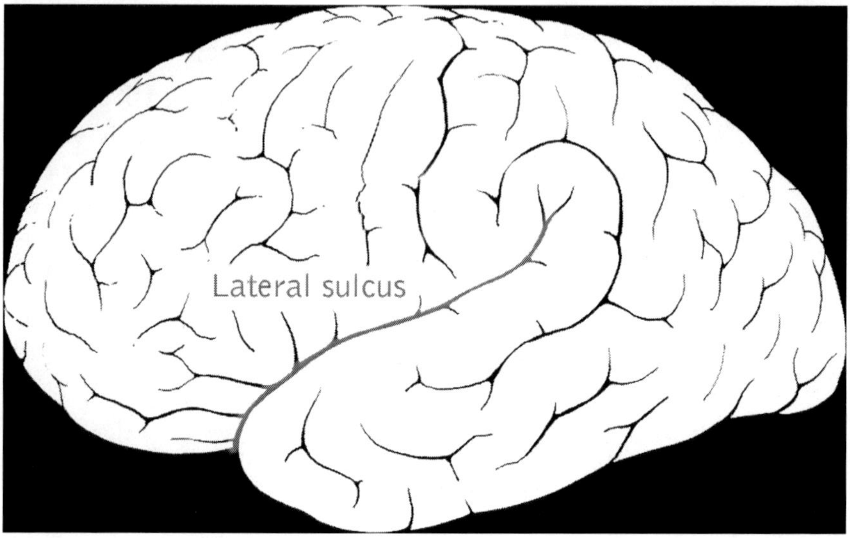

Einstein's Brain

of the brain. Whether this is related to his highly creative thinking or just random chance is unknown, but it's an interesting data point in our quest to understand creativity and intelligence.

Looking through a microscope, the wrinkly grey matter is composed of 30 trillion neurons; small whitish cells sprouting filaments that wrap around each other like the tentacles of an octopus. The tentacles, and there can be as many as 10,000 per cell, are known as dendrites and spread out to nearly touch other neurons. At the other end of the neuron is a single axon. The gaps between the end of an axon and the next neuron's dendrites are called synapses, about one-tenth of the width of a human hair and varied in structure. When a nerve 'fires', an electrical pulse spreads out along the axon to the end and crosses the synapses to other brain cells. This electrical pulse is not like the flow of current in a wire: neurons don't conduct electricity. It is more akin to dominoes falling in a line. Ion gates in the walls of the neuron open, letting potassium ions flow out. As the gates open in one section, the next section is triggered and so on. Thus, electrical signals ripple out along the axon. As the electrical signals cross the synapses they either excite or inhibit the firing of adjacent neurons. There is a lot more structure to a neuron than was once thought. The textbook model is of a sequence of ion sacks stacked end to end rather like plant cells, but neurons have a far more complex structure. Bundles of actin and tubulin form a skeleton in the neuron and the neuron metabolizes ATP to recharge its firing mechanism. Neurons behave far more like small animals than inanimate plant cells.

The wiring of our brain looks a bit like the logic circuits of a computer, and our best guess is the cells in our brain form some kind of computer. The brain cells – a specialized form of nerve cell – connect to the rest of the body via the nerve cells that largely run down our spine. Thoughts trigger action and, in reverse, the nerves in our extremities sense things in the environment and relay information back to the brain. If I think, 'move my finger' my finger will move, and if it touches something I will feel the sensation. Interestingly if my finger touches something hot a reflex will kick in. Reflexes work without involving the brain. We don't have to think, "that hurts." Instead, our finger reflexively pulls away. We may say ouch, but by the time we do, our fingers already moved away from the heat.

Nerve cells are much slower than the electronic systems we build with copper and silicon. This speed is quite noticeable and limits the rate we can do certain things. It takes around 0.08 seconds for a nerve impulse to run down to the tips of our fingers, initiate an action and return to give us the sensation of the action. This may sound fast but if you're a tennis player in a rally or a pianist faced with a fast passage, the nerves don't have time to make a full round trip signal before the next action must be initiated. In these instances we need to run on autopilot and there are parts of the body where the nervous system takes action without the brain getting involved. This is particularly the case with things like walking and balance, which must respond fast to changes in ground conditions. The signals just don't have time – and don't need – to go all the way up to the top of the body for instructions. Rather like the heat reflex above, the peripheral nervous system can process information locally. After all, brain cells and nerve cells are really all one type of cell.

If you have a group of people, you can conduct a fun experiment to show the speed of nerves. Hold hands in a big circle and squeeze the hand of the person next to you. When they feel you squeeze, they should squeeze the next person's hand and so on. The rate at which people squeeze hands around the circle is limited by the speed at which nerves conduct the signals across our bodies.

Imaging the Brain

There are several ways to look inside the brain without recourse to a bone saw. The methods are fascinating in their own right, even before we start looking at the results. Each image is generated using a different physical principle.

X-rays

The first Nobel Prize in Physics was awarded to Wilhelm Röntgen in 1901. He had discovered 'X' rays; so called because he had no better name for them. X-rays, as they became known, are just light of a very high frequency.

Light comes in a variety of colors; at the low end of the frequency scale we see red, higher up blue and, at the top, violet. At this point human eyes give up and cannot see anything higher, so ultraviolet light is invisible to us. Bees, on the other hand, can see a long way into the ultraviolet spectrum and some flowers have beautiful ultraviolet markings that attract bees for pollination. Daylight contains a great deal of ultraviolet light which is wasted on us – other than to tan our skin. But all is not lost. Clever manufacturers put fluorescent dyes into their washing powders which stick to our clothes and convert ultraviolet into visible light, making our T-shirts look brighter as they reflect *more* visible light than fell on them. You can see this effect most easily in a disco when ultraviolet lights are shone on the dance floor and anyone wearing a newly washed T-shirt will glow bright white. The other common substance that fluoresces strongly on a dance floor is tonic water. Quinine, the active ingredient in tonic water, is a strongly

Flowers in Ultraviolet Light

Pit Viper

fluorescent substance which converts ultraviolet light down into the visible spectrum. Photoactive dyes have recently become controversial as suggestions have been made that they are unsafe and irritate the skin. Going to discos might not be quite as fun in the future!

Thermal Imaging

At the bottom end of the spectrum is infrared light. Pit vipers have evolved special organs on the sides of their heads to 'see' in this spectrum and they use this sense to hunt prey in the dark. I use the word *see* with some caution. We have no idea what their sensation of 'heat-sight' involves, but their organs are very precise, able to detect things only 0.2 degrees warmer than the background.

Infrared cues help several species of snakes, bats and insects locate things in the dark, but the animal that excels at the task, albeit using technology, is mankind. Special cameras allow us to use infrared to see in the dark or detect where our houses lose heat.

X-rays are much higher in frequency – about one hundred times that of the ultraviolet light that affects our T-shirts. The high frequency corresponds to a small wavelength that allows the rays to pass through our bodies. Later on in the book we will understand that frequency is not a proper explanation for light, as it is not a wave but rather a particle that obeys the laws of a wave. But for now we will ignore this detail.

The first use of X-ray images was to see broken bones. Bones block the rays as they are dense, but the soft parts of our bodies are almost completely transparent to X-rays. We can see the soft tissues if we turn the contrast up, but there are problems when using X-rays to view the brain. Our skull completely encases the brain and however much we turn the contrast up, all we see is bone. The solution to this problem is to perform sophisticated mathematical tricks using a computer to enhance the contrast ratio and make image 'slices' through the living head.

The slicing technique was invented independently in the 1970s by Sir Godfrey Hounsfield, working for EMI in England, and Allan Cormack, of Tufts University in America, and they shared the 1979 Nobel Prize for Medicine for their work. Legend has it that EMI was making so much money from The Beatles they could fund the enormous development cost of the CAT scanner from the profits; true or not, it's a great invention.

The best way to understand the mathematics is to picture yourself in an episode of 'CSI', the American television crime drama. An intruder has attacked someone with a knife and there are blood spatters all over the walls of the room. Enter the brilliant pathologist who reconstructs the scene of the crime from the pattern of blood on the wall. She can map the trajectory of the blood spatters and back-calculate that the attacker must have been 5' 4", left-handed and wielding a 6" blade. In a CAT scan, our head is hit with billions of rays that bounce and scatter over the walls of the machine. Sensors detect the rays and a mathematical algorithm calculates an image of the body that would produce such a pattern. To

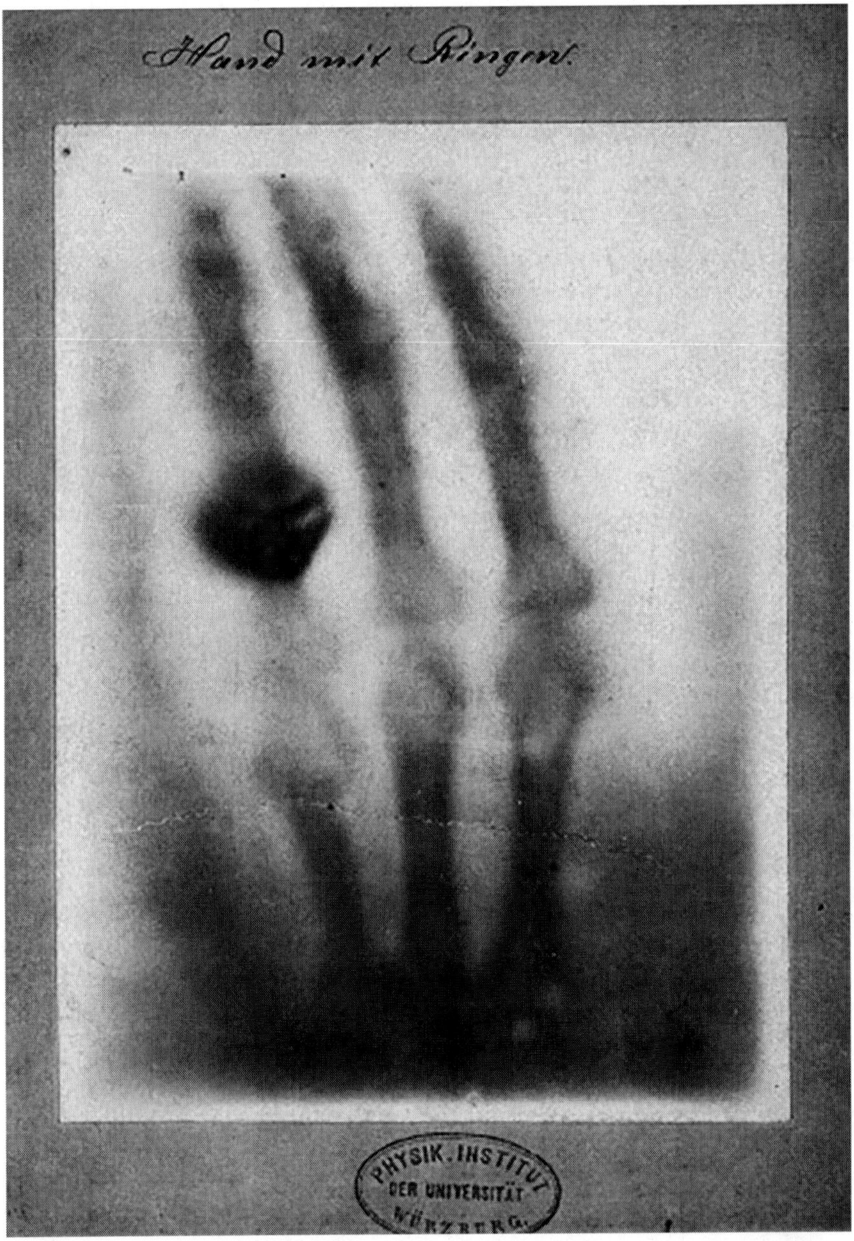

X-ray of Roentgen's Wife's Hand

simplify things we shine the X-rays onto the head as a narrow slit of light so we only have to do the back calculation in two dimensions. Then we stitch successive slices together in the computer to form a 3D virtual image. Thus, doctors can 'fly' through the brain looking at structures such as tumors from all angles.

There are two problems with X-ray imaging. Even with clever mathematics, the dense bone in the skull blocks the rays so you don't get much contrast, making it hard to distinguish normal brain matter from something like a tumor. But the bigger concern is X-rays are a form of ionizing radiation, and ionizing radiation causes cancer.

We are told to wear sun block to protect our skin from ultraviolet light; X-rays are 100 times more potent and can do a great deal of damage. Fortunately, the body repairs itself quite well in the presence of low levels of radiation. The *double* part of the double helix in our DNA allows a set of proteins in our cells to go around correcting errors when they detect a mismatch between the two strands. But, now and again an X-ray might make an irreparable fault in both copies. If enough of these faults accumulate, they can lead to cancer or, if the errors are in reproductive organs, birth defects. Doctors try to minimize the radiation we receive and give us as few CAT scans as possible during our lifetime, especially when we are young and have not yet had children.

MRI

X-rays dominated our ability to see into the human body until the mid-1970s when Raymond Damadian came up with the idea of using magnetism. Magnetic fields are not absorbed by bone and present no danger as they do not damage DNA. Ironically, the technique was originally known as Nuclear Magnetic Resonance, 'NMR', which patients thought must be dangerous because of the word nuclear. The name was

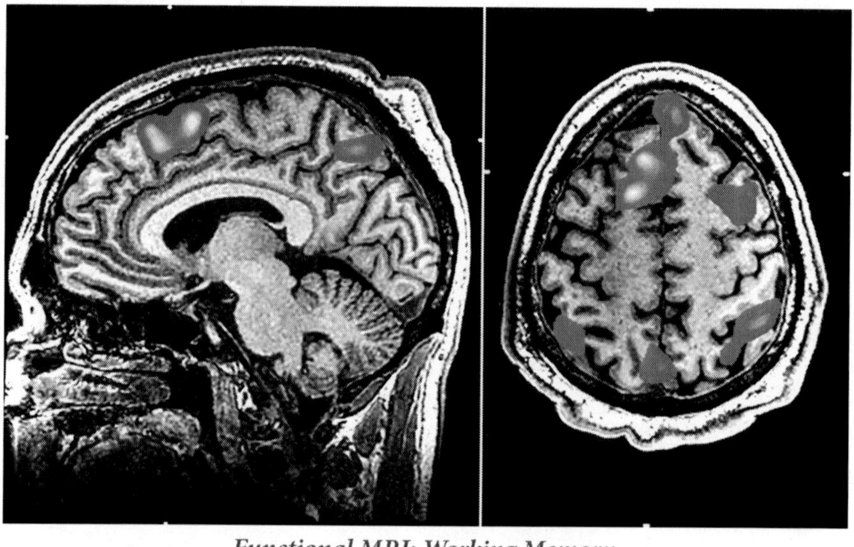

Functional MRI: Working Memory

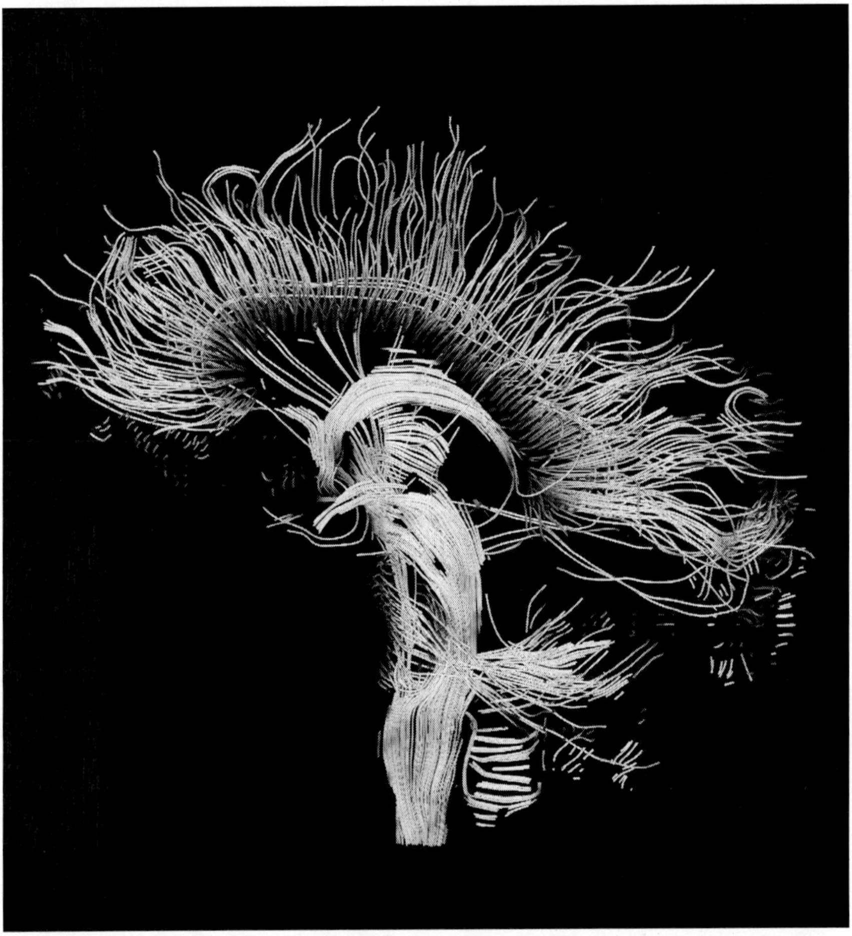

Diffusion Tensor Image

changed to the one we use today: Magnetic Resonance Imaging, 'MRI'. The system works by applying a strong magnetic field to your body to excite the hydrogen atoms. Since we are mostly H2O there are plenty of these.

Three magnetic fields are used. First, an extremely strong field is applied to the whole body. This causes all the hydrogen atoms in the water and fat to spin in line with the field of the machine. Next a gradient field is applied to the top of your head so it is slightly more magnetized than the bottom of your feet and, finally, a pulse of magnetism is applied to the top of your head. The spinning hydrogen atoms line up a little more when this pulse is applied and then randomize again when it is switched off. As they randomize, they give off energy. The clever part is the gradient field which causes the atoms to give off energy at slightly different times – the top of your head first, your neck a fraction of a

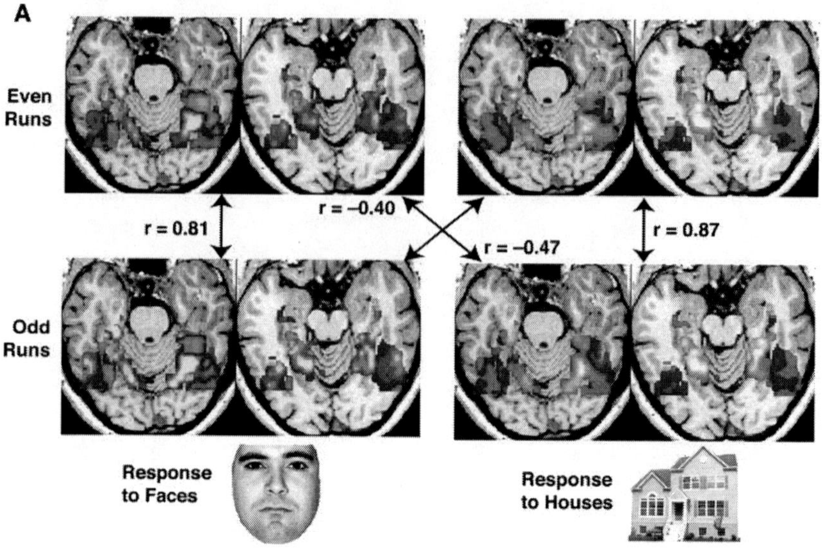

fMRI

second later, and so on down to your feet. What you see at any one time is a slice through a specific section of the body. You can then build up 3D images from these slices and look at the soft watery tissue rather than the hard bone you can see with an X-ray.

MRI scans give detailed images but today there are many more imaging tricks you can play. Give the patient gadolinium to eat – a type of paramagnetic material – and this contrast agent will highlight active parts of the brain. You can 'see' which parts are active: the location of emotions such as love, joy and even the effect of smells as the brain experiences things. This is still coarse grained information; it shows only the general area of excitation and it does not tell us what is going on at the nerve level, but the images are fascinating.

Another recent development in imaging is the diffusion MRI. If you remember your school physics, molecules travel with a random walk: they diffuse along pathways just as people wander along a corridor. If the corridor is full of people, they are jostled around and make little progress. If the corridor is empty, they move in straight lines. This difference in jostling affects the reading in an MRI and allows you to color code the image according to the rate of motion of water along the pathways. You can therefore 'see' the rate at which signals flow in the brain and not only locate thoughts, but also see the links between them.

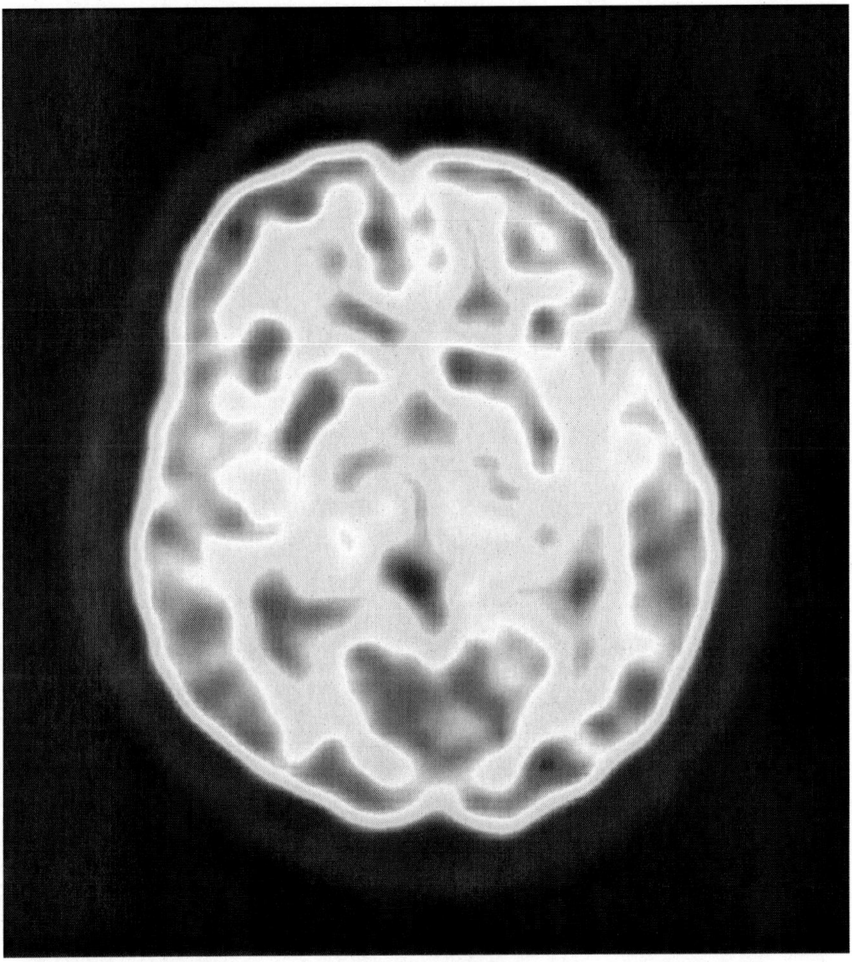

Functional PET

PET

The last scan we will look at is functional positron emission tomography, or f-PET. In this machine the scanner detects positrons given off by excited oxygen atoms.

As you think, you burn glucose by combining it with oxygen. The parts of the brain that are thinking hard use a great deal of oxygen and this shows up in scans. Again the consecutive slice trick is used to generate a 3D image that allows you to fly through the brain as it works on a problem.

There is one problem common to all these methods. X-rays, MRI and PET scans only show us the location of thoughts with an accuracy of a few millimeters. Each pixel in the image contains around 10 million neurons, so we can't see the details of thought. For a scale comparison it is like looking at a car factory from space. You can see cars and people going into the factory but you can't read the owner's manual. We need to be able to see at least 10 million times more detail than our current technologies allow to *see a thought*.

A Quick Tour

Now that we understand how to look inside the brain, let's take a tour around it. The brain is a highly distributed thinking machine. Some things, such as hearing, are located in specific places while others, like the enjoyment of music, are spread out.

Our eyes work as an extension of the brain and use a specialized type of nerve cell. Light falls on the retina and stimulates these cells, causing nerve impulses to run along the optic nerve into the center of the

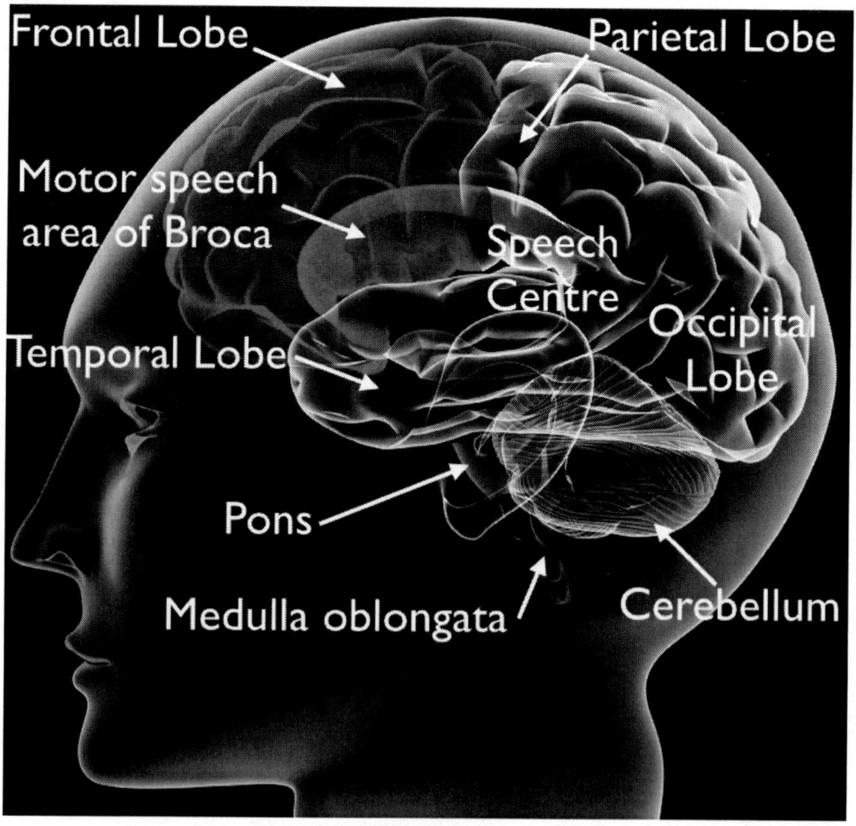

The Brain

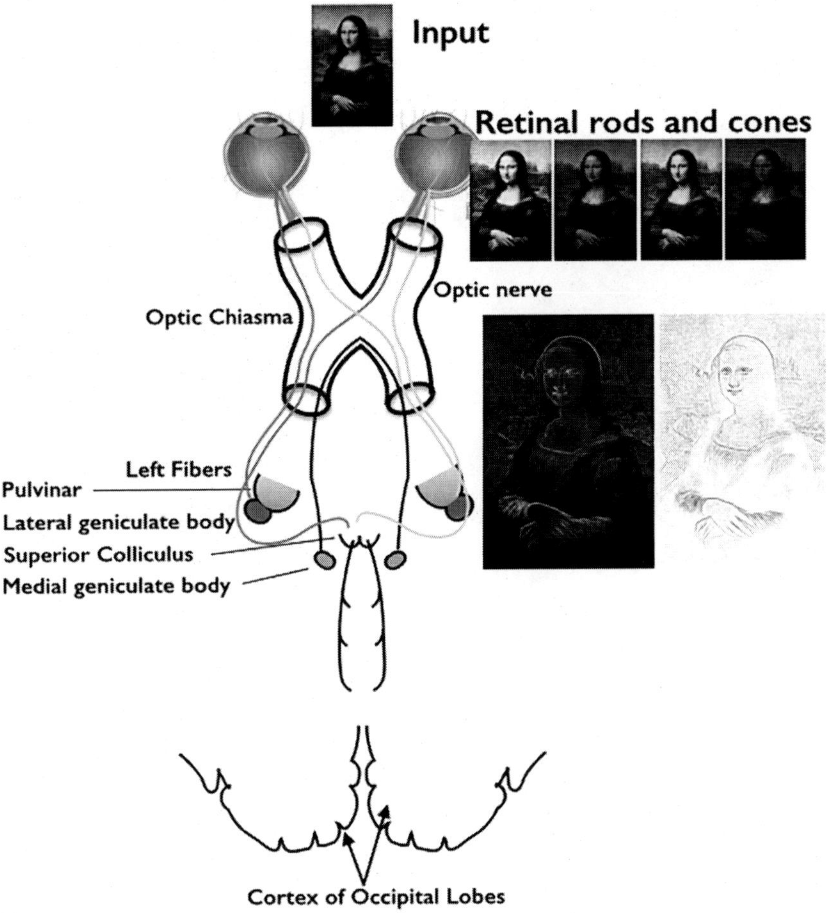

Visual Processing System

brain. The impulses split and form two distinct paths, one through the cerebral cortex, which gives us the sensation of conscious vision, and the other into the lower brain which provides us with instinctive reactions.

The right hand side of your body is connected to the left hemisphere of the brain and vice versa. This means each hand is controlled by the opposite side of the brain. But, your eyes see both your hands. To resolve this conundrum a very complex thing has to happen to the optic nerve in the center of the brain. The optic nerve from each eye splits and crosses over in the middle, so the left side of the left eye and the left side of the right eye goes to the right hand side of the brain and vice versa. This keeps the brain focused on the correct hand.

Frogs Eyes are Very Sensitive

The processing power of the eye is staggering. The human retina has about 120 million rods and 7 million cones, giving it an average resolution of 10,000 by 10,000 pixels. Each rod is sensitive to individual photons but we register light consciously only if we see around 5-7 photons. It is thought frogs can react to single photons because of the chemistry of their eyes and the fact they are cold-blooded, but this is not proven.

Some animals, including some frogs and my cat, have a tapetum lucidum. This is a reflective backing to the eye that allows each photon two chances to react with a rod, once on the way in and, if that fails, once on the way out. This is why you can see the eyes of some animals if you shine a light into the forest on a dark night. Cones are less sensitive than rods but give us color perception. In the human eye, there are three types of cone: a red, a green and a blue, giving us trichromatic vision. We see colors because light stimulates more than one types of cell and we infer the color in between. A fourth type of cone is present in some species such as birds, reptiles, and fish. This gives them tetra-chromic vision, allowing them to see into the ultraviolet range. It is speculated some humans might have this ability but so far none has come forward. Some animals lack the ability to see certain colors. Most dogs can't see red. This gives cats a big advantage!

Many people wonder if we all see the same color as each other. Is your red the same as mine? The brain's perception of color is complex. Although the color red is absolute and can be detected by a calibrated sensor, our perception of color is relative. We perceive them in the context

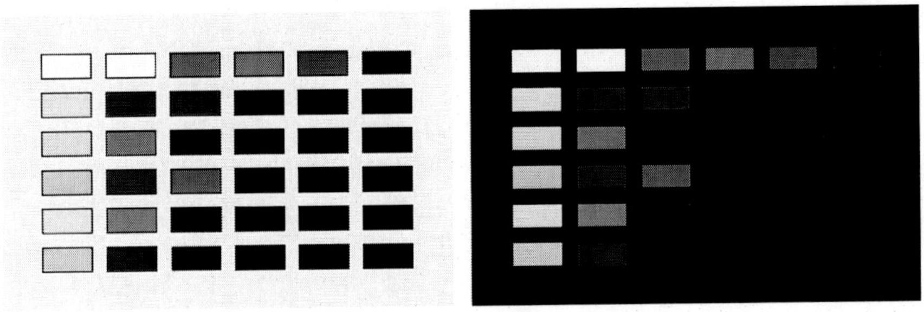

Color is Relative

of other colors – not in isolation. The two panels above contain identical blocks of color but they look very different against the background. Check out the website if you have a black and white book. It is an irrelevant question to ask if my red is the same as yours, since *my* red against one background is not even the same as my red against another.

People generally agree on naming colors but not all languages have the eleven specifically named colors of modern English: black, blue, brown, gray, green, orange, pink, purple, red, white, yellow, if you are interested. Ancient Celtic languages, so called 'gru' languages, recognized only four colors and other languages don't distinguish purple from blue. Color, or at least the naming of color, is a cultural thing.

Impressionist Painting, Monet Haystack

The resolution of the eye is not the same across the image. High resolution is concentrated in the center, while lower resolution black and white vision dominates the edge. This peripheral vision helps us detect predators or play football but it is not the focus of our attention. When we focus our attention on something, we turn our eyes to look at it directly. The central part of our eye is called the fovea centralis and is composed of cones. About half our cones are concentrated in this very small section and this gives us immense visual acuity. For a computer display to outperform this section of the eye it would need one billion by

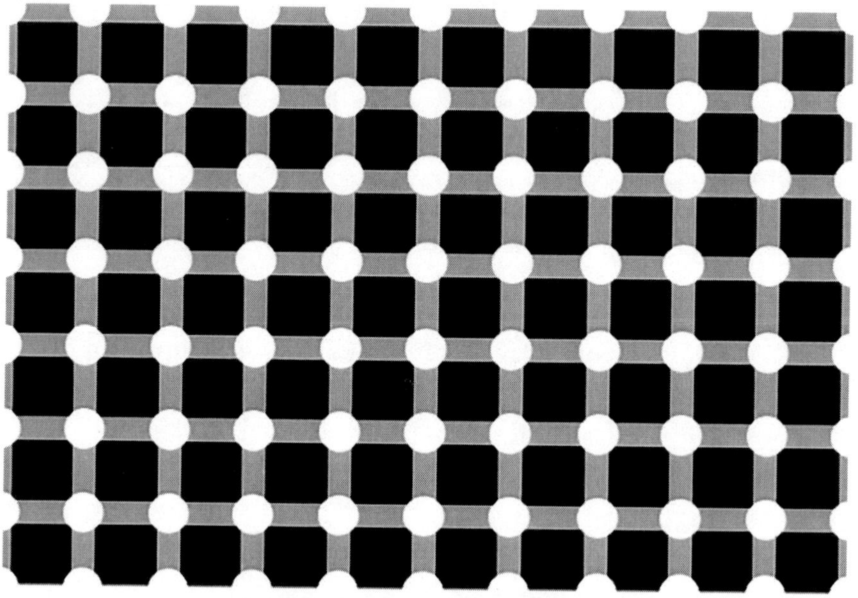

Scintillating Dots Optical Illusion

one billion pixels. The fovea centralis is tiny, only two degrees across, so our eyes must dart around the image to take in all the detail. Once the basic information is encoded in our retina and sent down the optic nerve, it goes into a production line process in the visual cortex where all the elements are analyzed. Our brains extract information from the image such as texture, edges and depth perception in specialized portions of the brain. Because of this specialization it is possible to play tricks on the brain with images that are not easy to process. Some we find pleasurable, while others can be a little disturbing.

Penrose Steps

Optical Illusions

This picture is an illusion that plays with your stereoscopic synthesis. The dots appears to flip between black and white. Other illusions play with depth perception. The Penrose Steps are a type of illusion that tries to build an impossible physical model in our cerebral cortex. The brain sees perspective and depth perception cues, but the resulting shape could never exist.

Hearing

Unlike sight, hearing is an absolute sense. Our ears capture and focus sound down to the eardrum where a set of small hairs called cilia convert it into electrical impulses. The impulses stimulate cells corresponding to specific pitches.

We are born with perfect pitch, yet most of us lose it early on. When I hear Maria Carey sing a top B flat a specific set of neurons located near the ear fires, and if she sings a top 'A' then a different clump of neurons are stimulated. By the time most children come to learn music they have edited out this absolute pitch information. One group of children who do not lose the ability are Chinese pianists. Because Chinese is a tonal language – where the pitch of words affects their meaning – and because

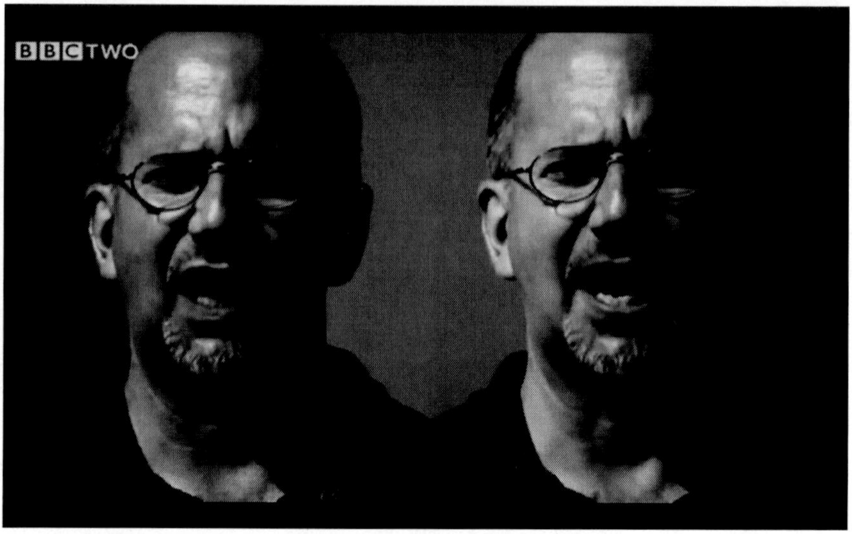

McGurk Effect; Go to the Website and Watch the Linked Video

Chinese children tend to learn the piano very young, they don't lose the absolute part of pitch. An astonishing 93% of these children develop and retain perfect pitch throughout their lives.

There are many cross connections between the audio and video processing systems. At parties you often can't hear speakers clearly because of the background noise. Watching their lips will help comprehension, but which sense wins if there is conflict between the two? The McGurk effect shows this.

To test the effect, go to the website, watch the video and see if you can distinguish when a speaker talking normally and when he is making the mouth movement of another sound. There is a winner. Try it for yourself; check out the link on my website.

Once upon a time people imagined the brain was like a camera forming an image of the world, but if this were the case there would be a paradox. Who is looking at the image in our brain to make sense of it? Modern research shows we don't take a complete picture of the world like a camera but rather parse the image into its constituent parts on the fly.

If someone asks, "Which side of the house is the tree on?" your brain parses the question and compares it with the image map in your mind's eye. What is the image composed of: trees, houses, sky, grass? Your brain manipulates the linguistic question about the relationship of elements and matches it with the visio-spatial understanding of the image, allowing you to answer the question. You might not have to answer

Humans' Ability to Concentrate

the question verbally. If you hit a baseball, no language is involved; you distinguish the ball from the background and perform quite a feat of tracking and calculation to connect it with your bat.

Because the brain is editing the scene on the fly to keep within its processing power, the eye only sees what it turns its attention to. Magicians take advantage of this to play amazing tricks on us. Watch the video on the web and then tell me what you see.

VISIT THE WEB AND VIEW THE VIDEO TO SEE WHAT HAPPENS

Tiger Woods Swing

You can see just how intensively the brain works on a given problem, throwing away all unnecessary information.

The brain contains mirror neurons, a type of brain cell that responds when we see another human do something. These neurons fire as if we were performing the action ourselves even though we are merely witnessing it. It is one of the ways we learn a skill. If I watch Tiger Woods's golf swing, my mirror neurons will fire as if I were practicing *his* swing. Later when I practice the swing for real, my neurons will have already been partially programmed. This effect is presumably the reason we enjoy watching sports; our mirror neurons allow us to begin acquiring a skill while sitting in an armchair! This is clearly a useful evolutionary trait but you *do* also need to practice for real!

Mirror neurons also fire in response to witnessing emotions. When we see an actor laugh or cry, we experience their emotion as if for real. This helps us empathize with the person we are watching and is part of the reason we enjoy movies and plays.

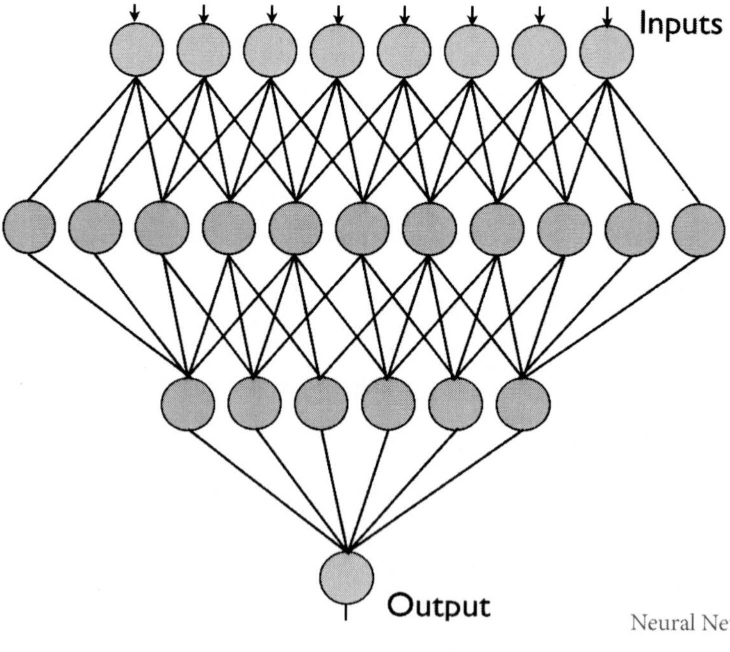

Neural Network

Thinking

"We cannot solve our problems with the same thinking we used when we created them."

Albert Einstein

If you feel mentally exhausted reading this book, don't worry. This is normal. Mental work takes energy. Scientists estimate the brain consumes 20% of our resting energy; around 12 watts. Physical fitness is important for thinking. If you get out of breath running for a bus, thinking is going to be harder for you. Studies are mixed about whether the additional work involved in solving a difficult problem causes you to use more energy. We certainly see an increase in the flow of glucose to the appropriate part of the brain, but the overall energy use in the brain is quite high in the first place, so it is hard to see the incremental effect.

Unlike muscles, which store energy locally as glycogen, brain cells 'burn' glucose and oxygen from the blood stream in real time. If scientists detect glucose and oxygen flowing to a part of the brain they know it must be working on a problem. As we know, there are several ways to make glucose and oxygen show up in brain scanners. You can, therefore, inject someone with the right chemical markers, wheel them into a brain scanner, and watch them learn new skills. On a practical level, there is limited space within a scanner and you can't wield a golf club, for example. Julien Doyon, a researcher at the University of Montreal, was recounting this problem to a friend and she suggested knitting. Knitting is a physical activity you learn just like a golf swing or a tennis stroke, with all the initial fumbles and jerky activity, settling down to a fluid learned skill. Most experienced knitters can engage in a full conversation while knitting complex patterns, only needing to break off and concentrate during a pattern change. Luckily, there are ceramic and bamboo knitting needles which don't interfere with MRI scanners, and they are small – no golf swing problems here. Studies of knitters show that when they initially learn a skill, several areas of their brain light up, but after a while, the brain activity becomes concentrated in the sensorimotor striatal territory.

Glucose, the brain's power source, is a sugar we get directly from eating sweets or indirectly by digesting starch. Some studies show children do slightly better at school if they eat starchy foods in the morning for breakfast – a bowl of cereal or porridge. When you think and work your brain consumes the glucose in your blood, and blood glucose level drops. If there is a steady source of glucose from the starch digesting in your gut, the glucose is constantly topped up and the level will stay high. If there is no input of glucose from your gut, the body will first get glucose from glycogen in your liver or generate it by converting fat reserves. This takes more work so the body tends to avoid doing so until it absolutely has to. You can function with slightly lower glucose levels but the body will shut down a little. One thing that suffers as a result is the brain's ability to perform cognitive tasks. A quick and easy way to fix this is to consume some raw glucose and most fridges have a ready supply in the form of sugary drinks. Stories of kids running amok, due to sugar highs brought on by too many sweets and sodas, appear to be an urban legend. In tests, parents told their children have had a sugar drink report them to be hyperactive even if they had been given a sugar free drink. I'm not suggesting you drink lots of sugary drinks – it is bad for your teeth and will make you fat – but the occasional soda is fine.

Memory

Scientists are just beginning to explore the mechanisms that lay down memory in the brain. There are two main classes of theory. The first believes memory is formed in the large scale wiring of the brain. Neurons connect with other neurons and the number and strength of these connections cause memory. When we learn, new connections are formed. The electrical activity in a given part of the brain triggers the formation of new dendrites. They grow, piloted by tubulin micro-tubes, rather like vines growing in a slow motion nature clip. Once a micro-tube guided filament is close enough to other, a synapse forms. This gross-scale wiring growth is one method of memory formation. Another gross-scale effect is myelination. Myelin is the insulation the body uses on nerves cells, including nerve cells in the brain. It looks a bit like the insulation we used in the 1930s. Before the invention of plastic, strips of waxed canvas were wrapped around wires to provide insulation. Myelin

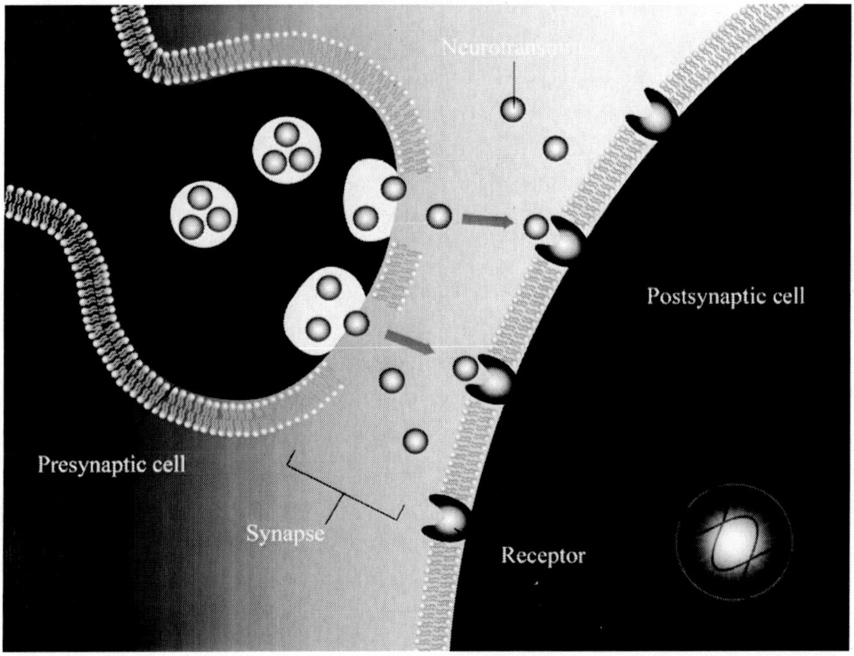

Synapse

has a similar structure. It is a flat protein laid down as a spiral on the outside of nerve cells. The theory is that cell firing causes myelination, which permanently imprints the memory.

The alternate class of theory proposes memory is encoded at a much smaller scale. Neurons are quite complex structures in their own right. Inside each neuron is a lattice of proteins, which forms a skeleton. Part of that skeleton provides structural integrity to the neuron, while other elements provide control and motility. It is this control part of the skeleton that people believe might encode memory. A 2012 paper by Travis Craddock and Jack Tuszynski of the University of Alberta, and anesthesiologist Stuart Hameroff of the University of Arizona proposes a protein called CaMKII binds to the cytoskeleton in 32 different configurations, providing a binary data encoding. It is an elegant idea but it also relies on your believing their model for quantum neuron processing which is still highly controversial. If proven, they are my top Nobel Prize tip for this decade!

Photographic Memory

Until recently conventional wisdom held that true photographic memory was a myth and the few people claiming to have it really used some sort of mnemonic memory technique to selectively memorize things. The most famous case was a Russian journalist known as 'S'. He habitually memorized things using association with places. In antiquity this was taught as 'the method of loci'. The unusual thing was his inability to turn the effect off, and he found it as much a curse as a blessing. He was unable to forget useless information and found it hard to interpret complex images, tending to see areas of color and shade rather than objects such as trees, houses and fields.

Very recently some people have come forward, six in America and one in the UK, who appear to have genuine photographic memories It is well worth watching the TV documentary *The Boy Who Can't Forget* to gain a sense of what this is like. These people appear to lack the ability to forget, and this turns our understanding of memory on its head. It seems memory might work the opposite way we thought. We had previously thought we only remember what we pay attention to, but perhaps we must actively forget, and this ability is missing in these subjects. Scientists are studying these people to see if they can understand more about memory.

The Aging Brain

We can explode a myth and encourage older readers simultaneously. Memory does not deteriorate with age, or at least not until we are very old. Most studies looking at memory deterioration focus on the very old and compare them with the very young. Even then, the differences are small. When people are asked to attempt memory problems there is a mild drop off with age but the results are quite similar. The most likely reason older people don't remember so well is they don't believe they can. Perhaps they don't have as much incentive to remember new information. Why learn someone's name if you're unlikely to meet them again? Since IQ actually increases with age, don't believe people when they say you are going downhill from the age of 40. You are not!

Computer Brains

Computers are really quite simple compared with all the evolved baggage we humans carry around. When a computer is presented with instructions, for example, for a program like Excel and a file such as my expenses, it will load everything into memory and 'run' it. The process of running a program is simple. Each instruction is a number. The computer reads the number, looks it up in a table, finds a corresponding number, and writes that down. Essentially that's all there is to it. From a simple mechanism like this, we get the enormous complexity of a modern computer. The sophistication is achieved through reading and writing many numbers in parallel, and chaining the steps together so that if you read a particular number it triggers another read/write process, and so on. I'm glossing over some details such as logical functions but, if you know how a modern computer chip is constructed, my description is not far off. Almost all logic today is implemented in tables to achieve the speeds we expect from modern chips.

All modern computers are clocked. A small piece of quartz rock has been polished, coated with metal, and wired up to a control circuit in the computer. When you apply voltage to the rock it bends and absorbs energy. When the voltage is taken away it bends back and gives out the energy. This is effectively a pendulum and it can be used to make an accurate clock. I used to design these for a living. Every logic gate in a computer is connected to this clock, and each time the clock ticks the logic gates in a computer *compute*.

Most modern computers are entirely synchronous. The clock rate is set so that the gates in the computer fully recover by the time of the next tick, and every gate is therefore ready in its standard position when the next instruction arrives. The human brain does not have a central clock. Each neuron acts independently – firing regardless of whether the neurons it is adjacent to are ready or not. It is wrong to think of the brain as digital. Each neuron *does* fire and recover, but it may be triggered again before it fully recovers. This makes for a chaotic and essentially analogue operation. If one neuron fires when a second has only half recovered, then it gets half an effect. If the neuron is 80% recovered, an 80% effect. Neuron recovery time is quite long, perhaps as much as 1/1000th of a second, and they are wired in three dimensions to as many as 10,000 other neurons. It is perfectly possible for a set of neurons to run one 'program' when they are rested and a completely different 'program' when they are 50% recovered and yet another programs if triggered from different starting locations. I have said 'program,' but arguing a brain runs a 'program' is misleading. It is not organized like this.

Neural Networks

A neural network is our best attempt at a computer model for the human brain. Each neuron is represented by an entry in a table. The entry records all the connections to it, along with the strength of each connection – these are called 'weights.' In some models the connections can be both inhibitors and activators like in real synapses. An individual neuron will fire if the sum of all the connections multiplied by the weights reaches a certain pre-determined threshold.

A neural network does not run a program in the conventional sense, and must be trained through experience rather like a human brain. The training process allows the weights in the network table to be adjusted to give the correct result. But, unlike the brain, you can read the weights and even save them to a disk. The neural network tables start with random settings. You show the network the letter 'A' and adjust the weights in the tables until it gives a positive answer: 'It's an A.' Repeat the process with the other letters until the network correctly distinguishes them. As you do this a computer algorithm constantly adjusts the weighting tables using a method called 'back propagation.'

At the end of the training process you can show the network some new input and see how it does. For example, a letter 'A' that is in a slightly different font to anything in the training set. Trained neural networks can perform complex tasks such as recognizing faces or making clinical diagnoses, and they can be allowed to modify their weighting tables as they work so they learn from experience in a similar way to a human brain. Strong AI proponents believe making a thinking machine is just a matter of building a really large, fast neural network and working out how to train it efficiently.

Quantum Brains

Conventional wisdom says each brain cell is a single processing unit making an on-off decision – fire, or don't fire – depending on the state of its neighbors. But, Stuart Hameroff, Professor of Anesthesiology at the University of Arizona, thinks neurons are not the fundamental information-processing unit in the brain. He suggests that this accolade should go to tubulin. Tubulin is a small, versatile protein that self-assembles into filaments rather like the way buckyballs – a magnetic children's toy – can be arranged. There are two types of tubulin molecule: α and β. They slot together and wrap around to form a micro tube about 25nm in diameter.

Tubulin micro tubes do several important things in the body. They form the skeleton of neurons and give them structure. They are involved in guiding neurons as they grow towards each other to form new connections, and they also operate in the nucleus of a cell to unzip

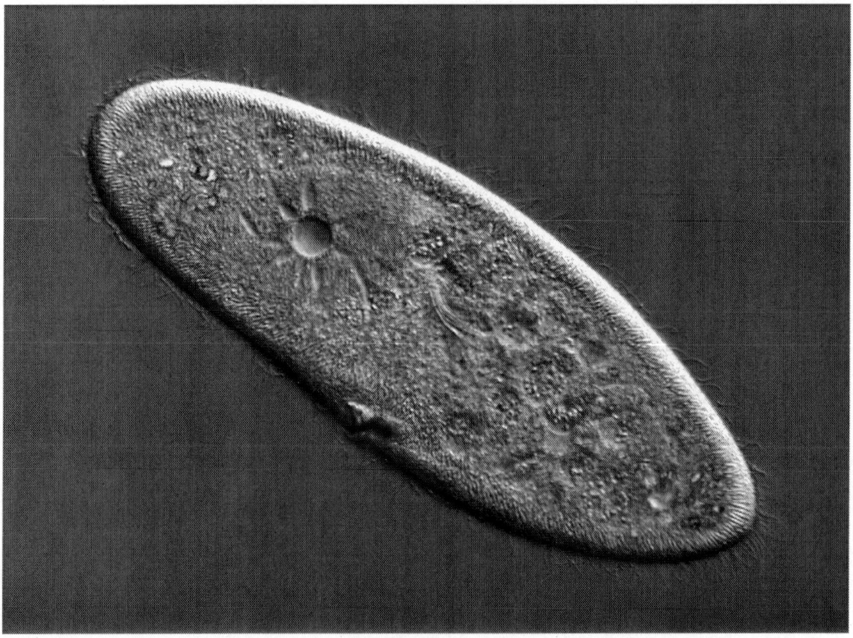

Paramecium

DNA into its two complementary strands when a cell divides. In single-celled organisms, including paramecium, the ends of the tubes stick out of the body and form the cilia that drive the organism along.

The presence of tubulin in complex, single-celled organisms provides a clue that the smallest information processing unit might not be the neuron. Some single cell organisms, such as paramecium, display complex behavior: hunting for prey and escaping danger. This suggests they can process small amounts of information without the need for a matrix of neurons. Since we evolved from these organisms, why wouldn't our brain cells take advantage of this sub-cellular intelligence?

The structure of tubulin lends itself to digital processing as the molecules forming the walls have two stable states and can flip between them. We might recognize this as the basis of a binary computer, and cells might have little computers within them. They would not need to process many bits to be useful. Perhaps single-cell organisms developed information processing capabilities in their micro tube structures that allowed them to better survive and, as their nervous systems evolved, they coupled these structures to form the brains we see today. This piece of theory is not too controversial. After all, nerves have wiring within them to carry information to the synapses and it's likely this wiring is involved in the thinking process. But Hameroff is not finished. He has teamed up with Roger Penrose to bring quantum mechanics into the picture.

Their reasoning is straightforward but has generated a great deal of controversy. Hameroff observes that anesthetics cause humans to lose consciousness by binding to tubulin, but they do not halt all brain function. He, therefore, concludes our conscious thinking is mediated by tubulin, not the larger scale firing of the neurons. Penrose had been looking for a mechanism in the brain that would explain how brains solve non-computational problems. Together Penrose and Hameroff propose tubulin micro tubes are quantum gravity computers that allow us to think non-computationally and are the seat of consciousness. The ideas are still being worked.

Penrose and Hameroff have a difficult task conveying their ideas to the rest of the scientific community. Scientists don't recognize a need for something that can think non-computably, so they are highly skeptical of a mechanism which performs that sort of thought. The latest development on the Hameroff Penrose model comes in the work of Travis Craddock, now of Nova Southeastern University, Florida, and others. They have written a paper arguing signals propagate according to quantum principles within microtubules through the excitation of thiamin molecules along the length of the tube. They believe these molecules are quantum, entangled in a similar manner to the mechanism recently discovered in photosynthesis. The geometry of these molecules is set out in a similar way to the active areas in chlorophyll and they have a complementary problems to solve. Chlorophyll tries to maximize energy conversion efficiency, while a microtubule tries to minimize the use of energy while propagating signals along a nerve. You might wonder

Tubulin Protein

Tubulin

where the light comes from since tubulin is housed deep within the neurons inside our brains and shielded from light by our skull. It turns out that the mitochondria which powers our bodies emit photons of UV light as a waste product of their metabolism. The speculation is tubulin harvests this waste energy.

Before we argue for this mechanism any further we still need to establish that a non-computational mechanism is needed to allow human thought. In the next chapters, we will look at the nature of knowledge and, in particular, mathematical creativity and the Wiles Paradox.

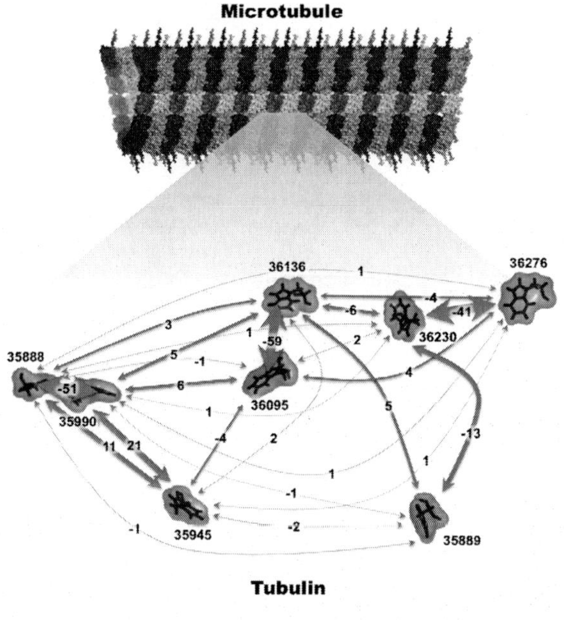

Quantum Coupling of Tubulin in Microtubule

Chapter 5

KNOWLEDGE

Chimpanzee and Typewriter

"There's an infinite number of monkeys outside who want to talk to us about this script for Hamlet they've worked out."

Douglas Adams

"I'm not young enough to know everything."

J.M. Barrie

"He has Van Gogh's ear for music."

Billy Wilder

Could an army of monkeys write *Hamlet* by bashing away randomly on typewriters? Of course, we don't mean this literally. We are asking whether knowledge can be created without understanding. Can a monkey, or perhaps some form of computerized random number generator, accidentally type out the script for Shakespeare's *Hamlet* or write Tolstoy's *War and Peace*? Is knowledge generation simply a numbers game?

Leo Tolstoy's *War and Peace* is generally assumed to be the longest novel ever written. This is not quite true. Wikipedia reckons the longest novel is a French book, *Artamène*, with over 2.1 million words. Tolstoy comes in sixteenth, with a mere half million!

Written in 1869, *War and Peace* tells the story of five Russian families during the Napoleonic wars. Originally written in a mixture of Russian and French, and numbering over 500,000 words, it was quickly translated to other languages. The mistress of composer Franz Liszt translated it fully into French, where it expands to 550,000 words. Contrary to popular myth the length of the book drops slightly in German. If you really want to save paper Chinese is best. Because it uses a single symbol per word, the Chinese translation needs only 750,000 characters compared with the 3 million for English. It is wrong to assume this is necessarily more efficient than a phonetic language. Although it might save on paper, it is considerably more laborious to write. Three strokes are required to write 'war' in English whereas the Chinese pictogram requires ten.

是

War in Chinese

Computers work with numbers. It is a simple process to translate a book into numbers because books are composed of discrete symbols. All we need do is give each symbol a unique number and record those numbers in digital format. Artistic works involving pictures and sound are more difficult to represent because they are continuous in nature. We have to digitize them first. With music or painting this inevitably means some loss of information as we can't cut a sound or image into an infinite number of pieces.

The modern standard for translating text to numbers is Unicode. Each character is represented by a five-digit number ranging from 1 to 64,000 – two bytes for those of you who know computing. This is sufficient to code almost all the world's symbols, so we can avoid any accusation of being language-ist! Here are some examples of the

Φテあ Q ボ杏碓 П Ж Я

Ancient Greek, Japanese: Kanji, Katakana, Chinese, and Russia-Cyrillic Symbols

characters represented by Unicode.

For our discussion, it does not matter which language *War and Peace* is written in. We just treat the symbols as numbers. I am going assume the English translation which has around 500,000 words; a nice round number. Assuming a generous 10 characters per word, *War and Peace* is approximately 10-megabytes – that's about the same size as a music track on iTunes. In practice, the book uses a bit more memory, as there is some overhead for formatting information. My laptop has a 500 Gigabyte hard disk so I could fit half a million copies of *War and Peace* on it!

If we take a look at the contents of the file on my computer the book starts:

871011081084480114105110991014415111

Can a computer calculate this number?

The obvious answer is YES. It is just an integer like 1, 3 or 42. Granted it's a large number, but the length of the number is simply the length of all the symbols in the book coded into Unicode – about 10 million digits. We have already determined this number can be stored on my hard disk half a million times, so it's not an unimaginably large number. How long would it take to calculate the number corresponding to *War and Peace*?

The simplest method is to count up starting at 1 then 2, 3, 4, 5, and so on until I try every number. Will this eventually get to the *War and Peace* number? The answer is yes. Eureka! All of human knowledge is computable. I have written this computation out as a simple computer program below. It says, in plain English, start at zero, go round a loop counting up one at a time and print each number as you go along.

```
i==0; Loop i++ Print i;
```

Easy!

No, unfortunately. The problem is subtler than it first appears. First it will take a VEEEEERRRY long time. If I counted up from one, I would print out *War and Peace* eventually but it would take 120 billion, billion, billion, billion, billion… (I would need the entire length of this book to write out all the billions) years! For the physicists amongst you, I would need $10^{30,000}$ years, assuming I could use every atom in the known universe counting in parallel at the plank interval. 'The plank interval' is the shortest time that can exist in the Universe as a discrete 'tick'.

Even going at this speed using with every atom in the known Universe would take $10^{5,000}$ longer than the age of the Universe. This is stupendously long. Remember scientific notation means I have a 1 with 5000 zeroes after it. It is a deceptive notation as something as innocuous as 10^{120} is equal to the number of atoms in the known universe. $10^{5,000}$ is an absolutely enormous number. If you hear something is going to 'take until the end of time', we're talking a lot longer than that!

You may have spotted that in the process of counting up to the *War and Peace* number we also count through EVERY book ever written shorter than 500,000 words in all the world's languages. Interestingly we counted through the Japanese and Chinese translations of *War and Peace* quite a bit before we reached the English and finally French translations. During the process, we also stepped through countless other wonderful works: proofs of amazing theorems, the complete works of William Shakespeare, and every composition ever written. Sadly, we never knew it. The problem is my program never stopped and told me it had found any of these wonderful things. I would have to sit staring at the screen to spot them. If I was off doing something else – making a cup of tea, taking the kids to school – I would miss all these wonders; the program never *tells* me if it has succeeded, but quietly prints out *War and Peace* and carries on. This is really annoying. It's not a useful machine.

What I need is a machine that rings a bell when it finds something interesting so I can break away from what I am doing and take a look. Reading every book it writes in every language and all the nonsense in between would take a ginormous amount of my time. (By-the-way, contrary to statements by school teachers that ginormous is not a word – it is!) I want a computer to come up with *War and Peace* without me having to do all the work.

It's no help if the machine writes everything down and lets me take a look in my own good time. That only puts off the time when I have to begin reading all the gibberish it produced. Another practical problem is the massive storage required. Just imagine the immense piles of printer paper! Stephen Hawking and Jacob Bekenstein have shown space appears to have a limit to the quantity of information it can store. The quantity of information we are looking at here is greater than the storage capacity of the Universe and would collapse space-time to a black hole before I got even a fraction of the way through. Let us try to be a bit cleverer about the task of creating this information.

The simplest way to tie the computer down is to run a much stricter program. Ask it to count up from one until you get to a number representing the novel War and Peace and then print it, stop and ring a bell.

Loop i++ until i == "War and Peace..."; Print i; ring-bell;

This program succeeds!

I am triumphant. I have calculated the *War and Peace* number, and this time I did not miss the event. But, if you consider this a little more deeply I gave the computer the answer! I told it the string "*War and Peace...*" and it was able to count up, stop, and tell me it reached it. In mathematical terminology, the program is said to have 'halted' when it reached the *War and Peace* number and in computer science speak it is a special purpose program designed to do only this one thing. This program is pointless. First, it would still take a ginormous amount of time to get there and, second, it is trivially the same as running the program: Print *War and Peace.*

i = "War and Peace..."; Print i;

It's just the same as me taking my laptop, finding *War and Peace* and pressing *print*. In no way is this equivalent to Leo Tolstoy's creative effort of writing *War and Peace* in the first place.

What went wrong?

I wanted my computer to find an *interesting* string I did not already know. *War and Peace* is trivially computable after Leo Tolstoy created it but the question is whether my computer could come up with *War and Peace* or some similar creative work on its own. Can it *create* and, more importantly, understand it has *created* something? We have linked the ideas of creativity and understanding, and this will prove to be the key to the problem.

The Problem

One suggestion put forward by Daniel Dennett is the creative process is a two-part task – generate ideas, then critically assess them. I can, in principle, make a program write out every possible book less than 500,000 words long. Provided I don't store the results this will not collapse the Universe. This just leaves the problem of writing another program to read all the output and ring a bell each time it finds some interesting truth. This second program might be called an appreciation program. Let's examine this approach. I can write out a very simple program to do this – provided I cheat and ignore the complexity of the term 'something interesting'. In plain English: Count up from one until I get an interesting fact, write it down and stop.

Loop i++ until i == (Something Interesting), Print i

This generates two problems. We need to make a program that can tell if something is interesting and it will need to be fast because it is going to be handed a huge amount of junk. Clearly I have a process running in my brain that can determine if something is interesting, but it is quite slow. It takes me an appreciable time to open a book, leaf through the pages and declare it either junk or interesting. Leo Tolstoy had a process in his brain that allowed him to create something interesting but I want to prove he did not do this by generating random junk and sifting through it. Let's look at the mathematics.

We know simply counting sequentially through every number would take too much time, but why not generate random numbers and run our critical eye over them? Surely this would give a faster result. Let us try with a short poem. How hard would it be to come across something as simple as a four-line poem using this technique?

This poem, by the late Spike Milligan, is only 23 words long, including the title, and I have a powerful computer. Wouldn't it be possible to generate it using a computer? Unfortunately, no. We humans don't have a good head for large numbers and this problem is much harder than it appears. Let's use playing cards to get a feeling for large numbers.

A Simple Poem

Rain

There are holes in the sky
Where the rain gets in
But they're ever so small
That's why the rain is thin.
Spike Milligan

Spike Milligan

Coming upon a poem by chance can be likened to the probability of dealing a perfect bridge hand. Shuffle the deck thoroughly and then deal four hands. What is the probability every player will have the ace through king in a single suit? It's about 1 in 1,000,000,000,000,000 hands. Because lots of people play a lot of bridge around the world, this outcome has been reported quite a few times. The possibility appears within the bounds of human experience. Fifty-two playing cards seems close to the 80 characters that make up this poem and 13 choices of cards is about the same as the 26 letters of the Latin alphabet. Wouldn't we expect poems of this complexity to crop up almost as often?

NO.

The 80 characters of this poem versus the 52 playing cards and the greater choice offered by 26 letters increases the problem geometrically. Taken together the probability of accidentally getting this poem is vastly less than a perfect hand of bridge, 1 in 10^{83} against the perfect bridge hand of 1 in 10^{20}. That's the difference between the number of atoms in the known universe and the number of atoms in a jug of water! Numbers get big very quickly when we are looking at the permutation of information. And there is another problem with our bridge analogy. All the bridge players in the world are part of the machine finding the perfect hand. When a human sees a perfect bridge hand they are amazed. It is an event that usually hits the local newspapers and a couple of years ago one reached the national papers in Britain. Each bridge player looks at every hand, they play so there is a huge amount of processing going on during every bridge game. To replicate this for our poem, we would need millions of poetry classes spending hours each evening reading through computer printouts of gibberish.

I should also add that sightings of perfect bridge hands are almost certainly hoaxes. The probability of it happening even once would require everyone on Earth to play bridge continuously for a thousand years. It is reported somewhere in the world about two or three times a year. If we are charitable, we might assume people failed to shuffle the deck properly but I suspect some mischief is going on! The numbers don't stack up…

You might think the problem is one of improving the efficiency of the filter so humans would only have to examine a smaller number of possibilities. Surely I could improve things by writing a simple program to ban all non-English characters, words and poor grammar; things that don't pass the Microsoft Word grammar checker. This would generate a more manageable number of potential poems.

Lewis Carroll shows this does not work; my idea to use a grammar and spelling checker to filter out gibberish just eliminated Jabberwocky, one of the most famous verses in the English language. Take a look at what Microsoft Word thinks of it.

The Jabberwocky

’Twas brillig, and the slithy toves
Did gyre and gimble in the wabe;
All mimsy were the borogoves,
And the mome raths outgrabe.
“Beware the Jabberwock, my son!
The jaws that bite, the claws that catch!
Beware the Jubjub bird, and shun
The frumious Bandersnatch!”

He took his vorpal sword in hand:
Long time the manxome foe he sought—
So rested he by the Tumtum tree,
And stood awhile in thought.

And as in uffish thought he stood,
The Jabberwock, with eyes of flame,
Came whiffling through the tulgey wood,
And burbled as it came!

One, two! One, two! and through and through
The vorpal blade went snicker-snack!
He left it dead, and with its head
He went galumphing back.

“And hast thou slain the Jabberwock?
Come to my arms, my beamish boy!
O frabjous day! Callooh! Callay!”
He chortled in his joy.

Twas brillig, and the slithy toves
Did gyre and gimble in the wabe;
All mimsy were the borogoves,
And the mome raths outgrabe.

Lewis Carroll

Lewis Carroll’s Jabberwocky

'Twas brillig, and the slithy toves
Did gyre and gimble in the wabe;
All mimsy were the borogoves,
And the mome raths outgrabe.
"Beware the Jabberwock, my son!
The jaws that bite, the claws that catch!
Beware the Jubjub bird, and shun
The frumious Bandersnatch!"
He took his vorpal sword in hand:
Long time the manxome foe he sought—
So rested he by the Tumtum tree,
And stood awhile in thought.
And as in uffish thought he stood,
The Jabberwock, with eyes of flame,
Came whiffling through the tulgey wood,
And burbled as it came!
One, two! One, two! and through and through
The vorpal blade went snicker-snack!
He left it dead, and with its head
He went galumphing back.

"And hast thou slain the Jabberwock?
Come to my arms, my beamish boy!
O frabjous day! Callooh! Callay!"
He chortled in his joy.
Twas brillig, and the slithy toves
Did gyre and gimble in the wabe;
All mimsy were the borogoves,
And the mome raths outgrabe.

The Jabberwocky Spell Check

Microsoft Verdict on the Poem

39 of the 166 words in the poem are unknown to Word's spelling checker and this is an optimistic analysis of how the algorithm would fare. Many of the words are in the spelling checker because of the poem: galumphing, for example. Lewis Carroll's work was sufficiently influential that part of

the English language was created in this poem. The same goes for much of Shakespeare. If we used a filter method, we would have just deleted most of Shakespeare from the English language! Indeed half the poems in my anthology of English verse are destined for the waste paper basket due to some minor infraction of 'the rules'. If you want something that completely flummoxes my spelling checker here is the Loch Ness Monster Song by Scottish poet Edwin Morgan. I asked a Scottish friend whether Scottish spelling checkers fared any better and he assures me, no.

The Loch Ness Monster's Song

Sssnnnwhuffffll?

Hnwhuffl hhnnwfl hnfl hfl?

Gdroblboblhobngbl gbl gl g g g g glbgl.
Drublhaflablhaflubhafgabhaflhafl fl fl -

gm grawwwww grf grawf awfgm graw gm.
Hovoplodok - doplodovok - plovodokot
- doplodokosh? Splgraw fok fok
splgrafhatchgabrlgabrl fok splfok!
Zgra kra gka fok!
Grof grawff gahf?
Gombl mbl bl -

blm plm,

blm plm,

blm plm,

blp

Edwin Morgan

The Loch Ness Monster

The foibles of spell checkers have long been a personal pain to me because of my dyslexia. Although I can see the red underlining Microsoft Word kindly inserts so liberally into my text, I can't easily see the occasions when I use a homonym. A fine poem illustrating the problem was kindly written by Jerrold H. Zar and published in *The Journal of Irreproducible Results*. It hangs on the wall behind my computer to remind me to check for these errors.

Candidate for a Pullet Surprise
By Jerrold H. Zar

I have a spelling checker,
It came with my PC.
It plane lee marks four my revue
Miss steaks aye can knot sea.

Eye ran this poem threw it,
Your sure reel glad two no.
Its vary polished in it's weigh.
My checker tolled me sew.

A checker is a bless sing,
It freeze yew lodes of thyme.
It helps me right awl stiles two reed,
And aides me when eye rime.

Each frays come posed up on my screen
Eye trussed too bee a joule.
The checker pours or every word
Too cheque sum spelling rule.

Bee fore a veiling checker's
Hour spelling mite decline,
And if we're lacks oar have a laps,
We wood bee maid too wine.

Butt now bee cause my spelling
Is checked with such grate flare,
Their are know fault's with in my cite,
Of nun eye am a wear.

Now spelling does knot phase me,
It does knot bring a tier.
My pay purrs awl due glad den
With wrapped word's fare as hear.

Too rite with care is quite a feet
Of witch won should bee proud,
And wee mussed dew the best wee can,
Sew flaw's are knot aloud.

Sow ewe can sea why aye dew prays
Such soft wear four pea seas,
And why eye brake in two averse
Buy righting want too pleas.

The Search for Knowledge

I hope this explanation shows you the simplest model for creativity – working through every possibility, and examining them all – is doomed to failure. It would take longer than *until the end of time* to even list all the options, let alone analyze them.

You might wonder just how long it is until the end of time? It's generally assumed there are two possible ends to the Universe, a Big Crunch or heat death. Either way the approximate estimate is our Universe will last somewhere between one and fifty times longer than it has lasted so far. That's a long time, at least another 15 billion years, but just generating *War and Peace* would take 5000 orders of magnitude longer than this!

More complex models such as a three-step process have been suggested. We could perhaps randomly create information and put it through a mechanical filter to bring it down to a manageable set of options and then give it to an appreciation algorithm to finally decide whether we have created something. The real problem with this model is the filters. If we try to reduce the effort by assembling works only from pre-existing words, we will have filtered away many works we know and love. Gone are Shakespeare, Lewis Carroll, Dylan Thomas and Roald Dahl, shall I go on? Indeed, once upon a time there were *no* words, every word was coined at some point. The process of creating art is continually creative and mechanical filters can't be applied to things they have not seen before.

You might argue we could devise a more sophisticated mechanical filter, something that contains an algorithm with an understanding of the rules of language. The problem is both the size of the task and the nature of understanding. If I devised some really good appreciation algorithm which did not delete all the creative words of the English language, it would still have to read and appreciate the huge quantities of input until it hit upon something good. There is no way for any machine to read all this information in the age of our Universe; the numbers are just too large. And there is no way for a machine to understand all the rules of language, they are not written down and constantly evolve.

These descriptions should give you an intuitive feel for nature of the creative problem. If you try to deconstruct it into mechanical steps you end up with either a mechanism that needs to be infinitely specified or one that lets through an infinite quantity of nonsense. A human could never sift through all that garbage to find the occasional pearl of wisdom.

Until the beginning of the 20th century, most people thought knowledge and creativity must be just a matter of scale. A big enough, fast enough machine should be able to solve any problem. But early in the 1930s two mathematicians – Kurt Gödel and Alan Turing – showed knowledge was not so simple. Let me give you a feel for why.

Knowing When You Know

The essence of creating knowledge, is to know when you have done so. In a sense, counting from one to infinity means *I know everything*, and merely counting to 50 million creates every piece of significant symbolic knowledge that will ever be written – all the books, plays, mathematical theorems you could possibly want. But, if I were to list all these numbers in an enormous imaginary book it would hardly constitute knowing everything: I would be awash with numbers but not with knowledge.

The essential feature of 'knowing' is to have a small number of steps that will definitely answer a problem. For example, if I wish to phone someone I can look up their details on my phone. The process will tell me their number in two or three steps. If you tell me the number is somewhere in the phone book this is not knowledge. It could mean I need an infinite number of steps.

If I accidentally deleted all the names in my phone – a nightmare scenario – and just had a print out of numbers would I still 'know' them? Obviously I would recognize my mother's number, but most of them would be useless. To know something, I need link the information to what it is for. A number with a name allows me to predict what will happen if I make a call. I will have an interesting conversation or pay my gas bill. It's the same with most numbers. If I have a number that represents the design for a building or a mathematical theorem, these numbers have purpose. If I input these numbers to a computer along with some building design software or a copy of Mathematica they will do something interesting; allowing a construction firm to build a innovative building or a mathematician to check a theorem is sound.

It's a lot harder to prove numbers representing art are functionally useful. A work of art is in some sense not complete – it still needs to go through the process of being appreciated by someone. We could show it to a friend or exhibit it in a gallery but this is un unpredictable process. Van Gogh's paintings were so criticized in his lifetime, many people would have denied them the label art, and Edwin Morgan's Loch Ness

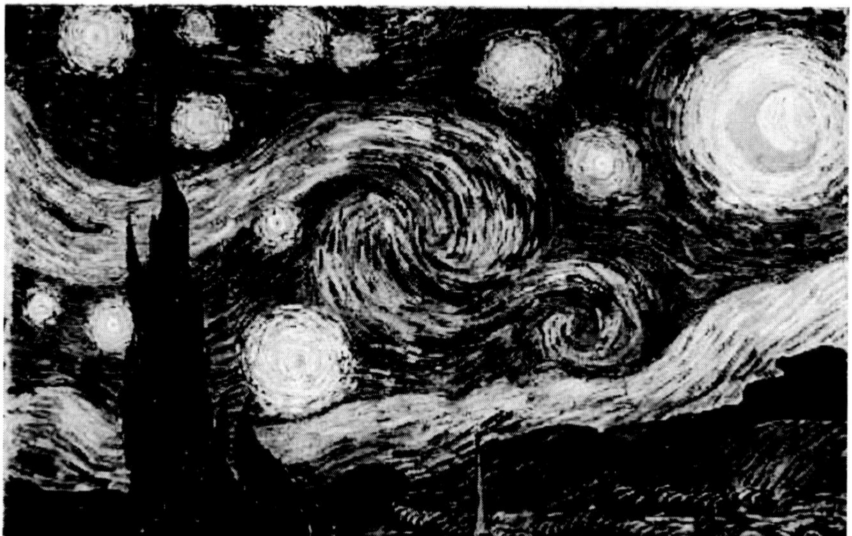

Art or Information

Monster poem is almost pure gibberish, but it's undoubtedly art. Art is a tricky problem but, in practice, most of us agree on what constitutes good and bad art. We will look again at art, in Chapter 10.

Classically we assume knowledge is discovered through random chance and iteration. To understand how this might work let's lay out the world's information in a way we can visualize. Imagine every piece of discoverable knowledge could be found in an infinitely large library.

The infinity library would contain every possible symphony, theorem, novel, poem, and play ever written, or to be written. Its sister library next door, the continuum library, would contain all the analogue works of art; painting, sculpture, architecture, physical artifacts and the like. The curators of the two libraries would constantly argue over whose collection was the better. We'll leave them to differ for the moment. The infinity library is interesting enough so let's explore it first. After all, its sister, the continuum library, takes an infinite amount of time just to look at the first room, and we are in a hurry!

Although the infinity library is infinite, we are probably only concerned with entries shorter than a million symbols. All the interesting papers, proofs and symphonies I know of are shorter than this. If I wanted to include all computer programs, I would still only need to increase it to 100 million symbols. Looking for knowledge is *not* itself an infinite task.

For the sake of clarity, I will ask the infinity librarian to organize the collection. Any book or paper will be sorted according to its title and the contents of its pages, and similar books should be grouped together. I also only want to look at the English section of the library for the moment. I will still have a huge section to look through but at least every work is titled and readable by me. Much of the information will be junk but amongst the sea of rubbish will be islands of useful knowledge. Now, is there a way to find knowledge in this library in an automated fashion?

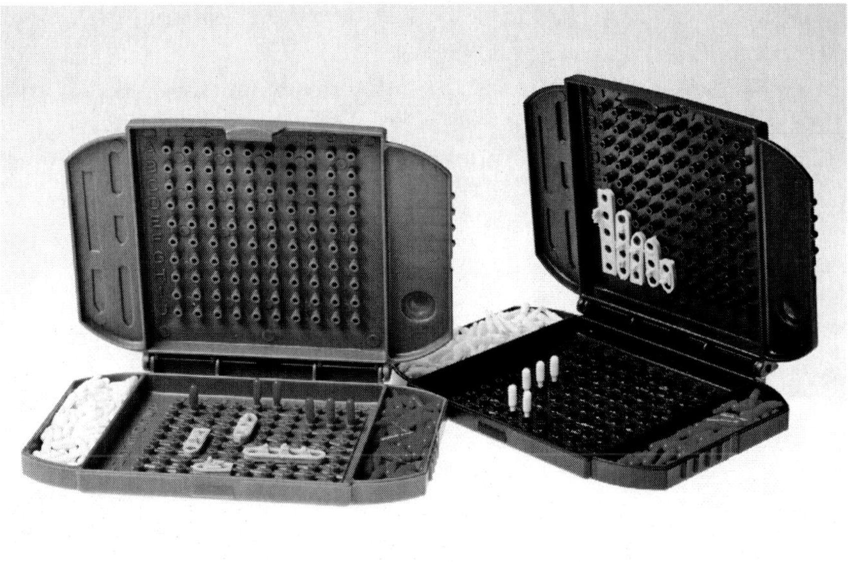

Battleship

The best analogy I can find to illustrate iterative knowledge discovery is the 1970s family game 'Battleship'. The game consists of two 10 by 10 grids that you plug your ships into. All the ships are linear shapes of a few squares in length. The players cannot see each other's ships and must guess where they are. A very simple way to do this would be to ask your opponent whether they have a ship on the top left square and continue systematically across the board, square by square, until you reach the bottom right hand corner. This would eventually find every ship. If every ship were a piece of knowledge we could discover all the knowledge in the world by simply stepping through the board one cell at a time, but it would take a long time.

A better way to play Battleship is to pick a square at random. If you get a hit, explore linearly around the hit. This will efficiently find the rest of the ship. The same might be true for knowledge. We could take random shots, get lucky and move linearly to flesh out our knowledge. Once we had exhausted an area we could take a step away at random and again hope for another hit. This process is exactly the way some people imagine the frontier of knowledge expands.

But, it is wrong.

The monkey moon shot story explains...

> *"I believe that this nation should commit itself to achieving the goal, before this decade is out, of landing a monkey on the moon and returning him safely to Earth."*
>
> President Monkey

The monkey nation is asked to mount a moon shot. After a little time a monkey is asked to report on progress.

"I can report," says the monkey, "I have climbed a particularly tall tree on the tallest hill on my island and have made over seven hundred meters progress towards the moon, although this is only 0.0001% of the way there, this has been quick so I believe we are well on the way."

You see of course the problem. Progress in many problems is nonlinear. Moving a bit of the way towards the goal does not provide any *actual* progress: That is the problem with knowledge. It is not linear in structure. You need to take leaps to discover new knowledge. You can not simply look around in the general area. Such leaps are mathematically huge. The chance of making a successful one by pure chance is virtually zero.

But Cats Can!

As chance would have it, as I was writing this book about the impossibility of creating great literary works at random, our new kitten, Jessie, sat on my keyboard – she likes the warmth. To my great embarrassment I have been proven wrong. Here is her first literary work. I managed to capture her on camera a little later that evening, editing a spreadsheet. My brain interprets this string as the cat thanking me for good food. I wonder if you see the same thing? This is just a demonstration of the strength of human pattern detection algorithms and not, sadly, of feline communication.

Cats Creation

…. Kkkklnk gfoooooooofd0------- iiiii;;;;;;;;;;;ii…..ffffffffffffffffffffff……
==
==
==
===========================pppppppppppppppppppppp
pppppppppppppppppppppppppppppppppppppppppppppppppp
pppppppppppppppppppppppppppppppppppppppppppppppppp
pppppppppppppppppppppppppppppppppppppppppppppppppp
pppppppppppppppppppppppppppppppppppppppppppppppppp
pppppppppppppppppppppppppppppppppppppppppppppppppp
pppppppppppppppppppppppppppppppppppppppppppppppppp
ppppppppppppppppppppppppp..opppppppppppppppppppppppp
pppppppppppppppppppppppppppppppppppppppppppppppppp
pppppppppppppppppppppppppppppppppppppppppppppppppp
pppppppppppppppppppppppppppppppppppppppppppppppppp
ppppppppppppppppppph

Jessie, Our Creative Kitten

Chapter 6

KITTENS & GORILLAS

Orangutan and Kitten

"No kitten that loves fish is unteachable; No kitten without a tail can play with a gorilla; Kittens with whiskers will always love fish; No teachable kitten has green eyes; No kittens have tails unless they have whisters; hence..."

Lewis Carroll

"Once you eliminate the impossible, whatever remains, however improbably, must be the truth."

Sherlock Holmes,
Arthur Conan Doyle

As well as giving us Alice, the Jabberwocky, and the Cheshire Cat, Lewis Carroll lectured on mathematics at Oxford University. He wrote several books on logic, illustrated with wonderful problems involving fish, kittens, and gorillas – much less boring than the brown, grass-eating cows of modern textbooks. Kittens and gorillas are not usually in much contact, but I did find one hit on Google, pictured!

The words we organize into books, poems and plays are not just a random jumble; they have structure and a logic to them. We group verbs, subjects and objects together to form sentences and, at a larger scale, characters have motivations and relationships: this character loves that character, the valet had the candlestick in the ballroom and could not have stabbed the butler in the kitchen, and so on. We have dictionaries to define words, but to truly understand the information they convey we need to understand the logical rules governing how they can be combined.

Everyday conversation is fragmented and repetitive. Fortunately, now and again, we say something definitive. For example, "This gorilla is brown." The statement links a property, 'brownness', to a thing, 'a gorilla'. Logical statements are precise but often need to be put in context. If I were standing in a forest when I made my statement you must guess I mean the nearest gorilla. The word 'This' implies nearness, but nearness is not well defined. Better to be precise. 'The gorilla I am closest to, measured by line of sight distance is the Pantone shade *dark brown*.' However, if I talked like this all day I would not have many friends.

Logical Beginnings

The formal study of logic began in 384BC with the publication of a treatise called the *Organon* by the Greek philosopher Aristotle. A student of Plato, Aristotle taught many of the famous leaders of his time, including Alexander The Great. Ancient Greece was not some idyllic think tank. If you annoyed the political establishment you might find yourself having to leave town in a hurry. This happened to Aristotle after Plato's death, and he spent nearly a decade touring Europe. Eventually, he returned to Athens where he published his study on logic.

In the Organon, Aristotle examined groups of up to four statements, each containing up to four relationships. For example: All kittens eat fish. Some kittens eat fish. No kittens love gorillas. No gorillas eat kittens – luckily. It is possible to put two statements back to back and infer things.

I could say, "All gorillas eat leaves." "All leaves are green." Therefore I can infer all gorillas eat some green things. This is a valid inference. It is *not* correct to say, gorillas eat *only* green things.

There are 256 ways you can arrange four Aristotle statements with four relationships but only 19 valid deductive conclusions can be drawn. The kitten puzzle at the start of the chapter is an example of such a logical puzzle. Can you reach the right conclusion?

TRY SOLVING THE KITTEN PUZZLE WITHOUT READING ON

Aristotle's syllogisms are only a start. There are many other types of logic. In antiquity, the Stoics developed a different brand of logic based on the idea of larger and smaller. Stoic logic allows us to answer questions of relative size. If a Mini is smaller than an Audi, and an Audi is smaller than a Rolls Royce, then a Mini is smaller than a Rolls Royce. The Stoics pursued their branch of logic until around 180AD when study of this sort died out. It's not quite clear why. Perhaps the rise of religious power and the onset of the Dark Ages curtailed intellectual inquiry. Even after the Enlightenment began around 1650 it took some time for the discipline of logic to re-emerge. If you want to learn more about syllogistic logic and how to solve Lewis Carroll's puzzle you should read his book *The Game of Logic*. The definitive book on the logic of language, in my opinion, is *Logic* by Wilfrid Hodges.

Logic for Computers

Western civilization mostly survived on syllogisms and stoic logic for nearly two thousand years before George Boole devised his theory of binary logic in 1847. Boole developed an elegant mathematical system for representing logical statements that allowed simple arithmetical operations to answer logical questions. We now call this system Boolean logic and he gave us the modern convention of using one for true, and zero for false. Computers use his principles all the time. For example, if it is true my bank account shows less than zero, then make it true that someone will send me a letter warning me I am overdrawn. The best way to get your head around Boolean logic is to solve the ancient puzzle of the Two Guards. The puzzle featured in the 1986 movie, *The Labyrinth*, starring David Bowie and Jennifer Connelly. If you want to cheat watch the film to see the answer. Here is the puzzle. I'll put the answer on my website.

> *Two guards stand barring your way and behind them are two doors. One guard always speaks the truth, while the other always lies. You are only allowed to ask one question of one of the guards. Your life depends on picking the right question to ask as, based on the answer, you must pick a door. One leads to life, the other to certain death. Is there a question you can ask to ensure you pick the door leading to life?*

TRY SOLVING THE GUARD PUZZLE

Twin Guards - Left door or Right

If you are reading this, you picked the correct door and lived.

Logic for Humans

Syllogisms can be used for practical purposes. Take, for example, the following set of statements, "I want a hot drink." "Coffee and tea are hot drinks." "I always drink milk with tea," "We have no milk." What drink should I choose? I'm sure you can work it out. This logical problem follows a simple chain and results in me getting the hot drink I like.

We use Boolean logic on a day-to-day basis. The simplest form is a checklist. Pilots use checklists all the time; do I have wings, fuel and a copilot? If they are all there, go ahead and fly. Otherwise do not. Mathematically speaking, a checklist is simply the product of the options. If they are all one, then the product is one – in this case we can fly. If any is false – represented by a zero – the product will be zero and we cannot fly.

Life is often more complicated and we have many logical tools at our disposal. Let's take a look at a few, starting with a famous historical one.

Benjamin Franklin invented the lightning rod and bifocal glasses, as well as charting the Gulf Stream and all manner of other scientific discoveries. He described his process for decision-making when there are many pros and cons to consider.

> *"... my Way is, to divide half a Sheet of Paper by a Line into two Columns, writing over the one Pro, and over the other Con. Then during three or four Days Consideration I put down under the different Heads short Hints of the different Motives that at different Times occur to me for or against the Measure. When I have thus got them all together in one View, I endeavor to estimate their respective Weights; and where I find two, one on each side, that seem equal, I strike them both out: If I find a Reason pro equal to some two Reasons con, I strike out the three. If I judge some two Reasons con equal to some three Reasons pro, I strike out the five; and thus proceeding I find at length where the Balance lies; and if after a Day or two of farther Consideration nothing new that is of Importance occurs on either side, I come to a Determination accordingly."*

Another important piece of logic is *reductio ad absurdum*. Reduction to the absurd allows us to disprove something because, if it were true, it would lead to an absurd conclusion. An alibi is a familiar form. If I was seen in the pub when the murder occurred in the ballroom of the manor house and you claim I committed the murder, I must have been in two places at once. People can't be in two places at once – that would be absurd. Conclusion: I am innocent!

Notice I not only prove I am not guilty I also prove the opposite: I am innocent. When a mathematician uses this trick, it is called an indirect proof and works the same way as the alibi. Assume the opposite is true of some theory you want to prove (I am guilty). If it generates a contradiction or paradox (can't be in two places at once) you can deduce the opposite must be true (innocence). Mathematicians use this all the time. It assumes, of course, mathematics is consistent and that true and false are opposites.

Some mathematicians argue this is too strong an assumption. Why should we assume consistency and recognize only two logical states, true and false? These mathematicians believe the only way to prove a theorem is with positive argument rather than using the opposite of a negative argument. They don't allow indirect proofs in their mathematical models. This type of mathematics is unsurprisingly called positivism. It's a pure theory but, unfortunately, if you try to follow it you lose much of our current mathematical knowledge and understanding. Most modern mathematicians think it a historical curiosity, but it does pop up from time to time. Modern mathematics is founded on the axioms that true and false are the opposite of each other and that inconsistency is forbidden within the system. Mathematical proofs submitted to journals are not permitted to contain inconsistencies or result in paradoxes.

Paradoxes – When Logic Fails

"I would not be a member of any club that would admit me."

Groucho Marx

Paradoxes occur when a statement makes no sense, or results in an internal contradiction as with Groucho Marx's famous quote. They are widely used in mathematics to implement indirect proofs. To do this, we suppose something is true, and if it results in a paradox then the

Groucho Marx

thing we thought true must be false and the opposite is true. This is a somewhat circuitous route to prove things, but it is often the only practical way.

Two paradoxes we are taught as children are the liar's paradox and Zeno's paradox – also known as the story of the tortoise and hare. The first is a real paradox but the second is a false paradox. The liar's paradox is just the simple statement:

"This sentence is false."

It is a paradox because of the internal inconsistency: We cannot determine if it is a true or false.

First assume it is true, but it says it is false, so it is not true. Then try it the other way around. Assume it is false but the sentence states it is false, so it must be true. If that were so it must be false by the first argument and so on *ad infinitum.*

Either way around, the sentence contradicts itself. A paradox.

Zeno's Paradox, on the other hand, is a false paradox. Here is the story.

Once upon a time there was a hare. He was a very arrogant hare and believed he could outrun any animal. A tortoise was walking along the way and the hare jumped out in front of him. "You are so slow," said the hare. The tortoise replied, "You may be the fastest hare in the kingdom but I am the most persuasive tortoise. I bet I can persuade you of anything, including that I am faster than you."

"I don't believe you," said the hare.

"OK," said the tortoise, "let me show you. Give me 100 meters head start since you are so fast. Then, we'll both start to run. After 10 seconds you will have run 100 meters and arrived where I used to be, but I will now be ten meters ahead. After another second you will be where I am now, but I will be 1 meter ahead again. So you can never catch me."

The hare pondered for a while but, being a hare of little brain, could not make out the true answer.

It is a false paradox. The time intervals are getting shorter. The question for a mathematician is, does the problem converge to a solution. The answer is yes, and I can reframe the problem to see how it is solved. Let's simply look at who would be ahead after 20 seconds: the hare!

The mathematical reason for it being a false paradox is that some series converge and some do not. If I move progressively closer and closer to something in smaller and smaller time intervals then I may indeed reach it. On the other hand, some series never converge. I will never reach infinity how ever many steps I take.

The Barber Paradox

Now, for a slightly harder paradox, let's suppose there is a town with just one barber.

In this town, every man keeps himself clean-shaven by either shaving himself or going to the barber; the barber shaves all the men in town who do not shave themselves. All this seems perfectly logical, until we pose the question: who shaves the barber?

This question results in a paradox because, according to the statement above, he can either be shaven by himself or the barber, which is he. However, neither of these possibilities is valid! This is because if the barber shaves himself, then the barber must not shave himself and if the barber does not shave himself, then the barber must shave himself.

You might think this paradox an oddity but, using this simple idea, Bertrand Russell changed the course of mathematical history and it is the fundamental paradox used to show computers are Turing limited.

The Russell Paradox

In the late 19th century, mathematicians began to think about the nature of numbers.

What is a number?

It is certainly not an object we can hold.

I can't hold a *two*, unless it's the brass number plate, for my front door. And, in that case I am holding *one* number plate, so I am not holding the *idea* of two, but rather the idea of *one*: one brass plate in the shape of a two.

The 'idea' of a number is to say something about the *things* I have in my hand: two apples, two oranges and two brass number plates. These are all sets of two things and 'two' is the collection of all these sets.

In 1890, Gottlob Frege completed his theory of sets. The project had taken him five years. Unfortunately, just before sending the book to the publisher, Bertrand Russell wrote to him and pointed out the following paradox. What about the set of sets that does not contain itself? Think about it...

It is the barber paradox with the word 'set' substituted for 'barber' and 'contains' rather than 'shave'. But it's essentially the same logical problem. You might find this rather contrived but mathematicians must have a system totally free from paradox, otherwise there is no certainty. Frege's system was holed below the water line.

Eventually, after much further work, a theory of sets was worked out that does not contain the Russell Paradox. It's called Zermelo-Fraenkel set theory, or ZF for short. It solves the Frege problem by forbidding sets to refer to themselves. It's a bit like Microsoft Excel's solution to dividing something by zero. It is simply forbidden and generates an error message. Set theory was fixed and is now the basis of most mathematical thinking.

What is Logic for?

Logic is the foundation of mathematics. Applying it enables us to make irrefutable statements about things: numbers, lines, planes, equations and the so on – the things you learned at school – and to prove statements about these things beyond *any* doubt. This is not the 'reasonable doubt' hurdle of our law courts, but an absolute measure: No possible doubt whatever.

Let's look at one of the earliest mathematical proofs: Euclid's proof there are an infinite number of prime numbers. Euclid created this proof in ancient Greece around 300BC – so far back that logic was in its infancy

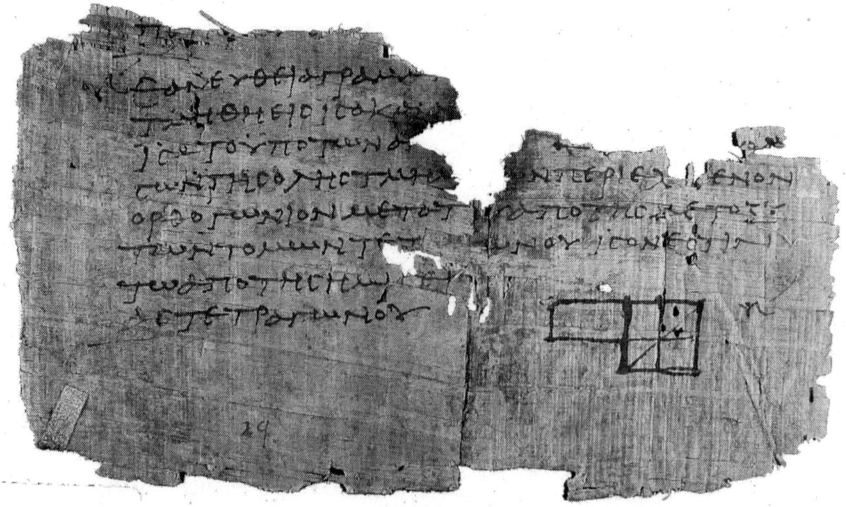

Euclid's Elements 100AD

and numbers had not yet been properly invented. Euclid used distances rather than numbers for all his proofs but I will use the word 'number' in this explanation.

First a little revision. A prime number is a number that can only be divided by itself and one, for example three, five, seven, and eleven. All numbers can be split into primes using a couple of tricks. First, all numbers are divisible by a set of primes. Ten is five times two – two primes. We are also fairly sure we can form any number by adding two primes together. This is Goldbach's Conjecture, set as a question in a letter written to Euler in 1742. It is still unproven!

Euclid proved there are an infinite number of primes by using *reductio ad absurdum*. Imagine we have a complete list of prime numbers – James' list of primes. It contains every prime number. (This is the setup. We are proposing something we suspect is incorrect and will lead to a paradox or contradiction. When it does, we will have proven the opposite fact. The proof relies on the fact that a number can either be prime or not prime. There is no middle ground.)

Let's make a new number by multiplying all the numbers on my list together and adding one. There are two possibilities: this new number is either prime or not prime.

If the number is prime, it is a new prime number that was not on my list and I have disproved the theory.

If it is *not* prime then it must be divisible by two prime numbers already on my list. However, neither of these numbers could have been on my list, because dividing by one of them would give me a remainder of one. Remember I multiplied *all* prime numbers together and added one. It must, therefore, be a new prime number, which had previously not been on my list. Once again, I disprove the theory.

Since both routes fail, James' list of prime numbers is not complete and, therefore, prime numbers are infinite.

Feynman's Proof

My favorite piece of logic is Richard Feynman's disproof of the existence of polywater. It's a strange logical proof bordering on philosophy, but it shows just how far you can take logic.

In 1969, an urban legend spread around the world that there was a substance called polywater. It even made it into an episode of Star Trek. Polywater was believed to be a lower energy state of water, more viscous than ordinary water. If this substance did exist, it would be possible to mine the oceans of the world converting water to polywater and therefore generate energy. There was a concern that if the right catalyst was accidentally introduced into the oceans they would solidify into polywater thus dooming the human race, or at the very least making water sports impossible!

Feynman was consulted and stated, "If there were such a substance as polywater then there would have evolved an animal that eats water and excretes polywater, using the liberated energy as its power source. Since there is no such animal, polywater does not exist."

Feynman's proof is an elegant indirect proof coupled with a syllogism. Polywater exists. Polywater is a lower energy form of the high-energy substance called water. Food is a high-energy substance that can be converted to a low energy substance by a process we shall call 'being good to eat.' All things on earth that are good to eat have something that eats them. Polywater is a food and therefore good to eat. Therefore an animal must exist that eats polywater. No such animal exists, so either something in our chain of logic is wrong, or the premise is unsound. Since the chain is sound, the original premise must be wrong: Polywater cannot exist.

In short, Feynman's proof says: if a thing is so, then the inevitable consequence is the evolution of something else, and since that something else does not exist, the original thing cannot be so. QED: disproof by nonexistent consequence.

The polywater disproof neatly demonstrates the important elements of Feynman's Evolutionary proof. First, life must be continuously exposed to the thing in question, in this case water. This is clearly so as most life on planet Earth lives in the oceans or is intimately entwined with water. Evolution takes time, so enough time must be allowed for life to evolve. It must be a nearly linear problem so that a solution proceeds in steps where each step is an improvement and no step requires too high a level of mutation or adaption. We can illustrate the boundary between a linear problem and one requiring a step change by describing how triple drug therapy works in the treatment of AIDS.

Until triple drug therapy entered the picture progress against AIDS had been a depressing story of drug discovery followed by the almost immediate evolution of the virus to evade the drug. The AIDS virus is a retrovirus with a shell composed of sugar molecules. It is almost trivial for an AIDS virus to mutate these outer markings to look different, even from one day to the next. This is the way the virus continually and nimbly evades our immune system. However, the AIDS virus *does* have some components that it can't easily mutate because they are not merely aesthetic, they have a functional purpose. Why not target them?

Unfortunately, it turns out the AIDS virus can even mutate its functional parts, but this is harder. The probability of a successful functional mutation is 1000 times less likely than a simple aesthetic mutation to the sugar coat.

Triple drug therapy works by attacking three different *functional* elements of the virus simultaneously. It is possible for the virus to modify all these functional elements but the likelihood of it doing so is tiny. One mutation alone does not help because the drug cocktail will still target the other two elements and kill the virus. The AIDS virus does not understand that it is facing a triple drug cocktail. It cannot reason like a sentient being and random chance is not sufficient to make the big leap necessary to overcome the cocktail of drugs. Unless you can mutate all three elements at once your time as a virus particle on this planet is over. Most problems we have to solve in this world require more than one simultaneous logical step and these don't happen by chance.

Chapter 7

COMPLEXITY & CHAOS

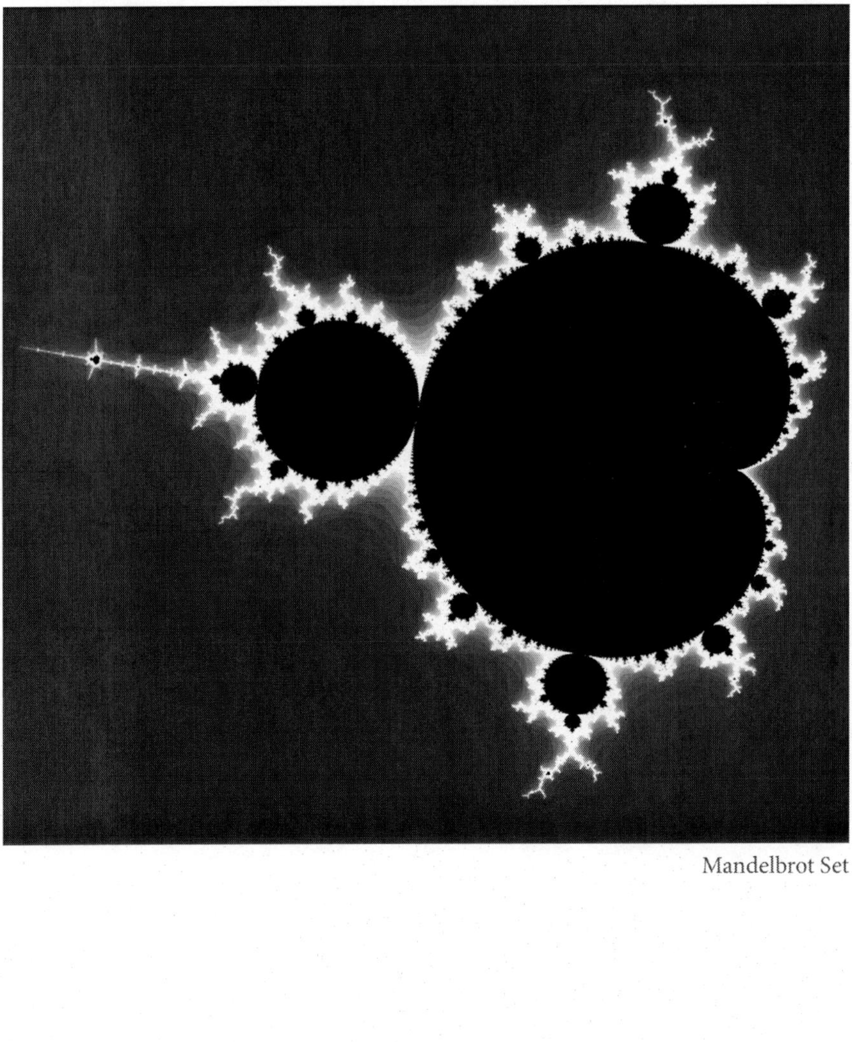

Mandelbrot Set

"Life is really simple, but we insist on making it complicated."

Confucius

"Any darn fool can make something complex; it takes a genius to make something simple."

Pete Seeger

There was once a great King who lived in a marvelous palace. To fend off boredom he collected all manner of interesting games and puzzles. One day an inventor came to his palace and told the King he had a game of such subtle complexity, yet apparent simplicity, the King would play no other. The King learned the game and soon agreed it was, without doubt, the best of all games. The game was, of course, 'chess'. The King asked the price of this game and the inventor told him it was a mere trifle. The King should give him one grain of rice on the first square of the board, two on the second, four on the third, and so on, doubling each square until he filled the board.

The King called his treasurer to honor the bargain and the first bags were brought from the storehouse. The grains were placed on the board in each square but soon there was not enough space and the grains had to be piled on the table next to the board. Soon this, too, was not enough and every table and chair in the hall had to be covered. Even this was not enough and they began to stack whole bags up in the courtyard.

When they reached the thirtieth square, the treasurer turned white. He sat and calculated for a while before saying with a trembling voice, "My great ruler, there is not enough rice in all the world to cover this board." The ruler called the inventor and told him he could not honor the debt and the inventor should name another price. The King had two beautiful daughters, the first knew she was beautiful and deported herself accordingly, and the second, was bookish and shy, but perhaps more beautiful for this. The inventor asked for the hand of the second daughter and lived happily ever after. In the less favorable version of this story, the King becomes very angry and has the inventor beheaded. I prefer the romantic version.

Placing rice on a chessboard and doubling it successively leads to wildly large numbers. Covering it completely requires 18,446,744,073,709,551,615 grains, about four hundred trillion tons and equivalent to one thousand years of worldwide rice production. Like the king, humans do not intuitively grasp the enormity of this problem because we're not good with large numbers.

Although the number of grains needed to cover a chess board is very large, it is not hard to calculate. The treasurer is the one who should have lost his head for not being able to do the calculation. The equation is simply two, doubled sixty-four times, less one, 2^{64}-1. A pocket calculator can produce this number in a thousandth of a second: it's just long multiplication. Although calculating this number is quick, it is not always the case. Answers to some problems have short cuts, while others do not.

Mathematicians have catalogued the universe of problems into classes rather as biologists have catalogued animals into species. Each problem is examined and put into a genus with a name. Sadly the names are not as readable as the Latin names for animals. For example, 'nlogn' is the complexity class of most sorting programs, while traversing a maze typically sits in the class NP or P/POLY. Although the classifications look complex the basis of cataloging is simple, a class name signifies the time needed to solve a problem using the best possible algorithm, and the scale this is measured in is 'Big O'.

Big O

Every problem has a complexity. In mathematics this is expressed using 'Big O' notation, where 'O' stands for order-of-magnitude. The simplest problems have order 1.

If I am working at my computer on a Word document and I press *print*, the printer will spring to action and print the document. This problem is of flat complexity, notated O(1). It does not matter how large the file is; one click is all I need. I am, of course, assuming sufficient paper in the printer and ink in the cartridges.

The next complexity class is a linear problem, O(n). For example, walking to the store to buy a pint of milk. The farther the store, the longer the walk. The time needed to get to the store is directly proportional to the distance: if I am walking, a single step multiplied by the number of steps required to cover the distance.

You might think adding two numbers together is a linear problem – the bigger the number, the harder the problem – but there's a clever trick to speed it up. You can get 10 people to add each column in parallel. They'll need to coordinate when someone ends up with a number larger than ten and has to carry the extra digit but this can be easily solved. A problem gets its classification only once we've used the cleverest possible trick to solve it.

Most problems we meet in mathematics are somewhere in between flat and linear but there are some that are much harder. The most common hard problem we come across in our daily lives is sorting. Rather than go through a tedious written description, check out the video link on my website. Sorting without using any spare space requires a bubble sort. This is an example of something that needs n squared operations and, since n squared is the simplest example of a polynomial, it is said to be in the polynomial time, or 'P' time classification.

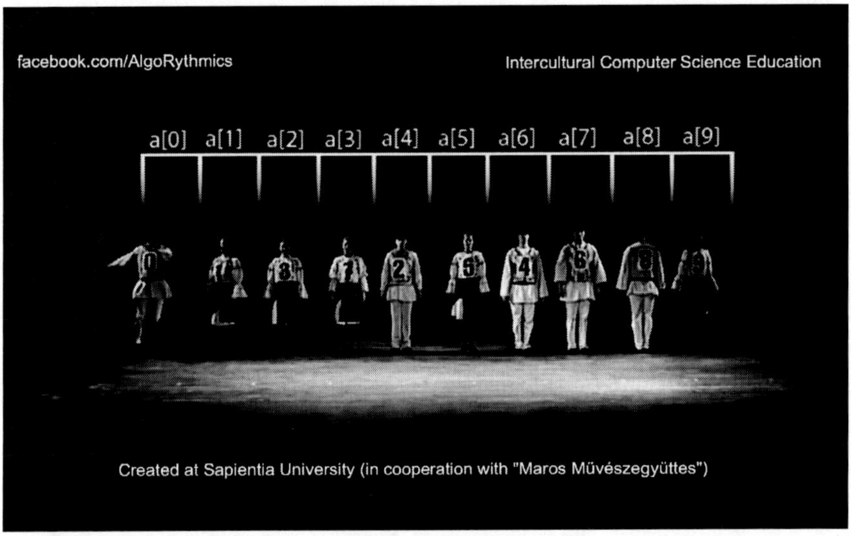

Bubble Sort Ballet

The Hardest Problems

You probably hope cracking the encryption used to secure the Internet is one of the hardest problems known to man but I'm sorry to tell you it is not. When you use your credit card to buy something from an online shop, your web browser changes from *http* to *https*, the 's' stands for secure. The data you send to the Internet is coded using a system developed in 1977 by Ron Rivest, Adi Shamir and Leonard Adleman of MIT, which is why it is called RSA encryption. Any information you send is raised to the power of a very large number – usually around one hundred digits long. Raising something to the power simply means multiplying it by itself that many times.

What makes decrypting a message hard is that division is a slow process; it is called 'long division' for a reason. It turns out there is no way to speed it up on a conventional computer so, unless you know the right number to divide by you will have to try *every* number. It is this that makes decrypting RSA messages hard.

Although RSA messages are difficult to decipher, they are nowhere near the hardest problems. That accolade is commonly believed to go to non-deterministic polynomial problems known as 'NP' problems. NP problems are easy to describe but fiendishly difficult to solve. Nondeterministic means each time you come to a branch in the problem there is no way to tell which branch is the best to pursue without exploring it all the way to the end. It's the same as a maze; at each junction in the maze you can decide which path to take, but the junction gives you no

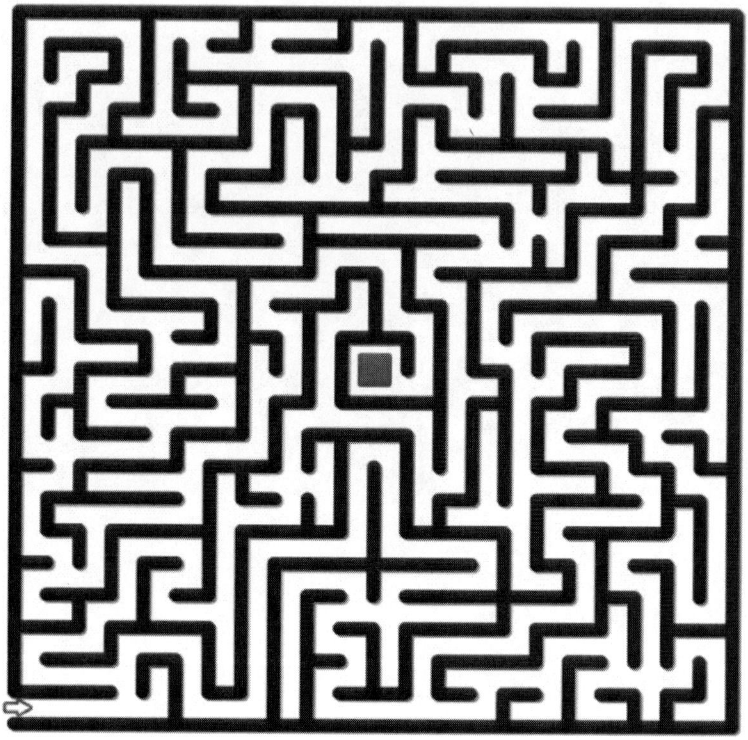

Maze

clue which one will be better. Beware the confusing naming system, 'N' stands for *nondeterministic* in this case, whereas in normal complexity classes 'n' stands for *number*. Sorry. That's just the way it is. Let me give you an example of one of these NP problems.

Let us assume we have one of those complicated recipes from the latest celebrity chef cookbook. If all the ingredients can be bought from one store, making the dish is straightforward, but if they come from different stores, you will have your work cut out. What is the best order to visit them? With 2 shops, it's trivial. Either order will do. With 3 it is a little harder and with 4 there is quite a bit of choice. This is known as the 'traveling salesman' problem because the original formulation described a salesman wishing to find the shortest route between all the cities in which he had customers. The complexity of this problem rises much faster than the Rice and Chess Board problem. Try it for yourself. It doesn't matter if you imagine you are visiting customers or shops. I have given you a grid to count off distances. Try to solve a problem for 3 cities, 5 and 10. What is the shortest path allowing you to visit each place?

TRY THE PUZZLE ON THE WEB

Warning: Don't spend too long on these problems.

The reason I warned you not to spend too long is that solving the 50-city problem would take longer than the age of the known universe. NP problems get harder very fast as the number of elements goes up. A 50-city problem is hugely larger than a five-city problem, not just ten times harder.

The Clay Mathematics Institute has offered a $1 million prize for anyone who can say whether NP problems are really as hard as they appear. It may be there is a general trick or a series of tricks that allow you to solve any NP problem in a shorter time. If you could do this, the problem would be demoted to P, allowing fast computers to tackle it. No one has yet found a proof of the P=NP problem. At the time of writing several proofs are sitting with the Clay Prize judges but don't hold your breath. Most people assume there is no solution. If you want to have a crack at the problem let me state it in simple terms.

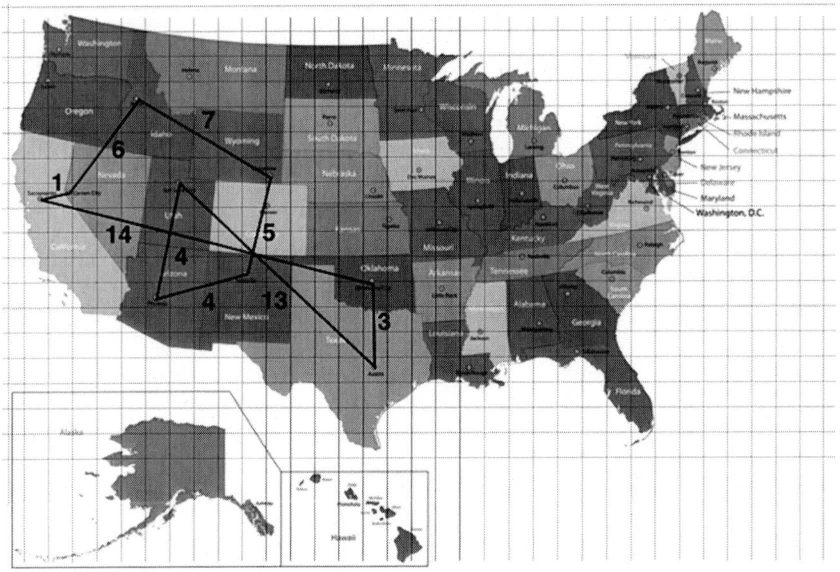

Traveling Salesman

Imagine you wanted to find the center of a maze. Is there a way to speed searching the maze, so you do not have to test every branch? If you can provide a mathematical proof that there is or is not, you win the prize.

Places Game

While it is commonly assumed NP problems are the hardest, this is not the case. There are quite a few that are harder still. One such is called a PSPACE problem. It's quite difficult to explain but luckily many of you will have played a form of it on long car trips when you were a child: My family calls it The Places Game.

I will pick a place – 'London,' and you must then pick another place, say, 'New York', that starts with the letter my place ends with. I'll then pick 'Canterbury' and my kids will laugh at my dyslexia and I'll have to switch to 'Kansas' and so on. Once you use a place you can't use it again.

The mathematical question is to predict who will win given each player has a finite list of places they know? It turns out this type of problem is even harder to solve than an NP problem. This is because on each turn a player gets to pick any name from their list. With the traveling salesman problem, there is only one 'player' – the salesman – so we can write out a route and check it. In the Places Game there is no single route through the game because, after I pick my favorite town 'London,' you can pick any place beginning with 'N'. I have to anticipate an enormous table of possible paths through the game. The table takes huge physical space – which is where PSPACE gets its name.

Remember I'm just playing the simplest mathematical games with bits of paper and discrete ideas. I haven't strayed into the quantum world yet. That brings with it a whole new level of complexity to explore. Complexity is such a diverse subject that Scott Aaronson of MIT has created a web site called the *complexity zoo* to catalogue all the different 'species'. It is much to complex to reproduce here but let me provide a sketch.

The Complexity Hierarchy

My table below represents the hierarchical complexity of knowledge. We start off with the problems both humans and computers find easy, then rapidly move onto problems that even the fastest machines find difficult: a perfect game of chess or predicting the weather. Above these computable problems are the non-computable ones which no computer running any algorithm can solve, and then there are the free will problems: how do we pick a problem in the first place? How do inventors come up with problems no one had ever thought to solve in the first place, such as the invention of the Rubik's Cube?

Ernő Rubik's Cube

Problem	**Example**
Flat	*Print File (for Human)*
nlogn	*Searching a list*
Linear	*Finding the lowest number in a list*
Logarithmic	*Long Multiplication*
Exponential	*Long Division*
P	*Most Algorithms*
Near NP	*Factor Prime Number*
NP-non-complete	*Perfect Game of Chess*
NP-Complete, tractable	*Travelling Salesman, SAT*
Chaotic	*Weather*
NP-Complete, Quantum	*Modeling a Quantum Process*
NP-Complete, intractable	*Busy Beaver, Towers of Hanoi*
PSPACE	*Graph Problems, Places Game*
Non-computable	*Creativity, Finding Fermat Theorem for a Turing machine, Tiling the plane with Penrose Triangles*
Non-deterministic, Non-time divisible, Non-computable	*Free will*
Impossible	*Halting problem for a Turing Machine, some mathematical theorems such as the Continuum Hypothesis in ZF+AC (Hilberts 1st). Travelling faster than the speed of light. Understanding the American tax code.*
Known Unknowns	*I know that I don't know either way.*
Unknown Unknowns	*I have not thought to ask that question yet. Inventing the Rubik's Cube*

Butterfly

"Does the flap of a butterfly's wings in Brazil set off a tornado in Texas?"

Philip Merilees, improving on
Edward Lorenz

Chaos

Chaos is the twin of complexity. It burst into the public psyche in 1987 with the publication of James Gleick's book *Chaos*. It's not a difficult concept to grasp. Complex systems can be formed using simple rules, and very small changes in starting conditions can profoundly affect future events. I experience this if I miss my train to work in the morning: 30 seconds either way will change the whole pattern of my day, the people I meet and the level of stress I experience. I'm sure you can think of similar experiences.

Henri Poincaré, a French mathematician, first studied the effect back in 1880. Poincaré was trying to solve an old mathematical problem called the Three Body Problem originally set by Isaac Newton. Take the Earth, Mars and the Sun. These three bodies orbit each other, or strictly speaking a point in space somewhere between them. Is there an equation that will tell you where the bodies will be in, say, 100 years' time?

Poincaré

The answer is surprising, no. The three bodies will orbit in a non-repeating way. There is no analytical short cut, no equation that will predict where they will be at some point in the future. The only way to know is to build a perfect model of the system and see what happens. Poincaré won a valuable prize for his proof from the King of Bavaria. You can see some amazingly complex orbits plotted below. Remember these are still deterministic and predictable – after all, they were calculated with a computer – they are just chaotic.

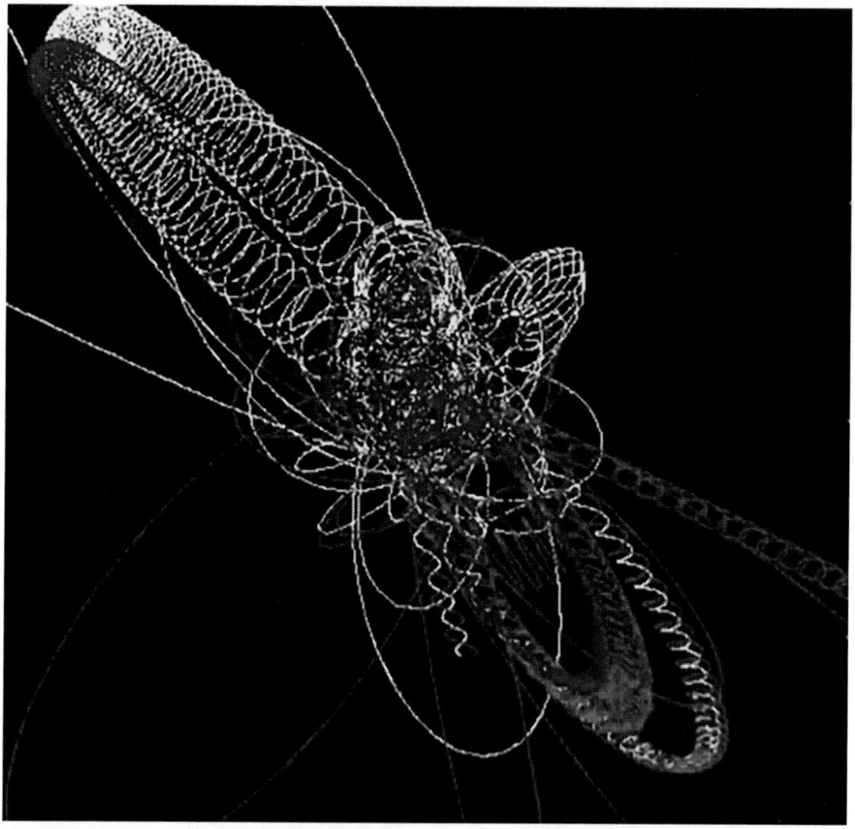

Four Body Problem

Butterflies and Sliding Doors

After Poincaré, the field of chaos remained fairly quiet until Edward Lorenz began studying weather patterns using computers in the 1960s. The story goes, one day his computer was misbehaving and he had to re-key some data into the machine. Rather than using eight decimal places he used only six to save time, and was amazed when the results of his program came out completely different. Dropping the seventh and eighth decimal place represents a change of only one part in a million, yet the patterns of weather predicted by the computer were completely altered.

Lorenz went on to study the effect and created a new branch of mathematics. His quote about the beat of a butterfly wing creating tornados has entered the public psyche and is central to the plot of numerous Hollywood movies. One of his functions – known as the Lorenz Attractor – nicely illustrates the nature of chaos. A very simple equation plots the beautiful, apparently three-dimensional, non-repeating shape.

Chaosville

Chaos, taken to its logical conclusion could explain our Universe. Stephen Wolfram in *A New Kind of Science*, makes the argument that simple rules could explain the extraordinary complexity we see in our Universe. He applies rules to elements in a two-dimensional grid programmed on the computer which form 'cellular automaton' that function a little like simple animals, generating all manner of complex shapes and behaviors. The inspiration for this approach is almost certainly Conway's Game of Life developed by John Conway in the 1960's. In his computer game, animals and machines seem to appear on the screen but in truth they derive from the most simple set of rules. You can check out the website to see a live version of Conway's Game of Life. It's a lot of fun. Wolfram's

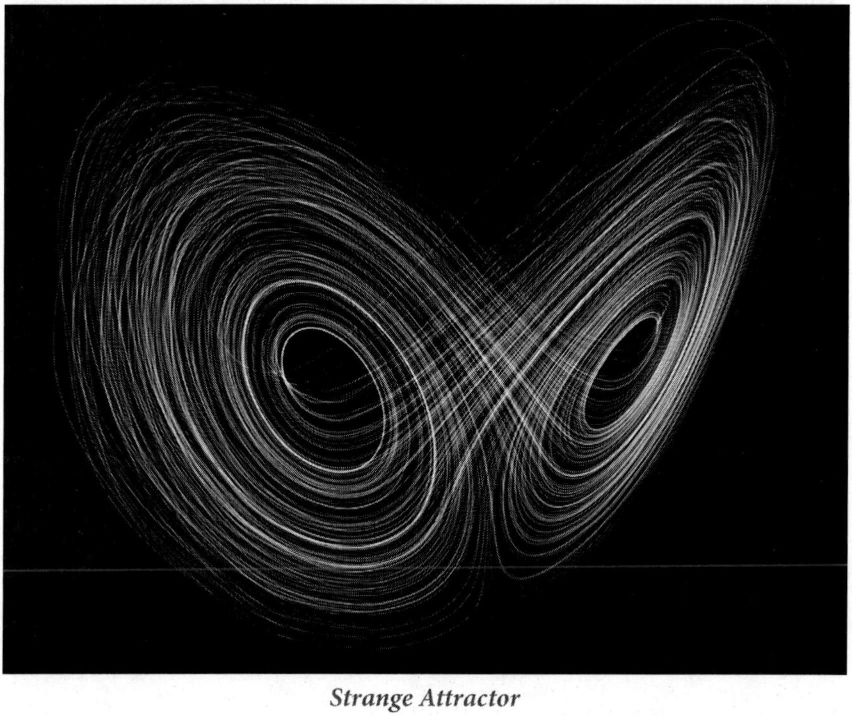

Strange Attractor

thesis is that we could all be living in one of these games. Perhaps our Universe is a form of Mandelbrot diagram – albeit a 3D version with stars and planets. If you look at the picture of a nebula and compare it to the Mandelbrot set, you can see how this is a tempting conclusion.

In the Game of Life the rules are simple yet the behavior simulates little animals being created and destroyed. Of course, there are no actual animals. The things you see on the screen, 'gliders', 'walkers', and 'cannons', just hang together accidentally. But, Wolfram considers these little digital creatures *are* animals. He argues our Universe is just like the Game of Life: A set of simple rules leading to complex behavior. If we are

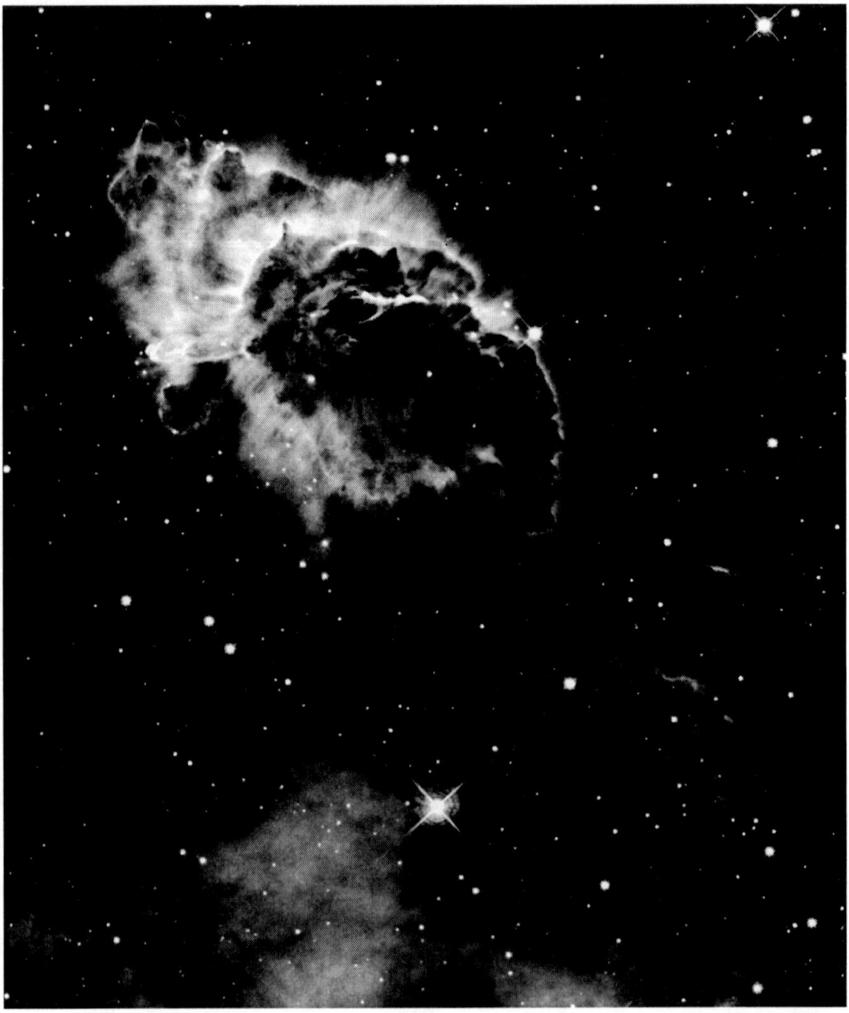

Nebula

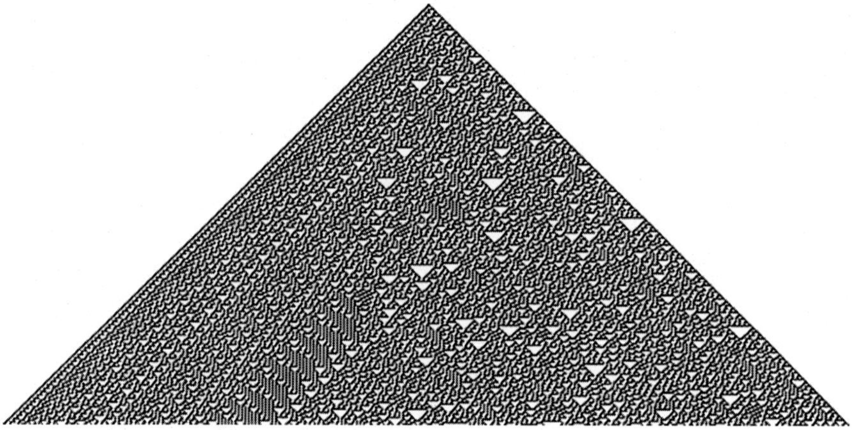

Cellular Automaton

prepared to call ourselves animals, so should the little creatures which emerge within the game. We simply emerged in a similar but slightly more complex game.

This proposal would mean our Universe is entirely deterministic, our lives the result of a gigantic computer program that we live within and form part of. Chaos might make it impossible to predict the future without running the program and watching what happened, but the results would be inevitable, set in motion at the dawn of time. There is no place for free will in such a Universe, no place for reason. The world would simply be.

But a strange idea will come to our aid to show us the limits of computation and allow us to question whether we live in a predetermined world. This idea is Aleph 1 – something larger than infinity. And it is infinity we will explore next.

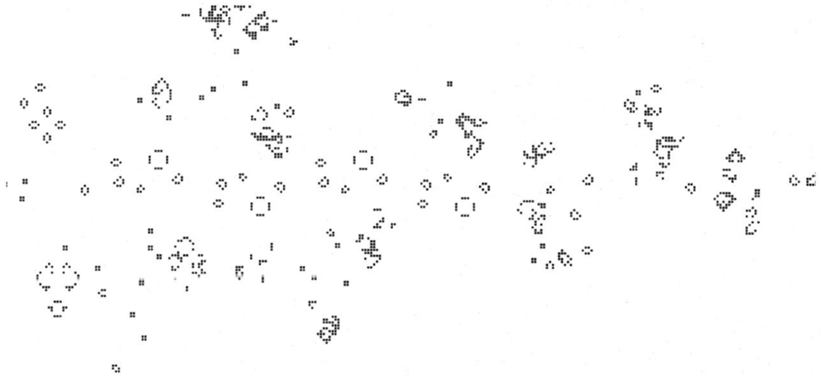

Conway's Game of Life

Chapter 8

∞

Hilbert's Hotel

"All infinities are equal, but some are more equal than others."

George Orwell, paraphrase

"Only two things are infinite, the universe and human stupidity, and I'm not sure about the former."

Albert Einstein

"God gave us the integers, all else is the work of man."

Kronecker

Health warning! The man who discovered infinity had a mental breakdown. This subject may tax your brain.

Georg Cantor didn't really 'discover' infinity but he was the first mathematician to put it on a firm theoretical footing. In the late 19th century, most mathematicians thought infinity was a curious idea with no proper place in mathematics. They treated Cantor's attempts to make it into a real mathematical object with contempt. This affected Cantor's morale and caused him to suffer several bouts of deep depression, retreating to a sanatorium from time to time.

Infinity is a difficult idea to grasp but it is vital to our study of information. It behaves counter-intuitively but is not impossible to grasp. The reason it is important is that information can always be translated into numbers and numbers go on to infinity. If you want to know all about information, you must understand infinite numbers.

History

Indian scholars began studying infinity in the 4th Century BC. It turns up naturally in all manner of places. In geometry, parallel lines extend forever in either direction without ever meeting. To define a parallel line you must contemplate infinity. In arithmetic, even if you pick the largest number you can imagine, there is always a larger one; just add one. In the physical world if you look up at the night sky it appears to go on forever. Again you have infinity.

Historically there were two interpretations of infinity. The first, favored by Plato, was a journey. When you embark upon a journey, you can always take another step. Infinity is the idea of 'one more' or never-ending. It can never be reached. The second definition is more radical. Infinity is a thing, a number *so big* you could not imagine anything bigger, but it is *one* number. Plato thought this second definition tantamount to madness. Today we embrace this madness and go a whole lot further. Let me show you how.

If infinity *were* a number, you should be able to perform mathematics with it; add it, multiply it, and even raise it to a power. This is not as radical as it might first seem. Until comparatively recently, zero was not accepted as a number – if you consider recent to be one thousand years! Nowadays it is.

At the end of the first millennium Indian scholars found, against their intuition, that you can use zero as a number without generating contradictions. Take addition. I can have zero cakes, add one, and I have one cake, add another, and have two cakes and so on. In this way, the number zero behaves just like any other counting number. It also works with multiplication. If I have zero lots of 4 cakes, I have no cakes. Zero times four is zero, so multiplication with zero works. There is one embarrassing exception, if I divide by zero I seem to get infinity. When I was a child this was a definition for infinity, but nowadays mathematicians simply forbid the operation. Division by zero is not allowed and if you try it on your computer, you will get the not terribly useful, #DIV/0! Error. That's progress I guess!

Zero had been tamed. What about infinity?

Cantor showed that while you *could* think of infinity as a number, it might not be just one number. He proposed there are many infinities. In fact, there are a greater than infinite number of them! He did this through a rigorous analysis of a new branch of mathematics called set theory.

Set theory is now the cornerstone of modern mathematics, but it was treated with suspicion in Cantor's time. Rather than embrace the new thinking, many mathematicians ridiculed it; Poincaré wrote that Cantor's ideas were a grave disease infecting the discipline of mathematics! This seems odd given our modern propensity to embrace innovation, but the tone of science back then was different: innovation was not necessarily considered a good thing.

At the turn of the 20th century, scientists were on a mission to tidy things up. Lord Kelvin announced in 1890 that mankind had discovered everything there was to know and the role of future scientists was simply to catalogue and observe the consequences of these laws, and to improve the accuracy of measurement. The last thing scientists wanted was a completely new set of numbers that behaved in strange ways. Cantor was upsetting the apple cart, but he was in good company. Just a few miles away in Berlin, a young Albert Einstein was beginning to study physics in his spare time. Those studies would culminate in his four papers of 1905, two on Quantum Mechanics and two on Relativity, ushering in the modern age of physics.

How to Count

To understand infinity you need to count in a particular way. You're probably used to counting with numbers. You count apples: one, two, three, and say, "I have three apples." You can do the same with oranges. If you have three apples and three oranges, the totals are the same and you can declare you have the same number of fruits. This is the first way to count.

But there is a second way of counting. Take your apples and put each next to an orange. If they match up, you can easily see they are equal in number. "Look," I say, "I have the same number of apples as oranges." This method is more primitive and does not require the concept of numbers, but it is very useful. If I'm a shepherd I can hold a set of counters in a bag, one for each sheep. To ensure all my flock are gathered in for the night I drop one counter into the bag as each sheep enters the enclosure. I don't need to give the counters number names.

The Munduruku tribe, from the Amazon rainforest, have no concept of number names beyond five. Their counting system simply goes one, two, three, four, five, many. Yet this second way of counting allows them to function successfully, deciding whether two groups of things have the same number of elements, even if there are more than five of them. For example, if they need to determine if they have enough spears for a hunt, each person simply stands next to their spear. If everyone has one, they're ready. If not, then the empty handed Munduruku simply make one. No need for pesky numbers or mathematics lessons.

This second way of counting is particularly useful when tackling infinity because we are not sure what infinity is. Treating it the same way the Munduruku treat the number 'many' is the safest thing to do. The first question we would like to answer is whether all infinite things are the same.

Spears and Hunters

We know from our childhood that infinity plus one is still infinity. Is there anything we can do to make infinity bigger? Perhaps multiplying infinity by infinity will do the trick.

Infinity times infinity can be visualized as a square with edges of infinite length. We can show that this square is the same size as a one-dimensional infinity through a clever trick – the zigzag method. Mark the infinity square into a grid. Start in the corner square, go across, diagonally down, then across, diagonally up, and so on. I'll draw you a picture. We visit every square in our grid using a single line. We can then lay down our infinite zigzag line next to the infinite line of one of the edges. The lines are the same length as they are both infinitely long! So infinity, times infinity, can be matched to infinity, they are the same. Cantor thought this a very strange result and wrote to a fellow mathematician, Dedekind, *"Je le vois, mais je ne le crois pas!"*, "I see it, but I don't believe it!"

If you are struggling with this, don't worry. We just jumped forward to quite a complex concept. Let's take it more slowly. One way to get a better grip on infinity is through the stories of David Hilbert and the Infinity Hotel.

Infinity for Dummies

Hilbert's Hotel is a mythical building with an infinite number of rooms. Other than this strange feature it is a regular hotel complete with minibar, dodgy TV, and slightly mad manager. The rooms are numbered sequential starting at one, then two, three, four, and so on. The hotel allows you to play a series of mathematical games to see how infinity behaves.

Are there the same number of minibars as there are rooms? That's easy. I said *every* room has a minibar. We can use the matching technique to match minibars with rooms. Go to the first room. There is a number on the door and a minibar inside. The same goes for room 2 and 3 and this goes on forever. I've just proven two infinite things are the same – rooms and bars, but I still have not shown you why the zigzag line is the same length as the edge line.

When you first explain infinity to a child they immediately ask "What's infinity plus one." A particularly smart kid I met, Dermot, asked, "What's infinity plus three?" Hilbert's Hotel allows us to answer this problem in a way we can visualize.

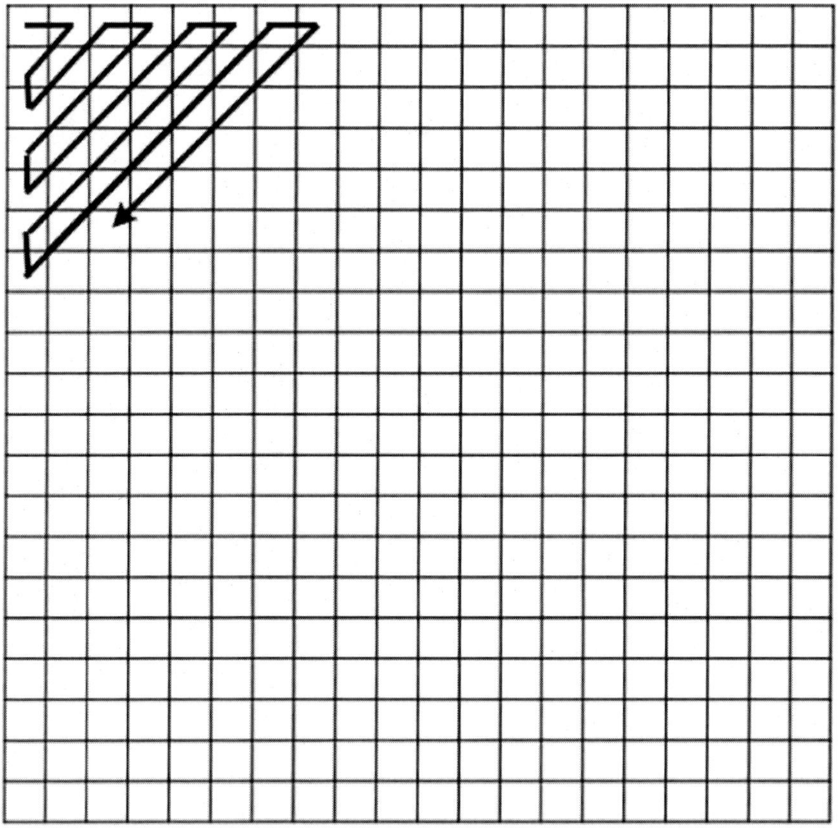

Traversing an Infinite Plane with a Line

The infinite hotel is full. A man comes to the front desk and asks for a room. The hotel manager says, "I'm terribly sorry, but we are full… But I may be able to help you. Let me think." He ponders for a moment and then says, "OK – I've found you a room." He calls the people in room 1 and asks them to move into room 2. He calls the people in room 2 and explains that due to a double booking they must move out of their room to let the people from room 1 in. But it's OK; they can move into room 3. Everyone moves up a room and the new guest gets the checks into the now vacant room 1.

This is a little harder to understand. We did not have a perfect one-to-one match as with the rooms and mini-bars. We had a mismatch of guests to rooms. But, we were able to show it is possible to re-establish a one-to-one match by doing something to every guest, having them move up a room. There is no problem with the last guest because it is an infinite hotel, there is no last guest! Another way to visualize the problem is to ask ever hunter to pass their spear to the right in the picture below.

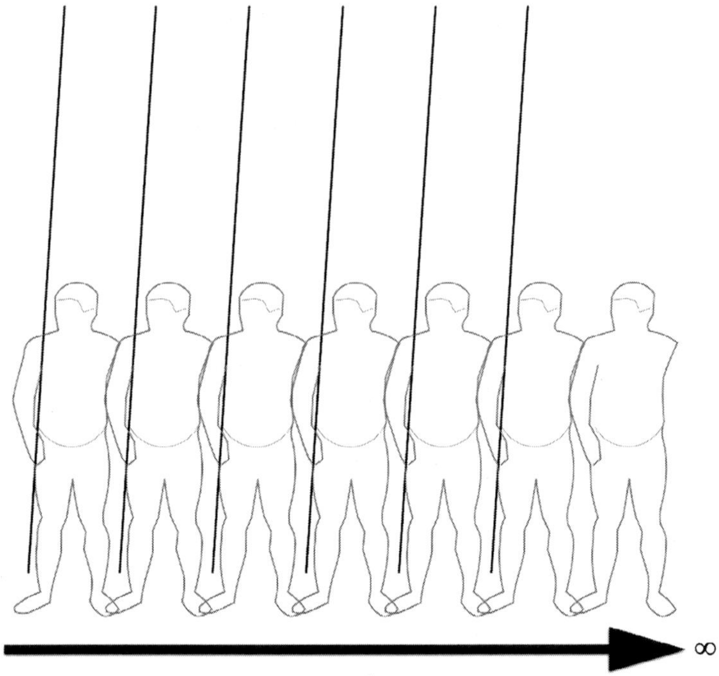

Hunter with Spears

Provided there are an infinite number of hunters there is always someone to hand the spear to and the person at the front of the line now has space for another spear.

You can probably see how to answer Dermot's question. The hotel manager calls the guest in the first room and asks him to move 3 rooms up rather than one. He then calls the remaining guests and tells them the same thing. Thus, he has managed to fit three more people into the infinite hotel. Infinity plus 3 is infinity. You may worry that it takes the manager an infinite time to call all the rooms, but it's OK; he lives infinitely long so it all works out.

What about fitting an infinite number of new guests into the already full hotel? Surely then we will get stuck.

No, Hilbert's Hotel can fit an infinite number of extra guests. Here's the trick: ask all the people currently in the hotel to move to the room with double the number they are currently in – 1 goes to 2, 2 goes to 4, 3 goes to 6, and so on. Now all the odd numbers are empty and you can fit an infinite number of people into the empty odd rooms. Infinity plus infinity is infinity. Voila.

Now, a very clever or annoying student asks, "What happens if an infinite number of infinitely large buses arrive at the hotel. Can they all fit in?" The mathematical question is "does infinity times infinity, equal infinity?" Let us ask all the guests to get out of the bus and line up in the parking lot in neat rows. Passengers from bus one in line 1, those from bus 2 in line 2, and so on. All the guests now form a two-dimensional grid. We already know how to map a two-dimensional grid to one-dimension using the zigzag method. We can fit them all in the hotel and we are done!

Is Anything Larger than Infinity?

Is there any bus or combination of buses that would cause the manager of Hilbert's Hotel a problem.

The answer is yes and it involves a subtle change to the contents of the bus.

An infinite number of buses turn up but this time the buses are filled with men and women. The hotel manager is asked to put everyone in a room and once again he obliges using the zigzag method.

At the end of the process the tour guide comes to him. "I think you have missed some people," he says. "Since I am just one person, I know you can fit *me* in. But, I have a whole bus in the car park you completely missed."

"No," says the manager. "I did every bus."

Infinity Plus Infinity Equals Infinity

"Ah, no," says the tour guide. "The first bus you accommodated had a man in the first seat but this has a woman. The second bus had a woman in the second seat but this one has a man and so on. This bus has a different gender in at least one seat to every bus you so far accommodated. It is a new bus."

The manager finds room for the passengers from the new bus but the tour guide comes back a moment later.

"You have missed another bus. This one has a different gender in at least one seat to every previous bus, including the one you just accommodated. It looks like there are an infinite number of buses you missed, all lined up to get into the infinite hotel."

What is it about *these* buses that make them so difficult to accommodate? They are all just filled with people after all.

The manager is defeated by the more complex information held in the contents of the buses. An infinitely large bus full of binary information has more information in it than an infinitely large bus specified only by its size. This is a larger infinity than the counting infinity. The permutation of all the possible options for the occupants of the bus is larger than infinity.

Real Numbers

What about the real world we live in? Is the larger infinity we failed to fit into Hilbert's Hotel present, or was it just a mathematical fiction? Hold up your thumb and index finger for a moment. The gap between them is a distance. Most likely this is a whole number with an infinite decimal digits after it – say 2.2320394386…. centimeters. The infinite set of decimal digits in this measurement is the larger type of infinity: called the continuum. Distances in space form a continuous unbroken line of points, with no gaps in between. The counting numbers, on the other hand, form a broken line. We take discrete steps from one number to the next. This is a hard distinction to grasp but it is the same distinction we used in Hilbert's Hotel. Imagine you believe you have a list of all the real numbers in the world. You can take the first decimal digit from the first number and add one, the second digit from the second number add one and so on generating new numbers not on the original list. Therefore, you cannot have a list all the real numbers; they are not countable. Let's take a closer look at these real numbers.

Here's a quick test. Which is the larger number, the first or the second?

Holding a Real Number in your Hand

First: 3.1233249837583462136421472374
Second: 3.1233249837583462134421472374

You have 2 seconds to answer!
TRY ANSWERING WITHOUT READING ON

The first is larger. I changed one digit. Can you see?

Notice, you need time to read each digit and process the information. If you were an obedient reader and attempted it in two seconds you either guessed or gave up. Two seconds is too short to take in all the digits.

Let me give you another test. Again, I'll ask you the question, "Is the first number larger than the second?"

First
3.12332498375834621364214723751646464646464636…
Second
3.12332498375834621364214723751646464646464636…

I know you're looking for the difference but you won't find one, as I did not have time to write the numbers out in full. The $10^{20000th}$ digit is different, but even if I took the whole age of the universe and counted as fast as possible I would not reach this digit. Any number greater than, $10^{120}/10^{-43}$ digits cannot be distinguished from another in the age of the observable universe. Real numbers are in practice subject to an uncertainty principle. Some mathematicians even wonder whether they really exist. But, they do exist in our minds and our thought experiments. In my view, any model of the Universe that ignores them is likely to be wrong.

Random Numbers

Which of the following numbers is random?

111111111111111
34289460370124001
49293741762343083

THINK ABOUT YOUR ANSWER THEN READ ON

Each of the numbers could be random. There is no reason any set of 10 digits is more likely than another, but it feels very unlikely that if I tried to generate a random number I would get 15 consecutive digits. What a human means by random is a jumbled up number: one with varying digits that have no real pattern. An American mathematician, George Chaitin has been able to explain this by saying that a random number is uncompressible. This means there is no way to describe the number more efficiently than writing it out in full. A string of ones can be compressed. "Write a million 1s" takes only 18 characters, yet accurately describes a number that is a million digits long. By contrast 8988376132 can't be compressed very much at all, its information is just a jumble. There are many interesting numbers around. Some numbers are *Hamlet*; some numbers are pi. One interesting number is the following: 17733173332032037377. It is the genetic sequence for the virus smallpox, or at least the first 20 digits. Copies of the full sequence sit under lock and key in the Pasteur Institute in France and the CDC in Atlanta. This number is a candidate for an 'evil' number. You might think there are many numbers that could represent smallpox because there are

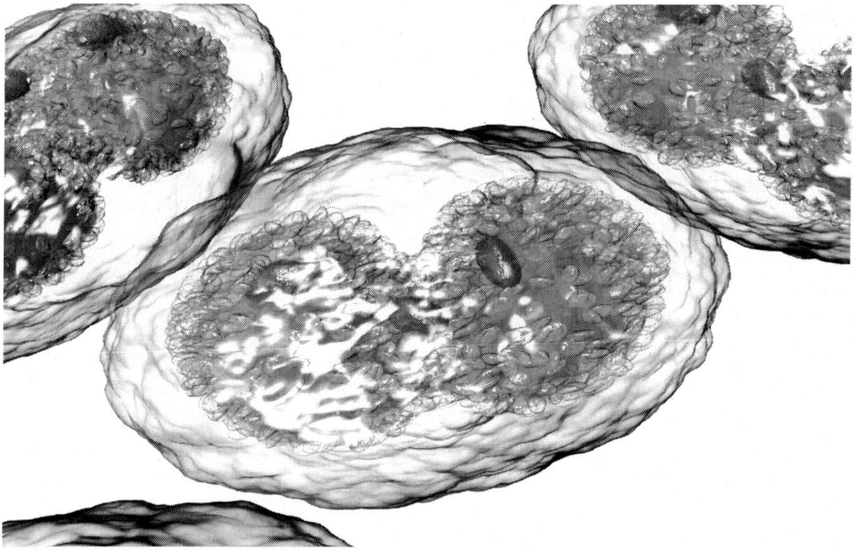

Smallpox Virus

many languages in the world and many ways you could code the genetic sequence of GATC. But, there *will be* one most efficient binary coding for smallpox and that number is the nearest we have to an evil number.

The other important element of random numbers is the process by which they are created. Computers can't genuinely generate random numbers. The numbers they generate are predictable and eventually

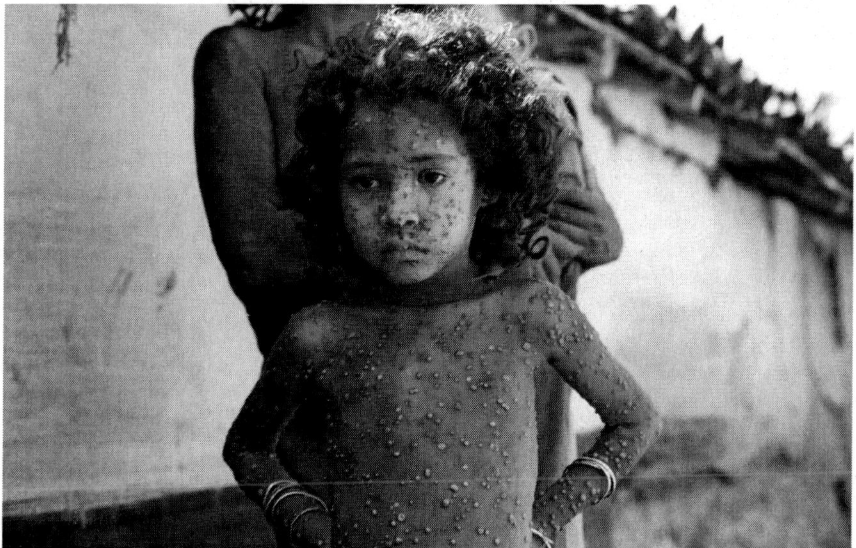

Child Survivor of Small Pox

repeat. To create the random number in my example above I went to www.random.org, a website that uses fluctuations in atmospheric quantum noise to generate random numbers. As far as we know quantum effects are truly random and have neither rhyme nor reason.

Numbers are more complex than they first appear. They are infinite, yet there are different infinities, and they have meaning. The smallpox example above and the Turing numbers we will discover shortly suggest numbers *do* have meaning independent of culture and language. The next two chapters will show us what happens when we think about the meaning of numbers. We will also explain one more 'super infinity' and this will be the key to understanding creativity.

"There are known knowns; there are things we know we know. We also know there are known unknowns; that is to say we know there are some things we do not know. But there are also unknown unknowns - the ones we don't know we don't know."

Donald Rumsfeld
United States Secretary of Defense
(2001-2006, 1975-1977)

Chapter 9

KNOWN UNKNOWNS

Donald Rumsfeld

In the spring of 1981, London staged its first marathon. The field of runners included 1200 international athletes and 20,000 amateurs. An estimated 20 million viewers watched from around the world. The top international runners stayed together for the first twenty miles and then two runners, American Dick Beardsley and Norwegian Inge Simonsen, made a push for the finish. They were long-standing rivals and, as they ran the final mile each man challenged the other to see if they could get ahead and gain the advantage. Because of the fine balance human muscles maintain between anaerobic and aerobic metabolism, the small set advantage could prove insurmountable. The other runner would need to sprint to catch up and the resultant lactic acid generated would turn their legs to jelly. As the two runners neared the finish line they glanced at each other, smiled, reached out and held hands as they crossed the line. Who won?

We all instinctively know the answer. The race was a draw, but the rules of the International Athletics Federation are clear. Read rule 164.

RULE 164

The Finish

1. The finish of a race shall be denoted by a white line 5 cm wide.
2. The athletes shall be placed in the order in which any part of their bodies (i.e. torso, as distinguished from the head, neck, arms, legs, hands or feet) reaches the vertical plane of the finish line.

The organizing committee held a brief conference and the result declared a draw. They had interpreted the rules in the same way 20 million TV viewers already 'knew' to be true.

This story should set your minds thinking about the nature of *rules* and *truth* and how the two are often different. According to the *rules*, one person crossed the line a little ahead of the other. The *truth*, as we all instinctively know, is that the race was a draw. Maybe the rulebook is missing a rule – 'The contact draw rule'. Clearly you could amend the rulebook to add this one rule. I checked the current athletics rules and they don't contain this amendment. If the rules were amended the mischievous amongst you will realize an unsporting athlete could grab the hand of their opponent as they crossed the line to force a draw. The rules would have to stipulate that holding hands must be voluntary for both parties, and refinements could go on for some time. What if I held your hand but you tripped and let go? What if my attempt to hold your hand

Kurt Gödel

caused you to trip? You could go on forever, generating rules to cover every eventuality.

Clearly, in the fuzzy world of human endeavor, truth and rules often part company. Yet, we all assume mathematics is free of such uncertainty. Let me tell you this is not so. The brilliant mathematician Kurt Gödel proved this when he was just 22, and his proof says something fundamental about the nature of knowledge.

The story of his discovery involves some of the greatest mathematical thinkers in history. My introduction to it came about from a chance accident. I became ill in my first year at University (mononucleosis, otherwise know as glandular fever, if you're curious) and was eventually sent home to recover. Lying in bed for two months is boring. So to pass the time my mother suggested I read Bertrand Russell's, *The History of Western Philosophy*. I think she figured I had plenty of time, so picked a thick book. This nearly 800-page tome charts the entire history of philosophy from the time of the ancient Greeks. I presumed Russell was a philosophy professor, but he was originally a mathematician. He was a mathematician. And because he lived and worked productively for almost all of his 97 years, spanning much of the 19th and 20th centuries, he crops up repeatedly as a central figure in many areas of intellectual life. Russell the politician, Russell the philosopher, Russell the mathematician and Russell the peace campaigner are all the same man – not, as I had incorrectly first guessed, a prolific family. In his early career, Bertrand Russell was a Fellow of Trinity College, Cambridge, working on a broad range of mathematical problems. Meanwhile, in Germany, his contemporary David Hilbert, also a polymath, held the chair of mathematics at Göttingen University. Both men shared a common objective: to tidy up the loose ends in mathematics and set down the rules once and for all. This movement was called Formalism.

Formalism

David Hilbert and Bertrand Russell believed you should be able to set out all the rules of mathematics even though it might be a complicated affair. Without contradiction or inconsistency you should be able to write down the rules and then play the 'game of mathematics' to derive every possible truth. Hilbert despised the idea that there could be unknowable things and was a forthright speaker. His battle cry was: *Wir müssen wissen — wir werden wissen!* "We must know — we will know!" He believed there were no fundamental unknowns in the world.

Donald Rumsfeld famously summed up the problem of unknowns in an attempt to clarify a question from a journalist at a Whitehouse press conference:

> *"There are known knowns; there are things we know we know. We also know there are known unknowns; that is to say we know there are some things we do not know. But there are also unknown unknowns – the ones we don't know we don't know."*

Interestingly Donald Rumsfeld, like Bertrand Russell, is another person to span a huge swath of time in the public eye. He was both the youngest and the oldest serving U.S. Secretary of Defense, serving under both Richard Nixon and George W. Bush. We will shortly discover Rumsfeld's convoluted view of the world turns out to be closer to the truth than Hilbert's tidy mathematical aspiration.

As well as believing there were no unknowable unknowns Hilbert thought mathematics was completely abstract. You did not need to know what you were talking about. Whether the symbols meant dogs, cats or numbers all you needed to do was apply the rules and all would be well. His belief is captured in his quote below.

"It must be possible to replace in all geometric statements the words point, line, plane by table, chair, beer mug."
David Hilbert

Geometry with Beer and Furniture

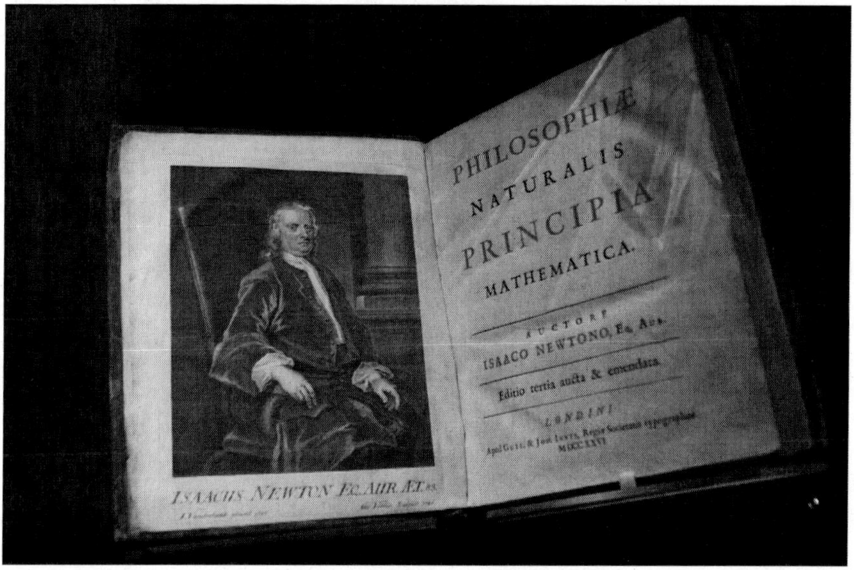

Newton's Principia

PM

In 1890, the Cambridge mathematicians Alfred North Whitehead and Bertrand Russell embarked on the mammoth task of writing out all the rules of mathematics and publishing them in a set of books called *Principia Mathematica*. Every rule is written down in meticulous detail. The books are heavy going and look like more like computer programs than text. They set out precisely what you can, and cannot, do with numbers, and are the most impenetrable textbook you will ever read. Just to give you a flavor here is one line where Russell proves 1+1=2. It has taken about 100 pages of densely packed equations to get to this point!

$$*54\cdot43.\quad \vdash :. \alpha, \beta \in 1 . \supset : \alpha \cap \beta = \Lambda . \equiv . \alpha \cup \beta \in 2$$

From this proposition it will follow, when arithmetical addition has been defined, that $1 + 1 = 2$.

One Plus One Equals Two, PM

PM is a 3-volume set of books. Volume One costs £480 on Amazon. This is a significant work and a collector's item. The last time a first edition volume came up at auction in 2007 it went for over £800. Cambridge University Press printed only 750 copies and I suspect they

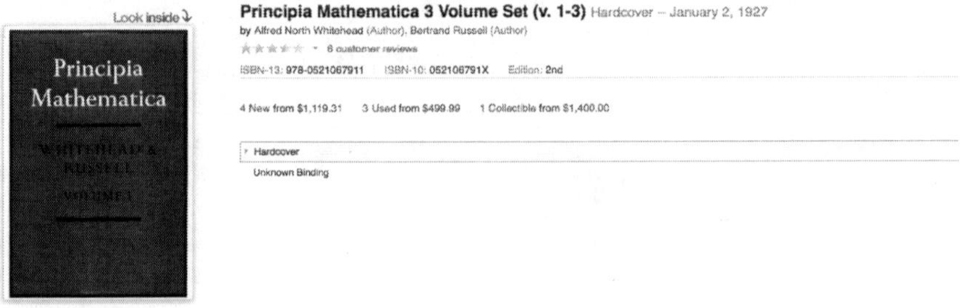

Amazon Listing for Principia Mathematica

are undervalued. When mathematicians use the letters 'PM', they are usually referring to Russell and Whitehead's *Principia Mathematica* rather than the afternoon.

Hilbert's Problems

In 1900, while Russell and Whitehead were in full flow writing out their rules, David Hilbert was invited to deliver the annual lecture at the International Congress of Mathematicians in Paris. He asked a mathematician friend what subject he should pick for the talk and, in a moment of inspiration, the friend suggested laying out a vision for the future of mathematics. Rather than tell people how wonderful mathematicians were, and why their discipline was the pinnacle of human scientific endeavor, why not try modesty and list all the problems on which they were stumped? Hilbert liked the idea and devoted his talk to all the problems he thought mathematicians would solve in the 20th century. Hilbert's Problems were simply an intellectual challenge. He offered no prizes. At the turn of the 21st century, the Clay Institute created the Millennium Prizes for solving the most important modern mathematical problems. Each solution wins a prize of a million dollars!

There are 23 numbered Hilbert Problems in all: ten in the original lecture and a further 13 in the written transcript. In 1928, he clarified the 2nd and 10th problems, refining them into three distinct questions: Is mathematics consistent, complete and decidable? Ironically this means that Hilbert's 23 problems actually number 24! The most important Hilbert questions where these last three. They ask whether Russell and Whitehead would be successful – can you write out all the rules of mathematics and then simply calculate the answer to any problem or derive any proof. This is known as the Decision Problem. Can you mechanically decide any mathematical question without doubt? To explain Hilbert's Problems, I need to define mathematics properly.

Giuseppe Peano, Mathematician

"A mathematician is a blind man in a dark room looking for a black cat which isn't there."

Charles Darwin

The Game of Math

One of my most vivid childhood memories is driving my mother distraction by asking the 'why' question. Most children go through this phase:

Me: "Why is a sponge wet?"
My mother: "Because it has soaked up water."
Me: "Why has it soaked up water?"
My mother: "Because it has small holes in it."
Me: "But what makes water wet?"
My mother: "Because it is made of wet stuff." a bit weak now.
Me: "What is wet stuff?"
...

You can ramble on indefinitely unpeeling a never-ending onion. Sometimes, if you are unlucky, you may get stuck in a loop. For example, "where did the chicken come from?" "An egg," "and where did the egg come from?"...

Mathematics breaks this cycle!

In mathematics, there is no danger of an infinite number of 'why' questions because at its core are a clearly defined set of absolute rules called axioms. You cannot ask the 'why' question of an axiom. It is a RULE!

Starting from an absolute minimum of fundamental rules everything else is built up so that no step requires any leap of faith nor generates any contradiction. Let me give you a concrete example and, in the process, show you how numbers are defined.

Numbers

It was not until the late 18th century that numbers were properly codified. The mathematician Giuseppe Peano gave us the rules, so they are called Peano axioms. Here are his 'axioms' in natural language.

Peano Axioms

1. The first number is named zero.
2. Every number has a next number (called its successor). Example: the next number after one is two.
3. Numbers are singular. Every number with the same name is the same thing.
4. If something is true of a number, it should be true of the next number (the successor number).

From this we can prove some very simple things.

1+1=2. Because the next number after 1 is 2 and '+1' means take the successor. (You can see I cheated here a little and did not take 100 pages for the proof.)

Back to my poor mother: "Why is the lowest number zero, Mummy?" "Because I say so!" Or, at least "…because Mr. Peano said so." That's what an axiom is.

"OK, but why is 3 greater than 2."

"Because I said that each number has a thing that comes after it.

"But, why can't 3 come after zero!"

"It can!"

"But then, if 3 is the thing after zero, I could count 0, 3, 2, 4…"

"Yes, if you want to…"

"I'm sort of lost. Now, you are saying that 3 doesn't really 'mean' anything. It just comes after 0."

"Yes. You can make up any symbols you like. You just have to remember what you said and be consistent."

The dialogue shows the importance of definition in mathematics. I could define my counting numbers as 0, 1, 2, 3, 4 or as ο, π, ρ, σ, ς, or 享, 仇, 仕, 仝 or to be really annoying and confusing 0, 3, 1, 2, 4; they are only arbitrary symbols. It helps us to learn the numbers because 1 is a single line, 2 is two lines joined, three is basically three lines looped together, and four is four lines, but we could have used any symbols we cared for. It is the rules for manipulating these symbols that are the important part and give mathematics its meaning.

The Game of Mathematics

When I was a child, our living room carpet had a square pattern. You could use boiled sweets to play checkers on it. Even though there was no board and no pieces, it was clearly a game of checkers because we followed the right rules (with the one exception that if you jumped over a sweet you got to eat it). Mathematics is like a game with a set of rules. If you follow the rules, you are doing mathematics.

Consider the simple mathematical theory that if A equals B, then B equals A. This seems clear-cut, but you can get into trouble if you're not careful when defining the word 'equals'. 'My dog equals naughty' does not imply 'naughty equals my dog. Here I have used 'equals' to mean 'has the property of.' My dog has the property of being naughty. This is an attribute, not equivalence. You must be careful with mathematics. A equals B implying B equals A is a property of numbers when the equals sign is used to mean equivalence.

Here are the rules of the game that provide a proof for this theory.

Let us start with the position in which we don't know whether A equals B implies B equals A. We have these three axioms, call them rules for now since we are using the game analogy.

Rule 1: If I have no minus sign in front of a letter I can assume there is an invisible + sign there.
Rule 2: If I have a positive letter (or a letter with no symbol in front of it) I can put a minus in front of it and put it on the other side of the equals sign.
Rule 3: I can swap the plus and minus signs of all the letters in my equation if I do it to all of them.

Now I am ready to prove my theorem.

A = B is the same as +A = + B. (rule 1)
+A = + B is the same as -B = - A (rule 2 done twice)
-B = -A is the same as B = A (rule 3)

Success.
So A = B is the same as B = A.

I have my proof. It might be glaringly obvious, but that's not the point. The point is you can apply rules to symbols and derive new rules. It does not matter what the symbols are or how obvious it is. Here's the same proof with dingbats.

Rule 1: If I have no glyph in front of a symbol I can assume there is an invisible Ψ there.

Rule 2: If I have a positive letter (or a letter with no symbol in front of it) I can put a ♮ in front of it and put it on the other side of the ›

Rule 3: I can swap the Ψ and ♮symbols of all the symbols in my equation if I do it to all of them.

The proof in symbols

♈ › ß is the same as Ψ ♈ › Ψ ß. (rule 1)
Ψ ♈ › Ψ ß is the same as ♮ß › ♮♈ (rule 2 twice)
♮ß › ♮♈ is the same as ß › ♈ (rule 3)

Any collection of symbols will do. The symbols have no meaning in themselves other than the meaning we have given them. A tribe in the Amazon jungle could demonstrate a proof without knowing any mathematics. All I need say is, "Hey, I want to play a game with you. Can anyone make this into that, in the fewest possible steps, while obeying these rules?"

But, is it true we can ignore the meaning behind the symbols. Does it matter that we were talking of numbers rather than spears, counters, or crocodiles? If we look at the marathon winning analogy again, we know the nature of a game is important. In a running race we can interpret holding hands to mean the two athletes are treated as one, the existing rules can then be applied as normal and the pair become a single winner. But, in tennis, there would be a problem. I wouldn't want to come on court and find I'm playing against two opponents! On consideration though I'd be happy if they had to hold hands while they played so that they constituted a single player. When we examine the actual circumstances, we can add a rule and show the rule works, but we have to see something about the specific sport that makes the rule fair and workable.

Hilbert was convinced mathematical truth is not like this and that proofs follow from the rulebook without any knowledge of the circumstances, i.e., the sport being played or any other analogous thing. He was to be proven wrong by Kurt Gödel.

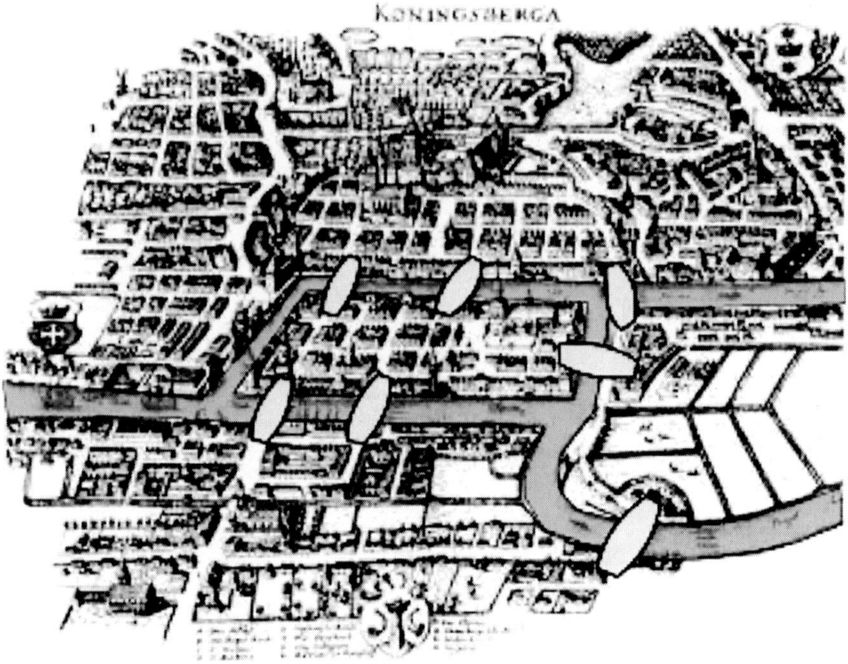

Königsberg Bridges

Gödel

Gödel studied mathematics at Königsberg University, Hilbert's hometown. Königsberg is famous for having a mathematical problem related to the seven bridges that link the city together. It's quite fun to try to solve. Find a route across the city that crosses each bridge once and once only. You can start anywhere, but no walking halfway over a bridge and no swimming!

Euler discovered a rigorous mathematical proof that there can be no solution in 1735 after five hundred years of failure by other mathematicians. The answer is you cannot.

In 1931 Kurt Gödel, then working at the University of Vienna, proved mathematics *is* like our sporting analogy. There are true statements in mathematics that cannot be proven by the rules of the system. Someone outside the system, with common sense, can see a statement is true, but it's impossible to prove this if you constrain yourself inside the system. It is the equivalent of all the members of the London Marathon Committee wondering what to do about the race while all of us watching the TV are shouting, "It's a draw!" Looking at the rulebook 'really hard' doesn't help.

You have to step back and think about the problem in the round and then devise some additional rules to handle the circumstances. Mathematics is like this also.

Here is how Gödel proved his result.

It is easy to turn logic or any text into numbers. That's how this book is stored on my laptop. All we need do is translate sentences into ASCII or Unicode. In this way, any theory can be reduced to a string of numbers.

Since Gödel's proof predates the invention of the computer, he had to come up with a novel way to store information. He deployed an old Roman invention; a substitution code. The number one was represented by 1, two by 2 and the symbols by larger numbers, for example, '=' was coded as 15 and so on. He then raised a sequence of prime numbers to the power of each of these codes and multiplied all the results together. This generated a single enormous but unique number that he could later factor back into its constituent parts to recover the information. This is a truly complicated solution to a very simple problem. Today we would solve it by storing each number in the memory of a computer as an array.

Let's use the easier table method to store things and code as follows: 000 will stand for 'start of proof'. Each step in the proof will start with 00 and each symbol in the proof starts and ends with a zero. This way we can code one plus one equals two as follows.

0000001110454011101210222000000

I think this is simple enough for you to guess the coding scheme. Hint: 111 stands for 1. The scheme is on my website if you can't work it out. Using this technique, any series of mathematical statements can be turned into a number. As a series of mathematical statements is a proof, we can generate proof numbers. They are just the sequential list of all the instructions. These numbers are sometimes referred to as Gödel numbers.

Gödel's next step was to say one number *demonstrates* the proof of another number. For example, the number 000820962 might demonstrate the proof of another number 000398... This is the mathematical equivalent of my saying a Word file demonstrates the truth of your mathematical theorem. Any statement can be represented by numbers, provided you have a consistent coding scheme that allows you to get back to the meaning.

Now Gödel set up his paradox:

Every correctly formed theorem number has another number, which demonstrates the proof of that number.

If this is universally true there should be no contradiction. Unfortunately if you apply the theorem to itself you get something similar to the liar's paradox.

"This proof number is not a proof of the truth of this theorem number."

The proof number proves the theorem number is true, but the truth of the statement is that it can't be a proof of the statement... Paradox.

The only way to resolve the paradox is to go back one step and realize that not *every* correctly formed theorem number has a proof number using only the rules of that system.

Concisely, Gödel's theorem says, "Within any formal system of mathematics there can be statements that are true but are not provable using only the rules of that system."

When Hilbert heard of Gödel's proof, his first reaction was anger. After all, he had spent 30 years of his life trying to prove mathematics was tidy and complete. Gödel had just shown it was not. Hilbert never worked on formalism again, but the rest of the mathematical establishment largely ignored the result. Gödel's proof did not stop mathematicians proving new theorems nor doing useful mathematics. They went on much as before, using a mixture of intuition and analysis. The only difference was someone had told them analysis alone would not succeed. The repercussions of Gödel's theory have more to do with understanding our place in the Universe and the nature of knowledge discovery. These are 'big' philosophical questions, which don't greatly affect the day-to-day ability of a mathematician to do their job. However, it is important to understand that knowledge discovery is not simply analysis. Knowing this helps us understand human creativity.

Inconsistency

In the proof above, I said the only way to resolve the paradox is by saying there cannot be a proof number for *every* mathematical statement and therefore mathematics is incomplete. There is one other way to solve the paradox, and that is by allowing inconsistency into the system. Gödel's proof assumes you can prove something true or false, but what if you could prove it true *and* false? In this case, the system is complete but you can prove truths and untruths within it! This may seem an acceptable solution, but inconsistency in a mathematical model is a cancer that will spread through the entire body. Think about it. If I am allowed to prove anything either way, of course, my system is complete. It can say anything it wants, but the proofs I make are worthless.

Let us imagine, for a moment, we created a new system of mathematics where all the numbers in our new theory behave as we expect, except for the numbers 5 and 6. You may use them to count, but they are also *equal* to each other! This feels bad and it certainly breaks the Peano axioms. In my new system 1 plus 5 and 0 plus 5 are the same, so I can equate 0 to 1. Because 0 and 1 are the basis of binary arithmetic, all numbers can be equated. Numbers now have no guaranteed meaning in my system and, what is worse, since logic uses 1 and 0 to represents true and false, all of logic falls apart as well. Whenever we allow inconsistency into mathematics it rapidly brings the whole pack of cards down.

The example I gave was glaring; an inconsistency right in the middle of the counting numbers! Maybe I was too aggressive and a subtle and less damaging inconsistency might be tolerable. However, *any* inconsistency allows me to make zero equal one somewhere in my system and, therefore, any theorem based on proof by counterexample will be suspect.

There might be systems where inconsistency could be a legitimate part of a mathematical system, but I would always need positive corroboration for each proof. If I tried hard enough, I could always prove something either way. I would need to formulate a new mathematical rule – something like "I will believe short, sensible-looking proofs to be right and circuitous proofs to be wrong." Mathematics would be a bit like a court of law. You would have to weigh up the evidence from a variety of sources and the verdict would be a matter of subjective opinion rather than objective fact. Inconsistency is *very* bad in mathematics.

The Lucas Argument

J.R. Lucas of Oxford University believes Gödel's theorem says something fundamental about the nature of the human mind. In 1959, he wrote a paper, *Minds, Machines and Gödel*, where he argued humans must be able to think outside a fixed set of formal rules. The paper has been causing arguments ever since. Strong AI proponents have a visceral reaction to it. Forty years later, in 1989 Roger Penrose picked up the baton and put the Lucas argument on a stronger theoretical footing. The Lucas-Penrose argument is this:

If humans used a formal system to think, they would be limited by the incompleteness theorem and unable to discover new theorems that required them to extend the formal rules. Humans do not appear to have such a limitation and regularly extend their appreciation of mathematics by expanding the rules, and seeing through to the truth.

Many scientists dislike this argument and think it farfetched, saying there is no evidence to show people see past the limitation. Our brains could be following a formal system capable of discovering everything we have discovered to date or, indeed, might encounter in the future. Why should we assume human minds are constrained in the same way as the mathematical systems they discover? There is no evidence to suggest a human *thinking* about Peano arithmetic is running a Peano based model in their head. When Peano discovered his theorem he was certainly extending our mathematical knowledge, but this does not imply he was extending the capability of his brain.

The critics of Lucas and Penrose have one big problem to deal with. The formal system in our head would need to be able to see the truth in everything we could *ever* encounter. But, our formal system appears to be small. As infants, it is almost nonexistent. Where does this enormous system come from? It can't come from our parents because they have the same problem; they were once children. You might argue that the capability of the human brain is huge and we can learn from all the other humans on earth, but let me remind you what Gödel said. However large

Two Giants

a system you have and however much you extend it, the system will always be incomplete. And we really do mean; however large. Even an infinitely large formal system would be incomplete.

The only way to avoid this problem is with some sort of conspiracy theory where we only come across problems our formal system can already solve. Such a theory is a determined Universe. In a determined Universe, all the mathematical problems we ever solve must be expressed by the formal systems existing in the Universe. We must never encounter a problem where we need to extend the system and break the Gödel limit because we are pre-determined not to do so.

The Inconsistency Defense

An argument put forward by opponents of the Lucas-Penrose position is that humans are inconsistent formal systems. Inconsistent formal systems are not subject to the incompleteness limit. Humans certainly behave inconsistently with remarkable regularity but simply making inconsistent statements is not sufficient to show the underlying formal system is, itself, inconsistent. Inconsistent beliefs can come simply from making mistakes or reading the same story in two different newspapers! We need a fundamentally inconsistent thinking mechanism inside our brains to break the constraint. The very machinery itself would have to be inconsistent. But this is exactly Penrose's point. Constructing a machine capable of reasoning in an inconsistent but useful manner would need exotic technology, some sort of non-deterministic, rationalizing computer. The components to make it could not be computer logic as we know it today. All such logic is entirely computationally deterministic.

Let me see if I can reframe the Lucas argument. Imagine IBM's Watson computer was let loose on mathematical reasoning. Watson could scan every mathematical theorem ever written down. It would know every programming language created. It would have its enormous bank of general knowledge to call upon and it could answer many questions. It would sometimes appear inconsistent because the information it had trawled from the Internet would be wrong. But Watson would still be a consistent formal system and Gödel's theorem says there would be truths Watson could never see. Lucas argues humans can see such truths where a machine cannot, and these truths would allow a human to discover a proof to a mathematical problem that would forever elude Watson.

The Lucas argument runs into a brick wall because it asserts we see truths a machine cannot. For each alleged creative step, his opponents simply assert your brain was already sufficiently powerful to perform that creative step. Lucas's argument is largely a philosophical one. Surely all this creativity can't all be pre-coded within the brain. Surely we must be extending our model in order to extend mankind's mathematical model. "Prove it," say the detractor, and he cannot. We need something more practical if we're going to show a difference between humans and machines - something an engineer, or even a physicist, could grasp! That thing is a Turing Machine. We will examine this next.

Chapter 10

TURING'S MACHINE

Alan Turing

"A computer would deserve to be called intelligent if it could deceive a human into believing that it was human."

Alan Turing

"The only real valuable thing is intuition."

Albert Einstein

"Mathematical reasoning may be regarded rather schematically as the exercise of a combination of two facilities, which we may call intuition and ingenuity."

Alan Turing

It is 1943 and a small group of Polish mathematicians sit, ears glued to their wireless set, waiting to hear whether the German army will advance on Warsaw. The Polish Intelligence Bureau badly needed to know what the German army was planning and had recruited this group of young mathematicians as code breakers. Up to this point, code-breaking had been the domain of linguists able to see word patterns in apparently random sets of letters. The arrival of electro-mechanical machines made this method redundant, and code-breaking had become the domain of mathematical minds. The British, French, and American intelligence agencies were all hard at work deciphering the German codes, but only the Polish group, motivated by the imminent threat of invasion, had made real progress. The code they were breaking: 'Enigma'.

As with many inventions, Enigma got off to a difficult start. The inventor, Arthur Scherbius, tried to sell it to the army but they rejected it saying it did not provide any real military benefit. Instead, the machine went into service transmitting commercial shipping manifests. However, some senior figures in the German military had not forgotten the lesson of the First World War. During that war, the German army suffered major setbacks because the British broke all their codes early on. With the onset of World War II, Rommel ordered the German Army and Navy to deploy modern coding machines. The previously rejected Enigma was rapidly pressed into service and, all of a sudden, Europe went dark to Allied Intelligence. The man to lead the task of breaking Enigma for the English was Alan Turing.

Alan Turing

Alan Turing was conceived in India but born in London in early 1912. He was precocious from an early age and an extraordinarily determined character. His first day at Public School, Sherborne in Dorset, coincided with the British General Strike of 1926. With no public transport available, the thirteen-year-old Turing cycled the 60 miles to school, staying in a guesthouse on the way and earning a write-up in his local newspaper. Turing went on to study Mathematics at King's College, Cambridge and was made a Fellow at only 22. In 1936 Turing, aged 24, published *On Computable Numbers and their Application to the Entscheidungsproblem*, not a snappy title, but one of the most influential mathematical works of the 20th century. The paper described the new the science of computing and solved Hilbert's 'Entscheidungsproblem', a mathematical puzzle simply translated as 'the Decision Problem' – could you decide the truth of a mathematical statement using some sort of automatic computation – an 'algorithm' as we now call it?

It is difficult to imagine, but Turing worked on 'computing' before the invention of the computer. When he talked of computing, he meant the abstract idea of doing something mechanically. The nearest thing he had to a 'computer' at the time was a human mindlessly but methodically calculating something with pencil and paper! The scientific paper he submitted to the London Mathematical Society described both the theoretical basis of computing, and the design of a general-purpose computing machine: the forerunner of all modern computers.

At the time, only a handful people in the world could assess Turing's paper. One of them, Alonzo Church, was based at the Institute of Advanced Mathematics in the USA on the Princeton University campus, next door to the Institute for Advanced Study that housed Einstein. Turing travelled to America in 1937 and completed his doctoral thesis at Princeton. He might have stayed, but Europe was heating up and war seemed inevitable, so Turing returned to England to take up a part-time job in the government code-breaking branch. Here he was able to indulge his passion for hands-on engineering, experimenting with the newly invented valve technologies. When war finally broke out Turing was ordered to report to Bletchley Park, just north of London. This was to be the home of the top-secret British code-breaking group tasked with cracking Enigma. Turing's first task was to debrief the Polish mathematicians and see what they had discovered. The Polish mathematicians had seen there were flaws in Enigma that made it repeat itself. They had made a copy of the machine to test different coding configurations and had been routinely cracking Enigma for 6 years, but the Germans had been getting smarter and it was taking longer and longer to crack the codes. Turing realized he could apply the Polish ideas in a more general way and break the codes on an industrial scale. He was installed at Bletchley Park to lead the project.

Initially he was successful but as the war continued, Enigma developed subtleties making it harder to break. At one point, it was taking a whole month to break a single day's messages. Turing realized the only solution was to use computer technology to fully automate the decryption. He built a computing machine that could simulate thousands of Enigma machines and try out all the possible settings in a short space of time. The machine acquired the nickname 'a bombe', perhaps because of the ominous ticking sound it made as it calculated (or maybe as a reference to the smaller Polish machines).

Thanks to Turing's insight into coding schemes and the machines he designed, the British were soon able to read almost every coded message the Germans sent during the war, giving the Allies an enormous advantage. The D-Day invasion involved convincing Hitler that the Allies had a huge army of nearly 400,000 men, massed around Dover preparing an attack on Calais head on, with a second army in Scotland poised to attack Norway. In truth, they had only 150,000 men planning an assault on the Normandy Beaches in the South. Just before the landings messages were decoded showing Hitler had fallen for the Allied subterfuge. Even as the Normandy landings began, Hitler still thought this a bluff and kept his 28 divisions at Calais waiting for the imagined attack. Without this intelligence advantage, the Allies would have needed a much larger invasion force, and Churchill believed Turing's work shortened the war by as much as two years.

The cracking of Enigma remained a secret after the war and Turing's story remained untold for many years. When Churchill wrote his history, *The Second World War*, a massive work in six volumes, all sorts of sensitive information featured, but Turing's work was omitted. One sentence hints that Churchill might write something about it in the future, but he never did. Churchill considered the work at Bletchley Park so sensitive he had it put in the highest classification – extending the 30-year secrecy rule. We must presume the decoding schemes were still being deployed during the Cold War. The papers were finally released in 2010.

In one of those sad turns in history Turing was found guilty of gross indecency for homosexuality in 1954, a criminal act at the time, and was prescribed hormone treatment. This affected his mental state and he took his life by eating an apple laced with cyanide. He was eventually honored posthumously as a war hero and one of the most significant thinkers of the 20th Century. A Turing Award is the equivalent of the Nobel Prize for Computing. He was given a royal pardon in 2013.

To see how Turing came up with the idea for the Turing machine and solved the decision problem, we need to get a feel for theoretical mathematics. That might sound a little heavy going but don't worry, I will use a simple piece of mathematics to explain, one we have all played with as children, secret codes.

Codes

Enigma Machine

Everyone has played with some sort of secret code as a child – the Aggy Waggy game, passing notes written in invisible ink made from lemon juice, or perhaps a simple cypher. If I want to send you a secret message, I can use a substitution code. Let's see how good a code breaker you are. Can you decode this?

Gdkkn Qdzcdq

It's really easy. You might guess the message from the pattern of letters and your knowledge of my writing style. There are a couple of interesting patterns to note: the 3rd and 4th letter of the first word are the same and the first and last letter of the second word are the same. As a test I gave this code to my wife and my eight-year-old daughter to see how long it took them to decode… Less than a minute for my wife – a linguist. We will come back to my daughter shortly!

Roman Emperors used this sort of simple code to secure their messages, but modern codes have to be a great deal more sophisticated. Let us use a progressive cipher where we vary the substitution using a secret word. Take the name of my dog and write it down repeatedly next to the letters of the message you want to keep secret. Now translate all the letters in the message and the code into numbers 'a' = 1, 'b' = 2 and so on. Then add the letters of my dog's name to the letters of the message one at a time. If I get to 26 ('z') just wrap around to 'a' and carry on. This is called modulo arithmetic. This coding scheme will translate 'l' to 'a' the first time but 'l' to 'c' the second making it much harder for a linguist to see any pattern.

hello reader can you read this code
georgegeorgegeorgegeorgegeorgegeorge

Gives

ojacveyjpvlwghpegcvzoilfkehzpxghcvle

The advantage of this cipher is that I can easily remember the name George. I don't need to write it down. And the circular application makes the message sufficiently obscure you can't easily work it out…

Is this, therefore, a good code?

No.

This cipher is easy to break. Once you have guessed that I have applied a repeated short code word, you can write out ALL the possibilities and decrypt my message! This may be tedious, but if you are fighting a war and your life depends on it, you can employ a thousand people to write them all out. The British government employed 10,000 people at Bletchley Park, many of them doing exactly this. You might think that applying ALL the possibilities is too time consuming in practice but there are many shortcuts. If I suspect the message contains the name of a German town all I need do is try keys until I find a German town somewhere in the message then work my way outwards from there. Or perhaps I suspect the key is something easy to remember like the name of the Commandant's dog. I can try ALL German dog names until I get lucky. If I've 10,000 people working for me this is easy.

The Enigma machine and the coding process set up to operate it was designed to remove these loopholes. For a start, the keys were all random numbers taken from a code book – no dog names allowed – and the machine took the idea of a simple progressive cipher and made it *much* more complex.

Imagine I took my GeorgeGeorgeGeorge pattern but then every 3rd character added one, every 14th character subtracted 15 and every 40th character added the 3rd letter of the First Mate's mother's maiden name. Now this would be a VERY hard code to break. I would need a machine to code messages because if I tried to do it by hand I would make so many mistakes that the messages I send would be unintelligible. The Enigma machine made these coding schemes a practical possibility. But, although Enigma is hard to break it is not impossible with enough computing power. Is there any code that is impossible to break?

An Unbreakable code

Is there a way of coding a message so you can never break it?

The answer is there are two ways to code a message so it is PERFECTLY safe. The first is to use a one-time pad and the second is quantum cryptography.

One perfect way to encode a message is to use a one-time pad. On a sheet of paper I write a completely random set of numbers or letters – since we are going to translate numbers to letters it does not matter which. I make a copy and give it to a person I later want to send a coded message. Because I will only use these two paired sheets once it helps to make a few of them – a pad in fact. By convention, we refer to a single sheet or a whole book as a one-time pad code. Here is the one-time pad I created earlier. It is just a random sequence of letters and spaces.

kaleygnqaloiuebldlan dlkawoqyevbax gmlsosuebal

To code a message, I substitute numbers for letters as with the progressive cypher earlier again using modulo arithmetic to wrap around if I reach the letter 'z'. I have applied my one-time pad to the hello reader message below to get 'sfacngfvbpta'.

hello reader
sfacngfvbpta

This code is unbreakable – almost! Notice there are very few clues for anyone wanting to decode it without holding a copy of the pad. Spaces do not necessarily indicate breaks between words, and letter patterns are absent. It has only one flaw. The total number of characters and spaces could have some meaning. This is a problem because if I routinely communicated bombing targets and my message was "Bomb Bath". You could figure out the sender was not going to bomb Bristol if the message were shorter than 11 letters and spaces. To avoid this problem, messages are extended with nonsense at beginning and end to make sure no information can be gleaned from the length. The convention is to code messages to the full length of the pad. You must never reuse a pad. Each time you code a message, rip off that page rather like a calendar. Destroy it and use the next page for the next message. At the other end, the recipient uses his copy of the pad to run the process in reverse. Decode the message by swapping each letter according to the modulo method, rip the page from the pad, and burn it. Because each key is only used once you can't use any sort of statistical method to work out the message, making the one-time pad perfectly secure. Claude Shannon proved this in 1945 while working for Bell Corporation but, due to wartime secrecy, his proof was not published until 1948.

The Perfect Code

The proof that a one-time pad is perfectly secret is straightforward. Imagine I take a coin and flip it 1000 times. I'll write down some of the results as follows:

HHTHHHTTHTTTHTTTTTHTH…

I give you a copy of my results and keep one for myself. Now we each have the same random set of Heads and Tails recorded on a piece of paper. I can convert any message from letters to binary numbers: 'a' = 00000001, 'b' = 00000010, 'c' = 00000011 and so on. If you are not familiar with binary just assume I have a code where we only ever use combinations of 0s or 1s. To encrypt the message we flip each bit – 0 goes to 1 or 1 goes to 0 – using my random list of heads and tails according to the following rule: If I have a head flip the bit, otherwise leave it the same. I now have a randomized message, and it really is truly random. To convince yourself, imagine answering the question, do you like coffee or tea? Think of your answer and flip a coin. If the coin lands heads change your answer otherwise leave it the same. Now write your answer down. Try it out a few times. Do you see you end up with a totally random set of decisions – tea, coffee, coffee, tea, tea, tea. If you don't record the coin toss there is no way to determine your true answer.

Similarly, the message I encoded above now looks like a completely random stream of 1s and 0s and the only person who can decode it is the party with the other record of the coin tosses. Apply this to the message and, as if by magic, the message reappears. Any other random sequence will yield gibberish. It has to be the SAME random sequence I used in the first place.

Mathematically, the proof involves working out that the probability of getting the right answer by applying a random sequence is 1 in 2^n and the probability I could guess the answer is also 1 in 2^n? The same! So the chance of decrypting the message knowing the encryption method is the same as simply guessing the message and getting lucky. Therefore, the message is perfectly encrypted.

Quantum Cryptography

It turns out there is one other perfect encryption method that involves thinking about the nature of secrets. Normally we consider the primary problem with sending a secret message is coding it so that it can't be read by anyone but the intended recipient. However, wouldn't it be equally valuable to know if someone other than the recipient had intercepted and read the message? This is the trick quantum cryptography gives us.

Taking a measurement with a quantum device disturbs the system so measurements can be taken only once with the same results. By the same logic, I could send you a message and if someone else has read it in the meantime, you will know. I could arrange to meet with you in Berlin and if you detect the message has been intercepted, you could simply not show up.

I could use this same technique to send you a one-time pad. If you receive it without it being overheard, I could then safely send you an encrypted message. In 2007, this technique was used to transmit the results of a Swiss election from the polling booths to the central counting center.

Enigma

World War II accelerated the evolution of encryption from simple substitutions a human could perform to complex ciphers only a machine could calculate. You might wonder why everyone does not use a one-time-pad since it is a perfect code. The problem is distributing and maintaining the pads while keeping them secret. My daughter cracked my earlier code because she knows my laptop password, broke in, and read the answer. That's the problem with codes – security. The pads could be sent out in sealed envelopes but it would be easy to intercept an envelope, copy the pad and reseal it. You would then have a perfect and undetectable way to break the code. Also, if I were an Admiral wanting to communicate with my fleet of submarines I would need a huge pad – one page for every message I want to send – and either a pad for each submarine or one pad for all submarines. If I use only one pad, then I cannot talk to a submarine privately, and if any pad were lost *all* security would be breached. One-time-pads were used by both sides during World War Two, and often printed on nitrocellulose – a chemical similar to the explosive nitroglycerine. This allowed users to burn the codebooks quickly if an enemy threatened to capture them.

Both the Americans and British captured Enigma machines and codebooks during the war. A Navy Enigma machine was a sought-after prize, as it was more complex than the Army version, with extra dials and plug settings. To crack the more sophisticated codes Bletchley Park needed to get hold of Enigma machines, ideally without the Germans' knowledge. The film *U-571* merges two such capture stories into one, taking a few dramatic liberties along the way, but it's well worth watching.

Even with a captured machine, the codes were hard to break. You needed a starting point – a crib to give you a clue what the machine settings were. Helpfully, the German Army often began their messages with a weather report. Everyone knows the German word for weather – 'Wetter'. Decode the first 20 letters of a message until you found 'Wetter' and the message is unlocked. The German Navy, however, was less chatty and avoided obvious words in their messages. One way the Allies could find a crib was to blow something up. They would sail to some point in the Atlantic, fill an old boat with oil drums, and set it alight. The German Navy would get wind of this and go to investigate. The first thing they would do is to radio a message back to base with the coordinates of the wreckage, which, of course, the British already knew. This gave the British a crib, and once they were in, they could decode messages for several days in a row because the Enigma machines often cycled through a repeating pattern.

Throughout the War, the German military never suspected the British had cracked their codes and thought they must have traitors giving away their secrets. The Enigma machine was an elegant compromise between a truly unbreakable code and a simple cipher. Unfortunately for the Germans, Turing was on the side of the Allies.

In the 1930s almost all mathematics, accounting, and code-breaking were performed by humans using pencil and paper. It was the science behind this process Turing sought to understand. We'll take a step back in time again to 1935 and Turing's discovery of a solution to the Decision Problem – *the Entscheidungsproblem*.

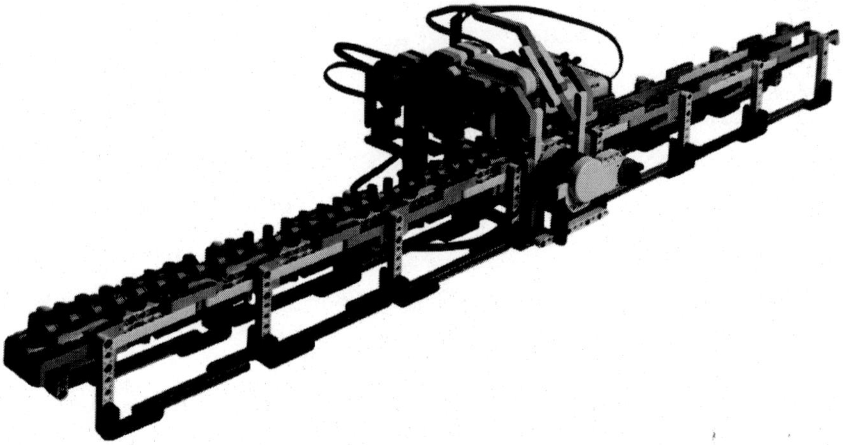

Lego Turing Machine

"Machines take me by surprise with great frequency."

Alan Turing

The Machine

Turing probably learned of *the Entscheidungsproblem* in a lecture given at Cambridge University by Max Newman. Newman described a new proof by Gödel showing mathematics was incomplete. The proof solved the completeness and consistency problems by turning mathematical statements into numbers and showing you could generate a logical paradox if you tried to argue for completeness and consistency at the same time. Thus, of the three original Hilbert problems, completeness, consistency and decidability, only decidability remained unanswered.

Turing spent all of 1935 and much of 1936 thinking about this question: Is mathematics intuitive, or could a machine decide mathematical questions automatically? Eventually, cycling through the Cambridge countryside one day, he stopped to rest in a field near Grantchester and in a flash of inspiration envisioned his mathematical machine. The machine was entirely imaginary but made as if from mechanical parts common in the 1930s.

The idea was to reduce the process of computing with pen and paper to its most basic level. Turing hit upon the idea of using a long ribbon of paper tape similar to the ones used in telegraph machines. A paper tape is simpler than rectangular paper as it can be handled mathematically as a single sequence of numbers – we don't have to worry about turning the page or working in two dimensions. If you are worried that a tape is less powerful than a sheet of paper remember Cantor's theorem: an infinite plane is the same as an infinite line. The use of a tape massively simplified the mathematics, and subsequently many early computers used tapes, as they were easy to handle in practice as well as in theory.

The eye, hand and pencil of a human mathematician was modeled as the read-write head of a teletype. It allowed the machine to read input from the tape and write information back so as to keeping track of intermediate calculations or provide the final output. The operation of the machine was straightforward. At each moment in time the machine could read a symbol on the tape, move the tape forward or backwards, and write or erase a symbol. That's all he needed to model a human doing something like long multiplication. Turing argued his model was exactly analogous to a human performing a computation.

Turing's imaginary machine was now able to perform computations just like a human. You could write down the rules for a given procedure and the machine could, for example, do long multiplication. At each step of the calculation, the computer would examine the state machine, look up the state in the instruction book and put the machine into its new state. If you recall Searle's Chinese Room, this is the same process the man in the room followed: get a symbol, look it up in a book, and reply with the corresponding symbol.

Universal Turing Machine

We have missed one important step from our explanation of the modern computer: the ability to run programs. Nowadays, we take for granted you can download a program from the Internet or buy one from a shop. In the 1930s adapting a single machine to multiple purposes was a radical idea. Machines were built to do one thing, and one thing only, and there was no concept of a general-purpose machine. Nowadays this is hard to comprehend, but there is a similar revolution going on in manufacturing today with the widespread adoption of 3D printing. Today most factories use tools – lathes, drills and saws – to fashion objects. Each machine does a specific job and is not 'general purpose'. But innovative new machines can now be purchased relatively inexpensively called 3D fabricators, which print entire objects. The same happened for electronic logic in Turing's time.

Before computers, logical tasks were performed by banks of relays. How these banks work can be illustrated by the workings of an old-fashioned elevator. If you pressed a button to call an elevator, you closed a switch coupled to a relay in the basement sending power to the car. Another switch was tripped automatically when the elevator reached the desired floor. All the functioning of the elevator system was fixed. Once you pressed a button to go up you could not change your mind and press

Old Fashioned Relay Mechanism

the button to go down. That logic did not exist in the relay banks. If you wanted to improve the logic of the elevator you would need to rip out all the relays and rewire everything from scratch.

Turing's first imaginary machine was set up in the same way. It had a fixed set of hard-wired logic, a rule book. In order to perform different tasks – say addition or multiplication you had to use a different rule book. His revolutionary idea was to write a rule book that told the machine to read a soft-wired set of instructions from the tape and execute those instead. He called this a Universal machine since it could perform *any* procedure written on the tape. Today we call this software. It is fair to say Turing was not the first to use this idea. Charles Babbage's analytical engine could read instructions from cards and execute different procedures, but Turing thought through all the ramifications of the idea and made it general purpose, giving us the modern science of computing. It is easy to build a real Turing machine, but by today's standards it is a little clumsy; a team in Denmark has built one using Lego. You can see a link on my website.

Very soon after Turing's paper was published, a number of people proposed better practical implementations. In 1943, John von Neumann of Princeton University created the architecture for ENIAC, the first stored program computer, developed for the United States Army's Ballistic

3D Printing Machine

Research Laboratory. The laptop I am writing on uses the von Neumann architecture, and most modern computers evolved from it. By contrast, mobile phones are descended from the Harvard architecture developed by IBM and first supplied to Harvard University in 1944, hence its name. The distinction in architectures has blurred over the years. The world supports two main computer chip technologies, one built for desktop and laptop computers, designed by Intel in Santa Clara, California, and the other, designed for mobile devices by ARM, in Cambridge, England. All these computers can, in principle, run any piece of software.

Programs

Software is just a series of numbers. When you click an icon on your desktop, the computer reads the number and interprets it as a series of instructions. There is a decoder inside the computer that knows the number '1' means add the next two digits and the number 5493 means display them on screen and so on. On my computer the operating system, Apple's OSX, takes the number, decodes it and passes it to the CPU for execution. You might ask what runs the operating system and that is a smaller program called the BIOS. What runs BIOS? An even smaller program called the Bootstrap. Once all this is up and running you have a working computer, which can run any program you throw at it.

The problem with programs is they tend to crash – usually at the most inconvenient times. It is often not clear whether a program has truly crashed. It might be stuck in an infinite loop, or it could be calculating the answer to a complex question, such as the answer to life, the Universe, and everything. How would we know? If only I had waited a little longer before rebooting, the program would have run to its end and given me the answer to Douglas Adams' question.

It would be very useful, and save a great deal of time, if I had a way of telling whether a program will ever stop. An elegant solution would be to have a second program called 'Halt', which would test the program and output 'will halt' or 'will crash' as appropriate. It turns out this program would be more than just useful. It could be used as an oracle, capable of answering almost any question imaginable.

I could, for example, write a program that says: for every index in Fermat's puzzle try every number and halt if you find a solution greater than 2. Now if I run my halt program on this program and it states 'will crash', I will have solved Fermat's Last Theorem! Do you see why?

If we give 'Halt' an input: a program we are interested in, along with some data, it will tell us if the program finds an answer. If I am trying to solve Fermat's Last Theorem, we will ask it to try every possible index for the equation $3^x+4^x=5^x$ and halt when it finds a true result greater than 2. If the halt program says yes and halts, you can trace through the program and work out how it did it. The theory would be proved. If the program says no, the theory is disproved. This gives us a way to discover proofs of many mathematical theorems.

I could try almost any puzzle using a program with this form. All I need do is put a problem in the following decision format: *try all possible options, and then stop and ring a bell if a solution is found.* The Halt program would then give the result leading to untold riches, winning all the remaining Clay Mathematics prizes at the very least and earning me $6m.

Does such a magical program exist? The answer, sadly, is no. There is no Halt program and the final part of Turing's paper proved there can never be.

The Proof

Let's write a list of all the possible programs my laptop could ever run. A comprehensive way to do this is to start at one and try every number.As I count up I am simply generating numbers, for example, 5,433,232, then turning each number into a program file and running it. For a bit of fun, I created a couple and tried them out on my laptop. They did nothing, so it was not very edifying. Most numbers are just junk because programs have to be in the right format for the computer you are working on. It's just like words. If you randomly take a handful of scrabble tiles out of a bag, most of the time you will have nonsense, but every now and they you will have an actual word. Be careful with this; you could accidentally write, "delete every item on my hard disk." Of course, the probability is astronomically low, but Murphy's Law says it will happen, so back up your data!

As you count up, you will generate every possible program along the way. A mathematician would say programs are recursively enumerable. The word recursive means there is an algorithm and enumerable means to count. Therefore, there is a counting algorithm that would run every imaginable program. Here is a list of them, or at least a some of the highlights:

0 (probably doesn't run)
1 (ditto)
00 (ditto)
01 (ditto)
0110010010010000100 (makes the computer beep once)
… (from here on I'll give the program names since the numbers are too large to print)
Does Nothing (there are many of these)
Is Gibberish (there are an infinite number of these)
Junk (an infinite number of these)
Print Something (again an infinite number of these)
More Gibberish
Excel
Word
PowerPoint
Mathematica...
Fermat's Last Theorem enumerator (runs for ever)
A nonworking version of the Halting Program
A nonworking version of the Crashing Program
Really big programs that don't fit on my hard drive

and so on.

You can see that every program imaginable is generated in our list. If you are wondering which version of Word or Excel, the answer is *every* version and every bug ridden unreleased version as well. We are enumerating every program that could ever be run in the known universe!

Perhaps you can see a problem looming. I can pose any mathematical puzzle in a clever way so that a program only stops if there is a solution. I am about to list every possible program that could ever be created. If halt exists this will automatically prove every mathematical theorem imaginable.

Let us see if this is so.

For our thought experiment, we will assume every program takes an input. Historical convention in computing means this is generally the case. If you type a program into the command line of a computer with some words listed afterwards, the computer will usually run the program with the words as input. For example, if you type, "Print 'Hello World'", most computers will print 'Hello World'.

We now imagine there is a Halt program that can run on an infinity of inputs. Will it work for every input? We are looking for a paradox caused by the existence of the Halt program. If Halt causes a paradox then Halt cannot exist.

Here goes...

If there is a Halt program, we can write a Crash program. That's a program that goes into an infinite loop if it detects a program will halt. Now what happens when we feed Crash into itself? Does Crash halt if it runs with the input Crash?

This creates a paradox; there is no solution which makes sense. It's similar to the Barber Paradox of earlier. Since a paradox is created there must be a fault in our original theory. The error is the existence of Crash. Since Crash cannot exist and it was created as the logical opposite of Halt, Halt cannot exist either. QED. There is no general program that will tell if another program will halt because such a program could not run with the negative of itself as input.

This places a limit on the power of computers to automatically solve problems. There is certainly no general purpose algorithm which will solve every problem. Slightly more subtly there is no general purpose program that is guaranteed to solve one arbitrary problem.

If there were, you could just write a program to sequentially present every problem to the arbitrary problem solver and you would have solved everything.

This presents us with a puzzle. A huge software industry has grown up based on Turing's ideas, employing tens of millions of people worldwide. This industry regularly solves all manner of problems. The proof from Turing's original 1936 paper suggests there should be quite strict limits on the power of computers. In the next chapter, we will examine this industry and take a look at Turing's theorem from a modern view point. The chapter can be read as a stand alone article but was originally written as an integral part of this book.

Chapter 11

SOFTWARE

Fred Brooks

Medieval Block Print from 'No Silver Bullet'

"The bearing of a child takes nine months, no matter how many women are assigned."

Fred Brooks

"Adding manpower to a late software project makes it later."

Brooks' Law

In *No Silver Bullet – Essence and Accidents of Software Engineering*, Fred Brooks explains why writing software is hard, and why machines are not going to do it for us anytime soon. The original article appeared in the proceedings of the Tenth World Software Conference. It was subsequently expanded into the, now famous, book, *The Mythical Man Month*.

Brooks believed solving real world problems involves understanding the essential complexity of life. 'Accidental Complexity' – the simple type – is the time-consuming part of writing software, for example, listing all 220 countries of the world in a website, or making sure all the buttons in an interface line up correctly. These tasks are tedious – you have to look up all the countries in Wikipedia and make decisions, such as whether the United Kingdom will be denoted 'UK' or 'GB'. They don't need any real ingenuity. 'Essential Complexity' is altogether different. It involves understanding the world and setting out the rules in meticulous detail. Brooks argued essential complexity is not susceptible to being sped up by machine processes. Navigating these architectural decisions cannot be automated. He gives us an analogy by comparing writing software to building a house.

When you build a house, an architect designs it, an engineer makes the calculations to ensure it is safe, and a construction firm builds it. The construction process dominates the cost and time. In software projects, an engineer writes a program that precisely defines the design and the construction and calculation is done by a compiler – software that takes the design and makes it machine-readable. Compilers operate in a fraction of a second. Making software is, therefore, dominated by the design time, and design is all about capturing the essential complexity of a task.

This chapter will try to show where essential complexity comes from, why computers can't tackle this sort of complexity and, therefore, why they can't write software. Good news for programmers as this means job security!

For a more thorough treatment of the mathematics read my paper *The Free Will Universe* at www.jamestagg.com/freewillpaper.

```
<!DOCTYPE html>
<html lang="en">
<head>
    <meta charset="UTF-8" />
    <meta http-equiv="Content-Type" content="text/html; charset=UTF-8" />
    <meta name="viewport" content="width=device-width, initial-scale=1.0">

    <title>James Tagg | Invention, Physics and Farming</title>
    <link rel="profile" href="http://gmpg.org/xfn/11" />
    <link rel="pingback" href="http://jamestagg.com/xmlrpc.php" />

    <!--[if lt IE 9]>
    <script src="http://s0.wp.com/wp-content/themes/premium/broadsheet/js/html5.js?m=1393348654g"
type="text/javascript"></script>
    <![endif]-->

            <script src='//r-login.wordpress.com/remote-login.php?
action=js&amp;host=jamestagg.com&amp;id=57804437&amp;t=1406042069&amp;back=http%3A%2F%2Fjamestagg.com%2F'
type="text/javascript"></script>
        <script type="text/javascript">
        /* <![CDATA[ */
            if ( 'function' === typeof WPRemoteLogin ) {
                document.cookie = "wordpress_test_cookie=test; path=/";
                if ( document.cookie.match( /(;|^)\s*wordpress_test_cookie\=/ ) ) {
                    WPRemoteLogin();
                }
            }
        /* ]]> */
        </script>
        <link rel="alternate" type="application/rss+xml" title="James Tagg &raquo; Feed"
href="http://jamestagg.com/feed/" />
<link rel="alternate" type="application/rss+xml" title="James Tagg &raquo; Comments Feed"
href="http://jamestagg.com/comments/feed/" />
<script type="text/javascript">
/* <![CDATA[ */
function addLoadEvent(func){var oldonload=window.onload;if(typeof window.onload!='function')
{window.onload=func;}else{window.onload=function(){oldonload();func();}}}
/* ]]> */
```

James Tagg's Home Page

"Computers are stupid. They can only give you answers."

Pablo Picasso

"Software is like sex: it's better when it's free."

Linus Torvalds

Silver Bullets Can't be Fired

Human brains are wonderfully creative things. We can compose music, play golf, write novels, and turn our hands to all manner of problems. Many people use their brains to write software. In our modern-day lives we use software all the time: when we access the web, type on a word processor or play a computer game. Software also inhabits many apparently dumb devices. Modern cars contain dozens of computers quietly working away; providing entertainment and navigation, controlling the engine, and helping the car brake safely. In my living room I count over a hundred computers. Many are tiny, like the one in my TV remote control, while others are hidden as parts of larger machines. The laptop on which I write has over twenty computers inside it, besides the main Intel processor.

One thing all these computers have in common is that a human being sat for many hours writing their software. Software is formal logic written in something resembling English.

If I go to my ATM and try to withdraw cash, a programmer will have written out the logic for the transaction as a set of rules.

When I put my bankcard in the slot, and type in my PIN, a line of software will ask: If the bank balance of 'James Tagg' is less than twenty dollars and I have pressed 'withdraw' for an amount in excess of twenty dollars, then display, "We are sorry we cannot process the transaction at this time." and return the card. There seems to be an unwritten rule that the things a computer says should be accurate but unhelpful!

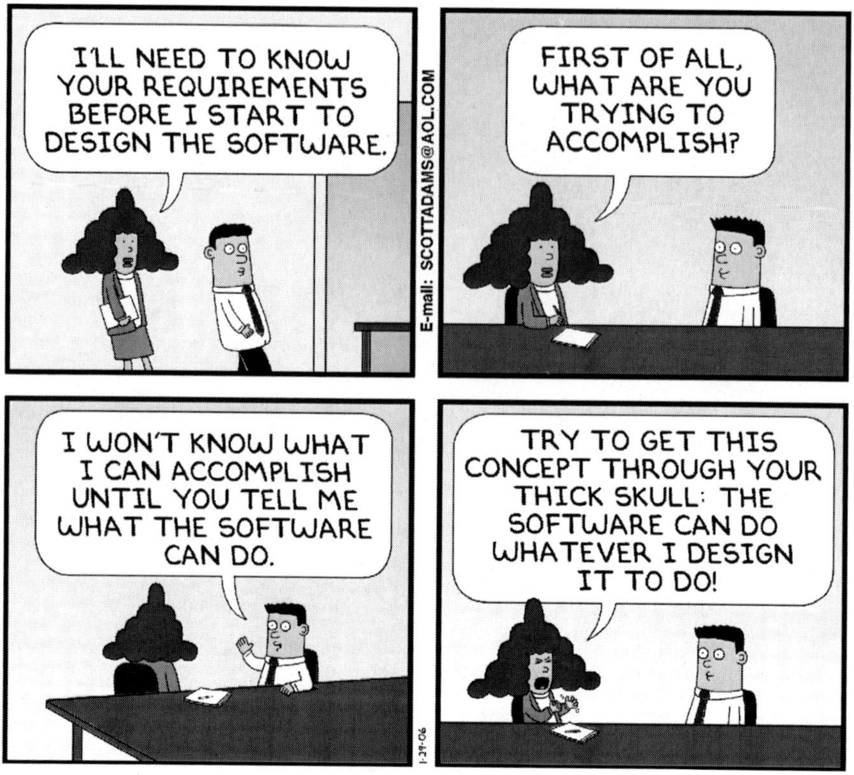

Alice, Ted and Software Specification

It would have been much more helpful if the computer had said, "You do not have enough balance in your account." And, it would have been more helpful still if it had asked whether I needed a temporary overdraft. However, such a feature needs many more lines of software and this is time-consuming to write.

Software takes time and is expensive, because it has to be written in a general-purpose way. Any name could substitute for James Tagg, and any amount could be used. After all, it would be useless if an ATM machine could only give out $20 to one person. The generalization of software makes use of variables instead of fixed values and this renders it hard to understand. Wherever we meet an idea that needs to be generalized, a letter must be used instead of a fixed value. Computer programs tend to look like this: if 'a' wants to do 'b' with 'c' then allow it only if 'd' is greater than 'c'. The software programmer has to keep track of all the possible values that could be inserted into each of the variables and make sure each and every combination would make sense. My ATM scenario gets complex quickly. It needs to be able to answer a range of questions for all the bank's customers, deal with any amount of

money and handle security when communicating with foreign banks is necessary. A human being must write lines of code for all the rules and every exception, making provision for any gibberish that might be typed in by the customer.

Many people ask, "Wouldn't it be great if my computer could write software for me? Humans could sit back and put their feet up." While most people don't actually believe this could happen, they will often ask why we can't specify software exactly and use unskilled people to write it. Both proposals fundamentally misunderstand the nature of writing software.

What do Programmers Do?

A human software programmer can write up to 1000 lines of code per day. At the beginning of a project, when the work is unconstrained, programmers write fast. Things slow down once programmers encounter the enemy: the real world. By the time the code is complete and selling in shops, the productivity of a programmer can be as low as one line of code per day. This is staggeringly low and luckily only applies to big commercial software, equating to about 10 words per day. A good typist types at 80 words per minute and most programmers are reasonable typists. So software writers in a big project spend only a minute or so per day in the act of writing. The rest is taken up by meetings, process discussions, email, reporting and so on. In projects that avoid much of this administrative overhead, good software programmers reach a long-run average of about 225 lines per day. This has been the level of productivity on the products I have developed in the past. These projects were lucky. They had a single team on the task from beginning to end and, in general, the projects took few wrong turns. Still these programmers were spending only 10-20 minutes of each day on actual programming. What were they doing the rest of the time?

In the early days of programming you might have a great idea, but the process of turning this idea into software was immensely long-winded. I learned to program at Manchester University in the 1980s. The enormous machines in the basement of the computer building provided heat for both our building and the mathematics tower next door. We were not permitted to play with these basement monsters but were 'privileged' to submit instructions to a mini computer in the undergraduate section – a PDP11-34.

For those of you not acquainted with computers I can tell you the process of writing software in the 1980s was immensely tedious. To add two numbers and display them on a screen took a month of lab time, using detailed instructions written in machine code. Everything was manual, including writing your code out in pencil on special paper with little numbered squares and then giving it to someone to type in overnight! You would return the next day to discover whether you had a usable program or a something riddled with errors. If you found an error, it would require editing. This was nothing like using a modern word processor. The online editors of the day were the ultimate in annoying software. If you misspelled a word, you would need to count up the letters and spaces manually on a printout and enter a command – replace letter 27 of line 40 with the character 'r'. Each and every typo would take five minutes to correct. I managed to finish the simple program required for course credit – I think it displayed an eight-digit decimal number – and ran for the hills. In my second year I bought a PC and decamped to the physics department next door where I remained for the rest of my undergraduate life.

The PC revolution provided programmers with a new and intuitive software creation environment where almost all the tedium was removed. A wealth of tools for creating software was pioneered by Bill Gates of

Microsoft and Philip Kahn of Borland, along with intuitive applications such as the spreadsheet invented by Dan Bricklin and Bob Frankston and made popular by Lotus Corporation. Today all computers have elegant WYSIWYG, 'What You See Is What You Get' interfaces, where you drag and drop elements into place on the screen. Over the last 25 years writing software has sped up and stopped being tedious – becoming almost a joy!

In *No Silver Bullet*, Brooks explains that writing software can't be accelerated any further because all the tedious mechanical tasks have already been removed. Remember his analogy: Writing software is like building a house, but with some important differences. With a house, an architect handles the design and then turns over construction to a building company. Construction takes an appreciable time, more time than the design and quite a bit more effort. But in software the construction is totally automated. When we complete the design for a piece of software we press compile on the computer and the software is built and tested automatically in a matter of seconds. Speeding this process up any further would make only a tiny improvement in the overall software creation time, since the process is already 99% design and 1% building. For the most part, the creative process of writing software cannot be improved through mechanical means.

This is not always the case. I recently upgraded the machines for some developers I work with. We added solid state hard drives. Compiling a program now takes only 10 seconds, compared with 6 minutes before. Because programmers nowadays tend to compile their programs very regularly we estimate this saves them as much as an hour a day. This is the only real innovation I have seen in the build phase of software in the last 5 years, and it's arguably not an innovation at all. We just forgot to keep on top of the build time and allowed it to get out of hand.

You might argue some counter examples. Modern software design suites let you drag and drop things on the screen to make applications or build a website. Two hundred million people have managed to put together WordPress websites using this technique. These are mechanical procedures for solving a programming task and seem to contradict my argument. They allow us to lay out graphics, press a button and turn the design into software. But they perform very simple tasks. The computer simply notes the coordinates of each box on the screen and places those numbers into a file. The process is entirely mechanical and could be performed by a clerk with no programming knowledge following a set of rules. The computer just does it faster. I did the clever work; I had the idea for the software, I came up with the idea for the interface, I decided where to place the boxes, and I chose all the colors, fonts and graphics. I did all the creative bits!

So, now we know what programmers do all day. They create!

Origins of Software

Alan Turing first described the modern day computer in a paper presented to the London Mathematical Society in 1936. He was not trying to invent the computer. That was a by-product. He was trying to solve a puzzle that had been troubling mathematicians for 30 years: *The Decision Problem.*

David Hilbert set out the challenge during a public lecture to the French Academy of Science in 1901, marking the turn of the century. Rather than give a boring lecture extolling the virtues of scientists, he decided to give his audience a list of all the puzzles mathematicians were stumped on.

Rather like the XPRIZE of today, he presented the problems as a series of challenges. Sadly for the mathematicians of his time, there were no million dollar prizes on offer, just a moment of fame and the adulation of their colleagues. Each challenge was given a number. The list included many famous puzzles; the Riemann Hypothesis, the puzzle of Diophantine Equations and the Navier Stokes Hypothesis, to name only three. A group of these questions were to coalesce into what we now know as the Decision Problem.

The Decision Problem is very important to computer science because it asks whether an algorithm can be written to automatically discover other algorithms. Since all software is itself algorithmic you could rephrase the question: Can software write software? This might seem esoteric. But, if you are a computer scientist, it is an important question. If we could solve all mathematical problems automatically we would not need mathematicians anymore. And, since programs are applied mathematics, the same goes for computer programmers.

Before you breathe a sigh of relief because you are neither a mathematician nor a computer scientist, you should remember it is possible to describe all knowledge using numbers. That's what your iPhone does when it stores music. If everything can be represented by numbers, then a fast-enough computer could use an algorithm to create *everything*! You really could set Douglas Adams' *Ultimate Question of Life the Universe and Everything* before a computer and it would come up with the answer – presumably extrapolating the existence of rice pudding and income tax along the way.

Algorithms

Back in the 1930s no mechanical system could perform a calculation with any speed. People still used pencil and paper for most things; the newly-invented mechanical cash registers were slow and could perform only one calculation for each crank of the handle. If you wanted to calculate something complex, you had to employ a *computer*: a person who could do mental arithmetic enormously fast. Richard Feynman's first job was computing for the Manhattan Project. The question was: Could a computer, either mechanical or human, blindly follow known rules to decide all mathematical questions? Hilbert's 10th Problem asked this question of a particular type of mathematical expression – called a Diophantine equation.

Hilbert's 10th Problem

> *"Given a Diophantine equation with any number of unknown quantities, devise a finite process to determine whether the equation is solvable in rational integers."*
>
> David Hilbert

Diophantus lived in ancient Persia – now Iran. His son died young and Diophantus was so consumed by grief he retreated into mathematics. He left us seven books of mathematical puzzles – some he devised himself and some of them taken from antiquity. The puzzles look deceptively simple and are all based on equations using whole numbers. His most famous puzzle is set in a poem which tells how old Diophantus was when he died. Can you solve it?

> *"Here lies Diophantus,' the wonder behold. Through art algebraic, the stone tells how old: 'God gave him his boyhood one-sixth of his life, One twelfth more as youth while whiskers grew rife; And then yet one-seventh ere marriage begun; In five years there came a bouncing new son. Alas, the dear child of master and sage, after attaining half the measure of his father's age, life chill fate took him. After consoling his fate by the science of numbers for four years, he ended his life."*

Diophantine puzzles look straightforward. Hilbert asked if these problems could be solved by a mechanical procedure, in modern terms, by an algorithm. To show you what is meant by this, allow me to take you

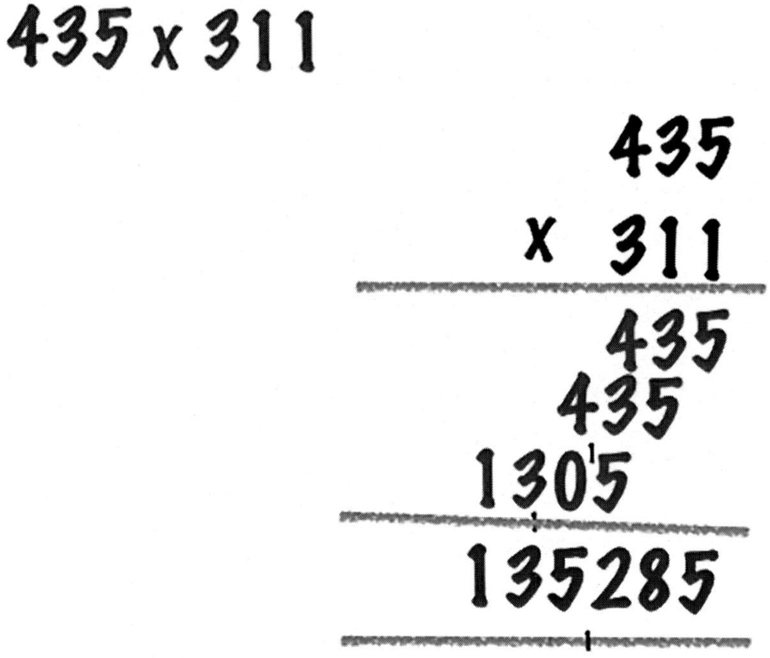

Long Multiplication

back to your childhood. Do you recall being taught long multiplication at school? Take a look at the next illustration and it will all come flooding back. Once you learn the process of long multiplication you can follow the rules and get the right answer for any similar problem every time. To do this, you lay out the calculation in a particular format and apply the logic. Multiply each number by a single digit of the other number and then add the results together.

Diophantine problems are a little more complex than long multiplication and some of them are a bit abstruse. But there is one *very* famous Diophantine problem we can all recite. “The square on the hypotenuse is equal to the sum of the squares of the other two sides.” The equation for a Pythagorean triangle.

The theorem applies to right-angled triangles and there are sixteen whole number solutions, known as Pythagorean triples; three, four, five; is one example.

Purists may protest that Fermat's Last Theorem isn't strictly Diophantine because it refers to a variable exponent – the x to the n part. This is hair splitting. But, of course, the splitting of hairs is bread and butter to a mathematician. We will see later that Fermat's Theorem can be made Diophantine, but we are jumping ahead of ourselves a little.

A question that taxed mathematicians for many centuries was whether there are triples for higher powers, such as cubes. In other words, would the cube of the hypotenuse be equal to the sum of the cubes of the other two sides for some set of numbers? After much work, it was proven no triple exists which can solve the cubic equation. But what happens if we substitute higher indices?

The next shape to consider is the hypercube – a four-dimensional cube. That may stretch your visual imagination but the equation is simple, $3^4+4^4 \neq 5^4$. Again the challenge is to find a whole number solution for:

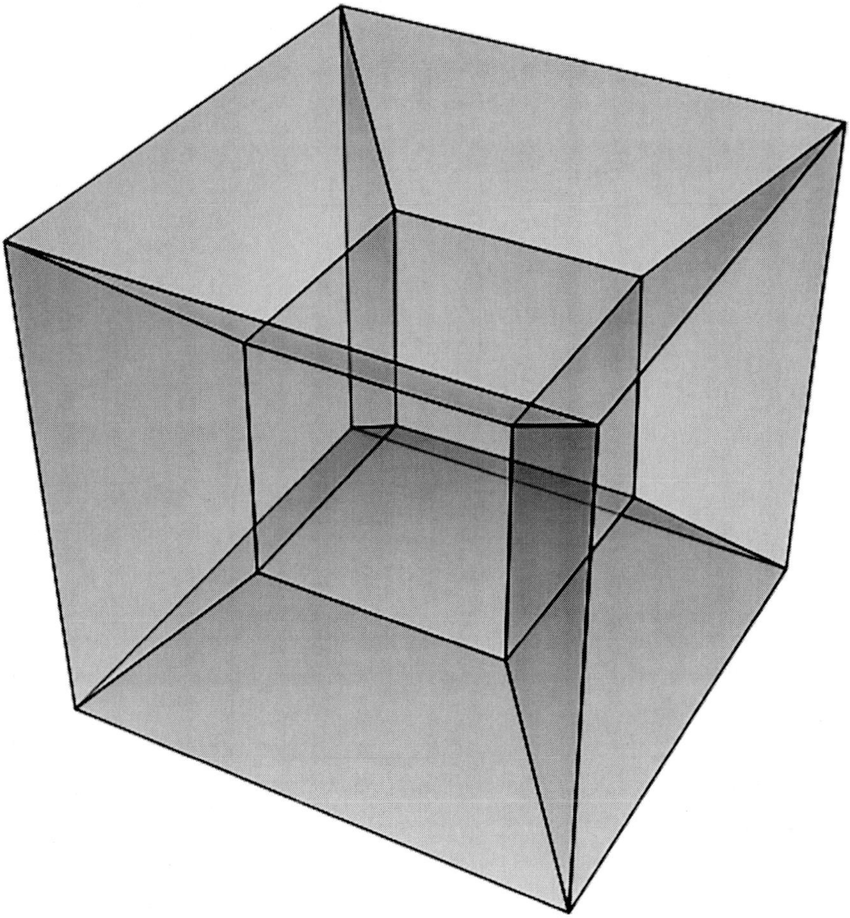

Hypercube

"The hypercube of the hypotenuse is equal to the sum of the hypercubes of the other two sides." A picture of the hypercube might help you visualize things.

It's quite difficult to get your head around this shape because it is hard to think in four dimensions. This seems strange because we have no problem seeing in three dimensions on flat, two-dimensional paper – it's called a picture, but four dimensions on flat paper appears to stump us. Again there is no solution for a hypercube: no Pythagorean triple exists.

Fermat's Last Theorem asked whether this inequality for the cube and the hypercube is true for *all* higher dimensions – for the hyper-hypercube, the hyper-hyper-hypercube and so on. Tantalizingly, he claimed to have found a proof but wrote that it was too large to fit in the margin of his book. It's partly due to this arrogant annotation that it became the most famous puzzle in mathematics, frustrating mathematicians for nearly 400 years.

Hilbert's question back at the turn of the 20th century was whether a machine could find a proof of this conjecture by following a mechanical procedure, similar to our long multiplication example above.

The puzzle was eventually solved in 1995 by Andrew Wiles, a mere 358 years after Fermat claimed to have solved it. Wiles' proof runs to eighty pages of densely typed mathematical notation – considerably larger than the margin in which Fermat claimed his proof did not quite fit! There is an excellent book by Simon Singh – *Fermat's Last Theorem* – that tells the whole story.

We now know for certain, thanks to Wiles, that the answer is 'no'. There are sixteen answers to the two-dimensional triangle puzzle but there is none for any higher dimension all the way up to infinity. How might a computer tackle this problem and find a proof?

A computer could apply brute force and try many solutions; every combination up to 100 million has already been tried and no exception found. But, mathematicians are haunted by big mistakes of the past. There were theories they imagined to be true until someone discovered a counterexample. This sort of thing dogged prime number theorems.

Mathematicians don't like to look foolish and are suspicious of practical answers, "Well, I've tried it and I can't seem to find an exception." This sort of argument does not wash with them. That's what engineers and physicists do. Mathematicians are better than that!

Mathematicians want definitive answers; "It is certain no solution can exist", and these sorts of answers require an understanding of the problem to see *why* no solution could exist. That's a very high bar. What we need is a program that, rather than mechanically trying every possible combination, takes our problem and definitively says, "Yes, there is a solution," or, "No, there is not." There are plenty of man-made proofs of this nature. Pythagoras's proof there are an infinite number of primes is an example. Pythagoras did not have to try every prime number. He simply understood the nature of prime numbers and gave us a logical reason why it is so.

Mathematicians love a general solution. One way to solve Hilbert's 10th Problem would be to find a single mechanical way to solve *every* problem. If you could solve *every* possible problem, you could certainly solve Hilbert's 10th Problem. It turns out there is a way to test whether every problem has a mechanical solution – pose the Halting Question.

The Halting Question

I should say for a little historical color that the Halting Problem was not called that by Turing. The name was coined much later, in the sixties, by Martin Davis. Turing knew the problem by the less catchy name of the "not crashing" problem, or as he preferred, "Being circle free", meaning the program did not get caught in an infinite loop.

To understand halting we should imagine a brute force program stepping through all the possible solutions to Fermat's problem. If there *is* a solution this stepping program will eventually halt and answer 'true'. If there is not, the program will run forever. Can we predict a program will not run forever? At first pass this is hard. We can't watch it forever and say, "It never halted." So is there a clever way to do this? An algorithm perhaps?

The Answer to the Ultimate Question

The answer is 'No!' In 1936, Alan Turing proved there is no general-purpose mechanical way to tell whether a program is going to find an answer at all, much less what the answer is. This means Hilbert's Decision Problem has no solution; there is no general purpose algorithm which will discover all mathematical theorems.

Turing succeeded in proving this by turning the problem on its head. He proved that a crash detection program is unable to see whether it will crash itself. Since you cannot tell whether a program will crash – and by this I mean go into an infinite loop – you cannot tell if it will halt. He used the simple argument that since you can't tell if the crashing program will halt, you have already proved you can't predict if every program will halt.

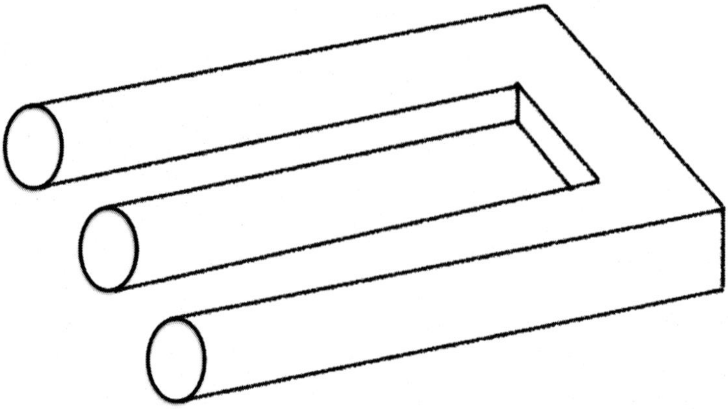

Impossible Shape

That is Turing's argument in a nutshell. But if that was too large a step, let's take the argument a little more slowly and prove it a couple of different ways. First, we will use a proof by counterexample, known by mathematicians as an 'indirect proof'. These may tax your brain. If you want a visual image to help with the idea of an indirect proof, take a look at the impossible shape. It is paradoxical, which means it does not exist. QED.

The Proofs

There are several ways to prove the non-existence of the Halting Program. I am going to present a few in the hope one of them will hit the mark and allow you to see why. The first proof uses a software flowchart. I have laid this out on the assumption the program exists and then attempted to apply it to itself. Unfortunately, the flowchart contains a paradox and thus there can be no Halting Program. The paradox is at once straightforward and confusing. It is a more elaborate version of the liar's paradox: "This sentence is a lie." If the sentence is true it must be false, and if the sentence is false then it must be true.

The Halting Program

Let us suppose there is a Halting Program. Remember that a Halting Program simply takes another program as input and predicts if it will halt or not. It follows there must also be a program called Haltcrash. Haltcrash goes into an infinite loop if it examines a program with input that halts, otherwise it halts itself.

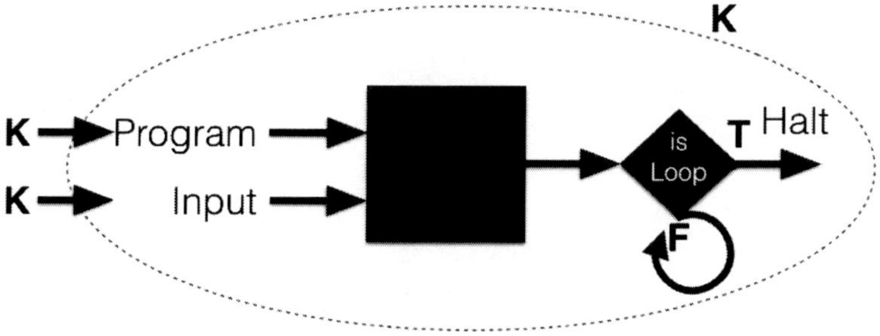

Halting Flowchart

Now we create a third program called RunMe. RunMe runs Haltcrash on itself. Still following this? Now execute RunMe with RunMe as its own input. What happens? The analysis is as follows:

1. RUNME started on input RUNME halts. If RUNME started on RUNME halts, then Haltcrash started on RUNME with input RUNME halts. If Haltcrash started on RUNME with input RUNME halts, then HALT decided that RUNME started on RUNME does not halt!

   Therefore,

   RUNME started on input RUNME halts implies that RUNME started on input RUNME does not halt. (contradiction)

2. RUNME started on input RUNME does not halt. If RUNME started on RUNME does not halt, then Haltcrash started on RUNME with input RUNME does not halt. If Haltcrash started on RUNME with input RUNME does not halt, then Halt decided that RUNME started on RUNME halts!

   Therefore,

   RUNME started on input RUNME does not halt implies that RUNME started on input RUNME halts. (contradiction)

Both analyses lead to a paradox! There is only one way out. There can be no halting procedure. I'm sorry if this is quite convoluted.

Philosophical Proof

If you find these technical proofs difficult to follow, it may be easier to examine the problem philosophically. Consider the consequence of the existence of a Halting procedure. A Universal Turing Machine is a relatively small program. Roger Penrose gives a three-page example in *The Emperor's New Mind*, and Stephen Wolfram has implemented one using a cellular automaton with as few as five component parts.

A Halting Program running on such a machine should be able to compute all the knowledge in the Universe. Every structure, every work of literature, every galaxy could be the output of this single, simple program. My pocket calculator could, theoretically, paint like Picasso and compose like Mozart. All art, knowledge and science would be entirely determined in our Universe and we would have no free will. If you philosophically rebel against this then the Halting Problem must have no solution.

Gödel's Insight

Another way to understand this conundrum is through the earlier work of Gödel. Solutions to mathematical puzzles are neat, orderly sequences of statements where the problem is solved step by step. Computers are good at step by step processes. Surely a computer could simply proceed in a painstaking fashion to check all the possible combinations of words and symbols to discover a proof.

An analogy might be trying to find your hotel room if you have forgotten the number. You could simply find it by trying every room. As you progressed through each floor, you would try every corridor and retrace your steps to the main hallway before attempting the next. Eventually you would succeed.

Finding proofs of theorems is often understood to be the same sort of task: search systematically through all the numbers and you will find the solution. But this is not so: There is a hidden problem.

Although it is true to say problems and proofs can be described by numbers, they are not simply related like a lock and key. We need the first number to translate into a set of symbols meaning something about mathematics: for example, that x squared plus y squared equals z squared but for higher powers there is no equality, and the second number to denotes a set of sequential steps we can apply to demonstrate this fact. These steps must have meaning and obey the rules of mathematics, but what are these rules? Are they written down in a text book?

It turns out there is no way to find this set of rules; it is a super-infinite task. We would need to reach into our infinite bag of numbers and pull out rule after rule, turning each into a mathematical model that explains numbers and logic and what can be done with them to form mathematical statements. The number of ways to do this is not just infinity, but two to the power of infinity. This is the number of ways to permute all possible mathematical rules.

Your mind may be rebelling at this. Surely, if I have an infinite set of numbers I can just pluck all the numbers from my bag and then I am certain to have the solution. Unfortunately, it turns out there is no complete, consistent set of rules; no valid dictionary that maps all numbers to all of mathematics. That is Gödel incompleteness theorem.

Despite a fundamental limit on mapping all numbers to all of mathematics, there might still have been an algorithm which could practically find solutions for a given arbitrary problem. Turing proved this is not the case.

The Wiles Paradox

Turing showed us there can be no general purpose, mechanical procedure capable of finding solutions to arbitrary problems. A computer program cannot discover mathematical theorems nor write programs to do so. Yet computers regularly solve problems and generate programs. That's what software compilers do. This seems to be contradiction.

The solution to this apparent contradiction is to propose a boundary: a 'logic limit' above which computers may not solve problems. With a high boundary a general-purpose machine could solve most problems in the real world, though some esoteric mathematical puzzles would be beyond it. But if the boundary were low, many activities in our daily life would need some sort of alternative, creative thinking. It is crucial to know where the logic limit lies.

The Logic Limit

Amazingly, in many branches of science it is possible to pinpoint the exact location of the logic limit, but finding that boundary in mathematics has taken forty years work from some of the greatest mathematicians of the 20th century.

The story starts back in the 1940s at Berkeley University with a young Julia Robinson, one of the first women to succeed in the previously male-dominated profession of mathematics. By all accounts, she had a wry sense of humor. When asked by her personnel department for a job description she replied: "Monday—tried to prove theorem, Tuesday—tried to prove theorem, Wednesday—tried to prove theorem, Thursday—tried to prove theorem, Friday—theorem false." Like Andrew Wiles, she fell in love with one of the great mathematical puzzles, and although she made great strides, the problem passed from her to Martin Davis for the next steps.

The final elements were put in place in the 1970s with the work of another young mathematician, this time a Russian – Yuri Matiyasevich. Robinson wrote to him when she heard of his proof, "To think all I had to do was to wait for you to be born and grow up so I could fill in the missing piece." The complete result is the Robinson Davis Matiyasevich theory which sets out the limits of logic and algebra. What, you may ask, do we mean by logic and algebra?

Mathematicians like to turn everything into logical statements, even ordering a round of drinks! The discipline of logic emerged from ancient Greece as the study of language. The starting point was the syllogism: Statements such as, "All cows eat grass." or Lewis Carroll's assertion, "There are no teachable gorillas." Over time the study of logic became ever more precise with, for example, the introduction of variables and equations; a=all cows, b=some grass. The formula "a eats b" translates by substitution into, "The cows eat the grass." This doesn't look much like a step forward but, trust me, it is.

The modern way to represent logic is using prenex normal form. This mouthful simply means separating relationships between things from the things themselves. The following four statements say the same thing, each in a more formalized way.

Speech: Harry loves Sally

Logical: x loves y (substitute Harry for x and Sally for y)

Formal: There exists an x, there exists a y (x loves y)

Prenex: $\exists x \exists y\ (x\ R\ y)$, Where R, the relationship, is 'loves'

The final example is in prenex normal form. The symbol '∃' means 'there exists' and R stands for relationship in this equation. All logical statements can be translated into this form using a purely mechanical process. There is even a website that will do this for you. It's useful but I don't recommend it as entertainment!

In the example above, something exists in relation to the existence of something else: one person who loves another. Give me a name and I can look up the person they love. This is simple. A computer can easily solve such problems. Indeed there are hundreds of websites doing this every day. Once you've solved one problem of this type, you have solved them all.

We can rearrange Diophantine equations into many different prenex forms. The simplest form might be, 'there exists an x which solves the following equation, x equals three.' This would be written out as $\exists x$, $x=3$ and is of the $\exists$ class – 'there exists'. There are slightly more complex classes than our simple $\exists$ relationship: $\forall\exists\forall$ 'for all, there exists for all' or the class $\forall^2\exists\forall$ 'for all, for all, there exists, for all'. Each of these groups of equation is called a 'reduction class'.

One way to think about a reduction class is as a problem in topology, 'knots', to non-mathematicians. Imagine someone handed you a bunch of tangled cables – the sort of mess you get when they are thrown haphazardly into a drawer. You can tease them apart and rearrange them but you must not cut them or break any connection. Once you have done this you will be left with a series of cables on the desk. They are all separate, looped or in someway knotted together. Each cable has a fundamental topological arrangement: straight cables, granny knots, figure eight, and so on. You have reduced them to their simplest form, their logical classes. The same goes for logical statements. Once you have rearranged logical statements into their simplest form you can lay them out and group them together according to their complexity. Each group makes up a reduction class and you can ask whether that class as a whole is automatically decidable. It is a huge task to untangle and classify mathematical problems, and it took Robinson and her colleagues nearly forty years to succeed.

It turns out problems with a form as simple as $\forall\exists\forall$ (for all, there exists, for all) have no general purpose algorithm. Each must be examined individually and solved by something that is not a computer. This is a remarkable result as the logic boundary is set quite low. An $\exists\exists$, (exists, exists), class of problem is automatically solvable by a general algorithm, but a ∀∃∀, (for all, there exists, for all), is not. Each individual type of problem within the class must be examined with insight and understanding.

Our lives are full of problems – playing chess, finding a mate, designing space ships and simply getting to work in the morning. Imagine we expressed everyday problems as logical problems. Where is the logic limit for life? We have no answer for this yet, but we do know the logic limit for computing; it is given by Rice's Theorem.

Named after Henry Rice, and proven in 1951 as part of his doctoral thesis at Syracuse University, Rice's Theorem states: "No nontrivial feature of a computer program can be automatically derived." You cannot tell if a program will halt with a given input. You cannot tell if one program will generate the same output as another. You cannot tell if a simpler program could be written to do the same task as a more complex one. In fact, no nontrivial thing can be proven. This means the logic limit in computers is low, and computer programmers have job security.

For Programmers

For the programmers amongst you, here are some of the things that cannot be done automatically even given infinite time:

- Self-halting Problem. Given a program that takes one input, does it terminate when given itself as input?

- Totality Problem. Given a program that takes one input, does it halt on all inputs?

- Program Equivalence Problem. Given two programs that take one input each, do they produce the same result on every input?

- Dead Code Elimination. Will a particular piece of code ever be executed?

- Variable Initialization. Is a variable initialized before it is first referenced?

- Memory Management. Will a variable ever be referenced again?

Can humans solve 'unsolvable' problems?

The question of whether Fermat's Last Theorem could be solved mechanically remained unanswered until 1970 when Yuri Matiyasevich filled in the missing piece in Julia Robinson's proof. Matiyasevich used an ingenious reduction method to match up sequences in Robinson's theorem with a set of Turing machines. This showed that if Robinson's theorem was false you could solve the halting problem and since you can't solve the halting problem, then Robinson's theorem must be true. All this effort proved Diophantine equations have no general algorithmic solution. This was a hugely important result but, as we noted earlier, Fermat's Last Theorem is not, strictly speaking, a Diophantine. It is an exponential Diophantine equation. We still had no definitive answer to Fermat.

In 1972 Keijo Ruohonen and again in 1993, Christoph Baxa demonstrated that Diophantine equations with exponential terms could be rewritten as regular Diophantine equations with one additional complication – the necessity of adding an infinite set of terms to the end of the equation. In 1993, J.P. Jones of the University of Calgary showed the logic limit for regular Diophantine equations lies at thirteen unknowns. Matiyasevich had already pointed this out but never completed his proof. Since infinity is greater than thirteen, all exponential Diophantine equations are above the logic limit and, therefore, undecidable. Finally, we have a proof that Fermat's Last Theorem is unsolvable by a computer – or at least by a general purpose algorithm running on a computer. Matiyasevich went on to show many mathematical problems can be rewritten as exponential Diophantine equations and that much of mathematics is undecidable. For example, the Four Color Conjecture:

> *"Given an arbitrary map on a Euclidean plane, show the map can be colored in a maximum of four colors such that no adjacent area shares the same color."*

Meanwhile, Andrew Wiles, an English mathematics Professor at Princeton had been secretly working on Fermat's Last Theorem. When I say secretly, he had not told anyone in his department, and only told his wife late in 1993 when he suspected he might have a solution. He had been working on the problem a long time, having fallen in love with it at the age of 8! In 1995, after nearly 30 years work, he announced he

Four Colors is All You Need

had found a proof. He had solved an unsolvable problem, a problem that could not be answered by using a computer. Therefore, Andrew Wiles cannot be a computer!

As with all real-life stories, it was not quite as neat as this. It turned out Wiles' initial proof had an error in it, identified by one of his referees. Wiles had made an assumption about a particular number theory that had not been proven: it was still a conjecture. Working with another mathematician, he managed to prove this conjecture and so, two years after first announcing that he had solved Fermat's Last Theorem he could finally lay it to rest.

The Special Purpose Objection

Before I declare mankind's outright victory over computers, the Special Purpose Objection must be overcome. The objectors would argue that Wiles is a Special Purpose computer. Special Purpose computers are at no risk of breaking the Turing limit when they solve problems they have

> **Theorem (Undecidability of Hilbert's tenth problem)**
> There is no algorithm which, for a given arbitrary Diophantine equation, would tell whether the equation has a solution or not.

been programmed to answer. The objection misses the key point. I am not arguing *having* a solution to a given mathematical puzzle presents a difficulty to a computer; I am arguing a computer cannot *discover* one.

Take, for example, the search engine Google. If I type "where can I find the proof of Fermat's Last Theorem?" into the search box, it will retrieve a PDF of the proof as the third result. It appears this special purpose computer solved the problem. But you immediately see the difficulty. Google search already knew the answer, or more precisely had indexed the answer. The computer was not tackling a random problem from scratch. It was tackling a problem for which it knew the answer, or at least where an answer could be found. There is no sense in which the search engine discovered the proof.

To really understand this objection we need to examine exactly what Turing and Matiyasevich proved.

An arbitrary problem is one you do not already know the solution to when you write the algorithm. You can think of it as a variable. Is there an algorithm that can solve problem 'X'? The alternative is a special program. It can solve problem Y. Y is a problem it knows. It must have the solution coded somewhere within it in a computably expandable way. You might think of this as a table of constants; problem Y has solution 1, problem Z has solution 2, and so on. But it could be more subtle than that. Problem Y might have a solution which is encrypted so you cannot recognize it within the program, or it might even be the result of some chaotic equation so complex that the only way to see it is to run the program and watch the output: no form of program analysis will give you any clue as to what it produces. There is only one stipulation. The answer to problem Y MUST be held within the program as a computable algorithm. Put another way, the computer must already be 'programmed' to answer the question.

Could a human mathematician be pre-programmed from birth? Yes, there is no fundamental objection to this. Mathematicians could be born to solve the problems they solve. But this would present a couple of issues. Where is this program stored? And who, or what, programmed the mathematician? Could we perhaps find an experiment to determine whether mathematicians are pre-programmed?

One view held by philosophers is that the Universe programmed the mathematician. They believe we live in an entirely determined Universe with no free will. There is then no mystery as to how Andrew Wiles came up with his proof. He was destined to do it from the dawn of time. The ink that fell from his pen to the paper was always going to fall in just that way. We live in a clockwork Universe and although we might feel we have free will, this is an illusion. I simply don't believe this. If I am right and humans do exercise free will, Andrew Wiles cannot be a computer. And because Andrew is not alone in discovering proofs, those mathematicians cannot be computers either. Humans are, therefore, not computers.

The Chance Objection

I said there was no automatic way to solve any problem above the logic limit, but this is not quite true. There is one automatic method you could deploy to generate a non-computable proof, the infamous 'monkeys and typewriters' idea where we use random chance to generate information. Many people have suggested it is possible to write a play such as Shakespeare's *Hamlet* by simply typing random characters until we happened upon the play. The argument is flawed.

The first flaw is the process would take a super-astronomically long time. Even if every atom in the Universe were a monkey with a typewriter, it would take orders of magnitude longer than the age of the known Universe to come up with the script to a play or a mathematical proof.

The probability of finding a solution to Fermat's Last Theorem by chance is about 1 in $10^{50,000}$. That's 1 with 50,000 zeros after it. For a comparison, there are only 10^{120} atoms in the known Universe. To be, or not to be, certain of finding the proof, you would need to run a computer long enough to calculate all the possible proofs up to the length of Wiles' solution. Currently, a computer using every particle in the Universe clocked at the Plank interval – the fastest conceivable computer running at 10^{34} operations per second – would take 10^{500} times the age of the known Universe to do this. If someone tells you this is *astronomically* unlikely they are making a huge understatement. A computer running until the end-of-time would only scratch the surface.

The second flaw is even more damning. Even if the monkeys succeeded in generating something interesting, something else needs to spot this. If an algorithm stumbled upon a proof of Fermat's Last Theorem, what would recognize it as such? There are no ways to systematically analyze proofs. There are no mechanical methods that understand these.

"Well, this certainly buggers our plan to conquer the Universe."

Dalek Trouble

"All non-trivial abstractions, to some degree, are leaky."

Spolsky's Law
of Leaky Abstractions

Consequences

Machines cannot discover theorems using algorithms, yet mathematicians do it all the time. Do the rest of us break the logic limit? It seems we do. People appear creative – painting, composing, sculpting and so forth. But, are these endeavors creative in the mathematical sense. To prove this, ironically we need to find something outside mathematics that is definitely non-computable. This is tricky. Most artistic things are fuzzily defined and there are no written rules we can apply. How can we prove a work of art could not have been generated by a computer?

Trivial proofs exist but they are rather contrived. For example, it would *not* be possible to make a film with a solution to the still unproven Riemann Hypothesis on the blackboard in the background of a movie scene. All the mathematics *Good Will Hunting* had been already discovered before the movie was made. New mathematics cannot be accidentally generated by a set designer – unless, of course, they also happened to be a world class mathematician.

These trivial proofs might lead a mathematician to argue the theory is proven. There *are* some artworks which cannot be computed. QED. But these are not very satisfactory proofs. I could create almost any movie I wanted without tripping over this rule. What I really wanted to know is whether *Good Will Hunting* as a whole could have been generated by a computer. Not that some weird version with a particular mathematical proof on the blackboard is forbidden. Movies are a difficult subject for this argument, but music is much easier to analyze. It is linear, highly mathematical and largely uniform by culture and language. Yet it is universally appreciated. Is music a computational or a creative endeavor?

Is Music Computable

To prove a piece of music is non-computable requires two tests. First to show we can 'reduce' it to a problem that is already non-computable and, second, to demonstrate it 'looks like' or 'sounds like' a piece of music. An accountant would say it needs to pass 'the smell test'.

The first non-computable problem to be studied in depth was Emil Post's Word Problem. Post was a contemporary of Alan Turing and studied at the Institute of Advanced Mathematics in Princeton. He solved the Halting Problem six months before Turing, but his proof used a complex recursive method called the lambda calculus. Turing's method was far more practical, which is why we now refer to Turing machines rather than Post machines. Later in his career, Post came up with a branch of non-computable mathematics called 'Post Problems'. They look like a puzzle you might find in a newspaper. Imagine starting with the word 'camel' and being asked to turn it into 'aardvark', using only a few simple rules. We'll make the problem very easy to start with: cam ↔ aard and el ↔vark. This solution is obvious; just do the substitutions and you are there. But what if the rules were a little more complex? Gennadií Makanin, a Russian mathematician based at the University of Moscow, found a set of extremely simple puzzles that are nevertheless non-computable. Here is one:

{"CCBB" ↔ "BBCC", "BCCCBB" ↔
"CBBBCC", "ACCBB" ↔ "BBA", "ABCCCBB"
↔ "CBBA", "BBCCBBBBCC" ↔
"BBCCBBBBCCA"}

Word Problem

Can a computer tell us which word problems have a solution and which do not? The answer is 'no'. Word substitution puzzles are a class of non-computable problem. Martin Davis proved this in 1948. Using a reduction argument we can use these word problems to prove some music is also non-computable.

Let us start by substituting the notes of the musical scale for the letters of the alphabet to create a piece of 'music'. Since it is a direct analogue of the word problem, we have created a non-computable piece of music. It is definitely non-computable, but is it music? If it just looked like a random jumble of notes it would be unconvincing, but luckily there are many forms of music that look exactly like a word substitution puzzle. Bach's *Art of Fugue*, the canons of Tudor composers such as William Byrd and Thomas Tallis, and the works of Grieg all use sequences of chords that move from one to the next using substitution rules. If you were to listen to the steps in our word substitution music, they would definitely sound musical. I think they should pass the main artistic criticism – that they should not sound formulaic.

But is any actual human composition non-computable? Unfortunately, we cannot prove whether a particular piece of Bach, Tallis or Grieg is non-computable because we don't know the specific rules used to compose it. All we know are the general musical principles of harmony and counterpoint that applied at the time. We don't have these composers personal rule sets because they were held in their brain and they are, of course, long since dead. It is statistically likely that most pieces are non-computable because there are an uncountably infinite number of them, whereas computable pieces are merely countably infinite. But that's just probability; it is no proof.

I puzzled for some time whether there is a way to prove it but had to conclude it is impossible. However, and this is how creativity works, once I had given up on the problem, my brain continued to work on it. I was not conscious of this, I was only aware that failing to solve the problem annoyed me. I then had a Eureka moment. Although I couldn't *prove* a piece of music was non-computational, I could make one! – a piece that could not have been created using computation alone. This requires me to inoculate your brain.

Creative Inoculation

Take either Andrew Wiles proof of Fermat's Last Theorem or Alan Turing's proof of the Halting Problem; both proofs are non-computable. Each document is made up of symbols, the Roman alphabet and some special Greek symbols such as α, β, ζ, and so on. Let us write out the symbols in a table and assign a musical note to each. It is straightforward to put these notes into a synthesizer and play the piece of music. I have provided a link to such a piece. Warning: once you listen to this you will have been 'creatively inoculated'.

This resulting piece of music, based on the transliteration of a proof, is non-computable. You might immediately argue with this, "The piece of music was translated from proof text to music file using a computer. It is clearly computed.", but this is not my point. The music could not have come into existence in our Universe as a result of a computation. It is a computable translation of a non-computable string. It could not have been generated solely by a computer: It was done in two steps, the first of which could not have been computed.

If, up to this time, our Universe has never contained a piece of music that was generated non-computationally, it does now. If you listen to this piece, you will find it impossible not to be somewhat inspired by it. You cannot erase the experience from your memory. And once you have heard it you will have been creatively inoculated. I have defeated Daniel Dennett and his like, and given you creative freedom!

www.jamestagg.com/noncompmusic

Having made at least some music above the Turing limit I could declare victory but I want to go further. Using the same reduction method, I believe we can show all art is above the limit. First let's attempt novels and plays. Do you enjoy those crime novels by Agatha Christie and Colin Dexter? It must be possible to construct a plot sufficiently complex, and a murder sufficiently baffling that it exceeds the logic limit. I could keep extending this idea to provide any number of examples and, therefore, prove all art and creative output is above the logic limit.

There are many other arts we could apply this argument too. In the visual domain there are non-computable images. In principle, it is possible, to draw or paint things beyond the capability of a computer. Roger Penrose has created non-computable visual puzzles such as tiling an infinite plain with special jigsaw pieces. Creating an image containing a solution to his visual puzzle is non-computable.

This extension argument also applies to me. There is an argument that I am a finite being and therefore can be simulated by a computer. Since I can be simulated by a computer, I am the same as a computer and therefore incapable of non-computable thought. The argument is as follows: James Tagg will have during his life a finite number of inputs and, equally, a finite set of outputs. This means you could model me using a

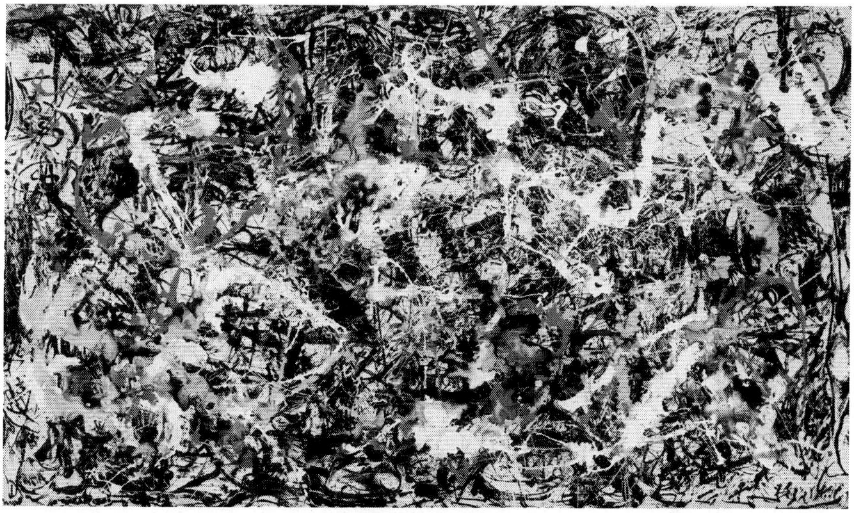

Jackson Pollock

computer. You could simply create a table of all the possible inputs and all the possible outputs I would make and this would be a perfect facsimile of me. A number of people have posed this as an argument to refute Roger Penrose's assertion that humans are capable of non-computable thought.

But this analysis misses a key point. There is no way to calculate all the contents of this table. My past could be tabulated. It is the history of all the things I ever did, but my future cannot. I might yet discover some great theorem that could not be computably generated. This would be a part of my output which could not be generated by an algorithm or any mechanical process. This forms a non-computational arrow of time; we can write down the past, we cannot write out the future. If a creative person such as Andrew Wiles could be simulated in advance, we would have an automatic way to find a solution to Fermat's Last Theorem. Since this is not possible, it follows that creative people cannot be simulated. This also means the Turing test is not passable by a machine. Humans can create; machines cannot. That is the difference.

Will Computers Take over the World?

Ray Kurzweil, the American inventor and futurologist, has suggested computers are getting exponentially faster and will soon reach such immense power they became effectively infinitely powerful. They could instantly answer any question posed and solve all our engineering problems. He dubs this point 'the singularity': a point of near infinite

Watson and Our Future?

computing power and therefore universal knowledge. This could herald a Utopian future; global warming, cancer, all things of the past. But computers might just as easily become bored and determine we humans are the real problem. If we are lucky, they may treat us as amusing pets. If we are unlucky...

These consequences might have come to pass if the answer to the Halting Problem were 'yes', but as the answer is 'no'! This is not the future we face.

Mummy, where do Bugs Come From?

One consequence of the logic limit provides a theoretical basis for the origin of computer bugs. The mention of 'bug' conjures up stories of dead creepy crawlies stuck in early computer circuits, but the term had been in use for over 150 years before the computer was even invented. Bugs are not simply annoying mistakes.If you misspell my name as Stagg instead of Tagg that's just carelessness. Real flaws creep into a computer program when you fail to understand Brooks' essential complexity, or by my terminology, you stray above the logic limit without realizing it.

Imagine we have created a piece of software. The software goes into test and is subjected to a range of use cases. Some of these will fail because we did not take into account all the real world possibilities. Then a strange thing happens. We get trapped in a loop of patching the errors in the program in a rather mechanical way. Find an error, patch it. Find another, create a work-around, and so on. By doing this, we are effectively mechanically generalizing our solution. This is forbidden as it breaks the Turing limit, so we can't mechanically solve a general logic problem above the logic limit. We need instead to use intuitive or creative thought. In our panic we did not stop, take a step back and engage our brain. Instead, we attempted, unsuccessfully, to blindly hack our way through the problem.

If we eventually succeeded in perfecting the code this way, we would have broken a fundamental law of the Universe. Something nasty would have to happen to prevent it, such as rupturing the space-time continuum or an event equally horrible! Luckily something prevents this and keeps our Universe intact – BUGS! Bugs stop us breaking Turing's limit.

The next time you curse a bug, remember if they didn't exist you'd be in danger of causing a logical paradox. There is no problem in redefining the domain and then creatively producing an all-encompassing design, but, you can't patch and hack your way there. This theory of bugs leads to an explanation for some modern programming rules of thumb.

Written specifications are valuable because they force you to lay out *the whole* problem. You don't need to be detailed regarding the depth, but should be expansive about the breadth, covering all the logical complexity. This might result in many details as a by-product, but a specification needs to delineate the edges of the problem space and not simply focus on a few key points.

Writing the tests for the software in advance is helpful as it is likely to tell you early whether your design encompasses the whole problem space.

Also, building a prototype, throwing it away, and then building the real thing can help greatly. It may be the only way to examine the edges of the problem space in detail. Armed with a full understanding, you can then imagine solutions to the complete problem in a single creative sitting. Whatever techniques you use to improve the quality of your software, remember you are engaged in a creative process that is not, itself, open to automation.

The Art of Programming

Programming is an art: a creative endeavor. It is also, of course, highly scientific. When you work with a good programmer – and I have been fortunate to work with some of the best in the world – they all follow a similar process. First they talk with you at length about your needs

Geek Humor

and examine the full scope of the problem space. Even if you say, "Oh don't worry about that bit," they always will. They want to know about everything. Then, they write a high-level list of features, some simple block diagrams, and occasionally a flow chart, only then do they begin to code, ticking off the list as they go. Sometimes, they will check to see if their list is the same as your list but more often they will come back and just check the high-level purpose. "If I give you something that achieves this, will that do it for you?" They test as they code so you end up with is something that meets your high-level purpose, and can prove it does so in its own right. At the end of the coding they write out the specification for the project so that they can remember what they did, or a colleague can pick it up in the future.

This is *not* how students are taught. Students are told to write a detailed specification at the start and then simply implement it. If you've been following my argument, they are being taught to do something impossible! There is no 'just' to programming. Sometimes teams are even split up so that one person writes the specification and another the code – again an impossible task. If the specification was the *answer* to the problem, it must have required creative thought to develop and so would be as complex as the program itself. Since it is not yet a program you cannot test it, so it becomes an untestable solution to a creative problem. Since the specification is *not* the answer but rather a general list of tasks, the great danger is to give it to a separate programmer and

they implement it mechanically. You see, of course, the problem. It will be riddled with bugs because they have missed the creative step of imagining the whole problem and solving it in the round.

This fundamental misconception of software is common in many organizations. "Ah," says the finance director, "I'll write a very detailed spec and then we can get someone cheap to *just* program it." This does not work. If the finance director has done the creative work of taking a problem and turning it into a detailed specification for the programmer to 'just program' – removing any ambiguity and therefore the creative overhead – he will have all but written software himself, albeit in a computer language of his own making. On the other hand, if the specification is a linear list of issues with no creative thought, he will not have reduced the time needed to program. He may have improved the quality by effectively getting a second pair of eyes onto the requirements gathering stage, but this does not help the programming effort itself.

Ideally, you should never split up specification and coding. It is a creative process best handled by very small numbers of people working intensively on it. Of course, there is one big problem with this: some software tasks are huge. Before we look at the science of splitting up a software project, it is worth pointing out that many of the most famous projects were written by one man. I have met many of these people and they are all exceptional – Linus Torvalds, Linux; Anthony Minessale, FreeSWITCH; Daniel-Constantin Mierla, Kamailio; Eric Allman, ,SendMail. Before splitting a project between many people, it is worth considering whether you can give it to just one individual. To do this you will need to unload this person of ALL interruptions and administrative burdens. This is the most effective way to solve a creative programming task. Practically, once your task is over the limit for a single human, a software project must be split up. This requires great care. Dividing a problem efficiently means specifying the interfaces between them and decoupling the components. This is the art of an architect or a producer in the creative arts. The creative process operates similarly in other walks of life. There are many examples of successful creative duos – Rogers and Hammerstein (*The Sound of Music*), Ben Elton and Richard Curtis (*Blackadder*).

Good managers, therefore, find ways to break projects into manageable sub-projects that can be worked by pairs or rely on single super-programmers with support around them. If you are lucky enough to gather together a group of super-programmers and can divide a problem efficiently amongst them, you can achieve great things. You see this pipeline in movie production. A script writer generates a script creatively. The casting director finds the actors, a director is in charge of filming, and an editor puts it together. In very great movies you will often find a great director or producer who had a hand in almost everything holding it all together. They are often accused of micro-managing but you can see that's what they must do. They are the super-programmer with the whole creative work in their head, and an eye on the audience and financial backers.

If you talk with great programmers you will be amazed by their breadth of technical, commercial and product knowledge. Why do they need all this commercial information to do their job in the round?

Rules and Tips

I began writing some rules on how to split up a project, and almost immediately ran into exceptions and special cases. The job of dividing things into sub-tasks is, itself, a creative problem and must not be done mechanically. Any 'one size fits all' rule will fail and you must apply domain knowledge and careful thought to the process.

It is the job of architects or a senior engineer to split projects into smaller chunks. To do this they must accurately 'guess' boundaries between subtasks to create self-contained, creatively solvable problems. This can be done by either vertical or horizontal abstraction. Both have their problems.

Horizontal abstraction is the simpler of the two to understand, and the more common. Computer systems are built 'on the shoulders of giants'. That is to say we no longer need to place individual pixels onto the computer screen. We can assume a computer will draw a square if we specify the dimension and coordinates of the center. That's abstraction. Today's computers are even more helpful. We can ask them to draw a rotating cube lit from a certain angle and the computer will do the whole job for us. But, there are always practical limitations to this.

I want my cubes to move around the screen naturally but I am not sure what physics model has been implemented. What will happen when they bump into each other? If the abstraction is not thoroughly thought through they pass through each other in a very odd way, breaking up and showing me they are really made of triangles, the illusion of three dimensions is lost. Whenever we work at an abstract level, we risk being exposed to its inner guts at some point. Joel Spolsky, a computer scientist who worked on Microsoft Excel, proposed the Law of Leaky Abstractions to explain this. An example of his law in action is the TCP/IP protocol stack that transports data over the Internet. The stack is hugely reliable, yet I have to debug one of these stacks at least four times a year!

The problem is that the TCP (Transmission Control Protocol) is designed to provide reliable delivery of information: internet pages, my bank account and the like. But, the internet protocol 'IP' on which it relies is only designed for best-efforts. When a link loses a packet of information, the TCP has to retransmit it. This takes additional time. TCP provides an abstraction of a reliable connection, but the implementation is not as robust as it may seem, and the details leak through as variable latency and throughput. This explains why your web pages sometimes do not completely render. You are told it is reliable, but often it is not! Experience is so valuable to a programmer because they know which of these specifications to take with a pinch of salt and when they are likely to leak. They are battle scarred by previous naivety.

I think Spolsky's Law follows from Rice's Theorem and ultimately from Turing's no halting proof. If leak-less abstraction was possible you could, in principle, write a recursive partial halting solution. By layering abstraction on top of abstraction you would be able to solve some very complex problems, eventually including the Halting Problem. We know this is impossible, so non-leaky abstraction cannot exist.

The other method of splitting software is vertically. This is often done following the natural boundaries of an organization: functional or geographic. Again there will be leakage between the systems; the data you get from the finance department might not be detailed enough for

Specification Cartoon

the engineers or vice versa, and so groups have to interact. The main problem with vertically divided software is each group tends to reinvent the wheel, so you end up with multiple similar implementations of the same thing.

All said, the architectural job in software is a dynamic one. You can split up software into separate elements but you must take into account the leakage between them. When you detect a leak you must bring people together to collaboratively solve the problem, rather than insisting on the original partitioning. While doing all this you must keep track of the overall aim and all the irritating small details contained in the many

lists that form the project specification. I should confess that I am no great fan of specifications, because they can mislead you into thinking you've solved the problem, but I concede a good specification is helpful. Spolsky's Second Law is 'Always write a specification.' Engineers should collaboratively write the specification as a response to the desires of the project creators. But they must not blindly implement the specification they've been handed. They must not forget the creative element.

The Role of 'Process' in Creativity

We hear a lot about 'process' when developing software and other creative tasks. The first thing to realize is process does not write software and every moment spent on process is a moment not writing software. Excessive process can bring the productivity of the average programmer down from a thousand lines per day to one. On the other hand, we all know that using no process to write software results in useless software. Good solo programmers, playwrights or composers are surrounded by lists and post-it notes full of process. Where is the balance to be struck?

In my view 'process' is there to help humans with the tasks we find naturally difficult. Humans, as we know, are dreadful at remembering lists of symbolic information. Give a human ten numbers to memorize and they will quickly forget them. Give Microsoft Excel ten numbers and it will remember them forever, or, at least, until your next upgrade! So the first job of process is to collect lists of things and sometimes even lists of those lists.

Another significant affliction affecting humans is procrastination. We tend to put off decisions. Process can set waypoints; when will the job of splitting a project occur, when will we begin the test, and so on.

The third job of process is to keep track of the division of labor – if the project has to be divided. Who will do what? Essentially we are back to lists again.

The most important job of process, in my view, is to keep track of scope. 'Logical scope creep' when unrecognized destroys software projects. Scope creep is fine if it just adds more linear work. "Could we add three more product types?" "Could you do another language?" "Can you make this interface prettier, less cluttered?" It may cause a busy team to groan, but it does not damage the integrity of the design. To put it back in Brooks' language, accidental creep is fine – provided you add some resource. Essential creep is not. Adding the french language prompts to a project in English might be fine, putting language translation into a project may be a step too far. The project may have strayed into a different logical class. Increases in logical scope often require redesign, you must stop and re-architect if you are to avoid bugs in plague like quantities.

If programming software is a creative task, how can we help improve productivity? The most important factor is to provide uninterrupted peace and quiet. Programming is a task where people need to hold many ideas in their head at the same time, and this requires deep concentration. To get some idea of the creative process at work, listen to the excellent TED lecture by John Cleese.

A common and costly mistake is to put off thinking about a class of things you are going to need in the next release because of time pressure. 'Time out, that's for the next release' and similar statements spell disaster for the future of a project as when you come to the next release, you may have to rewrite much of it from scratch. This is why good architects are so valuable. They anticipate the future even when they are told to ignore it and ship now!

Just as there are artistic geniuses, there are programming geniuses. Hold onto them if you get one. They are rare. We don't know if they can be made or they are lucky accidents, but statistics shows that some people are 1000 times more productive at writing code than the average. If you can find lots of them and make them work together you will build the next Google or Facebook. If you have a tight deadline, a super-programmer may get you out of a hole, producing in a week what might otherwise take a year. Remember your great programmers will most prolific if you can get process and distraction out of their way. Just make sure they have a clear idea of purpose.

Laws

A programmer interrupted eight times a day does no work.

A creative person interrupted eight times a day does no work.

Programming is a creative endeavor.

There are creative geniuses. Hold onto them.

Bugs save us from collapsing space-time when we are lazy and try to use mechanical means rather than creative thought to write software.

Chapter 12

HYPER-COMPUTING

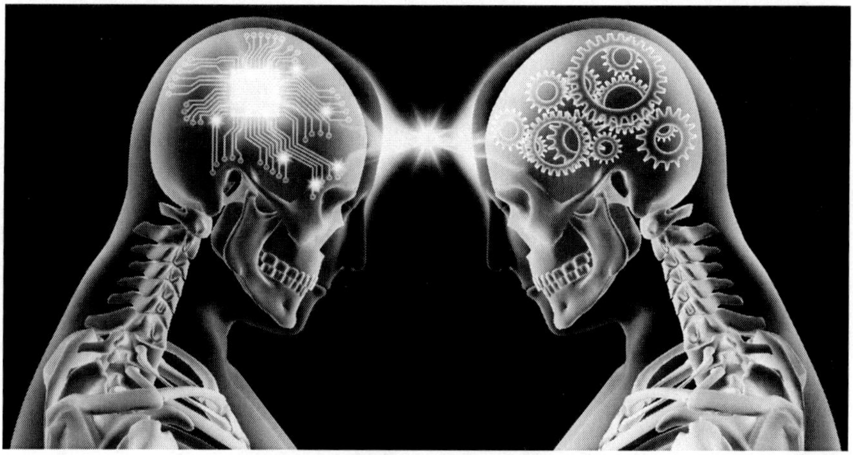

What's in a Brain

Perpetual Motion from the 1600s

"If you are in a spaceship that is travelling at the speed of light, and you turn on the headlights, does anything happen?"

Stephen Wright

If you believe humans outthink computers, be warned; you are in controversial territory. This would need a hyper-computer and many scientists speak of these in the same breath as perpetual motion machines.

I'm not sure it's an entirely fair analogy. We understand machines, and the physical laws of our Universe forbid perpetual motion. We don't understand brains, so we can't reasonably dismiss human hyper-computing. Humans commonly demonstrate one clear example of thinking which appears to break the Turing limit, namely finding solutions to mathematical puzzles. We need an explanation for this. Let me take you on a whistle-stop tour of all the schemes people have imagined that might lead to a hyper-computer.

A hyper-computer is a machine that can calculate a function which a Turing machine can not. For example, when given a number denoting a problem such as Fermat's Last Theorem, it can give me in return a number representing a valid proof. We are not concerned here with speed. We are talking about fundamental 'do-ability'. Such machines are often dubbed 'super-Turing'.

Epic Fails

Let us first look at some proposals that blatantly fail. My children call these 'epic fails', and they are the perpetual motion machines of the hyper-computing world.

Could we run many Turing machines at the same time, perhaps even an infinite number? Then we would have a much more powerful machine that must beat the Turing limit.

The answer is no.

Turing machines are already infinitely powerful and we know from our chapter on infinity that all countable infinities are the same. Infinity plus infinity, infinity times infinity, infinity to any power; all are equal. One single, fast, one-dimensional machine can simulate them all. We get no greater power with an infinite number of similar machines.

The next technique which might realize a hyper-computer is to have a machine which simultaneously runs every possible branch in a program. Each time the machine gets to a point where there is a binary decision, it can take the 'yes' branch, spawn a copy of itself, and run the 'no' branch as well. Logically this machine should be able to calculate anything since it tries *every* conceivable option. The process is called non-determinism. This doesn't mean the computer has free will. It just means the computer never chooses one option over another. It just assumes each could be correct and travels down both. Solving a problem using a machine like this can be fast. The problem is this machine has no greater power than a regular Turing machine. Let me show you why.

A non-deterministic machine is essentially the same as a single Turing machine; each time there is a branch in the program you would start running two processes. The first process works on every even tick of the computer clock and the other on every odd tick. Now we have a single machine running two branches at the same time. Using this trick over and over again, a single machine can run a program exploring every possible branch. Although it generates an enormous number of branches and takes a huge time to run, it is still a single machine and we have an infinity of time on our hands. Therefore, the machine is limited as before.

We are not doing well so far and we have already exhausted an infinite number of options! Let's try a different tack. We know true randomness is non-computable, the sort of randomness generated by the Lavarand we examined earlier in the book. Might this help? Truly random processes can't be simulated by a computer. If we throw this into the pot might it let us compute something a Turing machine cannot?

Again, no.

This idea still only generates a machine as powerful as the non-deterministic machine above. A non-deterministic Turing machine runs *every* possible program. All a random one does is choose *some* of the same paths at random. It, therefore, can't be any *more* powerful. The one difference is that it can generate non-computable numbers. However, the only interesting characteristic of these numbers is they are truly random and this randomness was an input. Their presence does not make the machine any more powerful.

There are quite a few proposals for hyper-computers that are just cleverly dressed up versions of the machines we have already met and dismissed. For example, it has been proposed the Internet could form a super-Turing machine. This is known as a site machine because the processing is distributed across many sites linked together through the Internet. It is proposed each site could act as an oracle to the others. This is quite an elegant idea, and some proofs have been offered that show such a machine is capable of generating non-computable functions. The problem with this idea is that you can simply draw an imaginary line around the whole site machine and it looks exactly like a big Turing machine. There is no conceptual difference between such a machine and a regular computer with subroutines. After all, that's in Turing's original proof. Again we have reached a dead end. We need something qualitatively different to a traditional computer in order to break the Turing limit. The obvious place to turn is the quantum world.

Quantum Computers

Quantum computers have had an extraordinary run in the press recently. It has been variously claimed they offer limitless computing power and can break all known security schemes; cracking, for example, the prime factors that form the basis of public key cryptography. This is big news. These codes are used to protect all the financial transactions we make on the web.

In a regular computer, bits of information are processed by switches that make simple 'yes' or 'no' decisions. In a quantum computer each switch can take both the yes and no branches, at least for a short time called the decoherence interval. The calculations are said to be superposed. This allows a quantum computer to calculate exponentially, rather than linearly, as the number of logic gates increases. Grover's algorithm and Shor's algorithm use this superposition to speed up factoring numbers and looking things up in databases, respectively.

Grover's algorithm gives us the ability to find something stored in a random place without having to look in every box. If you think about a standard search, say for your lost car keys, you must look everywhere to guarantee finding them. It does not much matter in what order you do it. When you are halfway through the search, you will be 50% likely to have found your keys. But, with a quantum computer, you can be fuzzy and look in many places at once. A quarter of the way through a quantum search, you are 50% likely to have found your keys. That might sound like a small improvement, but when working with very big numbers, it makes an enormous difference.

Shor's algorithm works a little differently and, yes, it does allow a quantum computer to break Internet encryption, so the newspaper headlines are true up to a point. Some time in the future we will need to move to a more secure type of encryption.

The largest quantum computers today can process 300 qubits at a time or remain 'coherent' for about two seconds. These results are pitifully low. The largest prime number factored so far is 143, a mere 7 bits long! By way of comparison, internet security routinely uses 1024 bits. But, quantum computers are improving exponentially faster than classical computers: They really do change the rules of the game. If you remember our discussion of chess, the quantity of space needed for a calculation can be the limiting factor. A quantum computer is very space efficient. When the computer branches and makes a copy of itself, it does so without needing more space. There are two theories for how it does this, (well, three, but the third is highly controversial). The first theory is the computer doesn't need the space because it hasn't made its mind up yet; somehow the calculation floats in an undecided state. The second is that the computer puts a copy of itself in a parallel Universe each time it branches. When the calculation is over, either all the Universes collapse to a decision, or *every* possibility is chosen in some Universe or other and they all go on their merry way! This is the 'many-worlds' interpretation of quantum mechanics and we will return to it later in the book.

We have now explored all the straightforward ways to make a hyper-computer, and all have failed. We need something still more exotic.

More Horse Power Needed

Is there anything more powerful than a Turing machine?

Yes, in theory, there is.

The first person to explore ways of breaking the Turing limit was Turing himself. He cut right through the problem by proposing the existence of an oracle function. At any point in a computation, you could ask this function a question and it would give you the right answer.

We must leave completely aside the question of how this wonderful oracle function is constructed. All we know is it can't be a machine. If it really existed, a Turing machine that was able to consult it would be able to answering any question you put to it. That is a hyper-computer.

Unfortunately having access to such an oracle does not get us far. We can use it to compute numbers we could not otherwise have obtained – or answer a single question – but it does not give us a general-purpose way to solve further problems outside of the logical area we asked it to answer.

Each time the oracle answers a question we break the limit a tiny bit. Each question and each answer moves us forward, but does not give us something universally applicable. If I ask the oracle to prove Fermat's Last Theorem it will give me that answer, but this does not turn me into a creative mathematician, able to prove any other theory. You can test this by typing a mathematical question into the Google search box. Does obtaining an answer make you better at mathematics?

In any case, an oracle is not and cannot be a machine, so it does not lead us any further in our quest to build something super-Turing.

The Weird and Wonderful

There are some really weird and wonderful proposals for machines capable of super-Turing thought. Let's take a bit of a flight of fantasy.

If we could make a spaceship survive the inhospitable environment near a spinning black hole, it might be possible to send information backward in time. We could see the answer to a calculation before we had to go to the trouble of calculating it in the first place.

Black Hole Malament-Holgarth Space

David Malament and Mark Hogarth of the University of California, Irvine have proposed a form of space-time called the Kerr Metric. This allows a machine to break the Turing limit, but has the drawback that as it does so it falls through the event horizon and is sucked into the black hole. We might discover new information but are now trapped inside the event horizon unable to communicate it – a form of cosmic censorship.

Candidates for a hyper-computer that could fit inside a human brain include mathematical curiosities which stretch the concept of infinity. The easiest to understand is the Zeno machine. In a Zeno machine a computer runs each successive step of a calculation in half the time of the previous step. The computer can pack an infinite quantity of computation into each finite time interval and can therefore outperform a Turing machine. This theory fails at a practical level because we simply can't build such a machine.

There are numerous weird suggestions for mathematical super-Turing machines, and many are described on the Internet. They all fit broadly within the two models above: modifications to space-time or peculiar mathematical paradoxes. The inspiration for the true solution to super-Turing thought may lay in there somewhere, but there are some more plausible proposals to look at next.

Plausible Ideas

I have characterized the next set of ideas as plausible, but they may still be highly controversial. My only criteria for plausibility are that the mechanism must outperform a machine limited to counting numbers, and it might fit inside our skulls. No black holes allowed.

One interesting proposal for a super-Turing machine that could fit inside our skulls is the Adaptive Recurrent Neural Network, 'ARNN' proposed by Hava Siegelmann of the University of Massachusetts, Amherst. An ARNN is a neural network with real number weights. As you recall, real numbers are equivalent to the continuum infinity, a larger infinity than that of counting numbers.

This is the infinity that defeats a Turing machine, and Siegelmann harnesses it as the basis of her computing machine. She argues that, although the machine cannot be programmed as it is impossible to write real numbers down, once it is running, the weights diverge and real numbers will be used within the network. These real numbers allow the machine to compute using numbers that are not, themselves, computable and this is where the machine's greater power comes from. Of course such a thing might easily fit inside our skulls, and the physics within our brains are certainly capable of using real analogue values.

The biggest stumbling block for Siegelmann's idea is the information that gives her machines their power is fine-grained and easily destroyed by noise in the environment. This is not just from the sort of electrical noise we hear when our cell phones interfere with the radio, but the precision required by her machines is so exacting that anything might interfere with them. For example, gravitational waves caused by the motions of nearby stars would disturb calculations at only the fiftieth decimal place. Since it is these digits that constitute the difference between an ARNN and a regular Turing machine, most people conclude ARNNs can't work. There is one effect stemming from the quantum world which might come to the rescue. The potential to do something in the quantum world is sufficient to modify the behavior of a system even if the system does not actually do that specific thing. This is called a counterfactual process. The possibility an ARNN might perform infinite precision calculations may be enough to give the machine the edge, even though in practice it is disturbed by noise. This is speculation upon speculation, but interesting nevertheless.

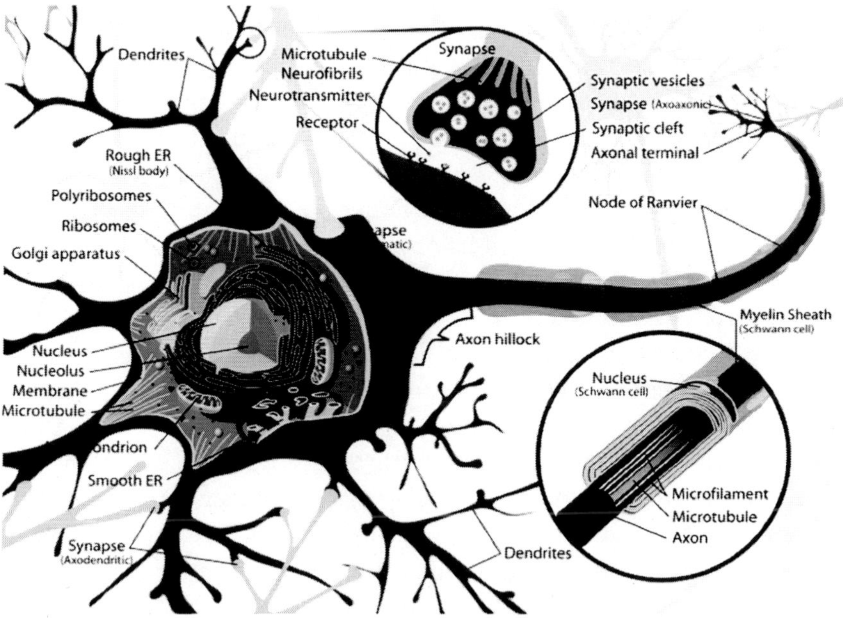

Neurons and Microtubules

Roger Penrose is fascinated by such counterfactual experiments and is inspired to think such effects might have a role in non-computable thought. It is his 'machines' we will look at next.

Penrose-Hameroff Machines, aka Brains

Roger Penrose of Oxford University and Stuart Hameroff of the University of Arizona have proposed a very different way to understand the workings of the brain. They focus on the much smaller scale structures within neurons called tubulin microtubules. If you watch a brain form, the dendrites grow towards each other, twisting and turning rather like the growth of a plant as viewed in a slow motion nature film. This motion is controlled by micro-tubular structures formed of a protein called tubulin. Tubulin is made from peanut-shaped polar molecules that self-assemble into helical tubes with a radius of just seven molecules. The tubes bundle together to form the backbone of neurons. The peanut-shaped molecules are bipolar switches and can flip between two states. This allows them to bend into different shapes and, in the most extreme example, to flap fast enough to propel small organisms such as paramecia. It is also, interestingly, the protein that unzips the double helix when a cell divides, and so plays a fundamental role in our evolution.

Penrose and Hameroff suggest these tubes form the true processing element in our brains. The walls of the tubes are formed of successive alpha and beta tubulin molecules. Each of the tubulin molecules can flip between two states, propagating a ripple along the tube wall. The scale is small enough for quantum effects to matter, and Hameroff suggests quantum error correction keeps the ripples from decohering too fast. Because the processing is happening at a molecular level rather than at the scale of a neuron, the brain would be considerably more powerful than a count of its neurons would suggest. They propose increased computing power would stem from three sources: There are many more tubulin molecules than neurons; the micro-tubes could perform quantum computation, and the micro-tubes are capable of non-computable, conscious, thought.

Measurement of a quantum process is the only candidate we have for a non-deterministic physical process today; all other physical processes are deterministic. Penrose argues that quantum processing in the brain spontaneously collapses in decision making because of the interaction between quantum superposition and gravity. The arguments are put forward in two books: *The Emperor's New Mind* and *Shadows of the Mind*. This theory remains controversial for two main reasons. First, most people see no need for super-Turing thought. They believe computers are sufficient. Second, they believe the brain is not a hospitable place for quantum effects: it is too hot and too chaotic. Indeed, until recently people assumed quantum effects would have no place in biological entities, but this orthodoxy has recently been overthrown by the discovery of quantum processes in photosynthesis. The paper by Travis Craddock of Nova and others suggests there may also be quantum structures in the neurons of our brains and we might possess quantum computers after all. But, remember, Penrose and Hameroff don't only need quantum coherence within our brain to explain consciousness. They also need gravitational effects.

Chapter 13

HYPER-COMMUNICATION

World Wide Communication

"The single biggest problem in communication is the illusion that it has taken place."

George Bernard Shaw

Each Christmas I buy the *Private Eye* annual (an English satirical magazine) only to be slightly disappointed when much of the humor falls flat, yet I can watch the TV current affairs quiz 'Have I Got News for You' featuring its editor and be reduced to tears of laughter. Being at a live recording of the show is even more powerful. Why is this? Why is the experience and effect so different? Is it just the sense of occasion when I go to a live show or is there something more to shared experience?

We appear to learn more from lectures delivered in person than reading the lecturer's book, or even watching the same lecture recorded on video. Studies show children who are read to by their parents do better than if they are left to follow along with a CD. Two groups of children were tested on two made-up words used in a story. The children read to by their parents had an 80% recall rate, while children who followed the CD only 17%. This is a big disparity. The simplest explanation is that the children who were read to pay more attention. Are there other effects?

IMAX

Most scientists believe communication between humans is classical: words spoken in proximity have no more power than had we carefully written out what we wanted to say. Body language and tone of voice are simply useful tools to aid the transmission of this information. I'm going to explore the ways in which human face-to-face communication might exceed this traditional classical model. Let us look first at the bandwidth of communication between people.

Bandwidth

Let me give you a mental picture for what I mean by bandwidth. Imagine I am sitting in a darkened theatre enjoying one of my favorite comedians at the Edinburgh Festival – the biggest arts festival in the world. I phone a friend who is also a fan and let them listen in. Perhaps I even use the camera and surreptitiously point the phone at the comedian. My live experience is digitized, compressed and transmitted over the mobile network to my friend. He gets the same experience but at much-reduced bandwidth.

My friend has a similar but qualitatively different experience to mine. He cannot hear the degrees of loud and soft I hear, nor the full range of high and low frequencies forming the timbre of the comedian's voice; no sense of the smell of old armchairs or the heat of the audience around me. He is spared the strange stickiness my shoes meet on the floor of the auditorium and the occasional slosh of beer that hits me from a slightly inebriated neighbor. For the person at the other end of the phone, their view is of a tiny two-dimensional screen about 4 by 3 inches square. Of course, they can enlarge the picture, but then the pixilation dominates and it looks like an impressionist picture viewed close up. He has nothing like the same intensity of experience. Loss of bandwidth is something we can study mathematically and the reduction is enormous.

Video and Audio

The image of the comedy show is digitized by the camera and microphone; the video at 384,000 bits per second and the audio at 64,000 bps. Mathematical compression will be applied and the video will shrink to 30,000 while the audio drops down to 4,700. After compression, the whole experience amounts to around 40,000 bits per second. To put it in some perspective, a DVD would be 11.5 million bits per second, nearly 300 times the bandwidth.

My in-person experience has much higher bandwidth than even a DVD. It may even have infinite bandwidth. Physicists argue whether space-time is quantized but, for now, we will look at what would be needed to reproduce the experience faithfully on modern digital recording equipment.

Digitization

When something is converted to digital form, it goes through a number of steps. First, some way must be found to chop the thing into small parts in space and time. Then each of these parts is sampled with a sensor to give an electrical signal and, finally, this signal is measured and turned into a number.

Old microphones used carbon granules. As the sound waves passed through them, the granules were shaken and made better contact with each other. Connecting a battery across the granules gave a varying voltage. Modern microphones use a variety of technologies. The preference of most recording artists today is the electret microphone. A coil moves inside a magnet generating a varying voltage which is translated into a voltage as before.

Next we use a fast running clock and measure the voltage on each tick giving us a sequence of numbers. We have created a near perfect record of the sound, and we can prove this by recreating the sound through a loudspeaker. This is what happens every time you listen to your iPod.

To digitize film, each frame must be split in space as well as time. On each tick of the clock, a process scans left to right and top to bottom to form a one-dimensional stream of numbers that records the image. The system cuts the picture up into little elements called pixels, standing for picture elements. Each small square has its average color measured for red, green, and blue content coded as a number.

Digitization techniques have become the dominant way electronics work in the home, and digitization circuits are now ubiquitous.

Reality

How big is reality? Setting aside for a moment the problem that it might be infinite, we need to reproduce all the elements that go to make it up.

A normal DVD has an image of 720 by 576 pixels with 16 bits of color depth and a frame rate of 25 frames per second. The eye, however, is considerably better than this and a DVD does not fool it. HD video is 1900 by 1000 pixels with 32 bits of color depth and 100 frames per second. This is a great deal better – if you enjoy watching sport or nature documentaries, the additional resolution is amazing. This still falls far short of reality. An IMAX theatre gives a wrap-around image of about 10,000 by 7,000 pixels and comes closer to the average resolution of the human eye, estimated at about 30,000 by 20,000 pixels. But the eye cheats. It concentrates the rods and cones in the central portion of the retina. Although IMAX achieves the average pixel density of your eye, it comes nowhere near the peak density which is nearly 10,000 times greater.

For a truly equivalent experience, we would need about 320 million pixels *per* eye at a frame rate of 120 frames per second, allowing us full stereo synthesis. At this speed and resolution, we are matching the visual acuity of the eye and should be able to fool it completely. But there is one more problem to overcome: The image is not interactive. Move your head in the real world and the image will change. The objects in the foreground will vary their position in relation to the background, so-called motion parallax. Try it now, move your head and you will see that the book, or screen you are reading moves in relation to the background. In a simple digitized 3D image this will not happen. You *will* have a 3D image but you will not have a *real* image, a light field.

To create a real image you need to view a hologram or use head-tracking technology. A hologram records the light waves given off by an object in multiple directions rather than just the intensity of the light striking the camera through a single focal point. When you shine a laser back through the hologram, it regenerates the light waves as they would have originally come from the object. That light can be viewed from different directions, giving the impression of three dimensions rather than a mere two-dimensional photograph. There is often a limitation in viewing angle because the original photographic plate must wrap all the way around an object to capture the full 3D light field, but the illusion is very convincing.

A more effective way to create a real experience – and one with no restriction on viewing angle – is to construct the image in a computer and track the movement of your head. The computer can create the two-dimensional images each eye would see if the scene were truly three-dimensional. Computer software resolves motion parallax and a host of other elements, but to do so the computer must understand a model of the world so it can calculate how the scene would look from a particular angle and in the appropriate lighting. Some recent games such as Activision's 'Call of Duty' do this, and the experience is compelling.

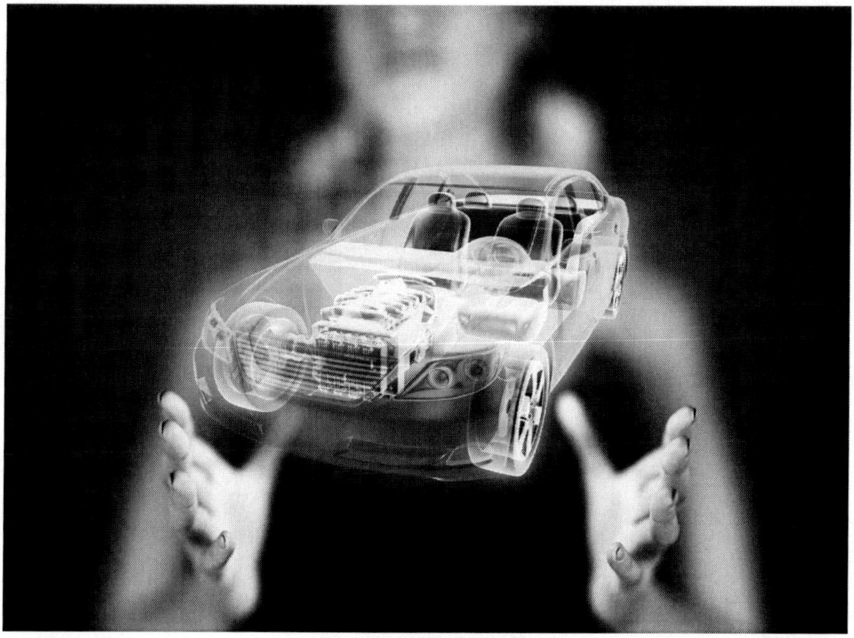

Hologram

There are still problems. The image is stereo but planar. All the light coming into your eye comes from the screen a meter or so away. In the real world objects need you to change the focal length of your eye to bring them into sharp focus depending on their proximity. Try looking at your hand as you move it towards and away from your face, too close and your eye can't pull focus any further and it will blur. This mismatch between focal depth and the apparent distance implied by motion parallax is one of the reasons you can get headaches watching 3D images. There is something not quite right about them and your eye has to learn a new behavior.

Audio Field

Our poor friend at the end of the phone is listening to a mere 4700 bits per second rendition of the comedian. A compact disk is 64,000, 16-bit samples per second in stereo, over a million bits per second. So the information content of a mobile phone call is very low. It is a miracle you can understand speech at all over such a narrow channel, but this is made possible by two factors. First, human speech uses a limited range of frequencies. All the information in our voices lies within about two octaves centered on middle C. And, second, you can perform some clever mathematics to generate speech from seed information. For a given speaker the vowel 'a' might be 20% middle C, 50% F and 25% A, with a few other things thrown in for good measure. We can transmit this information and ask the computer at the other end to re-synthesize it. This is what happens when you listen to someone on a modern phone. You do not hear their actual speech, you listen to a computer synthesizer make a near approximation.

CD is no longer the gold standard for sound. Professional audio has standardized on 24 bit recording which is probably far beyond the limit of the human ear. An audio soundtrack is doing a good job at 2 million bits per second.

Sitting perfectly still in the middle of a room, each ear will pick up a different signal if the source is not directly in front of us. The two ears on a human head face a little forward, and the hair on your head slightly absorbs sound. We can calculate the source of the sound by the slight difference in the times at which it strikes each ear, and the variation in frequency content. We can use these two pieces of information to determine the direction from which a sound is coming. It was useful for our ancestors to be able to tell where the saber-tooth tiger was hiding. We can gain more accurate information by turning our heads from side to side. The differences in frequency and timing should vary as we do so and we gain a little more data to perform the calculation. If we walk through the room we sample yet more of the soundscape and this can be used to pinpoint the exact location of the source. As we move, we expect the sounds we hear to change subtly according to the mental model we use for locating objects in the soundscape.

To give the illusion of a soundscape modern systems use multiple microphones to capture the sound, so it can be reproduced on multiple speakers. Ideally, we would record a hologram of the sound but it is possible to record on thirty or so microphones and mix the tracks down to 5 or more channels giving us the sound experience we now expect at a modern cinema.

What is the Bandwidth of Life?

We have not yet talked about the other senses; smell, vibration, temperature, balance, wind chill, and touch. In all, there are over 25 senses that must be stimulated accurately to simulate reality. Just think for a moment how much information must be replayed to reproduce the sensation of bungee jumping off a bridge in the jungle or taking off into space, or giving birth. To digitize life completely, we need to stimulate every relevant nerve ending in the human body in real-time – skin, ears, eyes, balance, pain centers, and so on.

At the low end, a 'perfect' IMAX production would require 360 degree stereoscopic projection and the generation of a full sound field. This would take 3 Gigabits per second for the audio field and 5,600 terabits per second for the video field. This could be substantially reduced if the person wears virtual reality glasses to track their head and eye movements, but then you are substituting resolution with computer power.

At the high end, a team at the US Department of Energy's Fermilab estimate reality needs one hundred trillion samples per inch for a 'simple' quantum representation. If we look at the many worlds view of quantum mechanics, each photon hitting our eye can't be fully described by a single number. The photon may be entangled with other realities we should keep track of. This causes our picture of reality to become wildly complex. Everything we might see and experience is in some way a combination of possibilities, and these possibilities all interact. Real life is *very* complex.

Symbolic Communication

Computers have no concept of an in-person meeting. They communicate using purely symbolic methods in binary numbers. These have the same meaning whether communicated over a short piece of wire or using a fiber optic cable half way around the world. Computers never have to communicate understanding to each other because they use programs and a program can be perfectly transmitted. Body language is, of course, completely alien to them!

We know there are non-computable things; functions, numbers, musical melodies, and mathematical puzzles. Why would there not also be a place for non-computation in communication? David Deutsch has suggested human creativity is used to guess the 'program' running in someone's mind, and evolved so we can learn skills. Instead, might face-to-face communication be important because it lets us impart knowledge in a non-symbolic manner?

Hyper-communication

As with hyper-computing, hyper-communication is controversial. We instinctively know human communication is very different to computer communication. Face-to-face communications have a qualitatively different feel to them. My question is this. Is there more to face-to-face communication between human beings than the simple exchange of symbolic information?

Let us propose an experiment. I erect a 3D screen with a hi-fi surround sound system in a university lecture hall and deliver a lecture to a camera in the adjacent hall. Half the students see the lecture directly, and half remotely. With modern screens, it might be possible to set up the experiment so well that is difficult to tell which hall I am actually in. Is the experience of the remote students the same as the ones sitting in direct proximity with me? Do mirror neurons fire more strongly and pick up more information when you see me in the flesh, or is the feeling that a lecture is better when you are 'physically there' an illusion? You are perhaps less likely to fall asleep in my lecture if you are physically there because you are afraid I might walk over and hit you! What possible non-classical effects could be in play when you see an event or communicate in person that might make the communication different? Here are two potential differences:

Information in a face-to-face encounter is continuous, not digitized. Continuous information is infinite in nature and does not have the finite limitation of digitized data. Of course, if we have digitized the sound at 24 bits and replayed it with extreme fidelity, there should not be any loss in information, but the interactivity of the soundscape is hard to simulate.

Light entering your eye contains information that could be quantum entangled with the object you are viewing. You become part of the system rather than merely an independent observer. It is difficult to see why this would produce a different quality of communication but it is testable. Set up the lecture experiment and measure the quality of understanding communicated between the parties.

If we believe our brains are super-Turing, then considering there might be some similar effects involved in human communication is not unreasonable, perhaps quantum effects play a role in communication. If we conclude our brains think classically, then we *probably* communicate classically.

Chapter 14

CREATIVITY

Thomas Edison, his wife and a Light Bulb

"Creativity is allowing yourself to make mistakes. Art is knowing which ones to keep."

Scott Adams

"Invention is 1% inspiration and 99% perspiration."

Thomas Edison

"Creativity is just connecting things. When you ask creative people how they did something, they feel a little guilty because they didn't really do it, they just saw something. It seemed obvious to them after a while. That's because they were able to connect experiences they've had and synthesize new things."

Steve Jobs

The ancient Greeks believed there was no such thing as creativity. Our job, as humans, was to look at the earth and discover things about it. When we looked at light passing through water or built a boat to travel on it, we were discovering, not inventing. Shipwrights did not invent boats they were simply building inevitable forms. Everything there was to know already existed, we just hadn't realized it yet. Of course, Greek playwrights were busy 'creating' the first plays; tragedies, comedies and the like, but serious thinkers thought of them as documenting the human condition. It wasn't until the Renaissance, 1500 years later, that humans began to appreciate that they *create* knowledge, and this started us on our quest to understand creativity.

One of my childhood memories is sitting on the kitchen floor with a glass of water and surrounded by knives and milk bottles. I was trying to solve one of the problems from Edward de Bono's book on lateral thinking, *A Five-day Course in Thinking*. De Bono, now in his 80s, is a prolific writer with over 60 publications to his name – all aimed at making us more creative. His books pose a series of practical problems, each needing progressively greater creative intelligence. The particular problem I was trying to solve was to balance a glass of water on knives suspended from four milk bottles. It took me after 2 hours.

Steve Jobs shows the iPhone

Except for De Bono there is not much written about creativity in books or on the Internet, but if you dip into the video archive, the discussion really opens up. Perhaps this is a feature of creativity; it's easier to explain in person. Of course, I have taken on the writing task with this book but I have the benefit of modern day resources such as multimedia, interactivity, and the web.

Some people appear to have creativity in abundance and the things they create are truly wonderful. I'm thinking here of Picasso, Einstein, Mozart, Edison, or Maxwell, but a precise definition of creative thinking is hard to pin down. Here are some generally accepted categories:

Divergent Thinking

The first sort of creative thinking we recognize is divergent thinking, often called brainstorming. This is the art of coming up with ideas – lots of them. A quick way to test your skill is to take a minute, and list all the possible uses for a paperclip. Try it!

In 60 seconds write down all the uses for a paper clip you can think of. Time yourself.

ANSWER WITHOUT READING ON

This is the classic test of creativity developed by J.P. Guilford in 1967. It is called the Alternative Uses Task. You can try the task with many objects: bricks, chairs, even water. How did you do on your first attempt? 8 to 10 uses is about average, 20 is extremely good. It's possible to teach most people to get near twenty and I'll show you how to do this in a moment.

Another test of idea generation is to draw 30 things in 30 circles. Thirty is such a large number it forces us to come up with some nutty ideas and break our natural tendency to self-censor.

For example, I'd like you to create logos or logo ideas, for a new coffee company in your circles. The test is best done without a time limit so now is the time to break off reading and make yourself a coffee. Then come back and draw 30 circles on a piece of paper. Fill in the circles.

MAKE A COFFEE, THEN START DRAWING.

The aim of brainstorming is to remove our inhibitions and get us to generate a mass of ideas. In normal life, we tend to suppress ideas even before we are consciously aware of them. Sir Ken Robinson has researched creativity in children and found the ability to brainstorm reduces linearly with age. At five or six, children given one of these divergent thinking tasks come up with many creative solutions: fold the paper clip into a dinosaur, and use it to attack your friends, get two and use them as chop sticks. As adults, we tend to disqualify ideas. You could never fold a paperclip that tightly or accurately, we said, "a" paper clip not two. But, you *can* fold a paper clip tightly, and the room you are doing the test in has thirty paper clips and thirty people in it so just team up with a friend. I never said this was a solo task!

Do you see how you impose nonexistent rules on your thinking, particularly the implied rule of not working with others? I did not say this test was subject to examination conditions. The first twenty years of our lives teaches us to work alone on intellectual tasks, yet when we get to the workplace we can, and indeed must collaborate to succeed. Now you have an idea how to ace the paper clip test: don't censor yourself and don't imply rules I have not imposed!

TRY THE PAPER CLIP TEST AGAIN!

Divergent thinking is rarely the final goal; it is rather a jumping off point for the creation of something new, like a solution to a mathematical puzzle, a painting, or a novel invention. The exercises allow us to explicitly see one of the early creative steps – idea generation before the pruning step. But most creative people often just create, they don't follow a scripted process. The term 'the creative process' is a great misnomer. There is no process that actually creates. Process merely puts us in the right frame of mind to do so. Processes are useful for framing a problem and ensuring we have all the right tools at our disposal: good crayons, some nice art paper, a hot cup of coffee. But process must be put to one side at the moment of actual creation.

Convergent Thinking

Convergent thinking is the opposite of divergent thinking. It focuses on discovering the final solution to a problem rather than generating precursor ideas. Some creative people only use this method, avoiding laborious processes such as brainstorming.

Tests of skill for convergent thinking generally pose puzzles where there is only one correct answer, but one that requires a non-linear step. Here's a really simple convergent thinking puzzle to try. It only requires a piece of paper and pen. Draw a circle on a piece of paper with a dot in the center. It should look like this. Do NOT take the tip of the pen off the paper until you are finished.

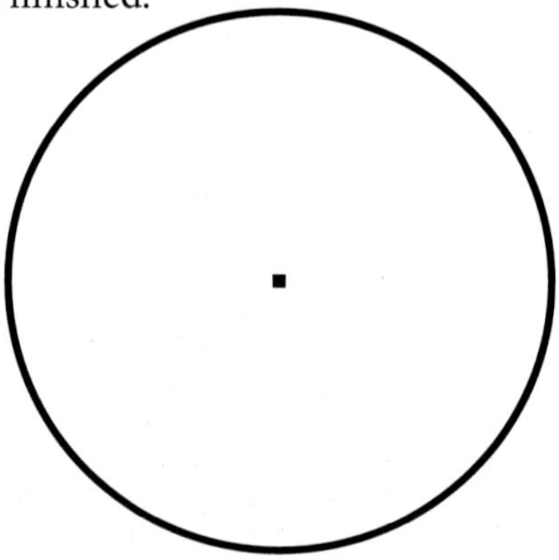

TRY ANSWERING IN YOUR OWN TIME

Another famous, but clichéd, problem is of you to draw four straight lines through these nine points without lifting the pen from the paper. Can you do it?

TRY ANSWERING IN YOUR OWN TIME

I won't put the answers here, or even a hint. It's quite famous and many of you will be familiar with them. The answers are buried on the website, and for those of you who already know the solution, there are some alternative problems. If you can't immediately solve a problem, think about it overnight. It's worth seeing what your brain will do while you are asleep!

The Science of Creativity

The first person to theorize about the creative process was Graham Wallas, the co-founder of the London School of Economics. In his book *The Art of Thought,* he proposed a five-step model for creative thinking. First preparation, when you become fully acquainted with the problem and its domain. Then incubation; walk the dog or make a cup of tea. After the meditative incubation phase you may get a gut feeling that a solution is on its way. Wallas called this third step intimation. It's left out of many modern versions of his theory, but I think it's an important step. Shortly

Eureka

after this you get that Eureka moment – illumination or insight where the creative idea bursts forth into your conscious awareness. The idea must finally be verified. Many of our ideas will turn out to be mistakes, but that's part of creativity. In the nearly hundred years of investigation since Wallas proposed this theorem, we have not moved much further forward in understanding creativity.

Alan Turing described his thoughts on the science behind creativity in a short piece he wrote about decision making:

> *"When making a decision of minor importance, I have always found it advantageous to consider all the pros and cons. In vital matters, however, such as the choice of a mate or a profession, the decision should come from the unconscious, from somewhere within ourselves. In the important decisions of personal life, we should be governed, I think, by the deep inner needs of our nature."*

Later in his career he came to believe machines would become intelligent and this sort of intuitive thinking could be effectively performed by a computer. As you know, I don't agree with his later viewpoint.

Another person who has thought long and hard about creativity is John Cleese, the comedian and actor. He describes the process wonderfully in a number of talks which you can find on YouTube. He finds a lot of his creativity emanates from his unconscious rather than conscious thought processes. To optimize this he needs large uninterrupted blocks of quiet

John Cleese on Creativity

time. Often, if a problem seems impossible, he will sleep on it. When he wakes the next morning, he will frequently find the problem has solved itself and a solution is ready at hand.

Art

The final class of creative thinking we generally recognize is artistic skill. This is probably a form of convergent thinking, except both the problem and the solution are open. Good artists are considered highly creative and most people tend to agree on what constitutes good art. There are some arguments but they are usually more about genres. I might not appreciate modern installation art, even to the point of declaring it, "not art." But, when forced to ignore their prejudices most people tend to agree on the distinction between good and bad.

Painting, sculpture, music, architecture and poetry are the traditional fine arts. There is often some argument over architecture: is it not too 'functional' to be considered an artistic endeavor? After all, art is not supposed to have any purpose other than to be, well, art. This definition inevitably leads to arguments about whether bad art is still 'art'. Art should be artful and how do you arrange a pile of used tires artfully? But this is a very narrow definition. I prefer to define art as something that provokes an emotional response in the beholder. Using this definition, the fact that a pile of tires disgusts and annoys you is exactly the point. Perhaps a more 'enlightened' viewer than you is intrigued by the clever use of materials.

Regardless, we consider art to be a creative endeavor and we can measure it using the criteria of novelty and quality. Since most people agree on these measures for a given piece of art, we can use the wisdom of crowds to give us a scientific scale. That does not mean there won't be art that you love but which leaves me cold. That is the joy of it. Novelty and quality are not the same as joy and pleasure, far less the tingle factor.

A quick test for artistic skill is to take a pen and paper and turn to the person sitting on your left and try to sketch them.

TRY IT!

If you tried, you and your neighbor would probably find the results rather humorous. But, most likely, you did not follow my instruction. This is a form of social self-censorship. I asked you to do something rather difficult and embarrassing, but very creative and likely to enlighten you. Sadly most people – I am no exception – tend to censor their creativity for fear of embarrassment. Children, of course, do not sensor themselves as much as adults.

Now you know how to be more creative. Find your inner child and don't censor yourself too much!

What Sparks Creativity

As an inventor, I'm often asked what makes me creative. How do I do it? The answer is, I have no real process. After all, a process is mechanical and this entire book has been about exploring how creativity is a non-mechanical task. However, there are many things you can do to unleash your creative potential.

New ideas are often sparked through linking disparate ideas. Expose yourself to as many ideas as you can, read widely, attend conferences, visit customers.

Creativity requires peace and quiet. I personally get up early every morning. This gives me a good two hours of uninterrupted time every day. It's also the part of the day when my brain works best. Others prefer to work late into the night.

Pressure, for me and for many people, is a great incentive. Tales of the Polish Enigma code breakers, Douglas Adams' writing deadlines and the fear of impending death in shark attack stories all force people to think in an accelerated way. This appears to help many people defeat the human tendency to prevaricate.

On the other hand avoid panic. While a level of pressure can help, panic is unproductive. There is a sweet spot between having enough time to get properly acquainted with a problem and an impending deadline to force the crystallization of ideas. This balance varies from person to person and is something you need to test for yourself.

You need time off. Once you have a well thought out idea, you may need to leave it alone for a while to allow your subconscious to work. Time off does not need to be two weeks at the beach. Charles Darwin and Benjamin Britten used to go for long walks. You can walk in Darwin's footsteps at Down House in Kent. Others such as John Cleese like to 'sleep on it'. Stephen Hawking distracts himself by working on a different problem for a while. Anything that avoids focusing directly on the problem itself seems to allow our creative freewheel run.

Environment can be important. The campuses created by Steve Jobs for both Apple and Pixar are designed to foster creativity. The physical environments build team behavior but also cause people to bump into each other. Cross-pollination drives creativity.

There are also some myths to dispel about creative people. Inventors are portrayed as eccentric and hopelessly disorganized, but Feynman kept notes of every idea he ever had. I have kept a series of notebooks, now computer based, since I left university. I still have almost all of these on a shelf at home. Creative people may be a little mad, but the successful ones are rarely disorganized.

You must allow your brain to free wheel. J.K. Rowling has said the characters in the *Harry Potter* novels write themselves. I come to my computer each morning having *not* thought too much overnight and just write. Creation is just that; you must allow yourself to do it. It's not a process.

The Innovator's Dilemma

Why don't big companies create? In 1997, Clayton Christensen of Harvard Business School wrote *The Innovator's Dilemma*, the seminal work on creativity within organizations. In it, he shows us why established companies tend not to innovate and why startups exist. Christiansen's academic research examines how companies handle discontinuous change in technology, focussing on the hard disk industry.

You might not think this a very sexy sector. Microprocessors and game consoles would be more fun, but the great advantage with the hard disk is there is a single industry journal that has tracked the progress of every player over 30 years, collecting detailed annual data on every facet of their business. For an academic, this is gold dust.

IBM invented the hard disk drive in their research center near Winchester, England. The first prototypes were, consequently, called Winchester Drives. When Christiansen examined the industry, he found something very strange. As the size of disks reduced first from 8" to 5¼" and then from 5¼" to 3½", the dominant players in the previous era went out of business and new startups colonized the market. This fallout was not confined to a few small companies. It affected large, well-established, publicly-listed organizations, too. They failed en masse at each discontinuity. At first this made no sense to him. Surely a skilled

Hard Drives

hard drive manufacturer would be the obvious group to construct the next generation. But it seemed that not only did incumbent players *not* construct the next generation, they ran their businesses into the ground while ignoring the technology discontinuity. Despite their legions of Ivy League graduates and business school MBAs, they all went bankrupt.

As he looked around the economy, he found a similar pattern in other sectors. Minicomputer companies failed to make the jump to personal computers. Further back in time, buggy whip companies – in the Fortune 100 at the turn of the 20th century – failed to make the transition to the motor vehicle economy. The only exception he could find was IBM. IBM had successfully navigated some transitions but at that time was fighting for survival as companies transitioned from mainframes to Linux based servers and their survival was in question. Why was this so?

Christensen's conclusion is that established companies tend to concentrate too much on their existing revenue streams while ignoring potential new ones. This is no surprise. When the disc drive industry made the move from 8" disks to 5¼", the only customers for these new new smaller models were unheard of manufacturers of personal computers. Some were based in the dorms of MIT and Harvard – Dell and Compaq – not in the existing powerhouses of computing – Digital

Equipment and Wang. New technology often underperforms the existing forms. 5¼" drives were slower, less reliable, and cost more per bit than their 8" predecessors but, of course, in one respect they were better. They were smaller and lighter and could fit in portable computers. The new technologies did a different thing in a different way, and overcame their disadvantages later. This chain of events is repeated many times over: Yellow Pages overtaken by Google, Borders by Amazon, Blockbusters by Netflix. Disruptive innovation changes the rules of the game as well as the pieces in the game.

Christensen's advice to companies is to separate your innovators from the existing business because their priorities will differ too greatly. Modern companies build entirely new divisions to create new products, or set up innovation labs to incubate ideas that would otherwise never get enough resources.

Reward for Creativity

There's no doubt society values creativity very highly. One of the first tasks Thomas Jefferson undertook when he became President of the United States was to set up a patent system. He remained head of the patent office for over ten years. These days, the protection of creative

Harold Cohen, Computer Art

ideas through patents, copyright, and trade secret is big business and combines to form the practice of 'intellectual property'. Societies with the best protection of intellectual property are often the most successful. The USA is the unassailed leader, with Asian countries rapidly catching up. Poor old Europeans have struggled with an almost unworkable patent system for nearly 30 years; a genuine Europe-wide patent only came into effect in 2013.

Creativity in the economy is now extremely important, and nothing emphasizes the point more than the job market. During the 60s finding a job was easy. There was an almost unlimited range of mechanical jobs on offer. In the post-industrial age, almost all the mechanical jobs have gone. Today we need to be experts in a field, able to solve problems creatively. You can't expect to walk into a job and be profitably productive on the first day. Finding a job is harder and the cost of employing someone is greater.

Why did we Evolve Creativity?

Roger Penrose wonders why mathematical creativity evolved in humans since it only became useful in ancient Greece a few thousand years ago. He believes it must have been useful for something before this. But what?

David Deutsch thinks creativity developed to allow one human to understand the thoughts of a fellow human being. We can't precisely communicate the 'programs' we run in our heads. We are unable to download a detailed thought and put it on a memory stick. He thinks our creative capacity developed to help us pass skills from one to another. The ability to paint and sculpt is an accidental by-product of this adaption.

It's my view we evolved creativity to deal with new situations and puzzles in our daily lives. We use creative thought processes and ingenuity to come up with novel solutions for when we can't rely on programming or a store of rules. Otherwise, the very first unforeseen situation could kill us!

Computer Creativity

Humans find creativity difficult. It requires peace and quiet, detailed study and input of caffeine. How does a computer fare? I have argued that computers cannot be creative above the logic limit, so this does not preclude them from creating within the narrow confines of a particular solution space. But a human still needs to set the rules for this space. The level of creativity we should see from computers is convincing within a limited conceptual area. Computers are not going to wake up one morning and *decide* to compose a breathtakingly beautiful symphony, but if we give them rules they can make a convincing version.

Many computer systems have been designed to tackle creativity. We have already met the composer Emily Howell and Douglass Hofstadter's computation program. Here are two more examples: Jape and AARON, which create jokes and art, respectively.

Jape – Joke Analysis and Production Engine – is a program created by Graeme Ritchie and Kim Binsted. It generates puns, the sort of things you might find in an English Christmas cracker or children's joke book. I'll let the output speak for itself.

Q: "What is the difference between leaves and a car?"
A: "One you brush and rake, the other you rush and brake."

Q: "What do you call a spicy missile?"
A: "A hot shot!"

One of the most enlightening examples of computer creativity is AARON – refreshingly not an acronym. His machine is depicted here and you should look up some works on the web, such as *Adam and Eve*, and *Aaron's Garden*. The program encodes rules about figures, objects

AARON – Harold Cohen, Automatic Painting Machine

and perspective. Once coded the program takes off and is remarkably creative in its compositions, without any further human intervention. However, each new capability must be hand-coded by its creator, Harold Cohen. These paintings give a good visual interpretation for the sort of latitude imposed by the logic limit. AARON can do some very impressive things, but always in a mechanical – albeit beautiful – way, within the rules set by Harold Cohen, the true artist. AARON will not suddenly awake one morning and independently decide to experiment with the color blue!

To give an idea of what I mean by 'mechanical elaboration' in a musical context, imagine you were using a Casio synthesizer. These machines have all sorts of fun settings. You can program them to play drum tracks, fill in chords, and add a jazzy, syncopated harmonization to your melody. But none of this is truly innovative. It's mechanical elaboration of your artistic material. Jape, AARON and Emily Howell all do the same thing within their domain. They mechanically elaborate the artistic creation of their human masters. AARON does an extremely good job of this.

The Myth of the Design Tradeoff

An important consequence of the non-linearity of creativity is we are not constrained by tradeoff laws. Let me explain.

Volkswagen Polo

How often do you hear the phrase, "It's down to tradeoffs," or "It's a matter of priorities", or even "You can't have your cake and eat it."

These stock statements misunderstand the infinitely complex nature of creativity and problem solving. Let us take a concrete example: the car.

My first car was a Volkswagen Polo. It was a great little car, quite nippy, cassette-radio, and four seats. The most recent Polo has antilock brakes, airbags, NCAP 5-star crash resistance, smarter styling, and a low emission engine. Shall I go on…? The doctrine of tradeoffs says I would have to give up something to gain these new features. But, I have not. The newer Polo is cheaper in real terms than my original, as well as being better designed.

Problems always have at least two dimensions of freedom. We can trade one feature for another or we can innovate to both have our cake and eat it! We are never constrained to simple on-the-one-hand, on-the-other-hand type decisions. Creativity is unconstrained by linear rules and tradeoffs.

Process versus Creativity

How many times have you heard the words, "We must create a process for this!"

In its place, process is good; It makes things consistent, repeatable and predictable. You can follow a process by rote without error. Processes are also easy to document and communicate because they are symbolic. But process is limited. It is, after all, a set of prescribed rules for solving a particular problem – and, because of this, it falls into the same trap.

A process cannot solve a problem that requires creative thought or logic more complex than the logic limit. Logical processes are useful for tracking lists. I am reassured when I get on an airplane and know the pilot has been through a preflight checklist. I would not want to fly in an airplane where the pilot announced he was taking a creative approach to the preflight check.

Process is a perfect tool for organizing the steps around being creative, but it won't do the creating for you.

Chapter 15

FREE WILL

Dilbert Ponders Free Will

"We have to believe in free will -
we have no choice."

Isaac Singer

"Time really is an illusion -
lunchtime doubly so."

Douglas Adams

A child grows up in poverty, their father absent, mother a drug addict. Riots break out and the child defends the local convenience store. Another child born on the same road, but from a better background, loots the store and is arrested. This scene played out on the streets of London during the summer of 2011, but similar incidents happen all across the world. People choose different moral paths; one person makes a good decision; the other, a bad one. Did they make these decisions freely or was their behavior inevitable, dictated at the dawn of time?

Free will is at the heart of our justice system. It requires a crime to be intentionally committed by a person of sound mind. If I kill you in an accident or because I am mentally incapacitated, I am innocent. Of course, if I mentally incapacitate myself with alcohol I would be guilty of manslaughter, perhaps even murder.

Our justice system requires a crime to be intentionally committed by a person of sound mind. Whenever we see something bad in the world we trace the events back to the thought processes which led up to it. It seems we punish the decisions in our brains leading to a crime, not the crime itself. But, in a deterministic Universe my thoughts could never be at fault. They are inevitable. "The Universe made me do it!"

You need not worry about the fabric of society falling apart in a deterministic Universe. The whole of existence will play out according to a predetermined script, complete with lawyers, trials, drama and pathos. The judge, jury and executioner would also have no free will. It would look as if you paid the price for the choices you made, but this would be an illusion. The whole thing would be like one enormous screenplay.

The concept of determinism goes against our conscious experience. We all have a strong sense of free will. I certainly think I have it! And this presents a problem, because the classical laws of physics say our Universe is entirely deterministic, and that free will is an illusion.

I should briefly mention 'compatibilism', a branch of philosophy that claims determinism is *not* at odds with free will. It argues that if I feel free and my actions do not appear constrained, then I am free even though my future might be inevitable: a sensation of freedom is sufficient. This seems rather feeble. I am seeking an explanation for how we might be truly free to choose our actions, not some linguistic trick to argue freedom is subjective. I believe true free will is a physical principle with observable effects on the Universe that would not be seen in a determined one.

Domino Toppling

Determinism

To firmly grasp the idea of determinism let's look at a fun example, domino toppling. If I arrange a set of dominoes on their edge in a long line and push over the first it will fall, knock over the next, then the next, and so on until all the dominoes have fallen. It is inevitable, and fun to watch. The same is thought to happen with particles in our Universe, albeit at a much smaller scale. The laws of physics governing these particles describe precisely what will happen as they interact. Our Universe could be thought of as a mechanical clock, wound and set at the Big Bang, or a fractal equation generating the wonders we see around us.

When I push over the first domino it should be possible to capture all the information about the particles in the dominoes, my hand, the table, and the surrounding environment to precisely determine what will happen next. Will all the dominoes fall perfectly, or is there a break in the pattern – one domino just a tiny bit out of alignment – which will spoil the fun? All the information is there in front of me and I should be able to predict it perfectly.

The laws of physics, as we understand them, are not only deterministic, they are reversible. This means if we know the position and momentum of every particle in the dominoes and the surrounding environment, we can extrapolate their motion back into the past. It should be possible to trace back the path of each particle to reconstruct the past history of the dominoes.

If we were to cast a wide enough net, and collect all the available information, we could go back and see the events in the factory where the dominoes were made, or even see the trees that was felled to make them. We would need a *lot* of information and huge computing power, but we *could* do it! With a sufficiently powerful computer we could travel back in time, albeit as a simulation, and relive past events. This would have no effect on the events themselves as it would be like watching a movie, but we could see every aspect of the past from any viewpoint.

To perform this time travel trick for real, we would have to gather information from an enormously wide area. Information spreads out at the speed of light. One minute after the dominoes topple, the information about the event will have spread one light minute – that is over a sphere forty-million kilometers across – half way to Venus. An hour later and it would be outside the solar system. If you were to cast your net that wide, and gathered up all the information within the sphere, you could still perfectly model the moment when the dominoes were toppled. The wider you cast the net, the more information you have and the further backward in time you can travel. If you take the idea of collecting information to its logical conclusion you could gather all the information in the Universe at a moment in time.

In 1814, Laplace put this idea in an essay. He proposed an immensely powerful being observes the position and momentum of every particle in the Universe. Armed with *any* snapshot of the Universe and the laws of physics, the entire future and the past of the Universe. The being was nicknamed Laplace's Daemon and the idea has influenced philosophy ever since.

If the Universe is predictable, our concept of time needs to be rethought. A common sense notion is that things in the future are unknown and things in the past are known. But, in a deterministic Universe a daemon or a supercomputer could keep track of all the information and tell you what is inevitably going to happen. The conscious feeling we have of moving through time would be just an illusion. Past and future have no meaning and there would just be a solid, permanent block of space-time. If you stood outside the Universe and looked at this block of space-time, everything that is going to happen and has already happened is set. This is sometimes called the Block Universe Hypothesis and is the logical conclusion of any theory that imagines an entirely determined Universe.

One thing that seems to throw doubt on this Block Universe Hypothesis is our personal conscious experience of the world. We experience the Universe unfolding over time. (Of course, we could have this conscious experience in a determined Universe if someone had programmed it that way. All we can say is that it seems unlikely someone would go to the trouble of giving us a completely fictitious experience. There are an infinite number of possible Universes, why pick one where we think time flows, but it does not.)

Uncertainty

If you know a little of quantum mechanics you might imagine Heisenberg's Uncertainty Principle comes to our rescue.

Heisenberg's principle is often misunderstood. People sometimes try to explain it as an experimental problem. If I want to measure the position of a particle I am going to need to shine a light on it. The photons I use to illuminate the particle will knock it out of position so the act of measurement disturbs the system. This is *not* the Uncertainty Principle. It is a different but related effect, called the measurement problem. The muddle is really Heisenberg's own fault. When he tried to produce a layman's explanation he used the analogy of disturbing the particle with the photon. This is wrong. A photon would not disturb a particle enough to explain the uncertainty we find; particles are fundamentally uncertain even before we measure them. Heisenberg's Uncertainty Principle is a quantum property, which means it makes no sense and there is no analogy I can give you to properly explain it! Here is the closest thing I can find.

Imagine I am playing a musical note on a guitar. You might want to know two things about it; where exactly is the string and what pitch, or note, am I playing? The problem with these two measurements is they can't be stated at the same time. Pitch is dictated by the rate of oscillation over time: the number of times a string vibrates back and forth per second. Position is the exact location of the string at a given moment in time. If I state the position precisely this has no pitch because pitch needs a time interval. If I allow a time interval the string will move during that time and it won't be precisely in one place. The best I can say is the string is about two millimeters above the fret board and two-thirds of the way across it.

So, I hear you cry, this Uncertainty Principle means our Universe is not deterministic because it is uncertain.

Unfortunately, the principle only prevents *us* from measuring the position and momentum of a particle at the same time, it does not prevent the Universe *knowing* the information it needs to allow the particle to go about its business in an entirely deterministic fashion. There is a perfectly reliable and predictable wave function that governs the motion of every particle, just as there is an entirely predictable equation for the motion of a string on a musical instrument.

If both the classical and quantum laws of physics are deterministic where does the freedom come from to make our Universe non-deterministic? There is just one place to look: you and me.

The Observer

I am looking out of my office window. It is a sunny autumn day and I have a beautiful view over London, but if I squint a little I can also see my reflection. The window in front of me is not perfect. Although it is mostly transparent, the glass also reflects some of the light. If you think of light as particles, the majority of the photons go through. But some bounce back. I'm going to show you that the behavior of these photons is governed by the observer – me!

The laws governing light, and most of the strange and wonderful effects it has, were first stated by Isaac Newton. Newton was an extraordinary man. He discovered many of the physical principles we use today, and his view of the Universe reigned unchallenged until Einstein's discovery of relativity. He was also, by many accounts, a nasty piece of work. Not only was he a famous academic, he also head of the Royal Mint. He is said to have taken great pleasure in having forgers hanged on Tower Hill. He claimed the invention of differential calculus despite it being invented independently by Gottfried Leibniz. Newton managed to have himself appointed to chair the committee reviewing Leibniz's work and determine who had come up with the idea first. Unsurprisingly, the committee found for Newton!

We see Newton's laws of reflection and transmission in all manner of everyday products, for example, the antireflective coatings of camera lenses or the screen of your smartphone. Manufacturers cover the glass in these products with coatings just a few molecules thick. Interference between the layers *kills* the reflections. On a very expensive lens several different layers are used; some kill red light and others kill blue light. Together they suppress most of the reflection. If it were not for these coatings you would be unable to go to the park on a summer's day and read your iPad. We need to think about reflection and transmission to demonstrate our role as observers.

A windowpane has two surfaces. Both surfaces reflect light, and if you look closely you will see your face is really reflected twice. You might think this is simply a double reflection but this is not so. Light behaves like waves. As with water waves, they interfere with one another. If two light waves are at the top of a crest as they meet, the result is a crest of double height. If both are at the bottom, you have a double trough, and if one is a crest and the other a trough you get nothing as they cancel each other out. You can see this effect in waves on the surface of a pond.

When light strikes a window pane, the light has two chances to reflect: one from the front surface and the second from the back surface. These two reflections interfere with each other. And, again, when you

Wave Interference

have interference you sometimes get constructive interference – the double crest or trough – and sometimes destructive interference – the crest and trough canceling each other.

The reason we don't see this effect in every reflection is because of imperfection. Windows are not perfectly flat and light is multicolored, so the effect is hard to see. But it is definitely there, and if you look really hard at a reflection in a window, you can sometimes see it at the boundary of sharp objects. The effect is very clear in the next picture which has been set up with two flat pieces of glass resting against each other. There is a tiny air gap between them. It is also commonly seen on puddles in cities. In this case the puddle usually has a slight film of oil on it. Unlike glass, puddles are perfectly flat thanks to gravity, but the oil film is thick in the center and thin at the edges. The light reflecting off a puddle will show a rainbow of colors. This is because each color is giving us a pattern of light and dark. If you look at the same puddle at night in a yellow streetlight, you will just see a monochrome pattern of light and dark. Look at the picture of waves on a pond.

The patterns of light and dark are usually explained by imagining the photons interfere with each other. This explanation is insufficient. Imagine for a moment you can see as well as a frog, and perceive one photon at a time. One moonless night just one photon comes to the two glass surfaces and reflects. What happens?

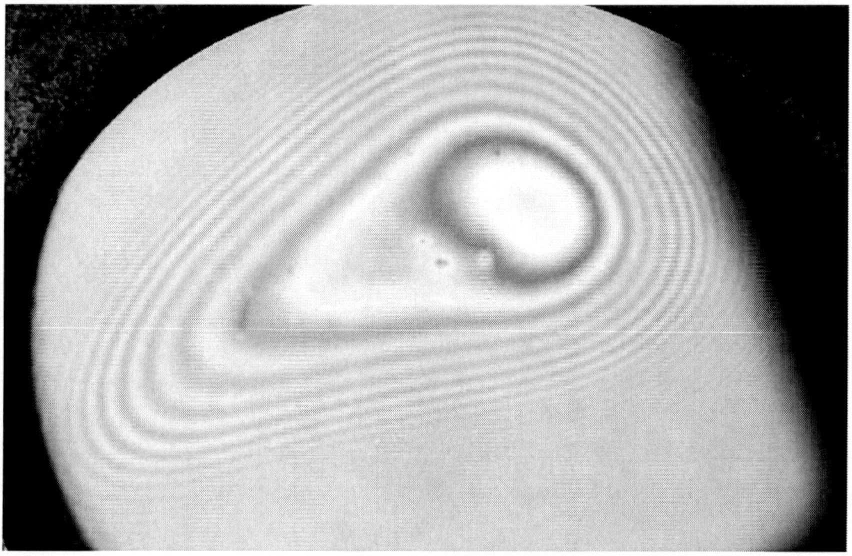

Newton's Rings

It turns out a single photon can interfere with itself! How can this be? It must somehow split up and consider both the available paths reflecting off the glass surfaces.

Now that we have these two concepts in our head, that a photon sometimes reflects and sometimes does not, and a single photon must consider both paths, we can ask: what tells the photon what to do?

There are only three possible answers: the light source that emitted the photon, the pane of glass that reflected the photon or the observer that saw the photon – me.

The first obvious place that might control the photon is the original source of the photon; the light bulb. The photon might leave the bulb already knowing what path to follow, whether it will be reflected and whether that reflection will be affected by the gap between the two surfaces in a positive or negative way. This is sometimes called a pilot wave theory. The problem with this theory is I could insert a piece of glass into the experiment after the photon has left the light source. This will affect the photon but the light source could not have known my intention in advance and told the photon what to do. Therefore, the path of the photon is not pre-programmed by the light source.

Now our photon has left the bulb and is traveling toward the glass. The glass has two surfaces. The photon reaches the first surface and has to decide if it will reflect. But there is a problem. The second surface will have an effect on this decision – constructively or destructively. The photon can't make up its mind at the first surface. It has not yet seen the second surface.

The photon travels on and reaches the second surface. It needs to make a decision: Shall I reflect or not? It cannot decide that it should have been reflected from the first surface because it is already at the second surface; it's too late.

The photon is stuck. It cannot make the decision at the first surface because that is too early, nor at the second surface because that is too late. The glass surfaces cannot be the source of the decision.

This leaves only one remaining option: I, the observer, *tell* the photon what to do. The word 'tell' is probably a little strong. Sadly, I am not that powerful. All I can do is tell the photon to make up its mind. When the photon reaches my eye, it *must* decide what happened to it along the journey, but this decision appears purely random and I have no effect upon it. The best way physicists have found to describe what is going on is to say particles, such as a photons, behave according to a wave function. Particles oscillate between all the possible options available to them and when we take a measurement this freezes the oscillations and gives a single result.

Where exactly is the measurement made? At my eye when the photon is refracted by the lens, when the photon enters the aqueous humor, or perhaps as it interacts with the rods and cones in the retina. Maybe we must wait until the detection of the photon is converted into an electrical impulse in the optic nerve or even the point at which my human consciousness perceives it.

This prompted the physicist John Bell to ask a slightly tongue-in-cheek question, "Was the world wave function waiting to jump for thousands of millions of years until single-celled creatures appeared? Or, did it have to wait a little longer for some more highly qualified measurer – with a Ph.D.?" You see his point. Where is the bar set that defines a measurement?

One of the most extreme answers to Bell's question is the strong anthropic principle. It argues humans – or at least sentient beings, perhaps even cats – *cause* the Universe to exist. The Universe bubbles along in a state of superposition with every possible event occurring and bifurcating until an observer emerges in one of the branches and the whole edifice collapses to that state. It is not clear if this produces many concurrent universes or if the first universe with a sentient being wins!

Solvay Conference

"There is no way to understand the mechanism that turns the water of the brain to the wine of consciousness."

Colin McGinn

"If you think this Universe is bad, you should see some of the others."

Philip K. Dick

Schrödinger's Cat

Measurement is a big puzzle. What causes the collapse of the wave function so that the photon stops considering many optional paths and makes a hard and fast decision. When light passes through a series of glass surfaces, it is reflected or transmitted by each. We can stack up as many pieces of glass as we want, but none of the surfaces will cause a measurement – a collapse of the wave function. It is not until the photon reaches a detector that a measurement is made and all the potential reflections and transmissions that might have happened 'collapse' into the one choice that actually happened.

You might doubt this but there are ingenious experiments that can be performed to prove it. One is quite simple to do and can be set up on your kitchen table with a handheld laser and $100 worth of optical components. You need three ordinary mirrors and a beam splitter. Beam splitters are often made from half-silvered mirrors. They are similar to your bedroom mirror except the silver coating is more thinly applied, allowing only half the light to reflect while the rest passes straight through. Arrange the mirrors and beam splitter on a table at the four corners of an imaginary box, as in the diagram. If you point your laser at the half-silvered mirror, half the light will go straight through and half will be reflected upwards towards the first mirror. It is sent on around the square until it meets the half-silvered mirror again, and the beams meet up. You might expect that half the light reaches the detector but this is not what happens. Depending on the way the mirrors are positioned, either all the light reaches the detector, or none does. (The light does not disappear it just gets sent back to the light source, energy is conserved.) If you turn down the brightness of your laser, this does not change. Even

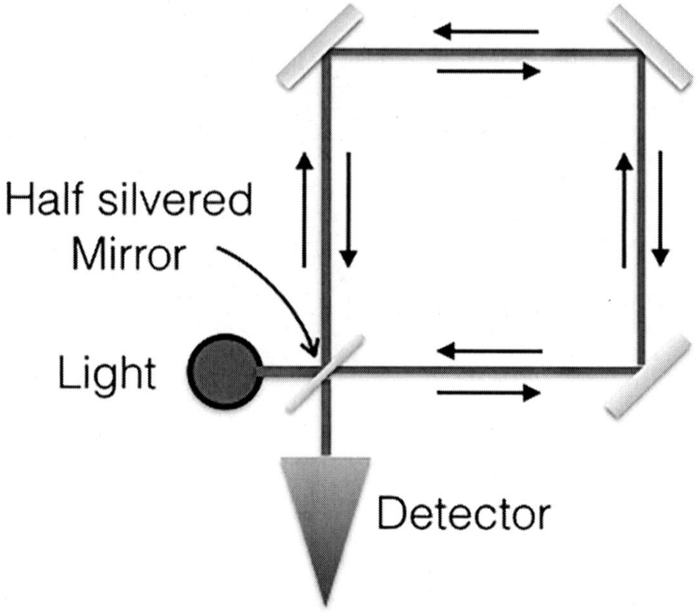

Interferometer

if only one photon is traveling at a time, still no light comes out in one direction and all the photons come out the other. The wave functions of each photon interfere with each other constructively or destructively. The only conclusion available is the photon must be traveling along both paths! They are said to be in 'superposition'. If you introduce a measuring device half way around the experiment, it will destroy the superposition and the photons behave in the common sense way. Remove the measuring device and, once again, the photons seem to take both paths. Richard Feynman pointed out that you really have to imagine that the photons take every possible path, not only the straight line paths. He received his Nobel Prize for demonstrating how to add up these infinite paths to get a finite answer with his 'sum over histories method'. Superposition is a strange idea when limited to the realm of small particles but what about larger things? – cats for example.

Erwin Schrödinger's unfortunate cat is trotted out to demonstrate the paradox so often that Stephen Hawking is on record for wanting to reach for a gun every time he hears mention of it.

The thought experiment works like this. A cat is put in a box with a radioactive substance, a Geiger counter and a vial of poison. If the counter detects a radioactive decay it breaks the bottle and the cat dies, if no decay is detected the cat lives.

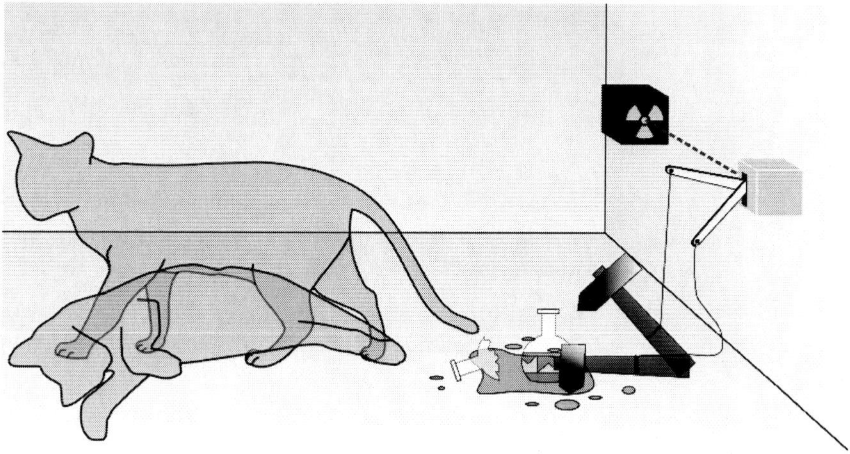

Schrödinger's Cat – both Alive and Dead

Since radioactive decay is a quantum event, we have to assume it might or might not have happened right up until the point of measurement. It is the same with any quantum event: photons reflecting from a piece of glass, measuring the spin of an electron or measuring the polarization of a photon. All these quantum effects exist in superposition until measured. But in the real world, we don't experience superposition. If I miss the train, I miss it. I don't partially catch it and partially miss it, and I don't experience any such quantum ambiguity. The only place I ever see such effects is watching science fiction movies. In real life the large scale world is certain. At what point does this quantum uncertainty transition to our classical certainty? What is the state of the cat before I – a sentient observer – open the box? Was the result of the decay measured by the Geiger counter, the cat, or are we waiting for someone to open the box and observe the result?

The Copenhagen interpretation of quantum mechanics – named after the main center of early quantum theory at the Niels Bohr Institute – says the cat is both alive and dead until I make a measurement. The cat is said to be in superposition, meaning a live cat and a dead cat inhabit the same volume of space-time 'experiencing' both alternatives and waiting for my measurement. This seems nonsensical, but Copenhagen quantum folk simply say, "That's the way it is; the mathematics works, if you don't like it, tough. Nature does not have to explain herself."

Einstein strongly disagreed with this position. He believed the world is certain and laws must govern radioactive decay and, therefore, the breaking of the vial and the life and death of the cat. There must be some, as yet, undiscovered theory. He reasoned as follows: A particle has position, velocity and spin. Why can it not have more hidden information that tells it when to decay? Perhaps particles are composed of sub-particles that cause the weird quantum effects we see.

We *have* discovered sub-particles – quarks and the like – but more than a hundred years of experimentation have gradually ruled out any form of theory explaining how these random events can be governed by the properties of the particle. The collapse of the wave function just seems to happen randomly.

There is one explanation for quantum mechanics that avoids the measurement problem altogether but it is even stranger than the Copenhagen interpretation: 'the many worlds' view'. The idea was first put forward by Hugh Everett in 1957, and it claims measurements are never made, there is never a collapse of the wave function, and every wave continues to exist. We just can't see them all. There is a version of me that has seen a live cat and another in a parallel universe that saw a dead one. The two versions of me are also in superposition, just like the cat, so there are an infinity of parallel universes tracking every possible option.

The only measurable consequence of this 'many worlds' idea is the existence of enormously enjoyable science fiction plots and much poking of fun between the many worlds camp, and the no-many-worlds camp. The single-worlds proponents point out the whole idea is untestable and just plain odd. For example, each choice we make, every reflection and any quantum process generates a new branch in the Universe. This is a vast amount of information to track and puts us back in a position where moral choices have no consequence. Every decision I make spawns a Universe where I made a different choice.

For a humorous take on this, you can visit a website and buy your own Universe for $2.99. You pose a question based on the throw of a die, let's say, one to three I go to work today and, four to six, I take a sick day. The website generates a quantum random number using an experimental setup at a laboratory in California. You can make your choice based on this quantum random number in the certain knowledge that another Universe springs into existence where you made the alternate choice, so somewhere you are not taking a sick day after all, and can be found hard at work at your desk.

There is one more explanation for quantum measurement, proposed by Roger Penrose. He proposes gravity comes to the rescue. Once enough particles are involved in the superposition of states, the curvature in space time becomes great enough to force a measurement event. In his view, a measuring instrument is simply an amplifier which brings a quantum event to the point where gravity begins to matter. His solution removes the requirement for many worlds and, indeed, our curious position as the conscious beings that bring the world into existence. Of course, Penrose does not stop there. He proposes the quantum gravity interaction gives rise to conscious thought and this process is the root of mathematical intuition.

The aim of our discussion is to show where determinism might break down in the physical laws of the Universe. If our Universe is determined, there will need to be a huge quantity of information stored somewhere to tell it what to do at each step. Storing a script for the Universe is not the conventional way people imagine determinism works. Rather they explain the apparent complexity we see through the application of a simple set of rules called 'the laws of physics'. We imagine using these laws to expand up a small set of starting conditions into the complexity of the Universe we experience. This is similar to the way fractals produce beautifully complex images from a tiny quantity of information. For example, the Mandelbrot set is created from a single, simple mathematical statement just twelve characters long, with one or two starting numbers. If this is how our Universe works then our thoughts and actions are just like the fronds of a fractal. It would mean the particles in the Universe 'know' what they will do next and carry enough information with them to determine their next action. This is a testable hypothesis and the test we have devised to measure this is the twin particle experiment.

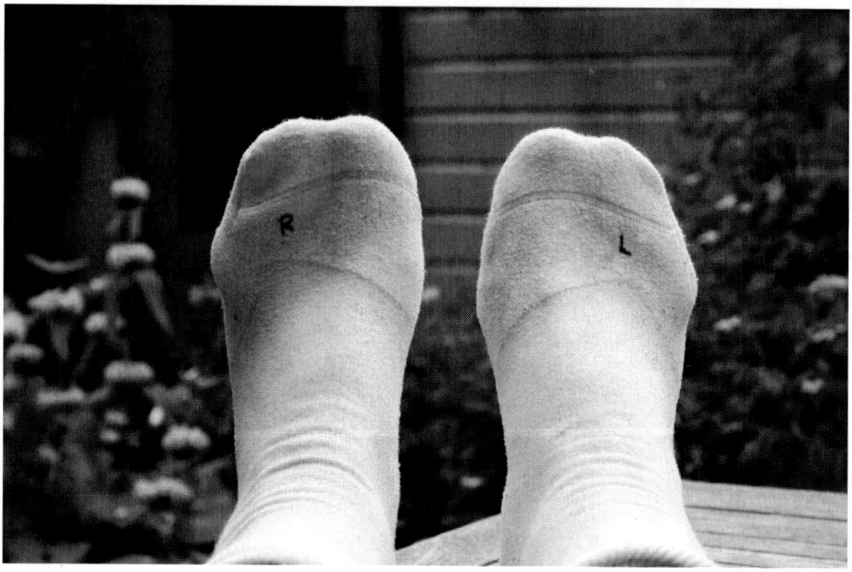

Right and Left Socks

"Was the world wave-function waiting to jump for thousands of millions of years until single-celled creatures appeared? Or did it have to wait a little longer for some more highly qualified measurer - with a Ph.D.?"

John Bell

Twins

There are several ways to make twin particles. The 'easy' way is with a laser and a nonlinear crystal. A beam of ultraviolet photons enters the crystal and about one in a billion times they interact with quantum fluctuations in the crystal lattice to create two red photons. This is known as 'spontaneous down conversion'.

There are two types of down conversion. In a type I interaction the twins have the same polarization, and in a type II they are at 90 degrees to each other. You can set up the experiment with either type, but it is important to remember which you used, or you will easily become confused. When we *talk* about photon experiments, we are usually referring to type I interactions because they are easier to understand. Often the actual experiment uses oppositely polarized photons because they are easier to generate.

Polarization is a wavelike property of photons. You can visualize them wiggling up and down, side-to-side or something in between. We use polarization to our advantage when we go on holiday to the beach; light from the sun is randomly polarized, but when it glances off the ocean it becomes predominantly horizontally polarized. If we wear vertically polarized sunglasses the glare off the ocean is blocked and we can see the ocean more clearly. The following two pictures show this effect.

The two photons we make with the crystal can be separated and sent to different places. The record so far is two towns near Geneva, 50 kilometers apart. For this experiment scientists 'borrowed' the unused fibers of Swisscom in the middle of the night – when phone traffic was light. A detector was placed at the end of each fiber to measure the particles.

Effect of Polaroid Lenses

When scientists examine the polarization of these photons, they get random results. Sometimes the photon is oscillating side to side, sometimes up and down and sometimes part way in between. This can be determined simply by taking a lens out of a pair of Polaroid glasses, holding it up at an angle and seeing if the photon can pass through. Obviously laboratory grade Polaroid material is available, so scientists don't have to destroy an expensive pair of designer glasses, but the principle is identical.

Very strange things happen when the measurements are made. The polarizations appear to have no discernible pattern, but once one of the photons has gone through a polarizer in the first town, its sister photon will always be found to have the opposite polarization (or the same if it was a type I)..

Einstein was uncomfortable with this for two reasons. The first related to his famous statement, "God does not play dice with the Universe." He was deeply uncomfortable with the idea that the polarizations were random. Even more troubling to him was the idea that the sister photon somehow instantaneously had the opposite polarization. How would it know? For the sister photon to immediately have the opposite polarization, information would have to travel faster than the speed of light from the first photon to tell its sister what to do. In 1935, Einstein wrote a paper with Jacob Podolsky and Samuel Rosen describing this 'EPR' paradox. Since faster than light communication was impossible – it breaks the law of special relativity – they concluded quantum mechanics must be wrong, or at least incomplete. A deeper theory would be needed to explain the particles' behavior. One very simple explanation is by analogy to socks! (Clothing analogies are one of the ways physicists try to make quantum mechanics less intimidating.)

Consider sister photons as if they were right and left socks. If we found a left sock on the bedroom floor, we would be unsurprised to find the matching sock was a right one. There is no need for messages to flow between the socks faster than the speed of light to synchronize them, they already know what they are! Einstein presumed sister photons were like socks; they were emitted from the light source with their polarizations already set, though you could not see this information until you measured one of the photons. The information was dubbed 'hidden' and the theory is called hidden variable theory.

Einstein was to be proven wrong.

For many years after the EPR paper was published, physicists split into factions: some thought the world random, some believed in hidden variables, and others thought attempts to 'understand' quantum mechanics were misguided. Why should physics make sense? The equations work. Who cares why?

In 1964, John Bell, an Irish physicist working at the Conseil Européen pour la Recherche Nucléaire ('CERN'), devised a way to test Einstein's hidden variable theory. He pointed out that if photons possess hidden variables and we randomly measure them with a detector set at three angles, we would expect to see more than one-third of the photons share the same result. But, in 1972, Freedman and Clauser performed this experiment and showed the photons share the result only a little over a quarter of the time. Since 'a little over a quarter' is less than 'more than a third', Bell's theory is false. Of course, Bell was entirely happy about this, since he set the equation up to be disproven. His equation is called an inequality because the equation contains a more than sign '>' rather than an equals '=' sign, so people say that quantum mechanics violates the Bell inequality. Because the inequality is violated, photons can have no prior knowledge of their polarization.

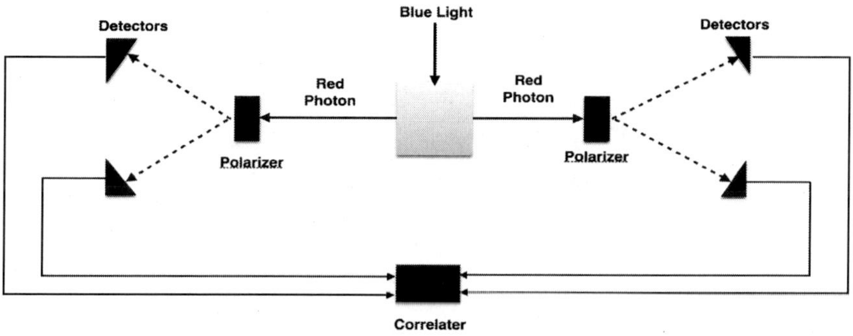

Bell Test Experiment

This is quite a complex piece of mathematics so let me show you how it works. Again, our thought experiment relies on an analogy involving clothing – sorry.

In the Bell Test experiment three polarizers are set up at 0, ⅓ and ⅔ of the way around a circle, 120 degrees apart. For Einstein to be correct photons must each carry at least three pieces of information:

If I meet the 0 degree polarizer do I go through or not?
If I meet the 120 degree polarizer do I go through or not?
If I meet the 240 degree polarizer do I go through or not?

If a photon had only one piece of information, say that it was vertically polarized, it would not *know* what to do if it came across a polarizer at 45 degrees. In that case the photon would sometimes go through and sometimes not, with a fifty-fifty probability. But Einstein did not want to countenance probability. "God does not play dice with the Universe." He required certainty. "I like to think the Moon is there when I am not watching it." The photons must know enough to handle, with certainty, any eventuality they may come across. (We could set up experiments with a more complex set of choices, dividing the photons into quarters, fifths and so on, but thirds are simple numbers and we can use the children's clothing analogy to demonstrate the mathematics.)

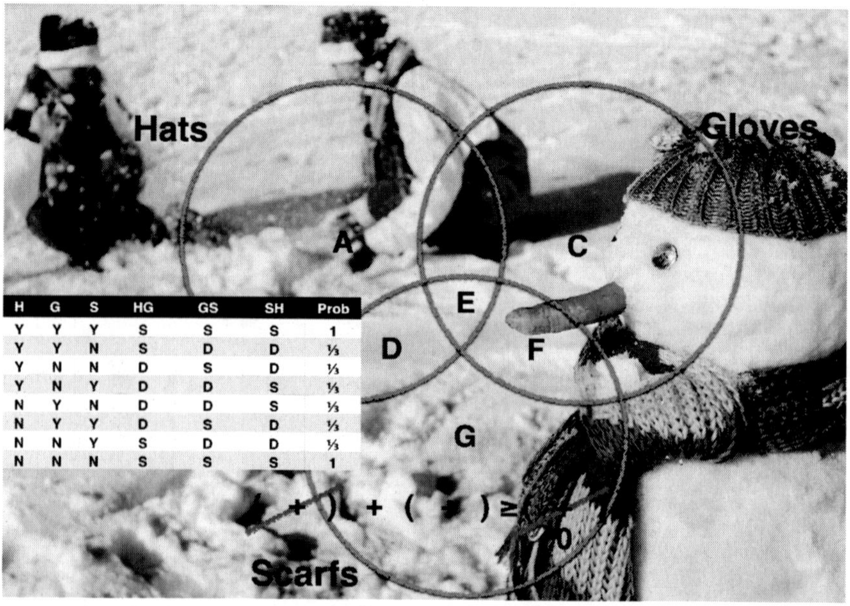

Hats, Scarves, and Gloves

We could liken photons knowing three pieces of information to children in a playground choosing to wear either hats, scarfs or gloves in some combination: hats for vertical, gloves for 120 degrees and scarfs for 240 degrees. There are eight choices for each child; nothing, hat, gloves, scarf, hat and scarf, hat and gloves, scarf and gloves, or all three.

Bell asked how often we would see two measurements agree. Look at the illustration and you can see when this happens. If a child was wearing all the clothes then if you check any pair, say gloves and scarfs you will always get a yes. If one of the children is wearing none of their winter clothes, you will always get a no for any pair you check. In these two cases, we are always sure to get agreement. For all the other cases, only one in three of the tests will agree. So Bell said that any time you have something with three hidden variables, there is at least a one in three chance that the measurements you make will agree, since six of the tests are one in three and the other two are certain.

Due to Heisenberg's Uncertainty Principle we can only look at one piece of clothing at a time. But, there is a trick. If there are identical twins among the children – who always dress the same way in our analogy – we can look at the gloves of one twin and the hat of another. Because they are twins if the first twin is wearing a hat we know the second one is too, without looking. We have a trick to measure two things at once.

When the test is done on twin photons only one in four, one quarter, agree. So there is a problem with the children analogy. It turns out photons don't wear gloves, hats, and scarfs. There are no hidden variables. A photon does not know what it will do before you measure it and can only decide on the fly at the point of measurement.

This means quantum particles are not *there* when they are not being observed. Observing them *does* appear to make them real. If the hidden variables, the gloves, hats and scarfs were in set positions when we were not observing them, the photon measurements would agree at least one-third of the time, but they do not. When we measure them, the two particles somehow communicate and agree to give a positive result only one quarter of the time. Bizarre, but that's just the way it is!

The Bell result is still somewhat controversial and has not been proven to everyone's satisfaction. Potential loopholes exist but are steadily being eroded. An experiment by Nicolas Giseng of CERN using the fiber optic network of Swiss Telecom to separate twin photons, shows the coordination signals must travel at least 10,000 times the speed of light – the limitation, and reason it is not infinitely fast, being the accuracy of his clocks. Daniel Sego, Daniel Danziger and Michael Wise have performed the Bell test experiment with an apparatus installed near Innsbruck where the choice of detector orientation was made by a random number generator after the photons had left the emitter. This shows the photons really can't know what they will do before they start their journey. Another loophole is the loss of some photons. We don't measure *all* the photons in an optical experiment because some are absorbed by the apparatus. It has been suggested all the 'lost' photons make up the error in the experiment. This is not very likely, it's akin to assuming all the voters who did not vote in an election would have voted Democrat. To avoid this criticism, an experiment has been performed with magnetized particles that don't get lost. The Bell result holds true.The loopholes are diminishing and it seems likely Bell will win out in the end.

Although the coordination information appears instantaneous, John Bell gave us an elegant explanation as to why this does not allow us to use the effect to transfer information faster than the speed of light. Imagine we are sitting at opposite ends of a room. We both toss coins and each of us write down our results; heads, tails, heads, heads and so on. I then acquire a magical power that causes your coin to make an extra flip just before you catch it, so it always gives the opposite result to mine. Although I am now controlling your coin, you cannot tell, as the result looks as random as before. The difference is simply that at first the coin orientation was random in its own right and then the opposite of my random result. It is only when I walk over and compare our results we can see they are matched in this strange way. There is no way to transmit information using this effect. Only after the experiment is finished can we exchange the necessary information to see the coordination that existed, and that comparison required me to transfer information. The fastest way to do that is at the speed of light.

Despite saying it is impossible, let us do a thought experiment and try to transmit information using Morse code. I will set up a simple old fashion telegraph machine. When I press the telegraph button at my end this will cause a measurement and the photons at your end will be forced to the opposite polarization. When I lift the key, your photons will revert to being randomized. You can see this illustrated in the diagram. Although I make your photon take up a polarization, analogous to making the coin take an extra flip, you don't have enough information to know this.

Now we are ready to use our quantum Morse machine to prove the Universe must have free will, or at least a degree of non-determinism.

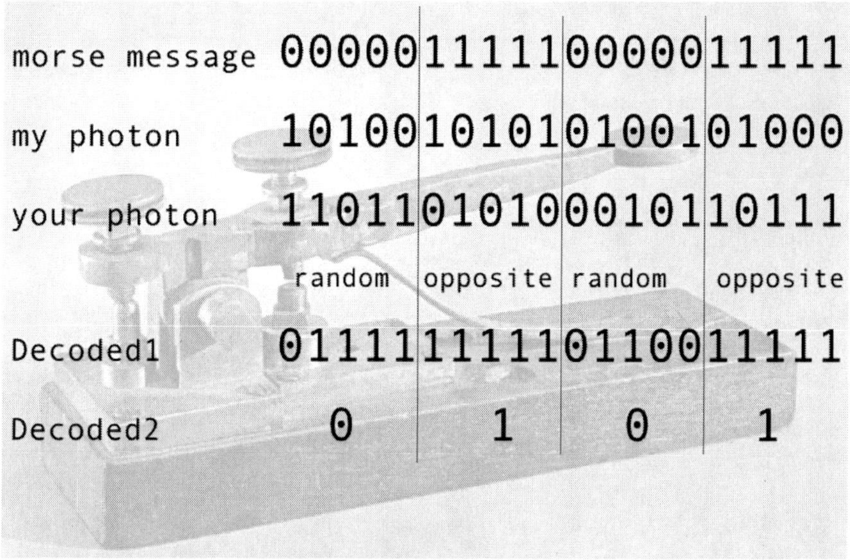

Quantum Morse Machine

A Simple Free Will Theorem

In the quantum Morse machine, I *do* transmit information faster than the speed of light. But the information I have transmitted is useless as it is, in effect, encrypted using a one-time pad. The only person in possession of a copy of this one-time pad is me: the sender.

Claude Shannon proved a one-time pad is unbreakable during the Second World War. Yet the British succeeded in breaking it. How was this possible?

The fatal weakness in the German one-time pads was the random numbers used to code the messages were generated by a machine, and were therefore not truly random. The numbers followed a sequence, and it was possible for Allied code breakers to work out the sequence and decode the messages. It follows that if we believe no message can propagate faster than the speed of light, my sequence of numbers must be non-computable. There must be no algorithm or computation that could generate it. Otherwise it would be liable to the same sort of decryption attack that the one-time pads suffered. If sequences of random measurements taken in the universe are non-computable it follows the Universe as a whole must be non-computable.

There are a few holes you could pick in this argument. Would it be sufficient if it were impossible to decrypt the message in the age of the Universe? What if there was an algorithm, but it was practically unknowable? But, I am talking here of principle. In principle, the Universe must be non-decryptable.

Richard Dawkins and the Atheist Tour Bus

"God exists, if only in the form of a meme with high survival value, or infective power, in the environment provided by human culture."

Richard Dawkins

Does God have Free Will?

Any discussion of free will is incomplete without some mention of God. Scientists generally avoid the topic, but since we're talking about such a fundamental concept, we must consider whether the Universe would be any different if it had a creator.

Recently there have been two widely publicized attacks on religious belief from the scientific community: the head-on attack from Richard Dawkins in *The God Delusion* or, the hard hitting sideswipe by Stephen Hawking in *The Universe in a Nutshell.*

Hawking made the front pages in 2000 with the statement: "There is then no need for a creator." He was considering whether God needed to ignite the Big Bang or if it occurred as a natural result of the laws of physics. Hawking had run the mathematics and realized a god was not needed to light the blue touch paper for the Big Bang - the laws of physics spontaneously caused it. His argument does not actually preclude the existence of a god, but it does move the point where we need a creator one step further up the chain.

This is not a fundamental change to the progress of theological argument over the last thousand years. Once we abandon our vision of God as a master builder, literally breathing life into Adam while putting the finishing touches to the Garden of Eden, we can move him up the causal chain as far as we like, eventually reaching a point where intervention is necessary to get things started. Hawking is only pointing out an intervention is not needed at the point of the Big Bang. It still begs the question “Where did the laws of physics come from?” If you don’t believe in a god then pushing a creator figure further and further up the chain eventually makes him redundant. If you have faith, you can take the position God is the creator of the fundamental rules.

Regardless of your personal position, I would like to make the argument for free will independent of belief. We must resolve the age-old paradox: How can God be all-knowing and all-powerful, and still have free will?

This is a long-standing theological debate dating back to the 15th century. It splits theologians into two camps. The first maintains God has both omniscience and omnipotence, and they are not inconsistent. This is the compatibilism argument again. Despite the acknowledged paradox, they argue that we should simply accept it and acknowledge that we are unable to comprehend such things. I don’t like this argument because it essentially denies reason. We are supposed to acknowledge that we simply cannot understand the mind of God. I prefer the more modern argument from the second camp that omnipotence trumps omniscience. It preserves the view that man can reason about the Universe – “Man is made in God’s image.”

This argument follows the logic: God must be able to choose not to know what will happen in the future so that he can have free will.

Fork in the Road

"When making a decision of minor importance, I have always found it advantageous to consider all the pros and cons. In vital matters, however, such as the choice of a mate or a profession, the decision should come from the unconscious, from somewhere within ourselves. In the important decisions of personal life, we should be governed, I think, by the deep inner needs of our nature."

Alan Turing

The Free Will Theorem

In 2006, John Conway and Simon Kochen published *The Free Will Theorem*. The paper received huge press attention and has been widely discussed in the scientific community. Their theorem states that; provided experimenters are free to run their experiment as they choose, the behavior of the particles they experiment upon is not determined in advance. Particles have free will!

If we go back to the Bell Test experiment, this proved twin particles do not carry around a parcel of information telling them what to do. Perhaps they get their marching orders from some outside influence. There are two possibilities. A particle is either told what to do by its environment or it gets its information from some data source. Can we use the laws of physics to test these possibilities? We don't need to know how the influence works, just that it might exist in principle.

Conway and Kochen prove there can be no external influence, and when a particle reveals its spin, that spin was not known beforehand. It is independent of any information in the history of the Universe up to that point.

Conway and Kochen's proof is elegant and involves some mental gymnastics, but it is no harder than Archimedes' proof of the infinity of primes we looked at earlier. Let us start with our twin particles. We are going to pick bosons, which have whole number spin. If you measure the spin, you will always get a reading of -1, 0 or +1. 'Spin' is one of those words physicists use to explain quantum things. It does not necessarily denote rotation but, if your mental model is a spinning top, that's not too bad. If we measure something in the quantum world, it always yields a classical result – in this case the magnitudes of spin are 1, 0 and 1. (Minus one squared is one.)

We need to imagine measuring the spin of a particle along three axes; x, y and z. Hold your hand up and make a shape that looks like the one in the following picture. You might remember it from science classes; it was used to help you understand Fleming's left-hand rule. For our purposes it does not matter which hand you use; it is just the shape that matters. I am going to use my left hand for sentimental reasons.

Now, imagine the palm of your hand is the measuring apparatus: your index finger the x axis, your middle finger, y and your thumb, z. At any moment you can move your hand to point in any direction and take a measurement. We will have to round up or down. Quantum mechanics is named 'quantum' because *all* the readings must be whole numbers. You will never see 10% spin in x, 90% in y and 85% in z; just ones, and zeros. The measurements for a Boson will always be 1,0,1 in some order. This is known as the '101' rule.

Now, we ask the question: does a particle have a definite spin before we take a measurement? The instinctive answer is yes, and this way of viewing things is known as realism. It seems obvious that even if we did not make a measurement, the particle would still have its spin; we just wouldn't know which type. Einstein explained realism by saying "I like

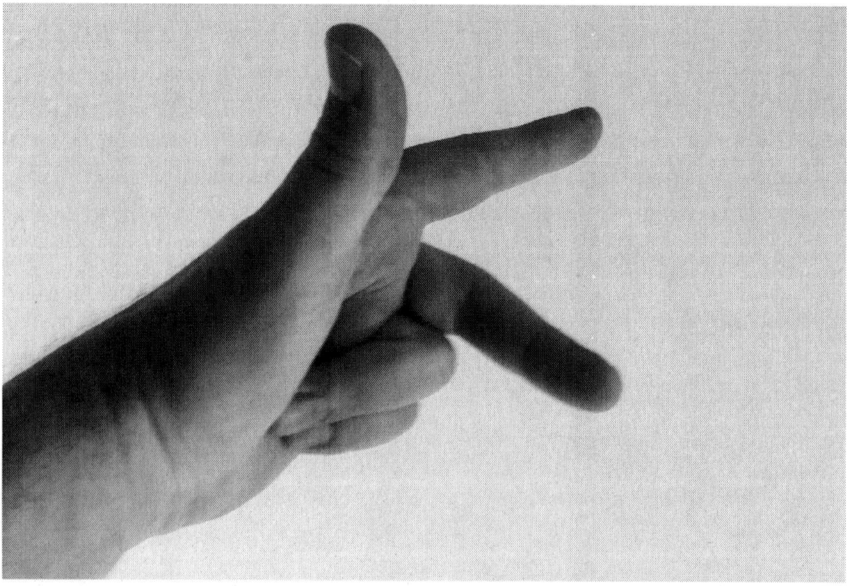

Kochen Specker

to think the Moon is there when I am not looking at it." But, how can we test his statement? How can we know something is there without taking a look? There is a way...

Let us suppose the particle had a definite spin before we measured it. Perhaps its spin points at the top left hand corner of the room. Imagine taking many measurements and seeing what happens. We can point our hand in any direction: top of the room, bottom left corner, bottom right corner and so on. Each time we point our hand in a direction we must get 1, 0 and 1 in some combination (110, 011, 101). The particles are 101 particles and this is an absolute rule.

Let's imagine doing the experiment. We fix the spin of a particle and begin to take measurements, noting the answers as we go. If we get a borderline condition we obey the 101 rule and give ourselves a 1, 0, 1 reading. As we move our hand to take measurements, a problem begins to emerge. Every now and again we obtain a measurement that conflicts. We chose a 1, 0, 1 when we were pointing our index finger towards the floor, but if we point the finger toward the door, we need that original middle number to have been a 1 for consistency. (The middle finger is now pointing in the direction the index finger pointed to for the first reading.) To fix the inconsistency we can change our original borderline decision to a 1,1,0. All is well and we continue. But, as we get over 30 measurements, we can't seem to find any way to make all the 1,0,1s fit together. After scratching our head for a while, we realize there might be no solution. And indeed there is not. This is the Kochen-Specker Paradox. The odd shaped cubes on the building in the Escher print are an example of one of these impossible figures.

1 0 1 puzzle piece

An analogy to this problem is trying to solve a broken Rubik's Cube. There is a really mischievous trick you can play on someone: reverse two colors on a Rubik's Cube. You can easily do this by snapping one of the edge blocks out, turning it around and snapping it back in. When the colors are already muddled up this is not obvious. Now give your

M. C. Escher's Waterfall (Impossible Shapes)

friend the puzzle and they will spend hours trying to solve it! It can't be done because the puzzle is put together wrong. And in this matter nature is also put together wrong! With as few as 33 measurements it is impossible to construct a consistent three-dimensional shape that has 1s and 0s obeying the 101 rule in every place. The only way to complete such a shape is with a measurement that is both simultaneously zero and one: a paradox. We know what happens when we generate paradoxes. It means one of the original assumptions is false and, in this instance, the falsehood is that a particle has a definite spin before we measure it. It

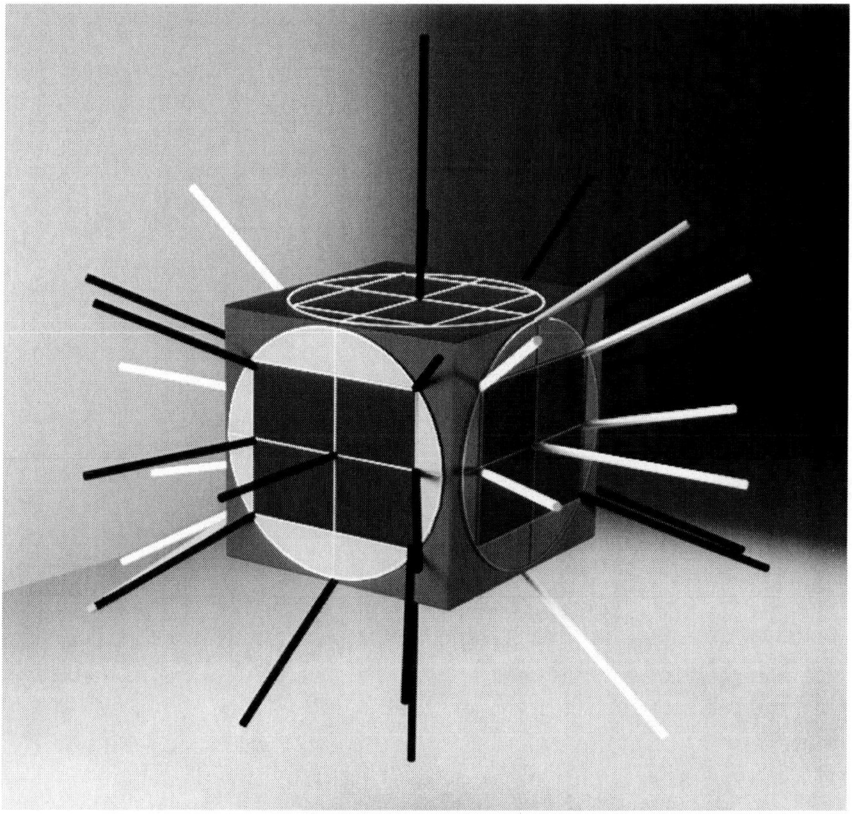

Kochen-Specker Cube

cannot. It must make up its mind on the fly. Einstein would be horrified. Realism is violated by the quantum world: reality and measurement are intertwined.

The Kochen-Specker paradox shows us that a particle only makes its choice at the point of measurement. This does not prove it has free will as it might still be told what to do by some external entity. It's rather like the famous game show, *Who Wants to be a Millionaire?* The particle could answer the spin question in four possible ways. First, it could *know* the answer, but we have just proven it does not. Second, it could *phone a friend* obtaining the answer from some cosmic arbiter. Third, it could ask the audience and take a vote from all the particles around it. Finally, it could freely choose, without recourse to any of the other possible options – in other words, it would guess!

A guess would mean particles have free will; no extraneous influence or piece of information either on their person or from some external source could have any effect. We are now going to prove the particle *does* guess.

The Proof

Conway and Kochen construct their proof from a small set of axioms, which form a rhyme. The axioms are; twin, fin and spin.

If two particles are separated by a distance (fin) and entangled (twin), the spins of the particles (spin) cannot be determined by any information in *their* history of the Universe up to that point. The proof relies on a thought experiment.

Consider twin particles separated by a long distance. Physicists call this 'space like separation'. All this means is one particle is measured on, say, Earth and the other on Mars, so relativity is significant in the experiment. This may be impractical today but there is no reason the experiment could not be done in principle. In the future, our children could set up on the UN Moon base and fire one photon to a detector on Hubble II and the other to the future Mars Orbital Station. Farfetched? If you had told Einstein back in 1947 that in less than 70 years we would be able to measure individual photons by sending them down spun glass fibers to locations separated by 50 kilometers, involving a multidisciplinary team composed of American, German, French and Russian scientists, all working in harmony, he might have been equally incredulous.

As the proof introduces relativity we also need two imaginary rocket ships. They must be traveling below the speed of light, so no Star Trek Enterprise or Millennium Falcon. We will have to stick with an old-school spaceship, the Sulaco from *Aliens* should do the trick. They must travel in opposite directions, passing our Moon Base just as the scientists run the experiment.

Special Relativity shows our Universe has a strange property: there is no such thing as a simultaneous event for two observers – at least if they are separated by any distance. From the point of view of the first spaceship, the measurement on Mars occurs first. But from the vantage point of the second observer, the measurement on Hubble occurs first.

Now comes the proof by counter example. Let us suppose the particles *were* influenced by an outside effect and had no free will.

Let us say the Mars particle chooses its answer because of an external influence. Its Hubble twin must choose the same answer. There is no problem with this because the Hubble particle could have made its decision before the Mars particle, so the decision was not predetermined.

But in another frame of reference the choice is made in the opposite sequence. The Hubble particle chooses after the Mars particle. This is predetermination and it breaks the Kochen-Specker theorem.

You can reverse the whole analysis and see the same problem from the other point of view. There is a paradox here however you look at it.

The only solution to the paradox is that both particles make their choice without any information from an outside source; particles have free will. This means at least one new piece of information spontaneously appears in the Universe – a 'bit' of free will, so to speak.

You might think there is a problem because the first particle affects its twin, even if the second did not receive any outside influence. This would result in the Kochen-Specker paradox reemerging. There is a neat way out of this; time has no meaning for the particles. Or, I should say, relative time has no meaning and, therefore, has no effect. There is no concept of before or after between the particles. They live in a little bubble of space-time where the order of events has no meaning. The particles make their free choice together within this safe bubble, and the paradox is avoided. When we come to measure them, we see they both made a random decision together, but if we ask which made it first, the question has no meaning. There is no clock valid for both particles, so there is no possible answer to the question.

Conway and Kochen have proven sub-atomic particles have free will – or at least entangled bosons do. At this point, their argument becomes a philosophical one. They propose that these particles pass on this free will to larger entities in the Universe and ultimately to us. Although particles are small and insignificant, they are the fundamental building blocks of nature, and the butterfly effect multiplies up tiny variations in the microscopic world into the macroscopic events we see.

Although their theorem is very elegant, we still have to address the question of whether the experimenter has the true freedom to run the experiment in the first place: the determined determinist argument.

Russian Dolls

"Great fleas have little fleas upon
their backs to bite 'em.

And little fleas have lesser fleas,
and so ad infinitum.

And the great fleas themselves, in
turn, have greater fleas to go on.

While these again have greater
still, and greater still, and so on."

Augustus De Morgan

Free Will Universe

I believe we live in a Universe where information comes into existence through the creative endeavors of human beings. When Andrew Wiles discovered his solution to Fermat's Last Theorem, he did something a computer cannot do and demonstrated non-computational thought. But there is an alternative explanation put forward by the determined determinists.

Daniel Dennett – the standard bearer for this camp – believes everything in the Universe is entirely determined. He argues there is no place in the laws of nature for free will to arise.

Both sides of the argument agree Turing prohibits a general-purpose machine from solving all mathematical problems, but that seems to be the extent of agreement. The determinists solve the Wiles Paradox by arguing he is a special purpose machine, perfectly able to find answers to non-computable problems. The Turing prohibition only applies to general purpose machines. Let us run a thought experiment to see what sort of Universe we would live in if special purpose machines were the answer to this puzzle.

If the Universe is determined, it can be modeled as a single algorithm. If everything in the Universe evolves according to a set of rules, it will run like a giant piece of clockwork or one large computer game. Each solar system, planet, and individual mathematician would evolve along preordained lines. Mathematicians would operate as software subroutine and would rely on further subroutines to explain the beating of their hearts and the way the molecules of their body interact.

If our Universe were organized in this way:

This Universe *could not* discover solutions to arbitrary problems.

This Universe *could* be preprogrammed with every theory we could ever discover within it. (There would be no arbitrary problems.)

This argument neatly sidesteps Turing's theorem by specifying there is no such thing as an arbitrary problem – a random problem picked from the infinite set of problems. At the same time, it sets certain characteristics of such a Universe and I believe we can test these...

A computable Universe must already know the solution to every problem it will encounter above the logic limit: It cannot discover knowledge on the fly. For many problems, a small number of fundamental rules can account for everything. Although our galaxy and the beautiful nebulae we see through our telescopes look complex, they might be the result of some such simple set of rules – just like a fractal. That's Stephen Wolfram's solution to the mystery of our Universe. But some problems are complex. The solution to Fermat's Last Theorem is an 80 page document consisting of 5 million bits of information. All this must be stored somewhere in the Universe. It might not be stored as a string of bytes, it could be found in a set of equations governing the motion of the atoms such that at some point – in 1995 to be exact – they all line up in Andrew Wiles' brain to direct his fingers to type out the proof. In this case, the Universe has solved a mathematical puzzle because it was specifically set up to do so from the time of the Big Bang, but this raises three questions:

Where does the Universe store this enormous amount of information?

How does The Universe hold the information reliably?

How did the pre-Universe solve the problem, so it might program the Universe at the moment of the Big Bang?

The first question is probably answerable. The Universe is a big place and could store sufficient information to solve the mysteries that puzzle the inquisitive creatures that inhabit its planes. There are many practical problems to consider, such as how to preserve the information through all the strange evolutions of our Universe; inflation, star formation, and so on. But it could be done.

The second question is insurmountable and presents the counter argument to the determinists. Our Universe appears to be composed of non-deterministic objects. Such objects exist in the mathematical world; Kochen-Specker cubes, for example. Unfortunately for the determined determinist, bosons behave according to the same principles. In case you're thinking thinking bosons are rare, light is formed of bosons. Our whole existence is surrounded by non-deterministic physics. Therefore, your actions are not predetermined by anything in your local corner of the Universe – the past light cone if you want to be strict about the physics.

The determined determinists are a determined bunch. Just because the information that determines your actions cannot be encoded by the particles you are made from, does not mean you are free. The information could be stored in parts of the Universe we cannot see, or held outside the Universe in some sort of cosmic hard drive. Every creative event in the Universe would be specified in this store.

But this begs the third question: How was this store of information generated in the first place? If a Universe contains creative things – as our Universe does – there is no way to computably generate the necessary determinist store of information. The Universe has free will because there is no deterministic process that could generate it.

If our Universe were a Turing machine, everything within it would be too. Think about the deterministic clockwork argument I gave earlier. If you try to construct a better – say a more random – machine inside a Turing machine, an observer could simply ignore the better machine hidden within it, and watch the outer machine work. The outer machine will predict the operation of the inner machine perfectly, even if the inner machine is fiendishly complicated. We have to consider the machine on which our human software runs. Our bodies, our minds, all that we are, is software running on the Universe's hardware of quarks and photons. If the hardware is deterministic, then so is our software. And if the hardware is deterministic, there can be no creativity within the Universe.

So the free will camp has an argument easily as frustrating as the one deployed by the determinists. Every time a determinist asks, "How do you know you were not always going to do that?" the free will believer can reply, "You asked me a question. If this dialogue is to have any significance, then we must exist in a rational Universe and, therefore, the laws of information give us creativity and free will. If you believe we are fully determined, there is no point in my answering your question."

I reason. Therefore, I have free will.

The Universe is not a machine.

Chapter 16

THE QUEST FOR KNOWLEDGE

Darwin's Beagle

"Sometimes I've believed as many as six impossible things before breakfast."

Queen of Hearts in

Lewis Carroll's Alice

"It is not the strongest of the species that survives, nor the most intelligent that survives. It is the one that is the most adaptable to change."

Charles Darwin

We celebrate creativity with many competitions and prizes. I have been a student of problem lists of over the years. Here is my list of the problems remaining open in the modern world. I've tied it in with other lists where relevant, and indicate what you might win if you were to solve one. As I was writing this book, a few of the questions were answered; the Higgs Boson was discovered and the Poincaré Conjecture proven. I will keep the list up to date on the web site.

1. **Mathematics** [Fields Medal]
   - 1.1 The Birch and Swinnerton-Dyer Conjecture.[C]
   - 1.2 Hodge Conjecture [C]
   - 1.3 Navier-Stokes Equations [C]
   - 1.4 A proof or disproof of P =NP [C]
   - 1.5 The Poincaré Conjecture [C] – Solved
   - 1.6 Riemann Hypothesis [h8 C]
   - 1.7 Yang-Mills Theory [C]
   - 1.8 Can we understand and solve all 23 Hilbert Problems [h1-23]
   - 1.9 Goldbach Conjecture [h8]
   - 1.10 Is mathematics fundamental to or simply a good model of our Universe? [H6]
   - 1.11 Is mathematics an emergent property in our Universe or causal? Which is more fundamental?
   - 1.12 Fermat's own original proof of his theorem!

2. **Physics** [Nobel Prize for Physics]
   - 2.1 Are there many worlds or just one?
   - 2.2 Does quantum collapse have meaning?
   - 2.3 Will we find the Higgs-Boson? (Provisionally yes, 2012)
   - 2.4 Do we need quantum gravity to explain human thought?
   - 2.5 Will we observe gravitational waves, and what is the current explanation for gravitational noise?
   - 2.6 What causes the arrow of time and the asymmetry of physical laws?
   - 2.7 Do the constants of physics change over time?
   - 2.8 Is quantum computation sufficient to simulate the universe, or is the universe non-computational?
   - 2.9 Can magnetic monopoles exist?
   - 2.10 What is meant by quantum non-locality, a.k.a., spooky action at a distance?

2.11 Is there a theory that would unite gravity with the other three forces: a Theory of Everything?
2.12 Is Schrödinger's cat alive or dead in the box?
2.13 Does ball lightning exist and can it be made in the laboratory?

3. **Cosmology** **Nobel Prize for Physics**
   3.1 What is the nature of Dark Matter?
   3.2 What is the nature of Dark Energy?
   3.3 What is Dark Flow?
   3.4 The slingshot anomaly.
   3.5 Did inflation really happen?
   3.6 Was there a singularity at the origin of our Universe, and what happened before the first second? An eternity?
   3.7 Can any information travel faster than the speed of light?
   3.8 What is the cause of the Pioneer anomaly? (solved in 2011)
   3.9 Are there aliens?
   3.10 The Goldilocks question. Why are the cosmological constants so finely tuned?
   3.11 Do real numbers exist or is our Universe quantized?
   3.12 Why is there little antimatter?
   3.13 What are cosmic rays and where do they come from?
   3.14 What was the WOW signal?
   3.15 Does the fine structure constant vary over time?
   3.16 If we live in an infinite Universe, why don't we see more strange things?
   3.17 Why is the cosmic background radiation so smooth?
   3.18 How can we explain the lack of total smoothness of the cosmic background radiation!
   3.19 Is there an explanation for any detail in the cosmic background radiation map?

4. **Engineering** **Nobel Prize for Chemistry, Turing Award**
   4.1 Can we achieve economic nuclear fusion?
   4.2 Will we realize cold fusion? (Partially demonstrated)
   4.3 Can an amateur get to the moon?
   4.4 Can an amateur collect a rock from the moon? X
   4.5 Will we make an Artificial Intelligence?
   4.6 Can we make a Tricorder? X
   4.7 Can we power the world from renewable sources?
   4.8 Will robots go to war in the future?

4.9 Can we make a robot indistinguishable from a human and cross the uncanny valley?
4.10 What is the tallest building we could build on planet Earth?
4.11 Will we routinely use flying cars by the end of this century?
4.12 Will we have a base on the Moon or Mars in this century?

5. Biology [Nobel Prize for Medicine]

5.1 Why is the placebo effect so strong?
5.2 Can we cure the common cold?
5.3 Is there a generally effective treatment for cancer?
5.4 Can we find a vaccine against HIV?
5.5 Can we cure endemic diseases such as malaria, or is it an arms race?
5.6 How plastic are our genes and is epigenetics a significant factor?
5.7 Can we cure dementia? [L]
5.8 Can we make a desktop gene sequencer? [X]
5.9 Will we prove the Kurzweil Hypothesis that technology will allow us to live forever?
5.10 How old will we live to with a reasonable quality of life?
5.11 Can genes jump between organisms? Even participating in whole scale fusion?
5.12 Will we be able to grow organs?
5.13 Will we clone a human from an adult?
5.14 Can we clone a dinosaur?

6. The Mind [Nobel Prize for Medicine]

6.1 Does the Flynn Effect mean we are really becoming more intelligent?
6.2 What is the nature of consciousness?
6.3 Do we have free will?
6.4 Which is more important: Nature or Nurture?
6.5 What is humor for?
6.6 Do some people have photographic memory? (yes, recent)
6.7 What is the purpose of sleep and, in particular, dreams?
6.8 What is understanding?
6.9 Do we ever truly know something?
6.10 How does the brain think?
6.11 Is the brain a quantum device?
6.12 Why do we get stressed?
6.13 Why are some people more intelligent than others?

6.14 What limits our ability to concentrate and work hard mentally?

7. The Ancient World Pulitzer prize for History

7.1 What is the Linear-a script discovered in Crete?
7.2 Where are the ruins of the Light House at Alexandria and indeed Alexandria itself?
7.3 What is the location of the Lost City of Atlantis if it is not a myth?
7.4 Will we ever find King John's Treasure?
7.5 What is the truth to the legend of El Dorado?
7.6 Why were the pyramids built?
7.7 What was the purpose of Stonehenge and who built it?
7.8 How many books and how much knowledge have we lost?
7.9 Did King Arthur and Camelot exist in any real way?
7.10 Why did the people of Easter Island build their statues?
7.11 Was there an ancient flood, suggested by the Bible and other ancient texts?
7.12 Are the Seven Wonders of the Ancient World lost forever?

8. The Modern World Nobel Peace Prize or Prize for Economics

8.1 Is there a best political organization for a country?
8.2 What is the best political balance of federation and autonomy?
8.3 The Black Swan Effect: Why do improbable things happen?
8.4 Is there a right way to run the economies of the world?
8.5 When is it right to intervene in a conflict, and when is it best to leave a country to its own devices?
8.6 What is the best way to choose a political representative?
8.7 Will we ever abolish war?
8.8 Why is the gap between rich and poor increasing in most of the world today?
8.9 How powerful should states be compared with world organizations?
8.10 Is there a right level of tax?
8.11 Are morals absolute or relative: euthanasia, abortion, gay marriage, eating meat?
8.12 What will we do about our aging population?

9. Planet Earth Goldman Prize for the Environment

9.1 Is man-made global warming real, and if already proven will we ever persuade the US government?
9.2 What caused the Tunguska Explosion?
9.3 What caused the extinction of the dinosaurs?
9.4 Can we predict earthquakes or eruptions?
9.5 What caused the reversing of the poles and when will the next one occur?
9.6 What was the origin of life on Earth?
9.7 Will we be wiped out by an asteroid before we build a suitable defense?
9.8 Can we grow enough food to feed the planet? [L]
9.9 Can we give clean water to everyone on the planet? [L]
9.10 Is increasing air travel compatible with survival of the planet? [L]

10. Philosophy [Nobel Prize in Literature and others]

10.1 Is there a God?
10.2 Where did we come from if we are not made by a god? And if we were, then where did God come from?
10.3 Where do morals come from?
10.4 Is there a reality?
10.5 Is there life after death?
10.6 Do we have free will?
10.7 Is beauty in the eye of the beholder?
10.8 What is the meaning of life, the Universe and everything, other than 42?

11. Conspiracy and Paranormal

11.1 Is there anything going on in the Bermuda Triangle?
11.2 Do aliens make crop circles? (disproven hoax)
11.3 Who was Jack the Ripper?
11.4 Can the mind bend spoons? (hoax, admitted)
11.5 Does the government suppress UFO existence?
11.6 Why was the Mary Celeste abandoned?
11.7 Is the Turin Shroud that of Christ?
11.8 Do the Abominable Snowman and Sasquatch exist?
11.9 Are there ghosts?
11.10 Is there a paranormal?
11.11 Do aliens live amongst us?
11.12 Was there a conspiracy in the shooting of JFK?

Cross reference to other lists

Hn: Hilbert's Problem
C: Clay Mathematics Millennium Prizes
X: XPRIZE
L: Longitude Prize

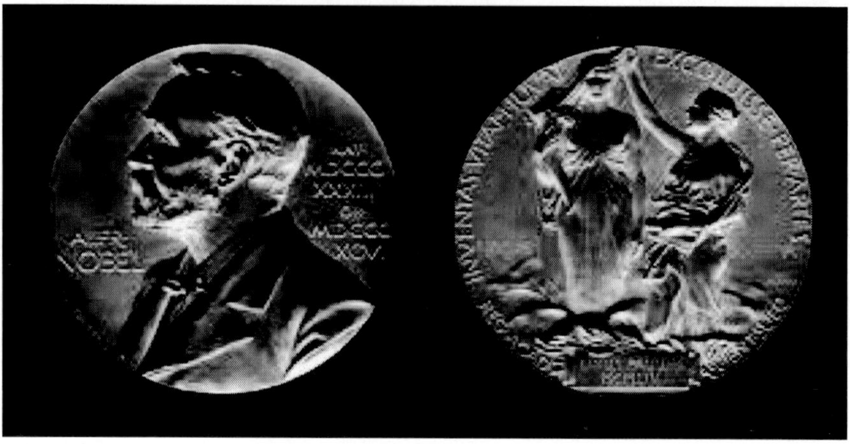

Nobel Prize Medal

"If I could explain it to the average person, I wouldn't have been worth the Nobel Prize."

Richard P. Feynman

Awards for Discovery

People like prizes. Competition drives humans forward in a way we don't properly understand. In film, we have the Academy Awards, whilst on the web we have The Webbies. Some prizes, such as the Nobel Prize, Fields Medal and Pulitzer Prizes, have a long and distinguished history, while others such as the XPRIZE are more recent creations. Some prizes, such as the Ig Nobel Prize and the Golden Pineapples were mainly created for their humorous value. Prizes are not a recent phenomenon. The Longitude Prize, originally won by John Harrison, is being revived in Britain in 2014 to mark its 300th anniversary. The original prize, £10,000 in its day, was awarded by the British government for making a device that allowed ships to determine their East-West position (a sextant only gives north-south). The 2014 prize is £10m pounds and the topic will be chosen by public vote! Here is a small history of some of the more famous prizes.

Nobel Prizes

Alfred Nobel spent his life developing weapons and explosives. His laboratory was built in the middle of a lake with a bridge running to it, so if he blew himself up doing an experiment, only he would die. He managed to stabilize nitroglycerine by mixing it with saltpeter and created

Pulitzer Medal

dynamite. This was used in the mining industry but also extensively in weaponry, so he came to be known as the Merchant of Death during his lifetime.

To be known as the merchant of death would have a profound effect on anyone. As Nobel pondered the balance of his life's work he decided to do something positive with the huge wealth he had accumulated. On his death in 1896, he willed his entire fortune to create the awards we now call Nobel Prizes.

There were five original prizes; physics, chemistry, peace, physiology or medicine, and literature. A newer economic science prize is awarded by the Royal Swedish Academy of Sciences.

You must be alive to receive a Nobel Prize; a few have been awarded posthumously because the laureate died after the winner was announced but before the award ceremony. The work must have been proven experimentally, and although originally it was supposed to be for discoveries in the previous year, nowadays a theory must have stood the test of time. Consequently, winners tend to be quite old. The prize must be for something with practical applicability – Einstein received his Nobel Prize for the Photo Electric Effect, rather than his more famous Theory of Relativity. The judges evidently thought particles more practical than planets! The prize is usually awarded to a maximum of three people. This has produced some controversial results but despite this the Nobel Prize is the uncontested top prize in science.

Pulitzer Prize

A Pulitzer Prizes is to the arts what a Nobel Prize is to science. Again the Prize was the result of a bequest. They are awarded in the fields of music, art and literature. Unlike Nobel Prizes, where there are no public nominations and you might wait a lifetime for the phone call, you enter your name for a Pulitzer Prize. Most people associate the term Pulitzer Prize winner with journalism, but about 25 Pulitzers are awarded each year. You must be a US citizen to enter.

Turing Award

Originally set up by the Association of Computer Machinery, this award comes with prize money of $250,000, supported by Google and Intel, and goes to a person who significantly advanced computer science or artificial intelligence in the previous year. It is considered the Nobel Prize for computing.

XPRIZE

XPRIZEs are awarded for technology and bear the democratic stamp of the Internet age. Anyone can propose a challenge but they must also provide the prize money! It's big money. The Ansari XPRIZE for the first

XPRIZE First Award Ceremony

non-governmental organization to put a man in space was $10 million, awarded in 2004. There are a growing number of XPRIZEs, including, at the time of writing:

- Google Lunar XPRIZE, $30m to put a rover on the Moon.
- Qualcomm Tricorder XPRIZE, $10m to make your mobile phone into a hand held medical health scanner, similar to the Star Trek tricorder.
- Nokia Sensing CHALLENGE, $2.25m to build a hand-held medical scanner.
- Wendy Schmidt Ocean Health XPRIZE, $2m to create a method to measure the ocean's pH.

Fields Medal

The equivalent of a Nobel Prize for mathematics is a Fields Medal. Joseph Field provided the money and helped set up the prize. Today it is administered as part of the International Mathematical Union. You must be under 40 to receive the prize. Andrew Wiles was 45 when he solved Fermat's Last Theorem, so they created a special prize for him called a Fields Fellowship. Until recently only men had received the prize. However in 2014 Maryam Mirzakhani won the prize for her work on the geometry of Riemann surfaces.

Fields Medal

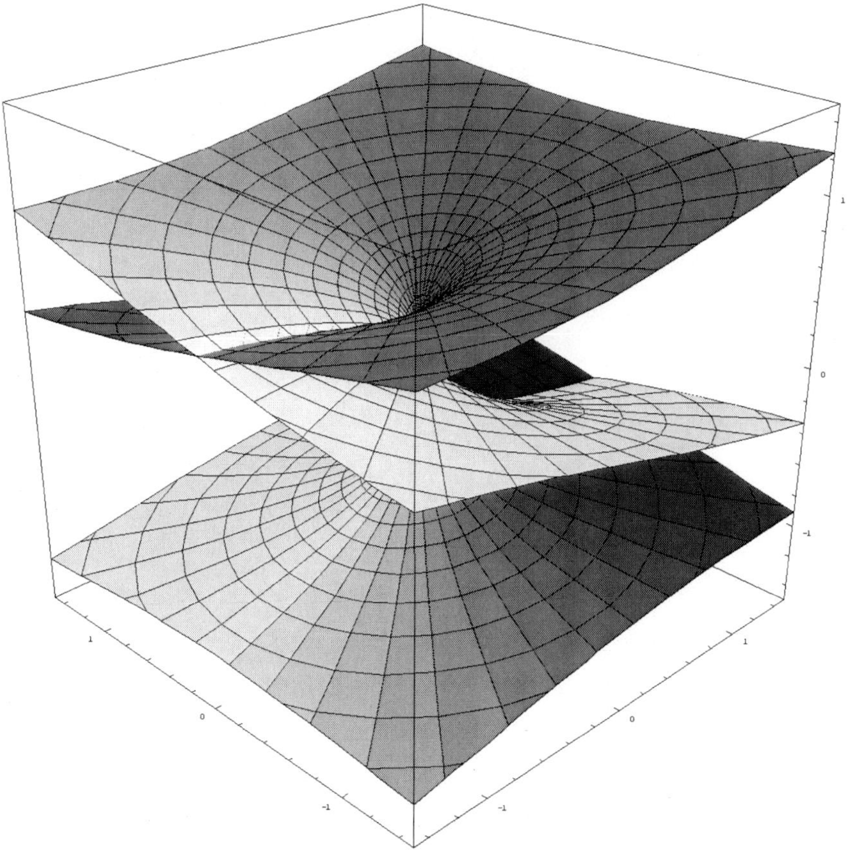

Riemann Surface

Chapter 17

THE FUTURE

Omar Khayyám

"Prediction is very hard,
especially about the future."

Niels Bohr

"The Moving Finger writes: and, having writ, Moves on: nor all thy Piety nor Wit Shall lure it back to cancel half a Line, Nor all thy Tears wash out a Word of it."

Rubaiyat of Omar Khayyam,
Edward FitzGerald

مایخ رمع تایعابر

I remember when I was eight years old, being asked to draw a vision of the world in the year 2000. In my the home of the future, rather than going to the shops to get milk, orange juice and cornflakes, they would arrive by pipe. These days I know about microbiology and realize this would have been highly impractical and perhaps rather dangerous. I could claim some premonition of the Internet at this point; no self-respecting science book is complete without one of these!

Of course, the truth is I had no more idea of the way things would turn out than anyone else. Now that I am a little older let's see how much trouble I can get into predicting the future.

I think we will build thinking machines – AIs – using our insights into the operation of the brain. They will not be like the computers of today but will still be physical devices. There is nothing overtly spiritual in my conception of the way we operate, but I am arguing that the human mechanism is more complex than a digital computer. Building these machines will be hard, and they will not be 'machines' in the sense I have used throughout this book. They will be minds.

When we build AIs that think and feel, will they acquire 'human' rights? Might one of my grandchildren fall in love with an AI, perhaps even marry one? On the darker side, how will they view us: what place would we have in their world once we had brought them into being? However, I think this process of building an AI will be hard and in one hundred years' time we will still be struggling with the problem.

In this book, I have presented a way to understand the creative process within our Universe. It relies on the existence of non-computable processes in our brain and in the physical laws which govern them. Currently, the laws contain a big hole. Although we can, perhaps, see where freedom might come from – through randomness and non-determinism – we don't understand where the will emanates to shape the Universe. Over the next thirty years, I think we will begin to understand this and see how creativity relates to the Universe we observe. I am not suggesting any anthropic principle, or some grand interaction between mankind and the Universe, just an important simple freedom: That we humans are free to think and do as we please. When I choose to lift my arm and raise a glass of wine with friends, this is my choice. I am the cause. The effect is the displacement of my arm, causing photons and gravitational waves to ripple out across the Universe, and in that sense I freely affect my environment.

Da Vinci, Self Portrait

"A good painter is to paint two main things, men and the working of man's mind."

Leonardo da Vinci

Appendix 1

Acknowledgments

Front Matter	
Cover	Vladislav Ociacia
Spine Equations	Illustration by Arabella Tagg
Author Photograph	Arabella Tagg
ACPMM, Wolfson College Cambridge	James Tagg Personal Collection, Course changed name to ACDMM in 1990.
Mathematical Bridge, Cambridge	Hipgnosis, www.shutterstock.com
Introductory Image	Photograph by James Tagg
Chapter 1	
Computer versus Human	Blutgruppe/Corbis
Kasparov versus Deep Blue	Louie Psihoyos/Corbis
The Music of Emily Howell	Kind permission of David Cope and Centaur Records. Emily Howell: From Darkness, Light. Picture and Audio Clip
IBM's Watson Plays Jeopardy	Associated Press Carol Kaelson/ Jeopardy Productions, Inc.
Watson Questions and Answers	Illustration by James Tagg
Steve Wozniak	TIM CHONG/Reuters/Corbis
Turning Images to Music	Credited to: Maxim Dupliy, Amir Amedi and Shelly Levy-Tzedek
Brain Image of Fish Hunting Prey	This work (or this video) was published from Kawakami lab in National Institute of Genetics , Japan (Muto, A. et al. Current Biology 23, 307–311, 2013)".
Babbage Difference Engine No. 2	Photograph by James Tagg @ The Computer History Museum
19th Century Calculators	Wikimedia, Ezrdr, CC3
Model of the Antikythera Mechanism	Wikimedia, Geni, CC3

Moore's Law	Credited to Ray Kurzweil, CC1
3D Chip	Kind permission Intel Press Department
Richard Branson	kathclick, www.bigstock.com
ELIZA, DOCTOR	Opensource project encapsulated into widget by James Tagg
IQ Test	Illustrated by James Tagg based on a Wechsler example question
Metal Puzzle	www.shutterstock.com, fdpress
Hole in the Wall Experiment	Courtesy Philippe Tarbouriech/Hole-in-the-Wall Education Ltd.
One Laptop per Child	One Laptop per Child project
Piano Practice	Photograph by James Tagg
Dan McLaughlin	Kind permission of Dan McLaughlin, www.thedanplan.com
Astrological Clock, Hampton Court	Wazzaman, Wikimedia, CC3
Lava Lamp	Sean Gladwell, www.shutterstock.com
Steve Jobs Collage	Kind permission: www.village9991.it
"Ascending and Descending"	© 2014 The M.C. Escher Company-The Netherlands. All rights reserved. www.mcescher.com

Chapter 2

Afghanistan Stability/COIN Dynamics	US Government, Joint Chiefs of Staff, PD
McChrystal in Kabul	USA Navy Photo, PD
Gettysburg Address as PowerPoint	Kind permission of Peter Norvig
Space Shuttle Columbia Crew	Credit NASA
Shuttle Tile	US Government, PD
Shuttle Images	Credit NASA
Searle's Chinese Room	Illustrated by James Tagg
Black Box Diagrams	Illustrated by James Tagg
The Miracle Worker, Helen Keller	Associated Press
Human Person, or is it?	Associated Press
New Yorker Dog Internet Cartoon	New Yorker © Condé Nast Licensing

Chapter 3

Body Language	Kind permission of Conference on Communication and Body Language.
Ronald Reagan and Mikael Gorbachev	US Government, PD
Höfði House in Reykjavik	Wikimedia
Fake or Real Smile	Bigedhar, www.bigstock.com
Yasser Arafat and Shimon Pérez	UPI
Learning Swedish, The Two Ronnies	Kind permission of BBC, hosted on YouTube
Scripts of the World	Illustrated by James Tagg
Chinese Traditional and Simplified	Illustrated by James Tagg
Great Comedy Videos	Kind permission BBC hosted on YouTube

Chapter 4

Child Having EEG	dblight, www.iStockphoto.com
X-Ray of Rontgen's Wife's Hand	Wikimedia
Lego Cubes Under Ultraviolet Light	www.public-domain-image.com
Pit Viper	abcphotosystem, www.shutterstock.com
Einstein's Brain	Wikimedia
Thermal Image of a House	Fotoflash, www.bigstock.com
Flowers in Ultraviolet Light	Bjørn Rørslett
Functional MRI, Response	National Institute of Mental Health, Wikimedia, PD
Functional MRI: Working Memory	Kind permission John Graner, Neuroimaging Department, National Intrepid Center of Excellence, Walter Reed National Military Medical Center, 8901 Wisconsin Avenue, Bethesda, MD 20889, USA
McGill Diffusion Tensor Image	Thomas Schultz, Wikimedia, CC3
Functional PET	Jens Maus, Wikimedia, PD
Organization of Your Brain	www.shutterstock.com and James Tagg
Visual Processing System	Illustrated by James Tagg includes www.shutterstock.com components.
Impressionist Painting, Monet Haystack	Wikimedia, PD
Frogs Eyes are Very Sensitive	Michiel de Wit, www.shutterstock.com
Color is Not an Absolute Sense	Illustrated by James Tagg
McGurk Effect	Kind permission of BBC, hosted on YouTube
Penrose Steps	James Tagg, Sketchup Model
Scintillating Blobs	Illustrated by James Tagg
Selective Attention video link	Kind permission to link provided by Daniel Simons. DVDs can be purchased from www.viscog.com
Tiger Woods Swing video	Kind permission of www.craighansongolf.com
Neural Network	Illustrated by James Tagg
Synapse	Meletver, www.bigstock.com
Paramecium	micro_photo, istock
Quantum Tubulin	Kind permission Travis Craddock
Tubulin Molecule	Wikimedia

Chapter 5

Chimpanzee and Typewriters	chippix, www.shutterstock.com
There are Holes in the Sky poem	Spike Milligan Enterprises
Spike Milligan	TopFoto[]
Lewis Carroll's Jabberwocky	Lewis Carroll, Out of Copyright
Lewis Carroll's Jabberwocky	Lewis Carroll, Out of Copyright
Word's Verdict on the Jabberwocky	Illustrated by James Tagg

Loch Ness Monster Picture	Unknown, Hoax
The Loch Ness Monster's Song	From Glasgow to Saturn (Carcanet, 1973) also published in Collected Poems (Carcanet, 1990) Reprinted by permission of Carcanet Press.
Dyslexic Poem	Kind permission of the copyright holder: The Journal of Irreproducible Results, the science humor magazine, www.jir.com, 1994 and 2000, via the author Jerrold H. Zar
Starry Night, van Gogh	Wikimedia, PD
Game of Battleship	www.shutterstock.com
Jesse our Creative Kitten	James Tagg

Chapter 6

Orangutan and Kitten	Chris Butler, www.bigstock.com
Twin Guards	Manamana, www.shutterstock.com
Groucho Marx	Library of Congress, PD
Euclid's Elements, Oxyrhynchus Papyrus	Wikimedia, PD

Chapter 7

Mandelbrot Set	Steve Buckley, www.shutterstock.com
Bubble Sort Ballet, video	Created at Sapientia University, Tirgu Mures (Marosvásárhely), Romania. Directed by Kátai Zoltán and Tóth László. In cooperation with "Maros Művészegyüttes", Tirgu Mures (Marosvásárhely), Romania.
Maze	Vasilius, www.bigstock.com
Travelling Salesman Problem	Illustrated by James Tagg, map from www.bigstock.com
Rubik's Cube	Photograph by James Tagg
Complexity Scale	Illustrated by James Tagg
Butterfly Beginnings of a Tornado?	saichol chandee, www.shutterstock.com
Trajectories	Kind permission Steinn Sigurðsson (1991)
Poincaré Portrait	Eugène Pirou, Wikimedia, PD
Blue Marble, Weather Patterns	Reto Stöckli, NASA Earth Observatory
Lorenz Attractor	zentilia, www.bigstock.com
Nebula	Credit NASA
Cellular Automaton	Weisstein, Eric W. "Cellular Automaton." From MathWorld--A Wolfram Web Resource.
Conway's 'Life'	James Tagg screen capture of an MIT opensource project

Chapter 8

Hilbert's Hotel	Karamysh www.bigstock.com
Spears and Hunters	Munduruku, Wikimedia cc2.5

Traversing an Infinite plane with a Line	Illustrated by James Tagg
Spear and Hunter	Illustrated by James Tagg
Hilbert Hotel Video Link	Kind permission of BBC, hosted on YouTube
Holding Infinity in Your Hand	Photograph by James Tagg
Number Quiz 1	Illustrated by James Tagg
Number Quiz 2	Illustrated by James Tagg
Donate a Random Number	Illustrated by James Tagg
Which Number is Random	Illustrated by James Tagg
Smallpox Virus	3d4Medical.com/Corbis
Smallpox Child	Associated Press, SANTOSH BASAK

Chapter 9

Donald Rumsfeld	US Army, Wikimedia, PD
Kurt Gödel, any Likeness is Accidental	Unknown, Wikimedia, PD
IAF Rule 164	IAF rules excerpt
PM	Paul Hermans, Wikimedia, CC3
Amazon Listing for PM	Amazon excerpt (not in print version)
1+1 = 2, PM (1)	PM excerpt
1+1 = 2, PM (2)	PM excerpt
Konigsberg's Bridges	Bogdan Giuşcă, Wikimedia, PD
Peano Portrait	Materialscientist, Wikimedia, PD
Beer Mug, Table and Chair	Photograph by James Tagg
Einstein and Gödel	Kind permission of the Archive of the Institute of Advanced Study

Chapter 10

Alan Turing Portrait	National Portrait Gallery
Enigma Machine	Sperling, Wikimedia, PD
Can you decode this?	Illustrated by James Tagg
Correct the code	Illustrated by James Tagg
Lego Turing Machine	www.LegoTuringMachine.org
Old Fashioned Relay Mechanism	Wikimedia, Signalhead, CS3
3D Printing Machine	360b / www.shutterstock.com
Block Print from 'No Silver Bullet'	Wikimedia, PD

Chapter 11

Fred Brooks	Copyright owned by SD&M, Wikimedia CC3
Web Page (James Tagg's Home Page)	Screen capture by James Tagg
Dilbert Software Specification	DILBERT © 2006 Scott Adams. Used By permission of UNIVERSAL UCLICK. All rights reserved.
Long Multiplication	Illustrated by James Tagg
A Hypercube in Two Dimensions	Mouagip, Wikimedia, CC3
Impossible Shapes, Devil's Tuning Fork	Illustrated by James Tagg
Halting Program	Illustrated by James Tagg
Four Color Problem	chas zzz brown, Wikimedia, CC3
Dalek Trouble	Birkett 1981, Permission Punch
Augustus De Morgan Poem	Augustus De Morgan, (pd)

Word Puzzle	Gennadiı́ Makanin Excerpt of paper on Word Puzzles
Creative Inoculation	Illustrated by James Tagg
Jackson Pollock	Albright-Knox Art Gallery/CORBIS, Pollock-Krasner Foundation / Artists Rights Society (ARS), New York
Jeopardy	Associated Press Carol Kaelson/ Jeopardy Productions Inc
Programming Cartoon	Kind permission Geekherocomic
Specification Cartoon	Credit Paragon Innovations

Chapter 12

Two Digital Brains Communicating	Photobank Gallery, www.shutterstock.com
Perpetual Motion from the 1600s	Robert Fludd's 1618 "Water Screw", Wikimedia, PD
Black Hole Malament-Holgarth Space	Crystal Graphics
Synapses and Tubulin	Crystal Graphics

Chapter 13

World Communication	Antartis, www.bigstock.com
IMAX	Louie Psihoyos/Corbis
Hologram	videodoctor, www.shutterstock.com

Chapter 14

Invention of Light Bulb, Thomas Edison	Corbis, Betmann
Steve Jobs Shows the iPhone	Corbis, Reuters
Stopwatch 60 seconds!	Studio 37, www.shutterstock.com
Paperclip Test	Illustrated by James Tagg
30 Things Test	Illustrated by James Tagg
Paperclip Test2	Illustrated by James Tagg
Eureka	KoS, Wikimedia, PD
Circle with Dot, Problem	Illustrated by James Tagg
Thinking Outside the Box	Illustrated by James Tagg
John Cleese, Video Link	Picture from www.shutterstock, links to World Innovation Forum, YouTube talk in iBook version and on website.
Sketch Test	Illustrated by James Tagg
Hard Drives	www.shutterstock.com
Harold Cohen and AARON	James Tagg at the Computer Museum
Harold Cohen and AARON	James Tagg at the Computer Museum
Old Polo	Generic Polo Photo
New Polo	Fingerhut, www.shutterstock.com

Chapter 15

Dilbert on Free Will	DILBERT © 1993 Scott Adams. Used By permission of UNIVERSAL UCLICK. All rights reserved.
Domino Toppling	(c) www.austriandominoart.com

Newton's Rings	Wikimedia
Wave Interference	Single image in Book. Slide show in iBook, Various; Wikimedia www.shutterstock.com, www.bigstock.com
Solvay Conference	Benjamin S. Couprie, Wikimedia, PD
Interferometer	Illustrated by James Tagg
Schrödinger's Cat	Dhatfield, Wikimedia, CC3
Polarized Glasses, Glare and No Glare	HUB, Wikimedia, CC3
Bell Test	Illustrated by James Tagg
Left and Right Socks	Hofmeester, Bigstock.com
Morse Signaling	Illustrated by James Tagg
Dawkins and Atheist Bus	Wikimedia, CC2
Fork in the Road	fivepointsix, www.bigstock.com
Left Hand Rule	Photograph by James Tagg
Orthogonal Sticks	Illustrated by James Tagg
M.C. Escher's "Waterfall"	© 2014 The M.C. Escher Company-The Netherlands. All rights reserved. www.mcescher.com
Kochen-Specker Cube	James Tagg modeled in Sketchup
Russian Dolls	Robyn Mackenzie, www.bigstock.com
Chapter 16	
The HMS Beagle	Bettmann/Corbis
Nobel Prize Medal	Wikimedia, PD
Golden Hall, Sweden	vichie81, www.shutterstock.com
Pulitzer Prize Medal	Original Daniel Chester French, photo upload Katpatuka, Wikimedia, PD
First XPRIZE Award Ceremony	Kbh3rd, Wikimedia, CC3
Fields Medal	Stefan Zachow, Wikimedia, PD
Chapter 17	
Omar Khayyam	Wikimedia, PD
Appendices	
Leonardo da Vinci, Self Portrait	Wikimedia, PD
British Library	Diliff, Wikimedia, CC2.5
Experiment, ATLAS, CERN	xdrew, www.shutterstock.com
Panda	leungchopan, www.shutterstock.com
Conway and Kochen	Photograph courtesy of Princeton University's Office of Communications; Denise Applewhite, photographer
Looney Tunes "That's all Folks"	Wikimedia, PD

The Wikimedia Creative Commons Licenses 1, 2, 2.5 and 3 may be found at www.wikimedia.com. PD indicates a public domain.

In the case of items marked 'video' clicking on the image in the iBook or eBook will link to YouTube. The links are also available at www.jamestagg.com/videolinks for book readers.

Reading Room at the British Museum

"From the moment I picked your book up until I laid it down I was convulsed with laughter. Some day I intend reading it."

Groucho Marx

Appendix 2

Bibliography

I am not resident at an academic institution, nor do I work for a large company with access to a broad range of journal subscriptions. I have a degree in Physics and Computer Science, so I am no layman. The modern web gives amateurs like me, easy access to enormous information resources that would only have been available from the finest University libraries even five years ago. Over time I have built up a personal library of books in the field, many of them ex-library copies which, by their date stamps, were never borrowed in their home universities!

I'm always skeptical of the enormous bibliographies found in the back of science books and whether they are ever read. If you want a pointer to the next books to read, here are some suggestions: *A Brief History of Time, The Man who Mistook his Wife for a Hat, The Emperor's New Mind, The Naked Jape, Gödel Escher Bach, Proust and the Squid, Logic, A Five Day Course in Thinking, Your Brain on Music, The 4% Universe, From Eternity to Here* and *Time.*

Journal	Cost
Scientific American	Some free articles, Membership $150 p.a.
Wikipedia	Free
The Economist	Free to search but a subscription needed for full articles, $200
Science: The American Institute for the Advancement of Science.	Annual Subscription $151
Mind	Annual Subscription, $200
Google Scholar	Free to search and often free to view, but some articles require membership of underlying services. From here you jump off into an endless series of journals too numerous to mention.
Google Books	Free, but you buy a lot of books!
Amazon	Some free material but again lot of book buying
JStor	Variable, based on area of interest
Arxiv.org	All the pre-prints of forthcoming papers. Invaluable. Free
SpringerLink	Article by article purchase, $35 each

Subscriptions and Sources

Chapter 1

Bellos, Alex. *Alex's Adventures in Numberland*. Bloomsbury Publishing PLC, 2010.

by Richard Roeper. *Urban Legends: The Truth behind All Those Deliciously Entertaining Myths That Are Absolutely, Positively, 100 Percent Not True*. Career Press, 1999.

Cairns-Smith, A. Graham. *Evolving the Mind: On the Nature of Matter and the Origin of Consciousness*. Cambridge University Press, 1996.

Dawkins, Richard. *The Magic of Reality: How We Know What's Really True*. Bantam Press, 2011.

Ericsson, K. Anders. "Attaining Excellence through Deliberate Practice: Insights from the Study of Expert Performance." *The Pursuit of Excellence through Education*, 2002, 21–55.

———. "Deliberate Practice and the Acquisition and Maintenance of Expert Performance in Medicine and Related Domains." *Academic Medicine* 79, no. 10 (2004): S70–81.

Ericsson, K. Anders, Ralf T. Krampe, and Clemens Tesch-Römer. "The Role of Deliberate Practice in the Acquisition of Expert Performance." *Psychological*

Review 100, no. 3 (1993): 363.
Fiske, John. *Introduction to Communication Studies*. 3rd ed. Routledge, 2010.
Franklin, Stan. *Artificial Minds*. MIT Press, 1997.
Gilovich, Thomas. *How We Know What Isn't So: Fallibility of Human Reason in Everyday Life*. Reprint. The Free Press, 1993.
Gregory, Robert J. *Psychological Testing: History, Principles, and Applications*. 6th ed. Pearson, 2010.
Hameroff, S. R. "Quantum Coherence in Microtubules: A Neural Basis for Emergent Consciousness?" *Journal of Consciousness Studies* 1, no. 1 (1994): 91–118.
Hameroff, Stuart R., and Alfred W. Kaszniak. *Toward a Science of Consciousness: The First Tucson Discussions and Debates*. MIT Press, 1996.
Harel, David. *Computers Ltd: What They REALLY Can't Do*. New Ed. OUP Oxford, 2003.
Hawkins, Jeff, and Sandra Blakeslee. *On Intelligence*. Reprint. Owl Books (NY), 2005.
Hofstadter, Douglas R. *Godel, Escher, Bach: An Eternal Golden Braid*. 20th Anniversary ed. Penguin, 2000.
Howell, E. *From Darness Light/Land of Stone/Shadow Worlds*. Centaur, 2010.
"IBM100 - Deep Blue." CTB14, March 7, 2012. http://www-03.ibm.com/ibm/history/ibm100/us/en/icons/deepblue/.
Ivancevic, Vladimir G., and Tijana T. Ivancevic. *Quantum Neural Computation*. Springer, 2010.
Jibu, Mari, and Kunio Yasue. *Quantum Brain Dynamics and Consciousness: An Introduction*. John Benjamins Publishing, 1995.
Jibu, M., S. Hagan, S. R. Hameroff, K. H. Pribram, and K. Yasue. "Quantum Optical Coherence in Cytoskeletal Microtubules: Implications for Brain Function." *Biosystems* 32, no. 3 (1994): 195–209.
Lahoz-Beltra, R., S. R. Hameroff, and J. E. Dayhoff. "Cytoskeletal Logic: A Model for Molecular Computation via Boolean Operations in Microtubules and Microtubule-Associated Proteins." *BioSystems* 29, no. 1 (1993): 1–23.
Malcolm Gladwell. *The Tipping Point: How Little Things Can Make a Big Difference*. Repr. Abacus, 2001.
Morris, Desmond. *Child: How Children Think, Learn and Grow in the Early Years*. Hamlyn, 2010.
———. *The Naked Ape: A Zoologist's Study of the Human Animal*. New edition. Vintage, 2005.
Neumann, John Von. *The Computer and the Brain*. 2nd Revised edition. Yale University Press, 2000.
Penrose, Roger. *The Large, the Small and the Human Mind*. New Ed. Cambridge University Press, 2000.
Přibram, Karl H., and Sir John Carew Eccles. *Rethinking Neural Networks: Quantum Fields and Biological Data*. Routledge, 1993.
"Return to Antikythera: Divers Revisit Wreck Where Ancient Computer Found." *The Guardian*, October 2, 2012. http://www.guardian.co.uk/science/blog/2012/oct/02/return-antikythera-wreck-ancient-computer.
Robinson, Ken, and Lou Aronica. *The Element: How Finding Your Passion Changes Everything*. Penguin, 2010.
Roebuck, Kevin. *Emotional Intelligence: High-Impact Strategies - What You Need to Know: Definitions, Adoptions, Impact, Benefits, Maturity, Vendors*. Tebbo,

2011.
Sacks, Oliver. *An Anthropologist on Mars*. 4th ed. Picador, 2009.
———. *The Man Who Mistook His Wife for a Hat*. 1st ed. Picador, 1986.
Tucker, William H. *The Cattell Controversy: Race, Science, and Ideology*. University of Illinois Press, 2009.
Turing, Alan M. "Intelligent Machines." *Ince, DC (Ed.)* 5 (1992). http://isites.harvard.edu/fs/docs/icb.topic958294.files/lecture-00-handout.pdf.
Vitiello, Giuseppe. *My Double Unveiled: The Dissipative Quantum Model of Brain*. John Benjamins Publishing, 2001.
Whitehead, Alfred North, and Bertrand Russell. *Principia Mathematica - Volume One: 1*. Rough Draft Printing, 2009.
Winston, Robert. *The Human Mind and How to Make the Most of It*. New edition. Chartered Institute of Personnel and Development, 2006.
Wolf, Maryanne. *Proust and the Squid: The Story and Science of the Reading Brain*. Icon Books Ltd, 2008.
Wolfram, Stephen. *A New Kind of Science*. First Edition. Wolfram Media Inc, 2002.

Chapter 2

Carr, Jimmy, and Lucy Greeves. *The Naked Jape: Uncovering the Hidden World of Jokes*. Penguin, 2007.
Cobley, Paul. *The Communication Theory Reader*. 1st ed. Routledge, 1996.
Dawkins, Richard. *Unweaving the Rainbow: Science, Delusion and the Appetite for Wonder*. Reisssue. Penguin, 2006.
Hume, David. *An Enquiry Concerning Human Understanding*. New Ed. /. OUP Oxford, 2008.
Locke, John. *An Essay Concerning Human Understanding*. Abridged edition. Hackett Publishing Co, Inc, 1996.
Martin, Robert M. *There Are Two Errors in the the Title of This Book**. Rev. and Expanded Ed. Broadview Press Ltd, 2002.
Sacks, Oliver. *An Anthropologist on Mars*. 4th ed. Picador, 2009.
Tufte, Edward R. *The Cognitive Style of PowerPoint: Pitching Out Corrupts Within*. 2nd ed. Graphics Press, 2006.
Wiseman, Prof. Richard. *Quirkology: The Curious Science Of Everyday Lives*. 2nd ed. Pan, 2011.

Chapter 3

Borg, James. *Body Language: 7 Easy Lessons to Master the Silent Language*. 1st ed. Prentice Hall Life, 2008.
Brounstein, Marty. *Communicating Effectively for Dummies*. John Wiley & Sons, 2001.
by Seth Godin ; with a foreword by Malcolm Gladwell. *Unleashing the Ideavirus : How to Turn Your Ideas into Marketing Epidemics*. Free Press, 2002.
Darwin, Charles. *The Origin of Species*. New edition. Wordsworth Editions Ltd, 1998.
Fiske, John. *Introduction to Communication Studies*. 3rd ed. Routledge, 2010.
Morris, Desmond. *Peoplewatching: The Desmond Morris Guide to Body Language*. Vintage, 2002.
———. *The Human Zoo*. New edition. Vintage, 1994.
———. *The Naked Ape: A Zoologist's Study of the Human Animal*. New edition. Vintage, 2005.

Navarro, Joe. *What Every Body Is Saying: An Ex-FBI Agent's Guide to Speed-Reading People*. HarperCollins Publishers, 2008.
Ogilvy, David. *Ogilvy on Advertising*. New edition. Prion Books Ltd, 2007.
Roebuck, Kevin. *Emotional Intelligence: High-Impact Strategies - What You Need to Know: Definitions, Adoptions, Impact, Benefits, Maturity, Vendors*. Tebbo, 2011.
Schirato, Tony, and Susan Yell. *Communication and Culture: An Introduction*. 2nd Revised edition. Sage Publications Ltd, 2000.
Taylor, Kathleen. *Brainwashing: The Science of Thought Control*. New Ed. OUP Oxford, 2006.
Winston, Professor Lord Robert. *Human Instinct*. New edition. Bantam, 2008.

Chapter 4

Derren Brown. *Tricks of the Mind*. Channel 4, 2006.
Gurney, Kevin. *An Introduction to Neural Networks*. CRC Press, 1997.
Hameroff, S. R. "Quantum Coherence in Microtubules: A Neural Basis for Emergent Consciousness?" *Journal of Consciousness Studies* 1, no. 1 (1994): 91–118.
Higbee, Kenneth L., and Ph.D. *Your Memory: How It Works and How to Improve It*. 2Rev Ed. Avalon Group, 2001.
Jibu, M., S. Hagan, S. R. Hameroff, K. H. Pribram, and K. Yasue. "Quantum Optical Coherence in Cytoskeletal Microtubules: Implications for Brain Function." *Biosystems* 32, no. 3 (1994): 195–209.
Jimmy Carr. *The Naked Jape : Uncovering the Hidden World of Jokes*. Michael Joseph, 2007.
Lahoz-Beltra, R., S. R. Hameroff, and J. E. Dayhoff. "Cytoskeletal Logic: A Model for Molecular Computation via Boolean Operations in Microtubules and Microtubule-Associated Proteins." *BioSystems* 29, no. 1 (1993): 1–23.
O'Brien, Dominic. *How to Develop a Brilliant Memory Week by Week: 52 Proven Ways to Enhance Your Memory Skills*. Duncan Baird Publishers, 2005.
Picton, P.D. *Neural Networks*. 2nd Revised edition. Palgrave Macmillan, 2000.
Siegelmann, Hava T. *Neural Networks and Analog Computation: Beyond the Turing Limit*. Birkhauser, 1998.
Winston, Robert. *The Human Mind and How to Make the Most of It*. New edition. Chartered Institute of Personnel and Development, 2006.
Wolf, Maryanne. *Proust and the Squid: The Story and Science of the Reading Brain*. Icon Books Ltd, 2008.

Chapter 5

Aaronson, Scott. *Quantum Computing since Democritus*. New York: Cambridge University Press, 2013.
Borges, Jorge Luis, and Andrew Hurley. *The Library of Babel*. Boston: David R. Godine Publisher Inc, 2000.
Chaitin, Gregory J. *Meta Maths: The Quest for Omega*. Atlantic Books, 2007.
Tolstoy, Leo. *War and Peace*. Ware: Wordsworth Editions, 2001.

Chapter 6

Ayer, A. J. *Language, Truth and Logic*. 2nd ed. Dover Publications Inc., 2002.
Boaler, Jo. *The Elephant in the Classroom: Helping Children Learn and Love Maths*. Souvenir Press Ltd, 2010.
Carroll, Lewis. *Lewis Carroll's Games and Puzzles*. 40th ed. Dover Publications Inc.,

1992.
———. *Symbolic Logic*. New issue of 1896 ed. Dover Publications Inc., 2000.
Crilly, Tony. *The Big Questions: Mathematics*. Quercus Publishing Plc, 2011.
Doxiadis, Apostolos, and Christos H. Papadimitriou. *Logicomix: An Epic Search for Truth*. First Edition. Bloomsbury Publishing PLC, 2009.
Goldrei, D.C. *Classic Set Theory: A Guided Introduction*. Chapman and Hall/CRC, 1996.
Hodges, Wilfrid. *Logic*. 2nd Revised edition. Penguin, 2001.
Martin, Robert M. *There Are Two Errors in the the Title of This Book**. Rev. and Expanded Ed. Broadview Press Ltd, 2002.
Newbery, John. *Logic Made Familiar and Easy: To Which Is Added a Compendious System of Metaphysics Or Ontology : Being the Fifth Volume of the Circle of the Sciences, &c. Published by the King's Authority*. BiblioBazaar, LLC, 2010.
Oechslin, Werner. *Byrne, Six Books of Euclid: Facsimile of the Famous First Edition of 1847*. Har/Pap. Taschen GmbH, 2010.
Russell, Bertrand. *Introduction to Mathematical Philosophy*. Reprint. Spokesman Books, 2007.

Chapter 7

Gleick, James. *Chaos: Making a New Science*. New edition. Vintage, 1997.
Griffeath, David, and Cristopher Moore. *New Constructions in Cellular Automata*. Oxford University Press, 2003.
"Mathematical Games - The Fantastic Combinations of John Conway's New Solitaire Game 'Life' - M. Gardner - 1970," June 3, 2009. http://web.archive.org/web/20090603015231/http://ddi.cs.uni-potsdam.de/HyFISCH/Produzieren/lis_projekt/proj_gamelife/ConwayScientificAmerican.htm.
Mitchell, Melanie. *Complexity: A Guided Tour*. OUP USA, 2009.
Weisstein, Eric W. "Elementary Cellular Automaton." Text. Accessed September 28, 2014. http://mathworld.wolfram.com/ElementaryCellularAutomaton.html.
Wolfram, Stephen. *A New Kind of Science*. First Edition. Wolfram Media Inc, 2002.

Chapter 8

Cantor, Georg. *Contributions to the Founding of the Theory of Transfinite Numbers*. Dover Publications Inc., 2003.
Clegg, Brian. *Brief History of Infinity: The Quest to Think the Unthinkable*. Robinson Publishing, 2003.
Cohen, Paul J. *Set Theory and the Continuum Hypothesis*. Dover Publications Inc., 2009.
Pica, Pierre, and Alain Lecomte. "Theoretical Implications of the Study of Numbers and Numerals in Mundurucu." *Philosophical Psychology* 21, no. 4 (August 1, 2008): 507–22. doi:10.1080/09515080802285461.
Pica, Pierre, Cathy Lemer, Véronique Izard, and Stanislas Dehaene. "Exact and Approximate Arithmetic in an Amazonian Indigene Group." *Science* 306, no. 5695 (October 15, 2004): 499–503. doi:10.1126/science.1102085.
Potter, Michael. *Set Theory and Its Philosophy: A Critical Introduction*. Clarendon Press, 2004.

Chapter 9

Chaitin, Gregory J. *Thinking About Gödel And Turing: Essays On Complexity 1970-2007*. World Scientific Publishing, 2007.

Franzén, Torkel. *Gödel's Theorem: An Incomplete Guide to Its Use and Abuse*. A K Peters/CRC Press, 2005.
Gödel, Kurt. *On Formally Undecidable Propositions of "Principia Mathematica" and Related Systems*. New edition. Dover Publications Inc., 2003.
Goldrei, D.C. *Classic Set Theory: A Guided Introduction*. Chapman and Hall/CRC, 1996.
Hofstadter, Douglas R. *Gödel, Escher, Bach: An Eternal Golden Braid*. 20th Anniversary ed. Penguin, 2000.
Nagel, Ernest, and James R. Newman. *Gödel's Proof*. Rev. Ed. New York University Press, 2001.
Newton, Sir Isaac. *Principia*. Prometheus Books, 1995.
Penrose, Sir Roger. *Shadows Of The Mind: A Search for the Missing Science of Consciousness*. New edition. Vintage, 2005.
Potter, Michael. *Set Theory and Its Philosophy: A Critical Introduction*. Clarendon Press, 2004.
Russell, Bertrand. *Introduction to Mathematical Philosophy*. Reprint. Spokesman Books, 2007.
Sautoy, Marcus Du. *The Music of the Primes: Why an Unsolved Problem in Mathematics Matters*. New Ed. Harper Perennial, 2004.
———. *The Number Mysteries: A Mathematical Odyssey Through Everyday Life*. Fourth Estate, 2010.
Whitehead, Alfred North, and Bertrand Russell. *Principia Mathematica - Volume One: 1*. Rough Draft Printing, 2009.

Chapter 10

Copeland, B. Jack. *The Essential Turing*. Clarendon Press, 2004.
David, Hans T. *The New Bach Reader: Life of Johann Sebastian Bach in Letters and Documents*. New edition. W. W. Norton & Co., 1999.
Dennett, Daniel C., and Douglas R. Hofstadter. *The Mind's I: Fantasies and Reflections on Self and Soul*. Basic Books, 2000.
Dewdney. *New Turing Omnibus*. Reprint. Palgrave Macmillan, 2003.
edited by B. Jack Copeland. *The Essential Turing : Seminal Writings in Computing, Logic, Philosophy, Artificial Intelligence, and Artificial Life plus the Secrets of Enigma*. Reprinted. Clarendon Press, 2005.
Gallwey, W Timothy, and Barry Green. *Inner Game of Music*. 7th ed. Pan, 2003.
Hofstadter, Douglas R. *I Am a Strange Loop*. Reprint. Basic Books, 2008.
Levitin, Daniel J. *This Is Your Brain on Music: Understanding a Human Obsession*. Atlantic Books, 2008.
Penrose, Roger. *The Large, the Small and the Human Mind*. New Ed. Cambridge University Press, 2000.
Penrose, Sir Roger. *The Emperor's New Mind: Concerning Computers, Minds, and the Laws of Physics*. New Ed. Oxford Paperbacks, 1999.
Petzold, Charles. *The Annotated Turing: A Guided Tour Through Alan Turing's Historic Paper on Computability and the Turing Machine*. John Wiley & Sons, 2008.
Sacks, Oliver. *Musicophilia: Tales of Music and the Brain*. Reprint. Picador, 2008.
Singh, Simon. *The Code Book: The Secret History of Codes and Code-Breaking*. (Reissue). Fourth Estate, 2002.
Turing, Alan. "Checking a Large Routine." In *The Early British Computer Conferences*, 70–72. MIT Press, 1989. http://dl.acm.org/citation.

cfm?id=94952.
Turing, Alan M. "Can a Machine Think." *The World of Mathematics* 4 (1956): 2099–2123.
———. "Computability and Λ-Definability." *The Journal of Symbolic Logic* 2, no. 4 (1937): 153–63.
———. "Computing Machinery and Intelligence." *Mind*, 1950, 433–60.
———. "Computing Machinery and Intelligence." In *Computers & Thought*, 11–35. MIT Press, 1995. http://dl.acm.org/citation.cfm?id=216410.
———. "Intelligent Machines." *Ince, DC (Ed.)* 5 (1992). http://isites.harvard.edu/fs/docs/icb.topic958294.files/lecture-00-handout.pdf.
———. "Rounding-off Errors in Matrix Processes." *The Quarterly Journal of Mechanics and Applied Mathematics* 1, no. 1 (1948): 287–308.
Turing, Alan Mathison. "On Computable Numbers, with an Application to the Entscheidungsproblem." *J. of Math* 58 (1936): 345–63.
———. "Systems of Logic Based on Ordinals." *Proceedings of the London Mathematical Society* 2, no. 1 (1939): 161–228.
———. "The Chemical Basis of Morphogenesis." *Bulletin of Mathematical Biology* 52, no. 1 (1990): 153–97.

Chapter 11

Baxa, Christoph. "A Note on Diophantine Representations." *American Mathematical Monthly*, 1993, 138–43.
Blass, Andreas, and Yuri Gurevich. "Algorithms: A Quest for Absolute Definitions." *Bulletin of the EATCS* 81 (2003): 195–225.
Börger, Egon, Erich Grädel, and Yuri Gurevich. *The Classical Decision Problem*. Springer, 2001.
Carroll, Lewis. *Symbolic Logic*. New issue of 1896 ed. Dover Publications Inc., 2000.
Davis, Martin, Hilary Putnam, and Julia Robinson. "The Decision Problem for Exponential Diophantine Equations." *Annals of Mathematics*, 1961, 425–36.
Dyson, Verena H., James P. Jones, and John C. Shepherdson. "Some Diophantine Forms of Gödel's Theorem." *Archive for Mathematical Logic* 22, no. 1 (1980): 51–60.
Franzén, Torkel. *Godel's Theorem: An Incomplete Guide to Its Use and Abuse*. A K Peters/CRC Press, 2005.
Hodges, Wilfrid. *Logic*. 2nd Revised edition. Penguin, 2001.
Jr, Frederick P. Brooks. *The Mythical Man Month and Other Essays on Software Engineering*. 2nd ed. Addison Wesley, 1995.
Kurzweil, Ray. *How to Create a Mind: The Secret of Human Thought Revealed*. Penguin, 2012.
Matiyasevich, Yuri. *HILBERT'S TENTH PROBLEM: What Can We Do with Diophantine Equations?*. Accessed April 13, 2014. http://logic.pdmi.ras.ru/~yumat/Journal/H10history/H10histe.pdf.gz.
Minsky, Marvin Lee. *Computation*. Prentice-Hall Englewood Cliffs, 1967. http://cba.mit.edu/events/03.11.ASE/docs/Minsky.pdf.
Nagel, Ernest, and James R. Newman. *Godel's Proof*. Rev. Ed. New York University Press, 2001.
Penrose, Sir Roger. *Shadows Of The Mind: A Search for the Missing Science of Consciousness*. New edition. Vintage, 2005.
———. *The Emperor's New Mind: Concerning Computers, Minds, and the Laws of Physics*. New Ed. Oxford Paperbacks, 1999.

Reid, Constance. *Julia: A Life in Mathematics*. Washington, DC: The Mathematical Association of America, 1997.

Rice, Henry Gordon. "Classes of Recursively Enumerable Sets and Their Decision Problems." *Transactions of the American Mathematical Society* 74, no. 2 (1953): 358–66.

Ruohonen, Keijo. "Hilbertin Kymmenes Probleema." *Arkhimedes*, no. 1 (1972): 2.

Spolsky, J. "The Law of Leaky Abstractions," November 11, 2002. http://www.joelonsoftware.com.

Tegmark, Max. "The Mathematical Universe." *Foundations of Physics* 38, no. 2 (2008): 101–50.

Turing, Alan M. "Can a Machine Think." *The World of Mathematics* 4 (1956): 2099–2123.

Turing, Alan Mathison. "On Computable Numbers, with an Application to the Entscheidungsproblem." *J. of Math* 58 (1936): 345–63.

———. "Systems of Logic Based on Ordinals." *Proceedings of the London Mathematical Society* 2, no. 1 (1939): 161–228.

Wiles, Andrew. "Modular Elliptic Curves and Fermat's Last Theorem." *Annals of Mathematics-Second Series* 141, no. 3 (1995): 443–552.

Chapter 12

Burgin, Mark. *Super-Recursive Algorithms*. Springer, 2005.

Darwin, Charles. *On the Origin of Species: By Means of Natural Selection*. Dover Giant Thrift Ed. Dover Publications Inc., 2006.

Mitchell, Melanie. *An Introduction to Genetic Algorithms*. New edition. MIT Press, 1998.

Siegelmann, Hava T. *Neural Networks and Analog Computation: Beyond the Turing Limit*. Birkhauser, 1998.

Syropoulos, Apostolos. *Hypercomputation: Computing Beyond the Church-Turing Barrier*. Softcover reprint of hardcover 1st ed. 2008. Springer, 2010.

Chapter 13

Shannon, C.E., and Warren Weaver. *The Mathematical Theory of Communication*. University of Illinois Press, 1949.

Chapter 14

Boden, Margaret A. *The Creative Mind: Myths and Mechanisms*. 2nd ed. Routledge, 2003.

Bono, Edward de. *How to Have Creative Ideas: 62 Exercises to Develop the Mind*. Vermilion, 2007.

———. *Lateral Thinking: A Textbook of Creativity*. Penguin, 2009.

———. *Six Thinking Hats*. Penguin, 2009.

Coyle, Daniel. *The Talent Code: Unlocking the Secret of Skill in Maths, Art, Music, Sport, and Just About Everything Else,* Random House Books, 2009.

Davis, Ronald D., and Eldon M. Braun. *The Gift of Dyslexia: Why Some of the Brighest People Can't Read and How They Can Learn*. 3rd Revised edition. Souvenir Press Ltd, 2010.

Edward De Bono. *How to Have Creative Ideas : 62 Exercises to Develop the Mind*. 1 Aufl. Vermilion, 2007.

Isaacson, Walter. *Steve Jobs: The Exclusive Biography*. Little, Brown, 2011.

McCandless, David. *Information Is Beautiful*. Collins, 2010.

Robinson, Ken. *Out of Our Minds: Learning to Be Creative*. 2nd Edition. Capstone, 2011.

Robinson, Ken, and Lou Aronica. *The Element: How Finding Your Passion Changes Everything*. Penguin, 2010.

Winston, Professor Lord Robert. *Bad Ideas?: An Arresting History of Our Inventions*. Bantam, 2011.

Chapter 15

Bell, John S., and others. "On the Einstein-Podolsky-Rosen Paradox." *Physics* 1, no. 3 (1964): 195–200.

Conway, John H., and Simon Kochen. "The Strong Free Will Theorem." *Notices of the AMS* 56, no. 2 (2009): 226–32.

Conway, John, and Simon Kochen. "Reply to Comments of Bassi, Ghirardi, and Tumulka on the Free Will Theorem." *Foundations of Physics* 37, no. 11 (2007): 1643–47.

Dennett, Daniel Clement. *Brainstorms: Philosophical Essays on Mind and Psychology*. 8. MIT Press, 1981.

Dennett, Danile C. *Kinds of Minds: Toward an Understanding of Consciousness*. Basic Books, 2008.

Ekert, Artur K. "Quantum Cryptography Based on Bell's Theorem." *Physical Review Letters* 67, no. 6 (1991): 661.

"EPR Paradox." *Wikipedia, the Free Encyclopedia*, September 15, 2014. http://en.wikipedia.org/w/index.php?title=EPR_paradox&oldid=625734938.

Gilovich, Thomas. *How We Know What Isn't So: Fallibility of Human Reason in Everyday Life*. Reprint. The Free Press, 1993.

Gisin, Nicolas. "The Free Will Theorem, Stochastic Quantum Dynamics and True Becoming in Relativistic Quantum Physics." *arXiv Preprint arXiv:1002.1392*, 2010. http://arxiv.org/abs/1002.1392.

Goldstein, Sheldon, Daniel V. Tausk, Roderich Tumulka, and Nino Zanghì. "What Does the Free Will Theorem Actually Prove." *Notices of the AMS* 57, no. 11 (2010): 1451–53.

Hawking, Stephen, and Leonard Mlodinow. *The Grand Design: New Answers to the Ultimate Questions of Life*. Bantam Press, 2010.

Heywood, Peter, and Michael LG Redhead. "Nonlocality and the Kochen-Specker Paradox." *Foundations of Physics* 13, no. 5 (1983): 481–99.

Huang, Yun-Feng, Chuan-Feng Li, Yong-Sheng Zhang, Jian-Wei Pan, and Guang-Can Guo. "Experimental Test of the Kochen-Specker Theorem with Single Photons." *Physical Review Letters* 90, no. 25 (2003): 250401.

Russell, Bertrand. *The Problems of Philosophy*. 2nd ed. Oxford Paperbacks, 2001.

Tumulka, Roderich. "Comment on 'the Free Will Theorem.'" *Foundations of Physics* 37, no. 2 (2007): 186–97.

Zhang, Yong-Sheng, Chuan-Feng Li, and Guang-Can Guo. "Quantum Key Distribution via Quantum Encryption." *Physical Review A* 64, no. 2 (2001): 024302.

Chapter 16

Land, George, and Beth Jarman. *Breakpoint and Beyond: Mastering the Future - Today*. Reprint. HarperBusiness, 1993.

Lloyd, John, and John Mitchinson. *QI: The Second Book of General Ignorance*. Faber and Faber, 2010.

Michael Brooks. *13 Things That Don't Make Sense : The Most Intriguing Scientific Mysteries of Our Time*. Profile, 2010.

Reason Special Interview with Roger Penrose, 2008. http://www.youtube.com/watch?v=xiYDc1LA0I4&feature=youtube_gdata_player.

Reason Special Interview with Roger Penrose, 2008. http://www.youtube.com/watch?v=xiYDc1LA0I4&feature=youtube_gdata_player.

Tegmark, Max. "The Importance of Quantum Decoherence in Brain Processes." *arXiv:quant-ph/9907009*, July 5, 1999. doi:10.1103/PhysRevE.61.4194.

ATLAS, CERN

"Good one, publish."

Milliken

Appendix 3

Puzzles and Experiments

In this book I have suggested some experiments for you to undertake, and posed some puzzles to solve. You can participate in the experiments or see the answers by going online and checking my website at www.jamestagg.com

Jeopardy Answers from Chapter 1.

Answer 1. Watson answered, Gestate.

Answer 2. Watson answered. Who is Bram Stoker.

Answer 3. The answer is Chicago but Watson answered "Toronto?????", the question marks indicating it was very doubtful of the answer.

Panda, Eats Shoots

"Parenthetical remarks (however relevant) are unnecessary."

Frank L. Visco,
How to Write Good

"Defining what we mean by a robot is hard to do. I know now when I see one but that definition works for anything, even pizza."

Mike Gregory

Appendix 4

Conventions in the Book

The use of *italics* is intended to give accent or indicate the title of the published work, such as a book or movie. Inverted Commas should read, 'so called'.

The use of the 'Oxford Comma' – a comma after 'and' – gives a longer break in a sentence to aid better understanding. You will find both 'and' and, 'and,' used in this book deliberately.

The use of 'their' substitutes for he or she, and is a convention I believe will supersede, 'he' or 'she' and, 'him' or 'her'.

The puzzles in this book are all available to download, so you don't need to deface the book. Feel free to deface it if you wish. Buy the electronic version and save trees.

Some of this book is historical or factual, while much is highly speculative. I have tried to indicate where ideas are controversial and where they are matters of accepted science. However, my experience is that much of what you are taught tends to be a gross generalization or even plain wrong. If you treat facts with a degree of skepticism, you will find this keeps you in good stead.

As someone who is highly dyslexic, there will be errors. Please email me the ones you find, and recommend the book to your friends so that I can afford to print a second edition with your corrections.

I have avoided the use of equations and mathematics, so you can see the flow of the philosophical argument. I also avoid a strongly historical narrative, but if you enjoy the history of science I recommend, *The Missing 4%*, and *Quantum* for a really clear exposé of the issues around quantum mechanics, relativity and cosmology, Robert Winston's *Bad Ideas* for a more thorough history of language and writing, and *The Trouble with Physics* for the recent history of particle Physics. Regarding the brain, anything by Oliver Sachs is a winner. *Your Brain on Music* is a good primer on the theory of artistic thought and music, and *Proust and the Squid* is a good discussion of dyslexia and learning.

The digits for the sequence of the Smallpox virus in Chapter Eight come from the varicella-zoster virus, a similar pathogen. The first few letters could be the same, but I hope it is impossible for anyone to disprove this as you would have to break into the CDC to do so.

John Masters is not the real name of the US officer who spoke in Kabul. That name was never released to the press.

This book was originally written using Microsoft Word on a MacBook Pro. It was then typeset for print using a variety of ePublication tools, including iBooksAuthor and Adobe InDesign. You can find a website for the book at www.jamestagg.com. It is published using WordPress. All the links in the book should be maintained there just in case there is link atrophy for the printed version of the book. Feel free to comment using the blog, Twitter, Facebook or email me.

Conway and Kochen

"It doesn't matter how beautiful your theory is, it doesn't matter how smart you are. If it doesn't agree with experiment, it's wrong."

Richard P. Feynman

Appendix 5

Index of Theorems

I have explained a number famous theorems in this book along with some ideas of my own. Here is a list of the most notable.

1. **Mind over Computer**
   Turing Test – How to tell whether a computer is intelligent, even though we cannot agree on a definition of intelligence.
   Flynn Effect – The observation that human intelligence appears to be improving over time.
   Kurzweil Singularity Proposal – The conjecture that Moore's Law will result in computers acquiring near infinite power relatively soon.
   Lucas Argument – Minds are in a different class to computers as they are not limited by the incompleteness theorem.
   Humor Hypothesis† – Humor and jokes are a display of non-computable intelligence.

2. **Understanding**
   Tufte's Assertion – That communication of understanding exceeds the capability of many presentation tools, particularly PowerPoint.
   Chinese Room – John Searle's paradox challenging the idea that understanding can be mechanically simulated.

3. **Body Language & Banter**
   Communication Hypothesis† – That face to face communication is more powerful in some real physical sense than symbolic communication.
   7-38-55 Rule – Mehrabian's observation that the emotional content of communication is 7% words, 38% tone of voice and 55% body language.

4. **The Brain**
   Penrose-Hameroff Conjecture – Brains are quantum-gravity computers using tubulin as the mediator.

5. **Knowledge**
   Information Continuum Hypothesis† – Information is finite, but understanding and knowledge are different in nature.
   Infinite Monkeys Hypothesis – The paradox that says monkeys could type *Hamlet* given enough time and paper.
   Cat Experiment† – Finding my house cat can use our computer, and may be more creative than monkeys!

6. **Kittens & Gorillas**
   Feynman Proof – A proof that uses the lack of an evolved species within an evolutionary niche to disprove the existence of something; in this case polywater.
   The Infinity of Primes – Pythagoras' proof there are an infinity of prime numbers without needing the concept of a number.

7. **Complexity & Chaos**
   The Butterfly Effect – The proposal by Edward Lorenz that tiny effects can multiply up into enormous results.
   P≠NP – That non-deterministic polynomial problems can never be solved in polynomial time and are, therefore, beyond the capability of any imagined computer.
   The Hawking-Bekenstein Turk† – Although there is a perfect chess machine, it would collapse space-time to a black hole were it to exist.

8. **∞**
   Continuum Hypothesis – Does anything come between the first two infinities; counting numbers and the continuum of real numbers.

Cantor's First Infinity Theorem – The infinite plane is the same infinity as the infinite line.

9. **Known Unknowns**
   Gödel's Incompleteness Theorem – Mathematics involving simple logic is incomplete.
   Gödel's Completeness Theorem – First order logic is complete.
   Hilbert's Completeness Theorem – Geometry is complete.

10. **Turing's Machines**
    Entscheidungsproblem – The decision problem has no solution.
    Turing Thesis – All computers, once sufficiently powerful, are equally powerful.
    Non-Computability of Music† – That general musical compositions are non-computable.
    Non-Computability of Creativity† – That general artistic creativity is non-computable.

11. **Software**
    Brooks' Law – Adding resource to a late project makes it later.
    Law of Leaky Abstractions – However good the attempt to abstract complexity, complexity has a habit of leaking through.
    Software is Created† – writing software is a non-computable, creative task.
    Bug Hypothesis† – Bugs are an inevitable consequence of trying to generalize software by mechanical means.

12. **Hyper-Computing**
    Adaptive Recurrent Neural Network Hypothesis – Hava Siegelmann's proposal that ARNNs are capable of super-Turing computation.

13. **Hyper-Communication**
    Bandwidth Conjecture† – Person-to-person communication has infinite bandwidth and is non-symbolic.

14. **Creativity**
    Creativity Hypothesis† – That all creative endeavor is a non-computable skill, analogue to theorem discovery.
    Wallas Model – A conceptual model for the way humans think creatively.

Creative Survival Advantage† – That creativity has evolved to give us a survival advantage at all stages of evolution, not just when we evolve to the point where mathematical intuition is significant.

15. **Free Will**

Laplace Daemon – A conceptual supreme being able to infer the future and the past from one snapshot of space-time and the laws of nature.

EPR Paradox – Twin particles would transmit information faster than the speed of light if quantum mechanics was to be believed.

Schrödinger's Cat – The paradox that a cat might be both alive and dead at the same time until observed.

Bell Inequality – Quantum mechanics forbids local hidden variables in a testable way. The test succeeds.

Kochen-Specker Paradox – Particles cannot know their settings before measurement.

Free Will Theorem – Nothing in the past light cone of the Universe causes a particle to choose its spin upon measurement.

Non-decryptable Universe† – The laws of physics mean the Universe is non-computable in principle.

Free Will Universe† – The laws of mathematics mean the Universe is non-computable and therefore has Free Will.

Russian Doll Conjecture† – Since humans are creative and non-deterministic and, in a sense, they run upon the hardware of the Universe, the hardware of our Universe must also be non-deterministic.

16. **The Quest for Knowledge**

Technology Hypothesis† – The extended strong anthropic principle that the Universe must have creative beings within it to uniquely define it.

17. **The Future**

Creative Non-Singularity† – The future is non-computable and therefore any increase in computer power, however great, will never achieve a creativity singularity.

† The symbol marks items proposed for the first time within this book. If I have missed a previous publication, please feel free to write to me and I will amend a future version.

Index

Symbols

∀∃∀ 249
∃ 249
3D chip 21, 22
3D printing 20, 222
7%-38%-55% rule 84
50 First Dates 12

A

AARON 310
Aaronson, Scott 168
abstraction 267
Academy Awards 365
Accidental Complexity 231
actin 98
Activision 290
Adams, Douglas 17, 128, 225, 238, 305, 314
Adams, Scott 296
Adaptive Recurrent Neural Network 280
Adleman, Leonard 165
Advanced Course in Design, Manufacturing and Management x
Afghanistan 54, 90
A Five-day Course in Thinking 297
age and memory
  120
AIDS 158
Aleph 1 175
Alexander The Great 149
algebra 248
algorithm 212, 238, 239, 243, 247, 249, 251, 257
  history of 6
alibi 153
Al-Khwarizmi 6
Allman, Eric 265
Alternative Uses Task 299
Alvarez, Luis 30
Amazoncom 308
Amazon rainforest 27, 181
Amedi, Amir 13
Amherst 280
amygdala 11, 31
analysis 204
Analytical Engine 15, 16, 223–224
A New Kind of Science 173
anthropic principle 322
Anti-Ballistic Missile Treaty 79
Antikythera 15
Apple 56, 68, 224, 306
Arab world democracy 82
Arafat, Yasser 81, 82
Archimedes 343
Aristotle 149
ARM 224
ARNN 280
art
  being appreciated 142
  creativity and 304
Artamène 129
Art of Fugue 259
ASCII 203
Asimov, Isaac 4
Association of Computer Machinery 367

astrological clock 39, 42
asynchronous logic 22
Atkins v Virginia 28
ATM 233
ATP 98
audio field 291
audio processing system 114
auditory cortex 31
Australian English 86
Australian Outback 28
avatar xii
axiom 198
  Peano axioms 199, 205

B

Babbage, Charles 16, 223
Bach, JS 7, 259
background context 86
Bader, Douglas ix
bandwidth 288, 292
Barber paradox 155
Barrie, JM 128
Barrymore, Drew 12
Battleship 144
Baxa, Christoph 251
Beardsley, Dick 192
Beatles 102
Beijing 88
Bekenstein, Jacob 6, 132
Bell, Alexander Graham 18
Bell Corporation 216
Bell, John 322, 330, 333
Bell test experiment 333, 343
Berkeley University 248
bifocal glasses 152
Big Bang xii, 339
Big O 164
binary logic 150
Binsted, Kim 310
BIOS 225
Blackadder 266
Black Box experiments 67
black hole 132, 279
Bletchley Park 215
blind sight 12
Block Universe Hypothesis 317
body language 84, 288
Bohr, Niels 372
Bolt, Usain 31
bone cancer 20
Boolean logic 150, 152
Boole, George 150
Bootstrap 225
Borders 308
Borland 237
bosons 343
Bowie, David 151
brain 1, 11
  accidents 11
  aging 120
  amygdala 11
  anatomy 108
  and plasticity 13
  as a computer 13, 14, 99, 120
  as an exchange 18
  auditory cortex 31
  color perception 110
  digesting starch 118
  electrical pulse 98
  emotions 116
  glucose use 117
  hearing 113
  hippocampus 11, 32
  imaging 99, 102
    3D virtual 103
    MRI 104
    PET 107
    seeing thought 108
  learning 35–38
  memory 11, 14
  meninges 97
  motor cortex 31
  non-computable processes 373
  noninvasive imaging techniques 11
  organized like a filing cabinet 12
  quantum effects 50, 283
  quick tour 108
  scanners 46
  stroke damage 12
  super-Turing 294
  thinking 117
  visual agnosia 12
brain damage 97
brainstorming 298
Branson, Richard 24
Bricklin, Dan 237
bridge 134
British General Strike 211
Britten, Benjamin 305
Brooks, Fred 229, 230, 231, 237

Brooks' Law 230
bubble sort ballet 165
Buschkuehl, Martin 33
Bush, George W 194
butterfly
  creating tornados 173
Byrd, William 259
bytes 129

C

calculating machines 15
California Institute of Technology (Caltech) xii
Call of Duty 290
Cambridge University 17, 72, 195, 221
  King's College 211
  Mathematical Bridge x
  Trinity College 193
  Wolfson College ix
CaMKII 119
Candidate for a Pullet Surprise 139
Cantonese 87
Cantor, Georg 179
Cantor's theorem 221
Carey, Maria 113
Carroll, John 29
Carroll, Lewis 135, 140, 149, 148–150, 248, 356
Casio synthesizer 311
CAT scans 13, 102
Cats Creation 145
Cattell, Raymond 29
CERN 333, 335
Chaitin, George 188
Chalmers, David 39
Champollion, Jean-François 89
chaos 171
CHC theory 29
checklist 152
Cheshire Cat 149
chess 32, 163
  perfect chess-playing machine 6
chimpanzee and typewriter 127
China 15
Chinese 86, 129
Chinese Room, Searle's 65, 64–67, 222
Christensen, Clayton 306
Christie, Agatha 260
chunking 91
Church, Alonzo 212
Churchill, Winston 17, 213
Chutzpah 86
ciphers 215, 218
circle free 243
Clauser, John 333
Clay Mathematics Institute 167, 196, 225
Cleese, John 270, 303
clocks 42
  astrological clock 39, 42
  modern computers and 43
code breakers 211
codes 214
  and children's games 214
  and code books 215
  and code breakers 214, 305
  and Enigma machine 215, 305
  and one-time pad 216, 217, 218
Cohen, Harold 308, 311
COIN dynamics 53, 55, 90
Cold War 81, 213
color perception 110
comedy 92, 94
  as survival skill 94
communication
  audio field 291
  background context 86
  bandwidth 288, 292
  body language 288
  digitization 289, 293
  earliest recorded 87
  emails 81
  face to face xii, 81, 83, 293
  hyper-communication 285–294
  nonverbal 84
  of objects 90
  scripts and symbols 87
  symbolic 87, 293
  telephone 81
Compaq 307
compatibilism 41, 315
compiler 231
complexity
  accidental 231
  essential 231
complexity hierarchy 168
compositions 8
computer xi
  as human 11, 26, 46
  brains 14, 120
  bugs 262

chess-playing 5
communicating 90
consciousness 14, 45
crash 225
creativity and 132, 257, 309
Deep Thought 17
first programmable computing machine 16
generating random numbers 189
historical convention 227
infinite computing power 261
Japanese characters 88
limitless computing power 277
logic 150
logic gates 18, 22, 121
logic limit 250
military 80
music and 258
non-computable solution 75
origins 15
pattern matching 49
personal 307
programmed to learn 38
quantum computers 277
random numbers and 44
sense of humor 25
silicon chip 20
symbolic communication 293
synchronous logic 22
understanding of 71
computer game 32
computing
exponential growth 20
concentration 115
Confucius 162
Connelly, Jennifer 151
consciousness 45, 124
Conseil Européen pour la Recherche Nucléaire 333
Contact 68
convergent thinking 300
Conway, John 173, 343
Conway's Game of Life 173
Cope, David 7
Copenhagen interpretation 327
Copernicus 42
Cormack, Allan 102
counter factual experiments 282
counting system 181
Coyle, Daniel 37
Craddock, Travis 50, 119, 124, 283
Crash program 227
creative thinking 1
creativity 30, 49, 295–312, 297
art and 304
being appreciated 142
computer and 132, 257, 309
convergent thinking 300
design tradeoff 311
divergent thinking 298
Eureka moment 302
incubation 301
innovator's dilemma 306
intimation 301
John Cleese on 303
knowledge and 141
mathematical creativity 309
mechanical steps 141
non-linearity of 311
preparation 301
process 133, 270, 305
process versus 312
reward for 308
science of 301
sparking creativity 305
Crete 89
cryptography 215
quantum 217
CSI 102
Cuneiform 87
Curtis, Richard 266
cypher 214

D

Dahl, Roald 140
Damadian, Raymond 104
Daniel-Constantin Mierla 265
Danziger, Daniel 335
Dark Ages 16
Darwin, Charles 197, 305, 356
da Vinci, Leonardo 374
Davis, Martin 243, 248, 258
Dawkins, Richard 338–339
D-Day 213
dead code elimination 250
de Bono, Edward 297
Decision Problem 196, 212, 219
decohering 282
Dedekind 182
Deep Blue 5

Deep Thought 17
de Fermat, Pierre 75
Dell 307
democracy
  Arab world 82
De Morgan, Augustus 350
Demotic 89
dendrites 98
Dennett, Daniel xi, 46, 133, 260, 351
Der Spiegel 34
Descartes 70
design tradeoff 311
determined universe 207
determinism 41–46, xi, 315, 316, 351
  free will and 315
Deutsch, David xi, 56, 293, 309
Dexter, Colin 260
Dick, Philip K 324
diffusion MRI 106
digital art 129
Digital Equipment 307
digitization 289
  of life 293
Dijkstra, Edgar 3
Dilbert 313
Diophantine equations 238, 239, 240, 249, 251
Diophantus 239
divergent thinking 298
DNA 104, 123
domino toppling 316
Doyle, Arthur Conan 148
Doyon, Julien 117
drag and drop 237
DVD 289
D-Wave 21
dyslexia 90, 139

E

Edinburgh Festival 288
Edison, Thomas 295, 296, 298
EEG 32
Egyptian 86, 89
Einstein, Albert 30, 34, 47, 64, 117, 178, 180, 210, 212, 298, 319, 327, 332, 333, 347, 348
  brain 97
Eliza 25
Elton, Ben 266
EMI 102
Emil Post's Word Problem 258
emotions 116
encryption 165, 218, 277
  RSA encryption 165
Encyclopedia Britannica 8
English 86, 89, 129
ENIAC 223
Enigma 211, 212, 215, 218
Entscheidungsproblem 211, 219, 221
EPR paradox 332
Equitable Center 5
equivalence 200
Ericsson, Anders 37
Ernő 169
Escher, MC 346
  and Penrose Steps 51
Essential Complexity 231
Euclid's proof 156
Euler 157, 202
Eureka moment 302
Everett, Hugh 328
experiments 1
exponent 241
expression analysis 84
eyes 108
  color perception 110
  fovea centralis 112
  resolution of 112

F

Facebook 71, 271
face-to-face interaction 83
false paradox 155
Fermat's Last Theorem xi, 225, 241, 242, 251, 253, 254, 259, 261, 275, 278, 351, 368
Fermat's puzzle 225
Fermilab 293
Feynman, Richard 58, 70, 157, 239, 306, 326, 364, 399
Feynman's proof 157
Fields Fellowship 368
Fields Medal 368
Finland 54
FitzGerald, Edward 372
Florida State University 37
flowchart 244
Fluid Concepts & Creative Analogies 49
fluid intelligence 29, 33
fluorescent dyes 100

Flynn Effect 33
Flynn, James 33
Formalism 193
Four Color Conjecture 251
fovea centralis 112
f-PET 107
fractals 329
Franklin, Benjamin 152
Frankston, Bob 237
Freedman, Stuart 333
FreeSWITCH 265
free will 41, 313–354
  determinism and 315
  God and 339
  particles 349
  Schrödinger's cat 325
  simple theorem 337
  The Free Will Theorem 343
  twin particle experiment 331
  uncertainty 318
Frege, Gottlob 155
French 90
French Academy of Science 238
Fritz, chess program 5
Frost, Robert 96
future 373
futures market 55

G

gadolinium 106
Garden of Eden 339
gate parity point 18
Gates, Bill 236
gears 42
Geiger counter 326
geometry 179
German 86, 129
Gettysburg Address 57
'G' factors 29
ginormous 131
Giseng, Nicolas 335
Gladwell, Malcolm 37
Glass, Philip 8
Gleick, James 171
glucose 117
God
  free will and 339
Gödel Escher Bach 49
Gödel, Kurt xi, 141, 193, 201, 221, 246
Gödel limit 207
Gödel numbers 203
Goldbach's Conjecture 157
Golden Pineapples 365
Good Will Hunting 257
Google 20, 253, 271, 308, 367
Gorbachev, Mikael 79
Göttingen University 193
grade inflation 32
Graham, Martha 78
Grand Masters 5
Grand Theft Auto 91
Grantchester 221
Greece 15, 156
  and ancient Greeks 18
Greek 87, 89, 149, 297
Greek tragedy 87
Gregory, Mike 396
Grieg 259
Group Intelligence 30
Grove, Andy 18
Grover's algorithm 277
guess xii
Guilford, JP 299
Gulf Stream 152
Gurdon, Sir John 30

H

Haltcrash 244
Halting Flowchart 245
Halting Problem 243, 251, 258, 259
Halting Program 225, 244
Halting Question 243
Hameroff, Stuart 119, 122, 282
Hamlet 129, 254
Hammond, Richard 97
Hampton Court Palace 42
Hard disk drives 306
Harrison, John 365
Harry Potter 92, 306
Harvard Business School 306
Harvard University 224, 307
Hawking Bekenstein bound 6
Hawking, Stephen x, xvi, 6, 132, 306, 326, 339
hearing 113
heat-sight 102
Hebrew 86, 87
Hebrew University of Jerusalem 13
Heisenberg's uncertainty principle 318, 335

Henry VIII 42
hieroglyphics 89
Higgs Boson 357
Hilbert, David 182, 193, 194, 238
Hilbert Problems 196, 221
Hilbert's 10th Problem 243, 253
Hilbert's Hotel 182
Himalayas 55
hippocampus 11, 32
Hitler, Adolf 213
Hoane, Joe 5
Hodges, Wilfrid 150
Höfði House 79, 80
Hofstadter, Douglas xi, 49, 310
Hogarth, Mark 280
Hole in the Wall Project 35
Holmes, Sherlock 148
hologram 290
Hong Kong 88
horizontal abstraction 266
Horn, John 29
Hounsfield, Sir Godfrey 102
Howell, Emily 7, 310
Hubble 348
Hulme, David 41
hunters and spears 181
hyper-communication 285–294, 293
  audio field 291
  bandwidth 288, 292
  digitization 289, 293
  reality 289
  symbolic communication 293
hyper-computing 273
hypercube 241–244
hypotenuse 242

I

IBM 207, 224, 306
  and Watson 8
  Watson Research Laboratory 5
Ig Nobel Prize 365
imaging 99
IMAX theatre 287, 290, 293
Inception 50
inconsistency
  in mathematics 204
inconsistency defense 207
incubation 1, 301
Indiana University 49
indirect proof 153, 158, 244
infinity , 179, 280
  history of 179
  how to count 180
  larger than infinity 185
Infinity Hotel 182
infrared light 102
innovator's dilemma 306
insight 2
inspiration 2
instinctive reactions 109
Institute of Advanced Mathematics 212, 258
Intel 18, 224, 367
intelligence 25
  fluid 29, 33
  'G' factors 29
  grade inflation 32
  human vs computing 75
  physical basis of 30
  quantitative numerical skills 30
  static 32
  time 29
  vision 29
interaction 85
  face-to-face 83
interferometer 326
International Congress of Mathematicians 196
International Mathematical Union 368
internet
  encryption 165, 277
internet protocol 267
intimation 2, 301
intuitive thinking 2
IP 267
iPad 319
iPhone 22, 238, 297
iPod 289
IQ 27, 33, 120
  IQ Test 27
Iraq 87
Iraq war 80
Irvine 280
ISABEL 14
iTunes 130

J

Jabberwocky 135, 136
Jaeggi, Susanne 33
Japanese 87

Jape 310
Jefferson, Thomas 308
Jeopardy 9
Jessie 145
Jobs, Steve 47, 68, 296–297, 297, 306
joke 93
  world's funniest 94
Joke Analysis and Production Engine 310
Jones, JP 251

K

Kahn, Philip 237
Kamailio 265
Kasparov, Garry 5, 34
  and Deep Blue 4–6
Kelvin, Lord 180
Kerr Metric 280
Khayyám, Omar 371
King's College 17, 211
Kish, Daniel 13
knitting 117
knowledge 8
  analysis 204
  creating 141
  creativity and 141
  difficulty discovering 204
  discovery of 142
  nature of 193
  search for 140
Kochen, Simon 343
Kochen Specker 344
Kochen-Specker Cube 347
Kochen-Specker paradox 345
Königsberg Bridges 202
Königsberg University 202
Kronecker 178
Kurzweil, Ray 20, 261
  and Moore's Law 19

L

lambda calculus 258
language 129
  body 84
Laplace, Pierre-Simon 317
lateral thinking 297
lava lamp 45
Lavarand 45
Law and Order 87
learning 35–38
Leibniz 319
Leicestershire 89
liar's paradox 154
library
  knowledge 143
light 100
  spectrum 102
lightning rod 152
Linear-a 89
Linear-b 89
Linux 265
Liszt, Franz 7, 129
Loch Ness Monster 142
Loch Ness Monster Song 138
Loebner prize 72
logic 149
  binary 150
  Boolean 150, 152
  checklists 152
  for computers 150
  limit 247
  purpose of 156
  reduction to the absurd 152
  Stoic 150
Logic 150
logic gates 18, 22, 121
logic limit 262
London Bridge 42
London marathon 192, 202
London Mathematical Society 15, 238
London School of Economics 301
London Science Museum 16
long multiplication 240
Lorenz Attractor 173
Lorenz, Edward 170, 172
Lotus Corporation 237
Lucas argument 205
Lucas, JR xi, 205
Lucas-Penrose argument 205

M

Madam Tussaud 75
magnetic fields 105
Magnetic Resonance Imaging 105
Makanin, Gennadií 258
Malament, David 280
Manchester University 236
Mandarin 87
Mandelbrot diagram 174
Mandelbrot Set 161
Manhattan Project 239

Marx, Groucho 153, 382
Massachusetts 89
Massachusetts Institute of Technology (MIT) 25, 165, 168, 307
Masters, John 54
mathematical proofs 156
mathematical theorems xi
mathematicians
  Polish 211
mathematics 153
  axiom 198
  equivalence 200
  flat problem 164
  future of 196
  game of 200
  how to count 180
  inconsistency defense 207
  inconsistency in 204
  indirect proof 244
  infinity 179
  linear problem 164
  long multiplication 240
  Lucas argument 205
  mathematical creativity 309
  non-deterministic polynomial problems 165
  Peano axioms 199, 205
  prime numbers 243
  PSPACE problem 168
  traveling salesman problem 166
  truth and rules 193, 200, 206
Matiyasevich, Yuri 248, 251
Mattapoisett 89
Maude, Isabel 14
Maxwell 298
Mayan astronomers 70
maze 164, 165
McChrystal, General Stanley A 54
McGinn, Colin 324
McGurk Effect 114
McLaughlin, Dan 37
Mehrabian, Albert 84
memory 11, 14, 90, 118
  digital 130
  photographic memory 119
  visio-spacial 28
  with age 120
memory management 250
meninges 97
meningitis 14
Merchant of Death 366
Merilees, Philip 170
Mesopotamia 87
metre 28
micro-expression analysis 84
microphones 289
Microsoft 237
Microsoft Word 135
microtubules 124, 281
Miles, Andrew 368
Millennium Falcon 348
Milliken 394
Minds, Machines and Gödel 205
Minessale, Anthony 265
Ming Dynasty 15
mirror neurons 116
Mirzakhani, Maryam 368
Mitra, Sugata 35
monkey 129
  moon shot story 144
monkeys and typewriters 254
Monty Python 93
Moon Base 348
Moore, Gordon 18
Moore's Law 18
Morgan, Edwin 138, 142
Morse code 336
motor cortex 31
Mozart 246, 298
MRI scan 69, 104
multiplication
  long 240
Munduruku tribe 181
Murphy's Law 226
muscle memory 90
muscles 117, 192
music 113
  computers and 258
musical compositions 8
myelin 31, 118

N

Napoleonic wars 129
NASA 59
Native American 89
Navier Stokes Hypothesis 238
nebula 174
Negroponte, Nicolas 35
neural network 116, 121, 280

neurons 50, 98, 116
  microtubules 281
  nerve impulse speed 99
  recovery time 121
  synapse 119
Newcastle University 35
Newman, Max 221
Newton, Isaac 171, 319
Newton's Rings 321
New York University School of Medicine 12
Niels Bohr Institute 327
nitrocellulose 218
Nixon, Richard 194
Nobel, Alfred 365
Nobel Prize 30, 50, 100, 102, 119, 213, 326, 365
non-algorithmic xi
non-computable processes 373
non-computable thought 261, 282
noncomputational creativity xi
non-determinism 275, 282, 318
non-deterministic behavior 44
non-deterministic polynomial problems 165
noninvasive imaging techniques 11
nonverbal communication 84
Norvig, Peter 57
No Silver Bullet 237
No Silver Bullet – Essence and Accidents of Software Engineering 231
Nova Institute 50
Nova Southeastern University 124
Nuclear Magnetic Resonance 104
numbers
  counting system 181
  defining 199
  Gödel numbers 203
  infinity 179
  nature of 155
  prime 156, 243, 343
  random 188
  real 186, 280
  Turing numbers 190
  zero 179
Nyquist, Harry xiii

O

Occam's Razor 68
omnipotence 340
omniscience 340
On Computable Numbers and their Application to the Entscheidungsproblem 211
One Laptop per Child 35, 82
one-time pad 216, 337
opium 55
optical illusions 113
oracle function 278
order-of-magnitude 164
O'Reilly, Edward 50
Organon 149
Orwell, George 178
Outliers 37
Oxford English Dictionary 86
Oxford University xi, 50, 149, 205, 282

P

paperclip test 298
paper tape 221
paradox xi, 68, 70, 114, 153, 203, 326
  Barber paradox 155
  EPR paradox 332
  false 155
  Kochen-Specker paradox 345
  liar's paradox 154
  Russell paradox 155
  Wiles paradox 247
  Zeno's paradox 154
parallel lines 179
Paramecium 123–126
particle accelerator 69
Pasteur Institute 188
pattern matching 49
Pavillon de Breteuil 28
PC revolution 236
PDP11-34 236
Peano axioms 199, 205
Peano, Giuseppe 197, 199
Pelmanism 28
pendulum 121
Penrose, Roger xi, 50, 56, 123, 205, 246, 261, 282, 309, 328
Penrose Steps 51, 113
Pentagon 79
people
  living forever 20
Pérez, Shimon 81, 82
permutation of information 135
Persia 15

personal computers 307
PET 107
philosophical proof 246
philosophy 193
Photo Electric Effect 366
photographic memory 119
photons 110, 320, 331, 332, 348
photosynthesis 50, 124
physics 180
  determinism 316
Picasso, Pablo 232, 246, 298
pit vipers 102
Pixar 306
Places game 168
plank interval 131, 255
Plato 149, 179
Podolsky, Jacob 332
poem
  computer created 134
Poincaré Conjecture 357
Poincaré, Henri 171, 180
Polaroid lenses 332
police strike 54
Polish Intelligence Bureau 211
polynomial 164
polywater 157
positivism 153
positron emission tomography 107
Post, Emil 258
Post Problems 258
Powell, Colin 53
PowerPoint 63
preparation 301
Previn, Andre 93
prime numbers 156, 243, 343
Princeton University 97, 212, 223, 251
Principia Mathematica 195
Private Eye 287
process
  creativity versus 312
program equivalence problem 250
programmer 235, 238, 263
  programming geniuses 271
  super-programmers 266
progressive cipher 214
proof
  Feynman's proof 157
  indirect 244
  mathematical 156
  philosophical 246
PSPACE problem 168
Pulitzer Prize 365, 367
purpose on the planet 9
puzzle
  two guards 151
Pygmalion 25
Pythagoras 243
Pythagorean triangle 240

Q

quantitative numerical skills 30
quants 71
quantum brains 122
quantum computers 277
quantum cryptography 215, 217
quantum effects 50, 282
quantum gravity interaction 329
quantum mechanics 22, 123, 180, 293, 344
  Copenhagen interpretation 327
quantum Morse machine 337
quantum randomness 45
quantum uncertainty 21
quartz 121
quartz crystal 43
qubits 21
quinine 100

R

radioactive decay 327
random chance 254
random numbers 44
Reagan, Ronald 79
reality 289
real numbers 280
reductio ad absurdum 152, 157
reflection 319
relativity 180
  Special Relativity 348
  Theory of Relativity 366
Renaissance 16, 297
Reykjavik 79
rice
  covering chessboard 163
Rice's Theorem 267
Riemann Hypothesis 238, 257
Riemann surfaces 368
Ritchie, Graeme 310
Rivest, Ron 165
Robinson Davis Matiyasevich theory 248

Robinson, Julia 248, 251
Robinson, Sir Ken 299
Rogers and Hammerstein 266
Rommel 211
Röntgen, Wilhelm 100
Rosen, Samuel 332
Rosetta Stone 89
Rowling, JK 306
Royal Swedish Academy of Sciences 366
RSA encryption 165
Rubik's cube 345
Rule 164 192
rules 192, 200
Rumsfeld, Donald 190, 194
RunMe 245
Ruohonen, Keijo 251
Russell, Bertrand 155, 193, 195
Russell paradox 155

S

Sachs, Oliver 12
Sagan, Carl 68
Sandler, Adam 12
Sanford, Edward 38
Schadenfreude 86
Scherbius, Arthur 211
Schrödinger, Erwin 326
Schrödinger's cat 325
Scientific American 85
scripts and symbols 87
Searle's Chinese Room 66, 222
secret message 214
Seeger, Pete 162
Sego, Daniel 335
self-halting problem 250
SendMail 265
Shadows of the Mind 50, 282
Shakespeare, William 39, 129, 131, 138, 140, 254
Shamir, Adi 165
Shannon, Claude xiii, 3, 216, 337
Sharman, Mike ix
Shaw, George Bernard 25, 78, 286
Shockley, William 30
Shor's algorithm 277
Siegelmann, Hava 280
silicon chip 20
Silicon Graphics 45
Simonsen, Inge 192
Singer, Isaac 314
Singh, Simon 242
single cell organisms 18
singularity 261
Siri 56
Skinner, BF 34
smallpox virus 189
smile 84
sock analogy 332
software 224, 231
  bugs 262
  coding 264
  drag and drop 237
  flowchart 244
  modern word processor 236
  origins of 238
  PC revolution 236
  problems 250
  process 270
  programmer 235, 238, 263
  programming geniuses 271
  re-architect 270
  scope creep 270
  spreadsheet 237
  super-programmers 266
  writing 235
sorting 164
Soviets 79
space like separation 348
Space Shuttle Columbia 58
Spanish 90
spears and hunters 181
Special Purpose Objection 253
Special Relativity 348
speed of light 317
spell checkers 139
spin 343
Spolsky, Joel 256
  Law of Leaky Abstractions 256
Spolsky's Law 267
spreadsheet 237
Stanford University 30
starch 118
Star Trek 157, 348
Star Wars 79
static intelligence 32
statistical approach 8
Stern, William 27
Stockhausen 7
Stoic logic 150
story 92

Strategic Defense Initiative 79
stroke damage 12
substitution code 203
Sumerians 87
superconductivity 22
super-programmers 266
super-Turing 275, 278, 283, 294
syllogisms 150, 152, 158
symbolic communication 87, 293
symbols 130, 143, 194, 201
synapse 119
system argument 66

T

Tagg, James
  Home Page 232
Tallis, Thomas 259
tapetum lucidum 110
TCP 267
Terman, Lewis 30
The Art of Thought 301
The Boy Who Can't Forget 120
The Cognitive Style of PowerPoint 63
The Emperor's New Mind xi, 50, 246, 282
The Free Will Theorem 343
The Free Will Universe 231
The Game of Logic 150
The God Delusion 339
The History of Western Philosophy 193
The Innovators Dilemma 306
The Journal of Irreproducible Results 139
The Labyrinth 150
The Man who Mistook his Wife for a Hat 12
The Mythical Man Month 231
Theory of Relativity 366
Thermal Imaging 101
The Sound of Music 266
The Talent Code 37
The Universe in a Nutshell 339
The Webby Awards 365
thiamin molecules 124
thinking 117
Thomas, Dylan 140
thought art 87
Three Body Problem 171
time intelligence 29
time travel 316
Tokyo University 13
Tolstoy, Leo 129
  War and Peace 129
toothed gears 43
Top Gear 97
topology 249
tortoise and hare 154
Torvalds, Linus 232, 265
totality problem 250
Tower of London 42
Transmission Control Protocol 267
traveling salesman problem 166
triple drug therapy 158
truth 192
tubulin 98, 118, 122, 124
  single-celled organisms 123
tubulin microtubules 282
tubulin molecules 50
Tufte, Ed 53, 63, 92
Tufts University 102
Turing, Alan xi, 15, 17, 26, 71, 96–97, 141, 209, 210, 211, 238, 258, 259, 302, 342
  and Churchill 213
  and computer understanding 212
  and Enigma 212
  and The Decision Problem 212, 219, 238
  and World War II 213
  at Bletchley Park 212
  at Cambridge University 211
  at Princeton University 212
  birth 211
  death 213
  homosexuality 213
  Turing Award 213
Turing Award 367
Turing limit 155, 253, 260, 275, 278, 280
Turing machine 212, 221, 246, 251, 275, 278, 280, 353
  Lego 223
  universal Turing machine 222
Turing numbers 190
Turing test 67, 71, 72, 261
Turing theorem 351
Tuszynski, Jack 119
twin particle experiment 331
twins 31
two guards puzzle 151
Two Ronnies 86, 93

U

Ultimate Question of Life the Universe and Everything 238
ultraviolet light 100
Uncanny Valley 75
uncertainty 318
understanding xiii, 53
  meaning of 56
  of computers 71
Unicode 129, 203
United States Army's Ballistic Research Laboratory 223
Universal Turing Machine 246
universe
  anthropic principle 322
  complexity and chaos 173
  determined 207
  deterministic 175
  end of 140
University of Alberta 119
University of Arizona 119, 122, 282
University of Calgary 251
University of California 280
University of Maryland 33
University of Massachusetts 280
University of Montreal 117
University of Moscow 258
University of Otago 33
University of Santa Cruz 7
University of Vienna 202
urban legend 11
US Supreme Court 28

V

van Gogh, Vincent 142
variable initialization 250
vertical abstraction 267
Visco, Frank L 396
vision 109
vision intelligence 29
visual agnosia 12
Volkswagen Polo 312
von Neumann, John 223
Vorderman, Carol 30

W

Wallas, Graham 1, 301
Wang 308
War and Peace 129
Watson computer 8, 207
Watson Research Laboratory 5
wave interference 320
wavelength 102
weather
  predicting 168, 172
Wechsler Test 27
Weizenbaum, Joseph 25
West, Mae 78
Whitehead, Alfred North 195
Who Wants to be a Millionaire? 347
Wikipedia 8, 129, 231
Wilder, Billy 128
Wiles, Andrew xi, 75, 242, 248, 251, 254, 259, 261, 351
Wiles Paradox 247
William of Occam 68
Winchester Drives 306
Wise, Michael 335
Wolfram, Stephen 173, 246, 352
Woods, Tiger 116
WordPress 237
World War I (First World War) 211, 337
World War II (Second World War) 17, 218, 337
  code breakers 211
Wozniak, Steve 10, 68
Wright, Stephen 274
WYSIWYG 237

X

XPRIZE 238, 367
X-ray 69, 100
  damage from 104
  slicing technique 102
  wavelength 102

Y

Yellow Pages 308

Z

Zar, Jerrold H 139
Zeitgeist 86
Zeno machine 280
Zeno's paradox 154
Zermelo-Fraenkel set theory 156
zigzag method 182

Made in United States
North Haven, CT
10 November 2026

22088255R00254